AN EAST END LEGACY

An East End Legacy is a memorial volume for William J. Fishman, whose seminal works on the East End of London in the late nineteenth century have served as a vital starting point for much of the later work on the complex web of relations in that quarter of the capital.

A number of leading scholars draw on Fishman's work to present a wide range of insights into the historical characters and events of the East End. The book's themes include local politics; anti-alienism, anti-Semitism and war; and culture and society. In pursuing these topics, the volume examines in great depth the social, political, religious and cultural changes that have taken place in the area over the past 120 years, many of which remain both significant and relevant. In addition, it illustrates East London's links with other parts of the world including Europe and America and those territories "beyond the oceans."

This book will prove valuable reading for researchers and readers interested in Victorian and twentieth-century British history, politics and culture.

Colin Holmes is Emeritus Professor of History at the University of Sheffield, UK.

Anne J. Kershen is Honorary Senior Research Fellow at the Centre for the Study of Migration,Queen Mary University of London and Honorary Senior Research Associate at the Bartlett School of Architecture, University College London.

ROUTLEDGE STUDIES IN RADICAL HISTORY AND POLITICS

Series editors: Thomas Linehan, Brunel University, and John Roberts, Brunel University

The series *Routledge Studies in Radical History and Politics* has two areas of interest. Firstly, this series aims to publish books which focus on the history of movements of the radical left. 'Movement of the radical left' is here interpreted in its broadest sense as encompassing those past movements for radical change which operated in the mainstream political arena as with political parties, and past movements for change which operated more outside the mainstream as with millenarian movements, anarchist groups, utopian socialist communities, and trade unions. Secondly, this series aims to publish books which focus on more contemporary expressions of radical left-wing politics. Recent years have been witness to the emergence of a multitude of new radical movements adept at getting their voices in the public sphere. From those participating in the Arab Spring, the Occupy movement, community unionism, social media forums, independent media outlets, local voluntary organisations campaigning for progressive change, and so on, it seems to be the case that innovative networks of radicalism are being constructed in civil society that operate in different public forms.

The series very much welcomes titles with a British focus, but is not limited to any particular national context or region. The series will encourage scholars who contribute to this series to draw on perspectives and insights from other disciplines.

Titles include:

The Radical Left Party Family in Western Europe, 1989–2015
Paolo Chiocchetti

A Political Family
The Kuczynskis, Fascism, Espionage and the Cold War
John Green

An East End Legacy
Essays in Memory of William J. Fishman
Edited by Colin Holmes and Anne J. Kershen

AN EAST END LEGACY

Essays in Memory of
William J. Fishman

Edited by Colin Holmes and Anne J. Kershen

Routledge
Taylor & Francis Group

LONDON AND NEW YORK

First published 2018
by Routledge
2 Park Square, Milton Park, Abingdon, Oxon OX14 4RN

and by Routledge
711 Third Avenue, New York, NY 10017

Routledge is an imprint of the Taylor & Francis Group, an informa business

British Library Cataloguing in Publication Data
A catalogue record for this book is available from the British Library

Library of Congress Cataloging in Publication Data
A catalog record for this book has been requested

ISBN: 978-1-138-12318-2 (hbk)
ISBN: 978-1-138-18604-0 (pbk)
ISBN: 978-1-315-64848-4 (ebk)

Typeset in Bembo
by Taylor & Francis Books

Printed and bound by CPI Group (UK) Ltd, Croydon, CR0 4YY

CONTENTS

ILLUSTRATIONS

Figures

Tables

CONTRIBUTORS

Michael Berkowitz, a native of Rochester, New York, is Professor of Modern Jewish History at University College London and editor of *Jewish Historical Studies: Transactions of the Jewish Historical Society of England* (UCL Press). He received his Ph.D. from the University of Wisconsin and has taught at the University of Chicago, Ohio State University and the University of Judaism (then West Coast branch of the Jewish Theological Seminary of America). His research in the last decade has been supported by Yad Vashem (Jerusalem), the United States Holocaust Memorial Museum (Washington, DC), the Center for Creative Photography (Tucson, AZ), the Ransom Center (Austin, TX), the University of London and the British Society for the History of Science. His most recent publication is *Jews and Photography in Britain* (2015). His previous monographs include *The Crime of My Very Existence: Nazism and the Myth of Jewish Criminality* (2007) and *Zionist Culture and West European Jewry before the First World War* (1993 and 1997). A volume co-edited with Martin Deppner, on the Jewish engagement with photography, is in press.

Todd M. Endelman is Professor Emeritus of History and Judaic Studies at the University of Michigan. He was educated at the University of California, Berkeley, and Harvard University, where he received his Ph.D. in 1976. He taught modern Jewish history at Yeshiva University, Indiana University and the University of Michigan. A specialist in the social history of European Jewry and the history of British Jewry, he is the author of *Radical Assimilation in English Jewish History, 1656–1945* (1990); *The Jews of Georgian England, 1714–1830* (1999); *The Jews of Britain, 1656–2000* (2002); *Broadening Jewish History: Towards a Social History of Ordinary Jews* (2014) and *Leaving the Jewish Fold: Conversion and Assimilation in Modern Jewish History* (2015). His currently writing a biography of the Anglo-Jewish race scientist, communal gadfly, and historian of the potato, Redcliffe Nathan Salaman.

Colin Holmes is Emeritus Professor of History in the University of Sheffield. He has published works on European economic history. But much of his research has focused on the histories of migration, race and fascism. In 1982 he co-founded the journal *Immigrants and Minorities* and retained an editorial role until 2011. His first excursion into this territory resulted in a pioneering study, *Immigrants and Minorities in British Society* (1978). His later major works include: *Anti-Semitism in British Society 1876–1939* (1979); *John Bull's Island* (1988); *A Tolerant Country?* (1991); and, most recently, *Searching for Lord Haw-Haw: The Political Lives of William Joyce* (2016). Amongst his other publications is the volume *Outsiders & Outcasts: Essays in Honour of William J. Fishman* (1993), which he contributed to and co-edited with Geoffrey Alderman. A *festschrift* marking his contribution to migration history is currently in progress and is scheduled for publication in 2017.

Anne J. Kershen was Barnet Shine Senior Research Fellow – the fellowship established for Bill Fishman in the early 1970s which he held until 1986 – in the Department of Politics (now the School of Politics and International Relations) at Queen Mary University of London from 1990 until her retirement in 2011. In 1995 she founded the Centre for the Study of Migration and became its Director, a position she held until 2011. Anne Kershen is now an Honorary Senior Research Fellow at QMUL and an Honorary Senior Research Associate at the Bartlett School of Architecture, UCL. She has published widely and her publications include; *Strangers, Aliens and Asians: Huguenots, Jews and Bangladeshis in Spitalfields, 1666–2000,* (2005); *Food in the Migrant Experience* (2002); *London the Promised Land* (1997); *Uniting the Tailors: Trade Unionism amongst the Tailoring Workers of London and Leeds 1870–1939* (1995); and jointly with Jonathan Romain, *Tradition and Change: History of Reform Judaism in Britain 1840–1995* (1995). Her latest book is *London the Promised Land Revisited, The Changing Migrant Landscape in the 21st Century* (2015). She is Series Editor for the Migration and Diaspora list for Routledge, acts as an advisor on migration in London for the media and has appeared on radio and television in migration-related programmes. She is a Fellow of the Royal Society of Arts and the Royal Historical Society.

Tony Kushner is Professor in the Parkes Institute for the Study of Jewish/non-Jewish Relations and History Department at the University of Southampton. His most recent book is *The Battle of Britishness: Migrant Journeys since 1685* (2012). He is currently working on a study of the construction of ethnicity in the British armed forces and two books relating to the Holocaust: *Journeys from the Abyss: The Holocaust and Forced Migration* and, with Dr Aimee Bunting, *Co-Presents to the Holocaust*. He is co-editor of the journal *Patterns of Prejudice* and deputy editor of *Jewish Culture and History*.

David Mazower is a senior staff journalist with BBC News and editor of a daily discussion show on BBC World Service. He is the author of *Yiddish Theatre in London* (1996), and produced the major exhibition of the same name for the Jewish

Museum, London, in 1987. He has published many articles on Yiddish culture and British Jewish history and is a regular contributor to the BBC News Magazine, The Digital Yiddish Theatre Project, History Workshop Online, The Mendele Review, *Pakn Treger* and Jewish Socialist.

His book chapters include: two major articles on the early history of the Ben Uri Art Society, most recently "Ben Uri and Yiddish Culture," in *Ben Uri, 100 Years in London* (London, 2015); "Stories in Song – the *melo-deklamatsyes* of Joseph Marko-vitsh," in J. Berkowitz (ed.), *Yiddish Theatre, New Approaches* (2003) and "Sholem Asch: Images of a Life," in N. Stahl (ed.), *Sholem Asch Reconsidered* (2004).

Wayne Parsons was a colleague of Bill Fishman at Queen Mary, University of London and had the pleasure and privilege of teaching a course on socialist thought with him in the late 1970s and through the 1980s. He was Professor of Public Policy at Queen Mary until 2013 and is currently Hon. Distinguished Professor at Cardiff University. His publications include: *The Political Economy of British Regional Policy* (1988); *The Power of the Financial Press: Journalism and Economic Opinion in Britain and America* and *Public Policy* (1989); *An Introduction to the Theory and Practice of Public Policy* (1996); and *Keynes and the Quest for a Moral Science: A Study of Economics and Alchemy* (2010).

Kerstin Sailer is a trained architect by background and Reader in Social and Spatial Networks at the UCL Bartlett School of Architecture. Her research explores the relationship between complex buildings and how they are perceived, used and appropriated by people. While the majority of her research has investi-gated large and complex buildings such as workplaces, laboratories, hospitals and schools where organisational behaviours are entangled with spatial layouts, she has an interest in a wide range of building types including religious and representative buildings. A principal theme in her research relates to how visibility and lines of sight are realised through the built environment and how these patterns shape human attitudes and behaviours. This has featured in several publications such as *Seeing and Being Seen Inside a Museum and a Department Store* (2015); *The Dynamics and Diversity of Space Use in the British Library* (2015); *The Generative Office Building* (2012); and *Creativity as Social and Spatial Process* (2011).

Trevor Smith taught at Exeter, Hull and York universities and was the founda-tion Professor of Politics and later Senior Vice-Principal at Queen Mary University of London. He subsequently served as Vice-Chancellor of the University of Ulster. He was knighted in 1996 and created a Life Peer in 1997. He has held non-executive directorships in a variety of cultural, publishing and NHS organisations, including the Joseph Rowntree Reform Trust Ltd for over thirty years and twelve as chair.

Daniel Tilles is Assistant Professor of History at the Pedagogical University of Cracow, Poland. He completed his Ph.D. at Royal Holloway, University of London in 2012, under the supervision of David Cesarani. He is the author of *British Fascist Antisemitism and Jewish Responses, 1932–40* (2015), editor of *Fascism and the Jews: Italy and Britain* (2011) and has published various chapters and articles on British fascist, anti-fascist and Jewish history.

Laura Vaughan is Professor of Urban Form and Society at the UCL Bartlett School of Architecture and a Fellow of the Royal Historical Society. Her research addresses the inherent complexity of the urban environment both theoretically and methodologically, most recently in a large study of London's suburban evolution from the nineteenth century till today – her book *Suburban Urbanities* was published by UCL Press in 2015.

She has been researching nineteenth-century Whitechapel for over two decades, with studies ranging from the spatial structuring of Charles Booth's poverty maps to a study of the Jewish East End. Her publications on the latter subject include: "Space and Exclusion: Does urban morphology play a part in social deprivation?" *Area* 37 (2007); "Mapping the East End Labyrinth," in A. Werner (ed.), *Jack the Ripper and the East End* (2008); and, with I. Geddes, "Urban Form and Deprivation: A Contemporary Proxy for Charles Booth's Analysis of Poverty," *Radical Statistics, Issue 99* (2009); and, with Anne Kershen, "There Was a Priest, a Rabbi and an Imam … : An Analysis of Urban Space and Religious Practice in London's East End, 1685–2010," *Material Religion* (2013).

Jerry White is Professor in Modern London History at Birkbeck College and a Fellow of the Royal Historical Society. He has been researching and writing London history since the mid-1970s. His early formation as a historian was with Raphael Samuel's influential History Workshop movement, and for many years he combined part-time research with a full-time career in local government, mainly in inner London at Islington, Haringey and Hackney. He ended his local government career in 2009 as a Local Government Ombudsman for England. He first met William J. Fishman in 1975 while researching his first book, *Rothschild Buildings: Life in an East End Tenement Block, 1887–1920*, which won the *Jewish Chronicle* Non-Fiction book award for 1980. Since then his research interests have encompassed London's history from 1700 to the present day. He is currently working on a full-scale history of London in the Second World War, due for publication in 2020. Professor White's most recent book, *Mansions of Misery: A Biography of the Marshalsea Debtors' Prison*, was published in October 2016. Among his many published works is *London in the Twentieth Century: A City and Its People*, winner of the 2001 Wolfson History Prize, and most recently *Zeppelin Nights: London in the First World War*, which was Spear's 2014 Social History of the Year.

A regular reviewer for the *Times Literary Supplement*, Professor White is also a frequent advisor to radio and television programmes and consultant as a London expert to national press and other publications. He holds an honorary doctorate from the University of London.

ACKNOWLEDGEMENTS

We thank all those who have helped in the compilation of this volume; our contributors, our editors at Routledge, and, of course, Bill's family and friends who have been so supportive of this project.

Colin would add his thanks not only to the usual suspects but also to James Pearson and Hilka Bronski.

For her part, Anne expresses thanks to Laura Vaughan for her cartographical guidance and her gratitude to Martin who has borne her involvement in this book with his usual good humour and tolerance.

Both of us appreciate Sybil Lunn's work in compiling the index.

Colin and Anne
December 2016
Sheffield and Shropshire

FOREWORD: WILLIAM JACK FISHMAN – A BRIEF BIOGRAPHY

Trevor Smith

Bill Fishman was born and raised in the heart of the East End and, military service apart in the Second World War, he spent his entire working career as both a teacher and a scholar in the East End.

I first met Bill in late September 1955, sitting next to him, quite by chance, in the Old Theatre of the London School of Economics. We were at the Freshers' Address being welcomed by the Director, the redoubtable demographer – Sir Alexander Carr-Saunders.

I don't recall a single point from the Director's speech, except that it was just the sort of dry and unexciting one you would expect from a statistician. By contrast, I can recall my introduction to Bill and we immediately recognised much in common with each other and became firm friends.

He was, of course, older than me by some seventeen years. That age difference was narrowed by the fact we had both been born in the East End – he in White-chapel and myself in Clapton. Also, I think he was fascinated to find an eighteen-year old *goy* with a good smattering of Yiddish phrases. I hadn't learnt these locally for I moved to the western suburbs as an infant; no, it was because my father's business partner and close friend was Jewish with the result that I had an early introduction into Anglo-Jewry. At the start of adolescence, therefore, I had atten-ded more *barmitzvahs* and Jewish weddings than baptisms and other Gentile rituals. From such serendipitous beginnings, a life-long friendship was sealed.

Bill was the middle of three sons born of a tailor – a *schneider* – and his wife – both from immigrant families from Eastern Europe. All three boys went to grammar schools as scholarship boys and were destined to become teachers.

Bill was educated at the Central Foundation School for Boys. On leaving he secured a clerkship with the London County Council – quite an achievement in the Depression of the inter-war years. He was also active in the Labour Party. While he developed a great interest in Marxism, he was not attracted to the

Communists to the point of joining the Party. He was an activist and joined in the popular resistance to the incursions of Oswald Mosley and his Blackshirt supporters in their frequent marches into the locality. Bill witnessed the infamous Battle of Cable Street in 1936 and recorded his memories both on paper and in broadcasts.

As for so many of his generation, it was the outbreak of hostilities in 1939 that brought about a marked change in his future life. He volunteered for the Army and joined the Essex Regiment and served for some years in India. It was a country that utterly fascinated him. First, the British Raj resonated with him in a Kipling-esque way. Then, India had something of the caste demarcations not dissimilar to those to be found in the *shtetls* and their environs which had been embedded in the Eastern European folk-memories of his family. His Indian experience stayed with him for the rest of his life and he wallowed in the memory of wearing an Australian-style military slouch hat with the left brim turned upright.

India was important in another respect. With the great extension of the activities of the Army Bureau of Current Affairs, he managed a transfer to the Royal Army Educational Corps where he rose to the rank of Warrant Officer. It was in the RAEC that he had his first taste of teaching that was to determine his future career when returning to Civvy Street.

On being demobilised in 1946, he immediately applied to be admitted on the twelve-month Emergency Teachers Training Course at Wandsworth Teachers' College, one of many such that had been hurriedly introduced by the Attlee government to solve the acute shortage of teachers. Bill always praised the training he received and thought it superior in many ways to the more conventional courses that succeeded it. It is interesting to note, in passing, that key elements of the Emergency Training scheme have been re-introduced in recent years.

Qualifying as a secondary school teacher, he returned to work as such in his native East End and spent seven years at Morpeth School. He made good progress, as he had done during his time in the Army, and in 1955 was promoted to be Principal of the Bethnal Green Junior Commercial College that focused mainly on night classes. It was soon after this appointment that we met. The new job entailed working from the late afternoon until about 9.00 p.m. Such hours meant that he could attend LSE in the mornings and early afternoons and contrive to complete a degree full-time. It would make for an extremely onerous schedule, combining as it did a full-time job with full-time study as well as having a young family. Life-long learning with a vengeance, you may think. Bill's application and assiduity were of the highest order but he was professionally and, even more, intellectually ambitious and driven.

He much enjoyed his time at LSE. He and I were in the British Government tutorial seminar conducted by Leonard Schapiro who was later to establish himself as a leading Kremlinologist and, in retirement, an expert in nineteenth-century Russian literature. He and Bill got on very well and had much in common, though their political views increasingly diverged.

His greatest friendship, however, and one which endured, was with his History tutor, the French specialist, Harry Hearder who later became a professor at Cardiff. Bill's Special Subject, as it was termed at LSE, was International History. Bill could speak French, was very attracted to the theories of the French anarchists, and Hearder could advise Bill how best to pursue his interest in this area. From this solid basis Bill was later to write his first book *The Insurrectionists* in 1970.

If I had to define Bill's political outlook, I would say, conscious of being deliberately oxymoronic, it was "anarcho-conformist" – he aspired to be constraint-free and individualistic, while knowing very well how to play the system and advance professionally. He managed to hold these two contradictory positions in a good balance throughout his life.

He advanced further with the re-designation of his Institute into the Tower Hamlets College of Further Education of which he remained Principal. I moonlighted there, supplementing my earnings, teaching Political Science along with his younger brother Al, or "Wiffin" as he was called, who took History classes. This further cemented my closeness with the Fishmans.

Bill had enjoyed teaching but could not abide the enormous amount of administration involved in running an FE College. He yearned also to engage much more in research and scholarship and produced a number of articles both on French anarchism and East End Jewry. These held him in good stead when he applied for and was awarded a Schoolmaster Fellowship at Balliol College, Oxford in 1965. Like India, this was a nirvana. There he met and was befriended by the Master, the Marxist Christopher Hill, by the Imperial historian Jack Gallagher, and especially by Richard Cobb, the distinguished Professor of Modern History and French specialist. Bill was deeply impressed by the micro-history methodology Cobb had developed and it influenced his own research. Cobb was a truly anarchic personality of the type Bill so admired.

Bill sought funds to enable him to continue with his research and leave the ILEA employment once and for all. Sybil Shine had been a contemporary of ours at LSE whose father, also an East Ender, was a wealthy benefactor and philanthropist. She encouraged him to finance Bill but his funds needed a suitable conduit.

Our paths had geographically diverged somewhat when I taught for five years at Hull University. On returning to work at QMC, I and my young family also lived nearby the Fishmans in Harrow. In addition to my post at QMC, I was running the Acton Society Trust, what would now be called a "Think Tank" which had charitable status and could administer, therefore, the Barnett Shine grant. Martin Paisner skilfully arranged the necessary legalities. That lasted for a year until I could arrange a transfer to QMC where Bill would become a Senior Research Fellow in the Department of Politics I had managed to create out of the Department of Economics. The History Department would have been a more obvious academic home for Bill but that could not so easily have been arranged.

As it was, Bill and I became colleagues for the third time. He stayed at QMC from 1972 to 1986 after which he returned to teach on a part-time basis as a visiting professor.

It was a very fruitful time for Bill who produced his main body of publications while at QMC. It saw the writing of his acclaimed prize-winning masterpiece *East End Jewish Radicals* that appeared in 1975. Its hero is Rudolf Rocker, the Gentile anarchist who led the Jewish radical movement. The book was published by

Duckworth. Sir Robert Blake had introduced Bill to the owner–managing director, Colin Haycraft, a distinguished classicist and yet another off-the-wall anarchic
and chaotic personality. The two got on very well and Duckworth continued to
publish Bill's later works. These included a photo-history tracing *The Streets of East
London* (1979) with Nicholas Breach, which was followed a decade later by a
sequel *East End & Docklands* with Breach and a QMC Geography colleague John
Hall. The year 1988 saw the appearance of another well-received book *East End
1888* that detailed the condition of the district a century earlier and drew attention
to the work of The Saints, the social reformers that included the likes of Charles
Booth, Thomas Barnardo and Frederick Charrington. For his published works he
was awarded a higher doctorate (a D.Sc. Econ.) by the University of London in
1989 and further recognition came when he was made a Fellow of QMC in 1992.
A *festschrift* in his honour, *Outsiders & Outcasts*, edited by Professors Geoffrey
Alderman and Colin Holmes, appeared in 1993.

Unsurprisingly, Bill held a succession of visiting professorships in the United
States. These included the universities of Youngstown, Ohio, Columbia, New
York City and others. He visited America frequently to teach and research. For
East End Jewish Radicals he sought out the memories of their children as many had
gone on to live in the States. This was during the years of youthful protest of the
late 1960s and early 1970s. He was amused to find these, by now, grandmothers,
often living in the homes of their offspring, being held in a new awe by *their*
rebellious grandchildren as they learned of the activism of their great-grandfathers –
much to the annoyance of their own Nixonite/Republican parents. The modern
impulses of youth were, it seems, ingrained in their DNA.

Unlike wartime India, his trips to the USA were not such a contrast or dramatically different for he took the East End with him every time. But he was pleased
to witness and savour the spirit of youthful dissent provoked by the Vietnam War
and racial segregation.

His scholarly achievements apart, as both researcher and charismatic teacher,
another love was for the *mame loshen* – Yiddish – and for its literature. These were
combined in his deep interest in the poetry of Avraham Stencl whose work he
promoted and helped to get translated.

Bill made his wide repository of knowledge of the history and peoples of East
London freely available to an extensive range of broadcasters from Britain and
abroad as well as to other authors with related interests including Roy Hattersley and
the novelist, the late Bernice Reubens.

Bill, as so many can attest, was renowned for his conducted tours of East
London which he very regularly staged. His accounts of the likes of Jack the
Ripper, the Elephant Man, Vladimir Lenin, Annie Besant and other denizens of
the area were legendary. He must have staged hundreds of such walks and they
were yet another hallmark of his life.

Bill came from a close-knit extended family. He likewise cherished his own
family of Doris, Barrie and Michael and he gave his love to the children of his
many friends. To my two sons and daughter he will always be "Uncle Bill."

He could not have achieved what he did without the unstinting love and support of his wife, Doris, whose beauty he would extol continuously to his intimates. He knew the debt he owed her over a very long and loving marriage. Doris cared for him, especially in his last years as age finally took its toll.

All those who knew Bill – the *doyen* of the history of East London – were all the better for it. His memory will long live on, especially in the minds of his former students. I conclude with the traditional Jewish blessing: may you all live long lives. Bill Fishman certainly lived a very long and full life.

FIGURE 0.1 Professor William J. Fishman

INTRODUCTION

Colin Holmes and Anne J. Kershen

Bill Fishman was born and raised in the East End. His dedicated research into the history of nineteenth-century East London resulted in publications which led to his being widely acknowledged as the leading authority on that area. He retired in 1986 and later a *festschrift* appeared which celebrated his contribution to academic scholarship.[1] Bill passed away in December 2014 at the age of ninety-three and we are proud to publish *An East End Legacy* as a memorial volume in his honour. Lord Smith of Clifton (Trevor Smith) was both a friend and colleague and Trevor's Foreword provides a moving portrait of the man we all knew as Bill.

Bill is widely recognised as the historian of a particular quartier and especially the streets of Whitechapel and Stepney. But his legacy is much more than the words on the pages of his books or his pre-satellite navigation guide to the streets of East London. His research provided a detailed record of the complex web of society, politics, culture and morality that was life in the East End of London at the end of the nineteenth century. His seminal works on this area have served as starting points for further research and writing. Indeed, he opened up a galaxy of opportunities and woven through the following chapters are threads that can be traced in his publications while others postdate the late nineteenth century.

As the vital background to the other essays in *An East End Legacy* Anne Kershen provides a demographic and cartographic survey of East London, roaming across the years between 1888 and 2016. In doing so she writes, citing Bill Fishman's *East End 1888*, that "the issues and images that created the 'overall picture of life among the labouring poor of East London,' more than a century ago are just as pertinent halfway through the second decade of the twenty-first century as they were then." This claim can be defended by observing the presence of the unequal provision of housing, extremes of overcrowding, a continuing large migrant population, as well as high levels of unemployment and the exploitation of vulnerable workers.

Though Bill Fishman is generally regarded as the major historian of East End life, his first published work, *The Insurrectionists*, was spatially removed from the landscape of East London, exploring as it did the progression of revolution and revolutionaries in France and Russia from the closing days of the eighteenth century to the second decade of the twentieth.[2] Yet it signalled what became a major theme in his second book – that of anarchism and the anarchists.[3] Bill's interest in anarchism, which fed into his libertarian Socialism, is the focus of Wayne Parsons's essay. He spent time as a colleague at Queen Mary and, while remarking on the influence of Dickens on Bill's work – noticing that they shared "a deep hostility to the onward march of the speculators, the utilitarians and the calculators in their modern incarnations as managers, target setters and number crunchers" – he observes that the wellspring of Bill's politics had other sources. It reflected partly a Jewish moral tradition which he probably learned from his *shtetl*-educated grandfather. But it also drew ideas from the anarchist Peter Kropotkin which appeared in works such as *Mutual Aid* and *The Conquest of Bread*. Bill's interest in anarchism was also influenced and inspired by Rudolf Rocker's *Nationalism and Culture*. All these strands of thought are woven into the texts of his *East End Jewish Radicals* and his *East End 1888* with their vivid tableaux of everyday life in a teeming metropolis.

The political philosophy of anarchism appears elsewhere in this memorial volume. And in tracing part of this tradition, Michael Berkowitz in "Anarchism, Jews, Relief – and Photography? Behind the Lens and Behind the Scenes, 1892–1946," takes an original approach to that "non-hierarchical institution" using photographic records as a tool in taking his readers into Eastern Europe and across the Atlantic. Bill would have been intrigued by the emphasis on Kropotkin – who was not Jewish – and the image of his filling "a messianic void for the mainly Yiddish-speaking faithful."

He welcomed the visual approach to the past and was renowned for his walking tours in East London. These included identifying tell-tale signs of the past as well as its more obvious reminders such the former synagogue on the corner of Fournier Street and Brick Lane which stands today as a mosque. Those who accompanied him had to use their eyes as well as listen to his commentaries. His awareness of the importance of that visual testimony can be found directly in the book on which he collaborated with the photographer Nicholas Breach, tracing the sights and significance of East London's streets and the daily life which came on display there from the late nineteenth century into more recent times.[4] That aspect of his historical interest is captured in Tony Kushner's "Doing the East End Walk, Oi! Heritage, Ownership and Belonging." This contribution ends on a pessimistic note, observing that "doing the East End walk," as imagined by Bill Fishman is now under threat – at a time when the area itself is awash with tourists and tours. Tony quite reasonably imagines Bill saying to him, when learning of the inordinate sums involved in purchasing or renting flats or houses in the former slums and homes of the dispossessed in Spitalfields such as the Providence Row Night Refuge: *Oi Veys Mir boychik!*

That emphasis on the visual is also to be found in David Mazower's essay on the Yiddish Theatre in London. He describes witnessing the destruction of the

Palaseum Cinema on Commercial Road which had been built in 1912. Seventy-five years later, when conducting a walking tour in the area, he was horrified to see a wrecking ball smashing the entire building to pieces. It was not only destroying the bricks and mortar, he observes, it was attacking "The [sense of] working class solidarity and the dreams of a brighter future that made the theatre a reality ..." Reflecting on what he had recently observed, he writes: "[Bill] would surely have found a grim humour in the way a *folks teater*, a people's theatre, was snatched away from its immigrant founders by the workings of the market." He can hear Bill saying: "Well, go on *boychik*, write it down, tell the story." In commenting in this way he reminds us that Bill was deeply concerned with preserving the heritage of the East End and shuddered at the prospect of the ways in which the City, so close yet such a markedly different world, might influence the world which had surrounded him when growing up. In keeping with that which has disappeared, David Mazower's present essay focuses on another lost part of East End Jewish culture, "The Rise and Fall of the Feinman Yiddish People's Theatre," which, as the accompanying photographs illustrate, offered a degree of magnificence to recently arrived Jews in London, one which is now scarcely imaginable other than through the visual record.

Concern with observing buildings particularly, is the theme of Laura Vaughan and Kerstin Sailer's essay, "The Metropolitan Rhythm of Street Life: A Socio-Spatial Analysis of Synagogues and Churches in Nineteenth-Century Whitechapel." It compares and contrasts the building and street relationships of synagogues and churches. In particular, it distinguishes *ad hoc* Jewish prayer spaces such as back rooms, from the more formalised sites, and in doing so, argues that "the East End provided a particular street setting which brought private, communal and public life into a nuanced balance."

Bill Fishman's sense of humanity meant his work noticed the outcast, the rejected, the problem individuals who lived out their lives in East London. As a result, his accumulated research conveys the reality of the Yiddish saying, "*Schwer und bitter is das leben*" (hard and bitter is life) and many of the faces which forlornly stare out at us from photographs in his *The Streets of East London*, offer graphic visual testimony to the human hardship present in this part of London. Working class Jews especially during the period of heavy migration from the Russian Empire – and even later – could act as a condensing rod for anti-Jewish sentiment when attention became focused on matters such as hygiene, sanitation and physical and mental health. Drawing on earlier initiatives, the established Jewish community realised in the early twentieth century, when eugenics thinking was influential in Europe and America, that such issues needed to be confronted and Todd Endelman's essay "The Jewish Health Organisation of Great Britain in the East End of London, 1923–1946," dwells on the work of a body that had East European antecedents and included in its ranks several well-known scientists including Radcliffe Nathan Salaman.

People lived, worshipped, plotted politics, committed crimes and died in over-crowded and insanitary buildings and the essays in this volume serve as a reminder of the tensions of life in the East End. Bill had an interest in East End criminality and such matters feature, even if very lightly, in his *The Streets of East London*. Jewish crime is the subject of Colin Holmes's contribution, which focuses on "The Reubens Brothers: Jews, Crime and the East London Connection," and takes as its centrepiece a murder committed in 1909 by two young Jewish criminals. At the same time it draws in other related examples of Jewish criminality in the thirty or so years before the Great War. Some of these criminals were anarchists who brought the violence of the Tsar's Empire onto the streets of London, others were established gangs which ran protection rackets and illegal gambling enterprises. The cumulative effect of such criminality during a period of high immigration was to generate and further reinforce anti-Semitism both in the East End and in government.

Even after the passage of the Aliens Act of 1905, which placed controls on immigrant entry, anti-Semitism remained in the East End and attitudes were heightened during the First World War, particularly after the introduction of conscription in 1916. In "Jews and Bombs: The Making of a Metropolitan Myth, 1916–1945," Jerry White notes the development of this hostility and the varied forms it took. Jews were accused of profiteering and creating tension by scrambling for shelter in the London underground – which led to their being described as alleged hordes of "excitable aliens." Contemporary comment also dwelt on the alien exodus from the capital to what were perceived as towns of greater safety such as Brighton – frequently regarded disparagingly as a Jerusalem-on-sea. Hostility relating to the number of Jews sheltering in the underground stations and the cowardly of nature of Jews, was soon to be reheated and reworked during the Second World War.

Interestingly these tensions provided a fertile seedbed for the Jew-hatred which came on display in the East End during the inter-war years from Britain's fascists, including the British Union of Fascists (BUF), led by Oswald Mosley. The iconic moment in the clash between the BUF and their opponents came with the so-called Battle of Cable Street which took place on 4 October 1936. The young Bill Fishman was present there to witness the action. Myths and legends surround the "Battle" and Daniel Tilles's essay weaves through the competing accounts, supplementing the claims of contemporaries with later evidence in an attempt to reach a conclusion on the significance of the event.

Britain's fascists never achieved power during the inter-war years and when the Second World War began, leading members of fascist groups including Mosley and his wife were interned. But anti-Semitism did not die away. Some of the claims made between the Wars echoed those voices heard earlier during the Boer War and the issues returned again during the Second World War. Bill Fishman was himself serving in the British Army at this time. But stereotypes are hard to shift; they sleep lightly.

Our essays range over a wide area of human life which underlines that Bill's East End legacy goes far beyond a single discipline and is not bound either spatially or temporally. Our hope is that they will inspire others to follow new pathways and develop fresh areas of research, analysis and record.

While illuminating, questioning, recreating and refining the past, the contributions also carry emphases relevant to today's London. In that respect, following the example set by Bill's own work, they have a public policy dimension. It is appropriate therefore to end by resurrecting George Santayana's observation in *The Life of Reason* (1905), which Bill used as the frontispiece to his *East End 1888*: "Those who cannot remember the past are condemned to repeat it."

Notes

1 G. Alderman and C. Holmes (eds), *Outsiders and Outcasts* (London, 1993).
2 W. J. Fishman, *The Insurrectionsts* (London, 1970).
3 W. J. Fishman, *East End Jewish Radicals* 1875–1914 (London, 1975).
4 W. J. Fishman and N. Breach, *The Streets of East London* (London, 1979).

1

FROM EAST END 1888 TO EAST END 2016

A Cartographic and Demographic Journey in the Life of an Inner London Borough

Anne J. Kershen

This chapter was inspired by Bill Fishman's literary excursion into the turbulent year of 1888 in his tour de force, *East End 1888: A Year in a London Borough among the Labouring Poor.*[1]

★★★★★★

The themes that Bill Fishman wove to produce the tapestry that is *East End 1888* are timeless and yet specific to the period in question. It was the severity of the conditions and the social and political reactions to the East End of 1888 that began the processes of change – and eventual amelioration – for those whom E.P. Thompson categorised as the "losers" of history.[2] The issues and images that created "the overall picture of life among the labouring poor of East London"[3] more than a century and a quarter ago, are just as pertinent halfway through the second decade of the twenty-first century as they were then. Inequity in the provision of housing and extremes of overcrowding, the presence of a large migrant population, local and national politics, high levels of unemployment, the exploitation of vulnerable members of the local work force and the fictionalisation of the East End – 1888 or 2016? This is not to suggest that the meanness and bleakness which was life for the poor in Tower Hamlets at the end of the nineteenth century is exactly replicated one hundred and twenty-eight years on. Rather than eradicated, time has changed the constituents.

Fishman devoted his book to the nine themes which enabled him to paint the portrait of what today is the area of London known as the Borough of Tower Hamlets.[4] It is impossible in one chapter to follow the course of all nine through the following years; rather I have chosen to focus principally on the cartographic and demographic records relating to the Borough in order to emphasise the continuity as well as the changes that have taken place in the East End.

Before exploring the East End in the years beyond 1888, one needs to consider the geographic and linguistic parameters of the East End and East London; locations and designations which are frequently interchanged and considered by some as coterminous. The East End is now commonly accepted to be the area lying within the boundaries of the London Borough of Tower Hamlets, though some contend its spread is wider, extending to Hackney, Shoreditch, Hoxton and even parts of Newham. In contrast, using a much smaller parameter, Fishman, in his *The Streets of East London* focused on Whitechapel – "the East End in the East End."[5] The area which by the mid-nineteenth century had become known as the East End, evolved from the cluster of hamlets which had, centuries earlier, grown up on the outer edge of the eastern boundary of the City of London; established by those who did not fulfil the required conditions of citizenship but serviced the needs of those who did. Over the centuries the hamlets expanded and fused to become one "place" – the East End. Proximity to the capital's heartland led to the area's becoming a first point of settlement for immigrants and refugees and a pattern of immigrant settlement was established by Huguenots and Jews from the mid-seventeenth century onwards. By the close of the nineteenth century the East End was considered by outsiders to be both exotic and hazardous; in the eyes of some analogous with the African Jungle. Writing of the time he spent there in 1902, the author Jack London recounted having been told, "You don't want to go down there … there are places where a man's life isn't worth tu'pence." It was, according to London, in its darkest corners, an "abyss."[6]

Today's East London was spawned in the early eighteenth century by the growth of Britain's industry and empire. The docks, the railways, ship building and light industry all spread eastward from the City of London, far beyond the limits of the East End. In 1963 Greater London was formally created an administrative county.[7] By the close of the twentieth century Greater London had expanded well beyond its original boundaries and East London became too large to consider as a single entity. Sub-regions were established and the northern area of East London became a sub-region, one of the five within Greater London, as designated in the 2011 London Plan. The northern sub-region currently extends over an area which covers the boroughs of Barking & Dagenham, City of London, Hackney, Havering, Newham, Redbridge, Tower Hamlets and Waltham Forest. It is a far cry from the East End where Bill Fishman grew up during the 1920s and 1930s.

Whilst we can clearly define both the East End and East London spatially, linguistically the task is far harder. In the minds of some, the "cockney" is synonymous with the East Ender, for others the cockney is a true working-class Londoner, born and bred within the sound of Bow Bells in London's Cheapside, having, as Gareth Stedman Jones explained, "a metropolitan pattern of speech, a species of humour and repartee associated with street markets and East End pubs."[8] Thus we must acknowledge the confusion associated with any attempt to tie the "cockney" by specific spatial boundaries, to the East End. The label Cockney is believed to have been derived from the usage of the term "Cock's Eggs," the derisive name given by rural people to Londoners. By the nineteenth century the appellation cockney and the use of the cockney language was considered to be a defining characteristic of someone who lived within five miles of St Mary-le-Bow Church. The exact location and image of the cockney has not been static. Stedman Jones suggests it was not until after the Second World War that the cockney "became firmly located in the docklands areas and the East End."[9] This spatial definition was reinforced in the 1960s and 1970s when television soaps such as *Till Death us do Part* and *East Enders* adopted the location. In his essay on "Cockney and the Nation," Stedman Jones suggests that the appellation cockney was not just figuratively used to denote a contribution to musical comedy; it had a political and social dimension that, he argues, has never been fully explored.[10]

While the remnants of cockney remain as a spatially identifiable pattern of speech, more recently others have taken the stage. Though not specifically tied to the East End, "Multicultural London English" has emerged from the capital's migrant population. Those whose home languages have their roots in different countries and continents, for example, the Caribbean, African, Indian and Bangladeshi, have created a creolised way of speech, one which heralds a distinct and important type of community language change. The East End input being from the Bengali community whose presence in Tower Hamlets, as will be shown below, is significant.[11] The geographic spread of East London has also had a linguistic impact, and a new pattern of "language" emerged in the 1980s – Estuary English.[12] Here again East London has enfolded the East End, this time linguistically.

Cartography and Demography

One of the celebrated characteristics of Bill Fishman's historiographical writing was the way in which he put meat on the bones of the people and places he wrote about. His descriptive passages brought the streets of the East End to life. In order to appreciate the changing nature of those streets and the population of East London, we need to consult the maps and demographic data that illustrate the evolution of the London Borough of Tower Hamlets over the past one hundred and twenty-eight years.

Cartography

The closing decades of the nineteenth century were ones during which, rather than accept poverty as a fact of life, early social scientists began to investigate its causes and effects. One of those was Charles Booth who sought, not to determine how "things come to be as they are," but rather to show "how things are" and, by so doing, provide grassroots-based aids for social reform.[13] One of those aids was his maps of poverty, the first of which appeared in 1889;[14] it covered the East End, at that time an area deemed to be one of the poorest places in England. Booth's Map of Poverty, produced in collaboration with the map maker George Arkell, colour-coded the streets of East London in gradations of wealth and poverty through a spectrum of colours descending from yellow/orange to black. Yellow conveyed an aura of wealth, indicating the upper-middle class; however, there was little, if any, of it visible in the East End. In contrast, the profusion of black and dark blue which coloured the streets at the western end of Tower Hamlets, created what the *Manchester Guardian* called, "a physical chart of sorrow, suffering and crime."[15] Booth's allocation of colours provided map readers with an instant graphic representation of the levels and volume of poverty in the East End. It was a visual, and in terms of poverty, shocking rhetoric. Black was used to represent the lowest class; vicious semi-criminal, "people living the life of savages." Dark blue denoted the very poor, in chronic want, whilst light blue signified those designated as living on the edge of Booth's twenty-one shillings a week poverty line – in reality they came within an income level of between eighteen to twenty-one shillings a week. The 1889 Map of Poverty was not the first map to alert the public, and more importantly politicians, to contemporary social hazards. John Snow's cholera map of 1854 graphically revealed the correlation of cholera cases to a dubious water pump in the St James district of Westminster.[16] But, significantly, Booth's was the first to draw attention to the inequities – and as some saw it threat – of late nineteenth-century society in a location which was only a stone's throw from the centres of government, finance and the Crown.

Booth's map provides us with a cartographical starting point from which to explore Bill Fishman's East End of 1888 and beyond. Booth's survey of the East End and the *Descriptive Map of London Poverty* which accompanied his two-volume *Life and Labour of the People of London*, was published in 1889 and concentrated solely on the East End.[17] The map was revised and extended ten years later to accompany his far more extensive nine-volume second edition.[18] By comparing and contrasting the 1889 and 1899 maps of the East End we can begin to appreciate the changes that took place in that one decade. The later map reveals that the area originally coloured black and dark blue around Flower and Dean and Thrawl Streets in 1889 was now coloured pink,[19] indicating that the newly built Rothschild Buildings, which had replaced the labyrinth of rookeries that previously covered those streets, was now occupied by residents in receipt of a regular wage, the latter a prerequisite of occupying a flat in The Buildings. The inhabitants were accordingly classified at a higher level of society. The 1899 map also shows the Boundary Estate, the nation's first council estate, which was in the throes of being built. Here again there is a significant change. What had been one of the most notorious slums in London, the Old Nichol, the rookery portrayed in East Ender Arthur Morrison's book, *A Child of the Jago* (1896), had metamorphosed in colour from the black/dark blue of poverty to a shade of pink which classified its residents as "fairly comfortable."

Booth did not just provide street maps of poverty and wealth. He was also concerned with the poor people's way of life and as a result provides us with another cartographical guide to the East End at the close of nineteenth century; this time it is a map which located places of worship, public elementary schools and licensed (public) and beer houses. The map not only emphasises the crowded nature of the streets of East London, where the three types of buildings were to be found cheek by jowl, it significantly reveals the multiplicity of public houses which played such an important role in the lives of the poor. Pubs were sanctuaries which provided a warm refuge from the often cold and stark rooms and tenements called home. The function, frequency and, as some saw it, danger of "drink"[20] as an escape from the misery of poverty is illustrated in a map produced by the National Temperance League in the mid-1880s. It presented an East End of London covered by red spots representing public houses – there were forty-eight along the one-mile stretch between the beginning and end of Whitechapel Road. Today most of the public houses are gone. In Brick Lane, which the National Temperance map showed blighted by spots, pubs now have been replaced by Bengali-owned curry houses, of which between Woodseer Street and Fashion Street alone, there are (at the time of writing) some twenty-six.[21] And, whilst at the close of the nineteenth century the "houses of drink" catered solely for locals, one hundred and twenty-eight years on the curry houses attract tourists and diners from all over the capital and beyond.

Booth was not alone in putting meat on the bones of the street maps of the East End. The expansion of the Jewish immigrant population in the East End did not take place without comment, much of which was negative. In an attempt to discover the true picture and evaluate the effect of Jewish settlement, Charles Russell and Harry Lewis carried out a survey of the area and, aided by George Arkell, produced a map of the Jewish East End to accompany their resulting book – *The Jew in London* – which appeared in 1901. They too used colours to identify volume and location, with the densest concentrations indicated in dark blue and lesser numbers in shades of red. And it is the coloured version of the map that provides an instant impression of the Jewish presence. However, one questions the purpose of the use of dark blue shading as the means of highlighting an area which was at least 95 per cent Jewish populated – only a decade earlier Booth had used the same colour to record the poorest and most useless members of society.

There is yet a further cartographical aid to our understanding of the East End at the beginning of the twentieth century and that is to be found in the collection of maps produced by Charles Goad to facilitate the fire insurance of buildings. These maps, which were updated every three to five years between 1885 and 1970, were a street by street record of buildings, as opposed to people. The maps revealed property usage, materials used in construction and proximity to fire services and sources of water. Yet the maps did much more than this; every tenement, cottage, shop and place of religion is shown, as are beer stores, fish curers, livery stables, in fact all forms of economic activity. A close perusal of the 1899 Goad insurance maps of Spitalfields clearly reveals the meanness of the houses that filled the streets, some back to back, and the growing number of tenement buildings which were beginning to dominate the East End.[22] In addition it shows the increasing number of small synagogues (*chevras*) which were frequently tucked between workshops, often invisible and unknown to all but those who worshipped within their walls.[23] By consulting Goad's range of maps produced during the final decade of the nineteenth century, we can trace the growth of tailoring workshops as an increasing number of Eastern European Jewish immigrant men found work in the areas' ladies' and gents' tailoring trade.[24] Charles Booth, Charles Goad and Charles Russell and Harry Lewis produced maps which, though intended for different purposes, all served to illustrate the density, overcrowding, poverty and diversity of the populace and economic infrastructure that was the East End at the end of the nineteenth century.

By consulting *Kelly's Post Office London Directories* for the closing decades of the nineteenth century, we are able to enlarge upon the cartographic picture provided by the mapmakers. *Kelly's* Street Directory section provided details of the principal streets in London, the traders and the trades carried on in the businesses along those thoroughfares. The listing of shops in the East End enables us to chart the emergence of new communities and, as will be shown later on, this applies to the late twentieth as well as the late nineteenth century. In the 1880s and 1890s it was the Jewish community, in the 1980s and 1990s it was the Bangladeshi community. In 1881 *Kelly's* records that there were just four Jewish-run shops in Middlesex and Wentworth Streets – these included a butcher and a grocer. In 1894, in those same streets, there were now eight kosher butcher shops, five grocers, two greengrocers, two pickle makers, two bakers, one egg merchant, one provision merchant, two fish shops and two fishmongers, all Jewish owned.[25] The notable increase in the Jewish population of the Jewish East End is most clearly demonstrated by the listings for 1896 in the *Jewish Year Book* for that year. It records the number of "butchers licensed to sell kosher meat and poultry," east to west between Aldgate and Mile End and north to south between Bethnal Green and Commercial Road, as totalling one hundred and twenty-six.[26] The density of the Jewish settlement in the East End was clearly conveyed by the Russell and Lewis map. It lay almost entirely in the west of what we know today as the London Borough of Tower Hamlets. The map shows that the Jewish community was settled predominantly from west to east between Middlesex Street and Bakers Row, and north to south between Quaker Street/Buxton Street and Commercial Road (East). The combination of maps and directories together build up a fascinating picture of the East End as it approached the outbreak of the First World War.

Forty years after the publication of Booth's first East End map of poverty, a revised map was published as part of the *New Survey of London Life and Labour* (NSLLL). Carried out under the auspices of the London School of Economics, the Survey was chaired by Hubert Llewellyn Smith who earlier had worked with Booth. Writing in 1936, Brinley Thomas described the *New Survey* as the "Intelligent man's guide to the mean streets and withered lives of London."[27] The purpose of the NSLLL was to assess working-class progress since Booth's earlier publication. The East London street survey was carried out between 1929 and 1931, just before the onset of the Great Depression in Britain, after which the numbers of those in poverty increased significantly. Households for possible inclusion in the Survey were selected at random. The intention was to focus only on working-class families; those that came within the category of middle class were subsequently rejected. Inclusion in the Survey was determined by head of household income and/or occupation. For those who were in employment, the NSLLL set the poverty line at forty shillings a week. However, doubts have been raised over this level, with suggestions that a more realistic figure would have been thirty-five shillings a week.[28] The self-employed threshold for inclusion in the Survey was set at a regular annual income of below two hundred and fifty pounds per annum. It appears that no thought was given to that fact that for many, particularly those working in seasonal trades or employed as piece workers, incomes were not static, but rose and fell throughout the year. Class categorisation by occupation has also been considered questionable. For example, a police inspector was deemed middle class whilst a police sergeant was considered working class. Hatton and Bailey argue that it was the misconception by those carrying out the Survey that the Jewish community was predominantly middle class, which led to its "large-scale exclusion."[29] This conflicts with Llewellyn Smith's view that the Jewish population of the East End was "on the whole a poor community, its proportion of poverty being slightly greater than that of the surrounding non-Jewish population."[30] However, the Jewish population of East London was not totally excluded. Henrietta Adler carried out research that was published in the Survey. Amongst her other findings she emphasised the fact that no more than 30 per cent of the Jewish residents of the area had been born overseas; data which accords with the fact that, following the outbreak of the First World War, severe restrictions had been imposed on alien entry into Britain.

As had its predecessor, the new map provided an instant visual guide to the levels of poverty found on the streets of East London. It has to be stressed that this must be taken only as a guide, for the Survey was carried out on a somewhat arbitrary basis, and has to be regarded more as an impressionistic, rather than accurate, representation. The noticeable difference between the 1889 and 1929–30 maps is the predominance of pink and red where previously there had been dark blue and black.[31] At first glance the East End section of the map appears strikingly red and pink, denoting the presence of skilled workers and the middle class, whilst the occasional purple street signalled the presence of unskilled labourers. Extreme poverty and/or deprivation represented by blue or black appeared infrequently. This confirms the Survey's findings that there had been an overall reduction in poverty; blue streets representing one-fifth of the East End's population as opposed to three-fifths in Booth's earlier survey. The map also underlined the fact that the late nineteenth-century clusters of poverty had dispersed away from Spitalfields.[32] The clusters of purple, blue and the occasional black streets are found to the northeast of Bethnal Green and to the southeast of Whitechapel Road. One explanation given for the changes in volume of poverty since 1888 was the introduction of welfare in the form of selective sickness insurance in 1911 and old age pensions for those over seventy in 1908.[33] These benefits contributed to the changed ratio of impoverishment in the East End from 1:3 to 1:4.

One thing the NSLLL maps did not show was the damage wrought by bombing in the First World War. Though nothing by comparison to the Blitz, an Air Raid Map of the Metropolitan Area and Central London 1914–18 shows that the East

End was one of the major targets of the bombing, with a resultant impact on housing.[34] The bombing reduced the number of affordable homes for the poor. This paucity of homes was further aggravated by the fact that many of the properties that had become empty as a result of a movement out of the East End to the suburbs, were beyond the pockets of those who needed somewhere to live. The 1920s saw a huge demand for social (council) housing, and a programme of slum clearance was begun in the 1930s. New estates were planned, one of the earliest being the Chicksand Estate, which was opened in 1937. However, all new building came to a standstill with the outbreak of war in 1939 and it would be a very different landscape that awaited mapmakers from the mid-1940s onwards.

In spite of the devastating force of the Blitz, miraculously some of the original Huguenot-built houses in Spitalfields remained untouched. Once again maps tell the story, this time of preservation and destruction. Material from the National Archives has enabled the construction of an interactive map which provides an impressive instant graphic representation of the impact of the blitzkrieg on East London. Using the bomb census created from data which recorded all the bombs that fell in the blitz between October 1940 and June 1941, "The Bomb Sight" reveals just how many bombs fell on the capital during those nine months. As with the mid-1880s map of public houses, red dots are used, this time to indicate bombs. The impression once again is that of a severe case of measles, this time of a more fatal kind. The *Bomb Sight Interactive Map*, highlights the way in which the bombing was directed at specific targets, most particularly the docks and the East End, particularly Stepney. In the case of the latter, the map illustrates the hazardous nature of the blitz bombing, for whilst some one hundred and seventy bombs fell on the area south of the Highway and the River between the Tower of London and King Edward Park, in Spitalfields over the same period, between Brick Lane and Commercial Street, bounded north and south by Bethnal Green Road and Whitechapel, only thirteen bombs fell.[35] From a map of the "bombing in Stepney," held in the Tower Hamlets Local History Archive, it appears as though a protective circle was drawn around Fournier, Princelet and Hanbury Streets. Some stray bombs did fall in Spitalfields but these knocked out single houses rather than the swathes of properties that occurred elsewhere. By the end of the war, a total of 2,221 civilians had been killed, 7,472 injured, 46,482 houses destroyed and a further 47,575 damaged, all as a result of enemy bombing.[36] The landscape of what is now the Borough of Tower Hamlets, was one of dereliction and depopulation. If the bombing achieved anything it was the eradication of some properties that were not fit for habitation. Sadly this did little to improve the overall housing conditions of the Borough's poorest residents, particularly at a time when the demographic map of Tower Hamlets was beginning to reflect the presence of the newest group of immigrant arrivals. Some slum demolition was carried out under the 1957 Housing Act but, as later maps of the Borough show, pockets of poverty and deprivation prevailed through to the twenty-first century.

There has not been a successor to the original Charles Booth Map of Poverty, or the NSLLL survey, but modern information technology has enabled area mapping which, as in the case of Booth and Llewellyn–Smith, provides instantaneous graphic knowledge – as well as now, interactive facilities. The *2010 Deprivation Mapper* tells the same story as was told one hundred and twenty years ago; that the London Borough of Tower Hamlets is still one of the most deprived in Britain.[37] However, as at the time of Booth, there are patches of "comfort," or rather, as in the case of Canary Wharf, extreme wealth. The Deprivation Mapper for Tower Hamlets shows a combination of sectors painted in shades which represent the very deepest level of deprivation and those which rank the least deprived. Whereas most of Tower Hamlets is categorised between one (the highest level of deprivation) and three, Canary Wharf – together with the City of London, one of the UK's two major financial centres – is ranked eight, the least deprived level on the map being ten. The colouring of this 2010 "map of poverty" is a reversal of earlier colour coding. The most deprived areas now appear in red, the least deprived shaded in royal blue. Seemingly in continuity with Booth and the NSLLL – yet telling a different story – the bulk of Tower Hamlets presents as pink/purple for, though many of the wards in the Borough are graded level one, there are clearly enclaves which are less deprived, the result being a mixture of shades. According to a government report published in 2015, overall deprivation in Tower Hamlets has reduced, and the Borough no longer features amongst the twenty most deprived in England. However this improvement has to be tempered with the fact that, "Tower Hamlets is one of the most deprived districts with regard to income deprivation amongst children and older people."[38]

Whilst a trawl through the Tower Hamlet maps of the past one hundred and twenty years enables us to identify the rise and fall of levels – and places – of poverty and wealth in the Borough, with the exception of the 1901 Russell and Lewis map of the Jewish East End, few maps have sought to put human faces on the streets of East London.[39] And whilst it is impossible to provide an in-depth account of the demographic changes that have occurred over the period, available data does enable us to explore the changing nature of the population of Bill Fishman's East End from 1888 until the second decade of the twenty-first century.

Demography

Bill Fishman's exhaustive portrayal of the East End in1888 brought the place and its people radiantly to life. It is impossible to be as detailed when covering a century and a quarter; even so some individuals will inevitably stand out. In what follows I will attempt to describe the social character of Tower Hamlets, in order to illustrate the continuity and change that has marked the landscape of the Borough over the past one hundred and twenty-eight years.

In his chapter on "The Ghetto," Fishman focuses on the increase in immigration and its effect on the East End of London.[40] It is significant that in 1891 the population of Tower Hamlets, standing at 584,936, was at its highest recorded level throughout the period covered by this chapter.[41] Twenty years later almost 54 per cent of all foreigners recorded in the capital were settled in Stepney, of which number 43,925 were Russian or Russian/Polish, many living in congested and unhealthy circumstances – a further 6,272 were resident in Bethnal Green.[42] By 1911 the western end of Tower Hamlets had become a multicultural repository.

In the midst of all the poverty and overcrowding of the East End before the First World War were havens of culture and escape, institutions created to provide moral and intellectual uplift for those who sought more than just a basic, and often grim, existence. In 1892 the Whitechapel Library, an institution which became known as the University of the Ghetto, was opened; its shelves lined with books in English together with a growing number in Yiddish – in the 1970s and 1980s the latter would be exchanged for books in Bengali and Urdu. Inside the Library could be found warmth, education and like-minded companionship. Nine years later, in a building directly adjoining, the Whitechapel Art Gallery was opened. Together these two edifices facilitated the cultural development of the inhabitants of Tower Hamlets. In the pre-First World War years, they fostered a group of Jewish immigrant youngsters who become known as the Whitechapel Boys; artists, poets and writers whose reputations and works would travel far beyond the boundaries of Tower Hamlets. Artists such as Mark Gertler and David Bomberg, and writers and poets such as Isaac Rosenberg and Joseph Leftwich fed their emerging creative talents within the buildings funded by John Passmore Edwards, himself encouraged by Canon Barnett, the founder of Toynbee Hall, the East End university settlement in Commercial Street. Within the space of less than twenty years, the physical and intellectual landscape of the East End had been enhanced by the construction of centres of cultural enquiry, stimulation and fulfilment within a radius of less than one-tenth of a mile. There were other writers, perhaps the most well-known being Israel Zangwill, whose novel *Children of the Ghetto* (1892), recorded in fiction the tragedy and hardship of life in the East End. Though not locally born, a number of authors recorded East London life as it was. These included Arthur Ward (Sax Rohmer), the creator of Dr Fu Manchu, and his contemporary Thomas Burke – who used the opium dens of Limehouse as the inspiration and settings for their fiction – as well as Jack London and the radical socialist Margaret Harkness, who published under the name of John Law and revealed the deprivation women endured in the slums of the East End.

As already shown, the First World War made its impact on the landscape and demography of the East End. By 1921 the population of the three boroughs that made up Tower Hamlets had reduced in number, a pattern that would continue until the beginning of the twenty-first century. Nevertheless Stepney continued to be the location that housed the largest number of aliens in the county of London; 37,260 Russian and Russian Polish Jews.[43] Even so, foreign-born Jews were continuing the move out of the East End which had begun during the First World War. The newly emerging suburbs to the northwest and northeast of the capital were a pull factor, but at the same time the anti-alien policies of the borough in not providing jobs or housing for aliens, or scholarships for their children, acted as a powerful push factor. These dynamics, added to the Anti-Alien Acts put in place by the National Government in 1914 and 1919, and subsequently renewed annually via the Aliens Order from 1921 until 1953, resulted in little or no new migrant arrivals to the area.

An additional factor which accounted for the decrease in the population of Tower Hamlets during and after the First World War, lies with the wartime departure, repatriation or internment of Germans, both naturalised and non-naturalised. Whilst repatriation and internment was applied to those without British citizenship, those who bore German surnames, even if naturalised or born in Britain, were subjected to attack and discrimination, particularly following the sinking of the *Lusitania* in May 1915. Germans in East London, and even those with German-sounding names, including Eastern European Jews, were subjected to the violence of rioters. In Limehouse, Bethnal Green and Stepney "every second German butcher's or baker's shop came under attack." In the area of the East India Docks alone sixty shops were vandalised and their contents stolen.[44] German families that had lived in the East End for decades came under attack. At the War's end, German communities that had thrived during the Victorian and Edwardian years had ceased to exist.[45]

By 1931 the total population of Tower Hamlets had reduced still further, that in Stepney down by almost 10 per cent. In spite of this, as a result of the shortage of adequate housing for the very poor, overcrowding persisted, in some places as high as two hundred and thirty-eight people per acre. Within this bubbling cauldron future writers including Wolf Mankowitz, Bernard Kops, Simon Blumenfeld and Arnold Wesker were cutting their literary teeth. After the Second World War they would follow in the footsteps of the Whitechapel Boys. Novels and plays, such as Wesker's trilogy – of which *Chicken Soup with Barley* was the first – and Blumenfeld's *Jew Boy*, provided audiences with an insight into life in the East End of the 1930s. In a poem he wrote some years later Kops described the impact of the Whitechapel Library on his intellectual growth:

> The reference library, where my thoughts were to rage
> I ate book after book, page after page.
> I scoffed poetry for breakfast and novels for tea.
> And plays for my supper. No more poverty.
> Welcome young poet, in here you are free
> To follow your star to where you should be.[46]

The Second World War put a stop to the planned improvements for housing in the East End. The East London that emerged after the war was a very different place, with a changed demographic landscape. In 1951 the population of Tower Hamlets stood at 232,860, less than half that recorded in 1891. It would not start to rise again until 1991, and take until 2011 to increase above the 1951 figure, at 254,096. During the 1950s and 1960s the Jewish community of the East End dwindled as all but a small minority made their way northwest and northeast to the suburbs of Edgware, Golders Green, Hendon, Hampstead, Ilford and Redbridge.

In the early 1950s, as the Jewish population was moving out, small numbers of Cypriot, Maltese, Somali, West Indian and Pakistani immigrants were clustering south of Whitechapel Road in and around Cable Street.[47] As numerous brothels sprang up, many run – it was alleged – by Maltese pimps, the district rapidly gained a reputation as a "refuge for whores" and soon became a no-go area for unaccompanied women; an echo of the "dangerous, degenerate and exotic" space that was the East End at the beginning of the twentieth century.[48] Stepney Council was so concerned that it went so far as to request that the government limit the entry of Maltese migrants.[49] In 1961 large parts of Cable Street were put under demolition order and the immigrants began to disperse, many of the single male Pakistani migrants moving north to Spitalfields, settling initially in Princelet Street and Old Montague Street.[50] The seeds of what would become the largest settlement of Bangladeshis outside Bangladesh were being sown.

As return home became a myth rather than a reality, from 1971 onwards family reunions began, as brides, wives and children travelled from Bangladesh to join husbands and fathers. The rate of rebuilding in Tower Hamlets had in no way kept pace with the 1960s programme of slum housing demolition and the provision of decent homes once again became an issue. Families in the newly emerging Bengali community regularly found themselves at the bottom of the housing list or, if allotted homes, were awarded the "worst housing … in the worst estates."[51] Eventually, as Charlie Foreman has described, a battle for homes began as the Bangladeshis fought against the iniquitous and discriminatory policies of local government.[52] Though the Bangladeshi population is now treated more justly in terms of the allocation of social housing, the issue of adequate housing stock remains. Halfway through the second decade of the twenty-first century there are over 23,500 on the Borough's waiting list for affordable social housing and an unacceptable number living in overcrowded conditions.[53]

In many ways, the evolution of the Bangladeshi community emulated that of the Jewish community one hundred years earlier. Provision shops catering for the needs of the immigrants – including those offering fish flown in fresh from Bangladesh – gradually opened in Brick Lane. Where there had been tailoring workshops there were now leather garment workshops, ladies' tailors were replaced by shops selling saris, shalwar kameez, jilbabs and hijabs; travel agents opened their doors to facilitate return visits to the *desh*[54] and, as the twentieth century became the twenty-first, Bengali banks, estate agents, lawyers and accountants were established to service the needs of the growing immigrant community. In 1997 a group of Bengali entrepreneurs conceived the idea of transforming the central section of Brick Lane into a mono-cultural enclave to be known as Banglatown. This was not the first time that the area had been given the name of its ethnic population. In the eighteenth century, when the area was home to thousands of Huguenots, it became known as "Petty France," in the late nineteenth century, as increasing numbers of Eastern European Jewish immigrants arrived, the district was given the name "Little Jerusalem," however, this was the first time that a resident immigrant community had provided its own designation and, by so doing, sought to overtly *own* a section of Brick Lane. The concept did not meet with immediate approval from certain local Muslims and some of the British press. The former perceived it as "an attempt to promote nationalism over Islamism," whilst the *Daily Telegraph* saw it as an attempt to create a "foreign ghetto" in the heart of the capital.[55] In spite of the objections, in 1997 Banglatown was inaugurated and soon after a decorative arch was erected which architecturally proclaimed the Bangladeshi presence in London's East End. Brick Lane rapidly became a magnet for those looking for an exotic experience. No longer the home of the poor and outcast living on the edge, it had become a destination for tourists and Londoners looking for a special night out.

By the early twenty-first century, Brick Lane was gaining attention for more than its restaurants and pavement tours. As had Margaret Harkness in the 1880s, so in 2003, an authoress who was not *of* the East End set out to expose life *in* the East End. Monica Ali was born in Dhaka, the capital of Bangladesh, of a Bengali father and English Mother. She came to Britain at the age of three, grew up in Bolton and studied at Oxford. Her first novel, *Brick Lane*, was located in the heart of East London. It told the story of a young woman from Bangladesh married to an immigrant living in the East End. The novel was acclaimed by the critics and its authoress selected as one of the best young novelists of the year. In contrast, it was strongly criticised by members of the East London Bangladeshi community, who said she had portrayed them as "uneducated and unsophisticated." They complained that the book "greatly offended the hard-working, industrious Bangladeshi community," many of whom had felt insulted by a passage in the book which described immigrants as having come over in the hold of a ship with lice in their hair.[56] In contrast, Margaret Harkness's criticism had come, not from the East End community she portrayed, but from the Marxist philosopher Frederick Engels, who accused her of writing of people who were "passive, docile and lacking revolutionary vigour."[57] Significantly, at the time of the publication of Harkness's novels no negative voices were heard from the residents of the East End even though they included members of the Social Democratic Federation, Socialist League, anarchists and trade unionists.

As the twentieth century drew to its close, the City began to encroach upon the traditional East End boundaries. The immigrant community in Spitalfields was gradually pushed eastwards, its place taken by young professionals prepared to pay three-quarters of a million pounds for a two-bedroom apartment on the Boundary Estate, or millions for Huguenot terraced houses – often formerly squalid multi-occupancies – in order to be close to their place of work in what was becoming a trendy and desirable part of the capital.[58] Brick Lane, considered by Christopher Wren as "remote and inaccessible," has become both the heartland of the Bengali community and a pulsating art and nightclub centre.[59]

However, it is not just Brick Lane and the western edge of Tower Hamlets which has metamorphosed. Between the closure of the docks in 1978 and 1995, what had been the derelict and rotting six thousand acres of forgotten land that had been London's Docklands was transformed into a vibrant and increasingly exclusive space. Canary Wharf is now one of the country's main financial centres.[60] It offers multi-million pound apartments for new young professionals and is the location of numerous banks, media companies and professional service firms, providing work for more than 105,000 people – though few are from the local community.

The changing commercial nature of Tower Hamlets together with its proximity to the City of London is illustrated by its current demography. Those of Bangladeshi origin or birth still dominate the ethnic graph, with 81,377 claiming Bengali ethnicity in the 2011 census, of which number 38,877 were born outside of the United Kingdom. The Bengali population is spread throughout the Borough, with the largest clusters located in the Bethnal Green South, Bromley by Bow, East India and Lansbury, Limehouse, St Dunstans and Stepney, Shadwell and Whitechapel wards.[61] The census also revealed the presence of an increased number of Eastern European Accession incomers. In March 2011 there were a recorded 2,674 Poles, 1,140 Lithuanians and 581 Romanians,[62] plus a diverse Western European presence of which French nationals made up 3,014 and Italian nationals, 3,037. However, when considering the demography of Tower Hamlets it must be emphasised that the largest single group is Bangladeshi, with British and "White Other" taking second and third places. Figure 1.1 reveals both the diverse nature of the non-UK-born population of Tower Hamlets and the predominance of Bangladeshi migrants, whilst Figure 1.2 illustrates the ethnic landscape of the Borough.

Chain migration, employment opportunity, proximity to the centres of finance (in the City of London and Canary Wharf), commerce, culture, religious diversity and tolerance in an established migrant-friendly infrastructure, ensures that the Borough's role as a first point of settlement for migrants will continue.

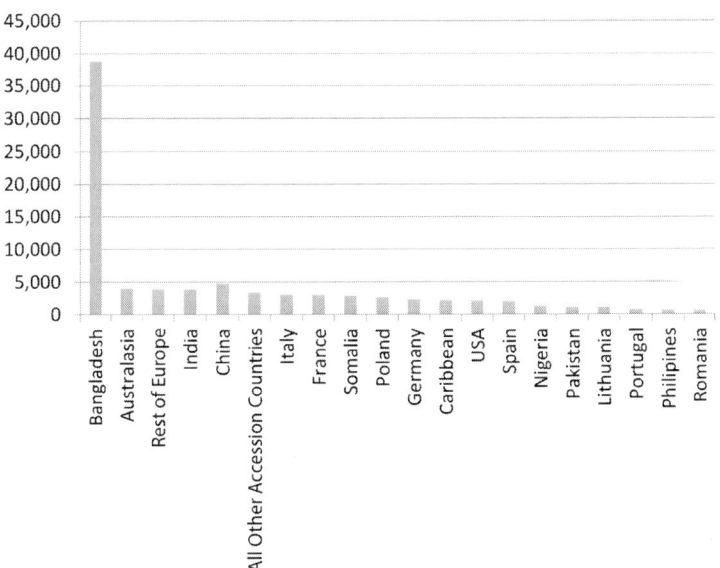

FIGURE 1.1 Residents of Tower Hamlets born outside of the UK as shown in the 2011 Census.[63]

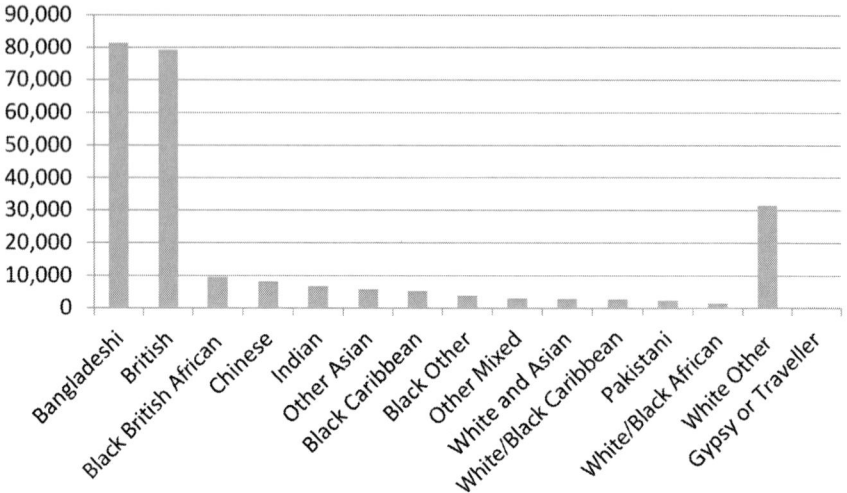

FIGURE 1.2 Recorded ethnic identity of population in Tower Hamlets as revealed in 2011 Census.[64]

The Politics of the East End

It is now time to consider the ways that local political activism has, from time to time found its way into national politics. Political expression and action by members of the local community is not new to Tower Hamlets. Contrary to Engels's assertion, Tower Hamlets has always been in the forefront of political radicalism. It was there in the late nineteenth century that the match girls, dockers and Jewish tailors went on strike in attempts to put an end to exploitation and low wages. However, these pockets of resistance, though initially successful, were short-lived and conditions frequently reverted back to their pre-strike state. In 1919, the Borough of Poplar gained national exposure following the refusal of Poplar Council, led by its Labour Mayor, George Lansbury – though not born in the East End, Lansbury spent most of his life there – to pay precepts which contributed to the funds of other, wealthier London councils. Instead Poplar gave the money to the local poor who were in need of relief. Lansbury's defiance and that of twenty-nine of his fellow councillors resulted in six weeks' imprisonment for the rebels and the term "Poplarism" entering the dictionary.[65] In 1922 Lansbury won the parliamentary seat for Bromley and Bow, which he held for the remainder of his life.

In the 1930s the East End and politics hit the national headlines again when, on 4 October 1936, Jewish East Enders and local Irish Dockers, together with members of the Communist Party, stood shoulder to shoulder to stop the British Union of Fascists marching through the East End.[66] The Battle of Cable Street has gained its place in history as the day when the fascists and their leader Sir Oswald Mosley, "did not pass."[67]

Local politics in the East End attracted local politicians whose roles and activities only occasionally gained attention from beyond Tower Hamlets. In 1993 the

Borough gained national media coverage when the British National Party's first elected representative, Derek Beackon, won the Millwall seat in a council by-election. His support came from local (white) residents who had become disenchanted with all three mainstream political parties as, after more than a decade, little had been done to ameliorate their poor living conditions. Housing was one of the main issues. In the run-up to the Council elections a rumour had been circulated around the Borough that the Bengalis were being awarded "all the best flats with showers."[68] Disillusioned and discontented, long-term residents made a protest vote and elected Beackon. Ironically, his term as councillor lasted barely one year. A fellow councillor recalled that during his brief time on the Council, on the rare occasions he attended meetings, Beackon never spoke.[69]

Early twenty-first-century local politics in Tower Hamlets have been, as so often in the past, somewhat tumultuous. Traditionally a Labour stronghold, in 2005 George Galloway was elected Member of Parliament for Bethnal Green and Bow for the Respect Party.[70] The following year twelve Respect members – all local Bengalis – were elected onto Tower Hamlets Council. Whilst there had been a tradition of socialist support in the East End, in the past it had not been linked to religion. Indeed many of the Jewish supporters of the Communist Party in the 1920s and 1930s had eschewed religion. Now it was different, for in order to gain backing from the Muslim population Respect was encouraging political support through religious organisations such as the Muslim Association of Britain and the Muslim Brotherhood, thus merging politics with religious identity. At the time, the Respect Party's popularity was reinforced by Muslim disillusionment with Labour following the Iraqi war. In the event Galloway did not prove a popular or effective MP and did not stand for the Bromley and Bow seat again at the 2010 General Election; he was replaced by Labour candidate Rushanara Ali, while Jim Fitzpatrick, also Labour, was elected for Poplar and Limehouse. In the Council Elections of that same year the number of Respect Councillors was reduced to one.

The face of Tower Hamlets local government was placed under the national microscope once again in 2010 with the appointment of Bangladeshi-born, Tower Hamlet's local, Luftur Rahman, as the Borough's first elected Mayor. Though Rahman initially stood on behalf of the Labour Party, he was subsequently rejected by the Party when it was learnt that he had committed a fraud in order to get selected. He then stood as an independent candidate. In 2014, Rahman founded Tower Hamlets First, giving a politically recognisable umbrella to himself and the group of independent Bangladeshi Councillors, some of whom had originally been members of Respect. In the local elections of 2014, eighteen of the forty-five Council seats went to members of Tower Hamlets First and Rahman was re-elected Mayor. However, his second term ended in ignominy in April 2015 following exposure by the media and a petition raised by local Labour Party activists. He was found guilty of corrupt and illegal electoral practices and disqualified from office by an Election Court. In that same month the Electoral Commission removed Tower Hamlets First from the Commission's Register of Political Parties.[71] In June 2015, former Labour leader of Tower Hamlets Council, John Biggs, was elected Mayor. At the time of writing the Council consists of forty-six Councillors, twenty-four of whom are Labour, twelve from the "Independent Group," five Conservative and five Independent. Of the forty-six on the Council, twenty-seven are Bangladeshi. The Labour Party is once again in the majority. The Bangladeshi community has politically matured to a point at which it constitutes a majority on the Council; a mark of the political commitment and support of both ethnic minority and local populace.

Conclusion

In many ways the East End of 2016 bears little resemblance to that of 1888. To the east of the Borough is Canary Wharf with its towering office blocks, abundance of million pound plus apartments, luxury shopping malls and cosmopolitan inhabitants. It is a space far removed from the docks that stood there one hundred years before. However, just over the Limehouse Link, dwarfed by the skyscrapers of Bank of America, HSBC and Credit Suisse on Canary Wharf, is a reminder of a less affluent past. The Will Crooks Estate is social housing constructed in the 1930s, which today provides homes for the local community, many living in overcrowded conditions, struggling to find their weekly rent. Continuity and change in one postcode.

At the western edge of Tower Hamlets is Brick Lane. At its southern end is the heart of the Bangladeshi community, Banglatown. In contrast, at the northern end, are the vibrant nightclubs, modern art exhibitions, gentrified homes and eating places of post-modern London. And whilst Canary Wharf has totally changed the landscape of the southeastern edge of the Borough, at its northwestern boundary, parts of Spitalfields remain – externally at least – much as they appeared in the mid-nineteenth century, or even earlier. Fournier Street has reverted back to the century before Fishman's 1888. What were multi-occupancies and tailoring workshops at the end of nineteenth century are once again elegant single occupancy Georgian homes. Architecturally the main artery of Spitalfields, Brick Lane, is a mixture of the past – from the eighteenth century – to the recent present. It still retains many of its original buildings, these now intermingled with 1950s and 1960s replacements for those destroyed by bombing or by slum clearance. On the corner of Brick Lane and Fournier Street is to be found a most unexpected example of continuity and change. The Great London Mosque occupies a building that was originally the *La Neuve Église*, the church constructed by the Huguenots in 1743. In 1899 the building became the ultra-orthodox *Mazhike Hadath* synagogue. Seventy-five years later it opened its doors to the local Muslim community as the *Jamme Masjid*. Externally, over the past two hundred and seventy-three years, no changes have been made to the building's architecture. But in 2010 the area's landscape was dramatically altered when a ninety foot high minaret, which is lit up at night, was erected immediately in front of the mosque's Brick Lane façade.[72] Here is both continuity in the ongoing arrival of outsiders and contrast in that the Bengali migrants overtly and proudly proclaim their religious and cultural presence.[73] Their nineteenth-century Eastern European Jewish counterparts kept a far lower, more discreet profile, content to have left the restrictions of Tsarist Russia and to have found economic opportunity and religious freedom in their "promised land."

Tower Hamlets is unique amongst the boroughs in Britain. Comparisons can be made with other places but its location, in proximity to the nation's centres of government, commerce, finance and monarchy for more than one thousand years has created a provenance that cannot be equalled. Bill Fishman's *East End 1888* brought to us a space that was more darkness than light, peopled more by victims than by victors, where brutality scored over tenderness, and where human life had little value and opposition to alien incomers was openly voiced. And yet within this space there was also hope, happiness and laughter as well as tears. There was fellowship and brotherhood in a place where Jewish tailors and Irish Dockers stood side by side in the fight for ameliorations of pay and working conditions. One hundred and twenty-eight years on Tower Hamlets, though still seen as a stepping stone to a better life, for many is now a luxury terminus. It is a borough where politics are still a point of contention between left, right and centre; a place where the names of Jack the Ripper and the Kray Brothers are indelibly inscribed on the area's criminal ledger and where artistic talents are accommodated and encouraged in what has become known as "London's trendiest area."[74] It is a borough whose Council is constantly working to reinforce and improve its infrastructure, particularly in the areas of education, social welfare and communal facilities.[75] Yet it is still a place where the divide between the haves and the have-nots exists, indeed the dichotomy has expanded. It is a space where overcrowding and hardship persists and where, tragically, radicalism has become a dangerous addition to the locality's downsides. A traveller from 1888 would certainly find the "East End" changed, and for the better, but that traveller would also recognise that the characteristics that gave the location its reputation as a very special and unique place have not gone away.

Notes

1 W.J. Fishman, *East End 1888: A Year in a London Borough among the Labouring Poor* (London, 1988).
2 E.P. Thompson, *The Making of the English Working Class* (New York, 1971), p. 12.
3 Fishman, *East End*, p. xi.
4 The London Borough of Tower Hamlets was created in 1965 following the fusion of the borough councils of Bethnal Green, Poplar and Stepney, all three created in 1900.
5 W.J. Fishman, *The Streets of East London* (London, 1979), p. 7.
6 J. London, *The People of the Abyss* (London, 1977 edition), p. 11.
7 Greater London consists of 32 London Boroughs plus the City of London.
8 G. Stedman Jones, "The 'cockney' and the nation, 1780–1988," in D. Feldman and G. Stedman Jones (eds), *Metropolis London: Histories and Representations since 1800* (London, 1989), p. 272.
9 Ibid., p. 276.
10 Ibid.

11 See J. Cheshire et al., "Contact, the Feature pool and the Speech Community: The Emergence of Multicultural London English," *Journal of Social Linguistics*, Vol. 15 (2011), pp. 151–96.

12 For a discussion on the changing nature of the language of East London, see J. Wells, www.phon.ucl.ac.uk/home/estuary/estuary.pdf, accessed 19 October 2015.

13 C. Booth, *Life and Labour of the Poor in London: First Series: Poverty (1)* (London, 1902 edition), p. 10.

14 However, most of the research for the map had been carried out by 1888.

15 *Manchester Guardian*, 17 April 1889.

16 See T. Koch and K. Denik, "Crediting his critics' concerns: Remaking John Snow's map of Broad Street cholera, 1854," *Social Science & Medicine*, Vol. 69 (2009), pp. 1246–51.

17 Confusingly the second volume of the first edition bore the title, *Labour and Life of the People of London*.

18 In 1903 the collection was completed, by that time running to seventeen volumes.

19 Pink on Booth's map represented those living above the poverty line and higher-class labour, those on "comfortable good ordinary earnings."

20 We should remember that beer was cheaper than water at this time.

21 The majority of so-called Indian Restaurants in the UK are owned by Bangladeshis, who though gradually changing the names to "Bengali" restaurants, in most cases retain the more familiar Indian nomenclature. The author counted these restaurants in September 2015, however, they come and go with rapidity so the number may well have changed by the time of this book's publication.

22 Goad Fire Insurance plan, Vol. 11, sheets 322, 336, 338 © Crown Copyright and Landmark Information Group Ltd.

23 There were also instances of workshops being converted into *chevra* at weekends and high holy days. A.J. Kershen, *Strangers, Aliens and Asians: Huguenots, Jews and Bangladeshis in Spitalfields 1660–2000* (Farnham, 2005), pp. 86–7.

24 See A.J. Kershen, *Uniting the Tailors, Trade Unionism Amongst the Tailoring Workers of London and Leeds 1876–1939* (Ilford, 1995).

25 Kershen, *Strangers*, pp. 90–1.

26 Ibid.

27 B. Thomas, "The New Survey of London Life and Labour," in *Economica*, New Series, Vol. 3 (1936), p. 461.

28 C.A. Linsley and C. Linsley, "Booth, Rowntree and Llewellyn Smith: A Reassessment of Interwar Poverty," *Economic Review*, Vol. 46 (1993), pp. 91–2.

29 T.J. Hatton and R.E. Bailey, "Unemployment Incidence in Interwar London," *Economica*, February 2002, accessed via www.researchgate.net/publication/4989811, accessed 7 September 2015,

30 T. Endelman, *The Jews of Britain from 1650 to 2000* (Berkeley, CA, Los Angeles, CA and London, 2002), p. 205.

31 The map's legend shows that most streets had a mixed population and in an attempt to show this, single colours had a stripe imposed upon them to indicate the minority difference. Booth overcame this problem by colouring many streets purple and thus creating a question mark over the exact nature of the residents.

32 Linsley and Linsley, "Booth, Rowntree and Llewellyn Smith," p. 93.

33 In 1925 the threshold for pensions was lowered to sixty-five and at the same time a widow's benefit was introduced.

34 www.greatwarlondon.wordpress.com/category/air-raid, accessed 30 October 2015.

35 www.dailymail.co.uk/sciencetech/article-2243951/The-astonishing-interactive-map-EVERY-bomb-dropped-London-Blitz.html, accessed 4 November 2015.

36 R. Taylor and C. Lloyd, *The East End at War* (Stroud, 2007), p. 21.

37 http://apps.opendatacommunities.org/showcase/deprivation, accessed 4 November 2015.

38 Department for Communities and Local Government, *The English Indices of Deprivation 2015*, 30 September 2015, p. 1.

39 A map which appears in G. Dench, K. Gavron and M. Young's, *The New East End: Kinship, Race and Conflict* shows the variance of Bangladeshi settlement as appeared in the 1991 and 2001 Census reports, see G. Dench, K. Gavron and M. Young, *The New East End: Kinship, Race and Conflict* (London, 2006), p. 56. While in A.J. Kershen's, *London the Promised Land Revisited* (Aldershot, 2015), there are maps which show the distribution of Polish, Indian and Irish residents of London, see pp. 14, 17, 18.

40 Fishman, *East End*, p. 131.

41 www.visionofbritain.org.uk/census/SRC_P/4/EW1891GEN, accessed 24 November 2015.

42 http://www.histpop.org/ohpr/servlet/PageBrowser?path=Browse/Census%20(by%20da te)&active=yes&mno=141&tocstate=expandnew&display=sections&display, accessed 24 November 2015.

43 www.histpop.org/ohpr/servlet/PageBrowser?path=Browse/Census%20(by%20date)&active =yes&mno=169&tocstate=expandnew&tocseq=500&display, accessed 25 November 2015.

44 www.TheGuardian.com/world/2015/may/13/anti-german-riots-1915-first-world-war, accessed 25 November 2015.

45 See P. Panayi, *Germans in Britain during the First World War* (London, 2014).

46 Permission to reproduce these lines given by Bernard Kops to the author, on 24 February 2016 and this acknowledged by the publisher of the poem, David Paul on 16 January 2017.

47 For an account of the African and African Caribbean community in and around Cable Street in the early 1950s, see M. Banton, *The Coloured Quarter: Negro Immigrants in an English City* (London, 1955).

48 See www.literarylondon.org/london-journal/september2005/newland.html, accessed 11 January 2016.

49 See G. Dench, *The Maltese in London: Case Study in the Erosion of Ethnic Consciousness* (London, 1975).

50 Almost all of the Pakistani migrants in East London originated from East Pakistan, the area which after 1971, and a bloody civil war, became the independent nation state of Bangladesh.

51 Bob Brett (previous Director of Housing for Tower Hamlets) in discussion with the author, 12 February 2003.

52 C. Foreman, *Spitalfields: A Battle for Land* (London, 1989); see also Kershen, *Strangers*, pp. 66–70.

53 http://citizensuk.org/wp-content/uploads/2014/05/Tower-Hamlets-Citizens-Report-FI NAL-use-this.pdf, accessed 26 January 2016.

54 Bengali word for home.

55 Kershen, *Strangers*, pp. 71–2.

56 http://news.bbc.co.uk/1/hi/uk/5229872.stm, accessed 11 December 2015.

57 http://www.victorianweb.org/gender/harkness.html, accessed 14 December 2015.

58 Indeed any "house" in the western part of East London is, at the time of writing, marketed at over one million pounds.

59 Kershen, *Strangers*, p. 55.

60 Initially the Canary Wharf scheme appeared a failure and Olympia and York, the company developing it, went into bankruptcy. It was rescued in 1995 and now provides not only offices for leading international companies but also luxury homes at multi-million pound prices.

61 www.ons.gov.uk/ons/datasets-and-tables/index Table QS211, accessed 1 February 2013.

62 www.ons.gov.uk/ons/publications/re-reference-tables.html tableQS202EW, accessed 11 December 2010. It should be noted that the other Eastern European countries are not listed separately so migrants from those countries would appear under "White Other" category which totals 31,550 and would also include incomers from Australasia, Western Europe and North America.

63 www.ons.gov.uk/ons/datasets-and-tables/index Table QS203EW, accessed 11 December 2012.

64 www.ons.gov.uk/ons/datsets-and-tables/index Table KS202EW, accessed 11 December 2012.
65 The giving of out-relief on an extravagant level. For details on Poplarism see, N. Branson, *Poplarism 1919–1925: George Lansbury and the Councillors' Revolt* (London, 1979).
66 For more on the Battle of Cable Street, see Daniel Tilles's chapter in this volume.
67 *No pasarán* – "They Shall Not Pass" was the battle cry used by the anti-Fascists in the Spanish Civil War.
68 Information from Bob Brett, in 1993 Housing Director for the Isle of Dogs, in discussion with the author 18 February 2004.
69 Information given to the author in May 1994 by a Labour Councillor who wishes to remain anonymous.
70 Galloway encouraged a bringing together of the Stop-the-War Coalition and the Muslim Association of Britain into the Respect Party, one which, particularly in Bethnal Green, would get strong support from the Bengali population. For details of the creation and life of the Respect Party, see S. Glynn, "Muslims and the Left: An English Case Study," in *Ethnicities*, Vol. 12, Issue 5 (2012), pp. 581–602.
71 www.electoralcommission.org.uk/i-am-a/journalist/electoral-commission-media-centre/n ews-releases-corporate/media-statement-on-removal-of-tower-hamlets-first-from-the-elec toral-commissions-register-of-political-parties, accessed 16 December 2015.
72 The Council allowed the construction of the Minaret on condition that, if the building on the corner of Fournier Street and Brick Lane ceased to be a mosque then the Minaret must be removed – arguably the same applies to the Gate should Banglatown change cultural identity.
73 Less than half a mile away is the East London Mosque in Whitechapel Road which can accommodate 7,000 worshippers.
74 http://worldnews.nbcnews.com/_news/2012/07/04/12545648-londons-east-end-from -haven-for-gangsters-to-olympic-showcase?lite, accessed 19 January 2016.
75 See M. Keating, "Knowing our Communities: It doesn't have to be that difficult," in A. J. Kershen (ed.), *London the Promised Land Revisited: The Changing Face of the London Migrant Landscape in the Early 21st Century* (Farnham, 2015), pp. 55–76.

Select Bibliography

Charles Booth, *Life and Labour of the Poor in London: First Series: Poverty (1)* (London, 1902 edition).
Anne J. Kershen, *London the Promised Land Revisited* (Aldershot, 2015).
Anne J. Kershen, *Strangers, Aliens and Asians: Huguenots, Jews and Bangladeshis in Spitalfields 1660–2000* (Farnham, 2005).
Jack London, *The People of the Abyss* (London, 1977 edition).
Michael Young and Peter Willmott, *Family and Kinship in East London* (London, 1970 edition).

PART One
Politics

2

ANARCHISM, JEWS, RELIEF – AND PHOTOGRAPHY?

Behind the Lens and behind the Scenes, 1892–1946

Michael Berkowitz

Anarchism in the late nineteenth and early twentieth centuries, as Bill Fishman demonstrated, must be taken seriously as a secular movement noteworthy for its embrace of the Jewish working class.[1] Immediately before the outbreak of the Great War, Fishman argued, "the Anarchists were the most dynamic element in [London's] East End political life. By the 1920s they were already an anachronism, shadowy ghosts of another era."[2] Individual anarchists and anarchism as a general outlook have long been shunned for obliviousness to practicalities, a willingness to use violent means, and disrespect of social conventions, especially against private property, bourgeois respectability, and organised religion. I will argue that Jewish anarchist sympathies were not dormant while the movement was increasingly marginalised and under siege – despite being judged a "failure" in London's East End in the inter-war years and elsewhere until the 1950s.[3]

The largest share of scholarly attention to anarchism, following the Russian Revolution, is in the context of the Spanish Civil War (1936–1939), which ended in disaster for anarchists and anti-fascists.[4] In addition to anarchist fervour for that much-mythologised conflict, the attraction of, and mutual support afforded to anarchists by Jews from 1918 to 1946, can be attributed partly to the veneration of their past leaders as well as the movement's remaining stalwarts. In certain respects this chapter is consistent with the recent history of Jewish participation in the Spanish Civil War by Gerben Zaagsma, which "analyses the symbolic meaning of the participation of Jewish volunteers and the Botwin Company both during and after the civil war." Zaagsma situates this "in the broader context of Jewish involvement in the left and Jewish and non-Jewish relations in the communist movement and beyond." He explores "representations of Jewish volunteers in the Parisian Yiddish press (both communist and non-communist)" and "the various ways in which Jewish volunteers and the Botwin Company have been commemorated after the Second World War tracing how discourses about Jewish volunteers became decisively shaped by post-Holocaust debates on Jewish responses to fascism and Nazism, and discusses claims that Jewish volunteers can be seen as 'the first Jews to resist Hitler with arms.'"[5] What follows may be read as a complement to Zaagsma's excellent study.

Almost invariably seen as more ethical and less prone to egotism than other politicians, anarchist luminaries were important among the faithful for the substance of their speech and actions as well as their symbolic value. The figures to be considered here include Peter Kropotkin, Erich Mühsam, Emma Goldman, Alexander Berkman and, in a supporting role, the lesser known Modest Stein. The community of anarchists, worldwide, rallied around images of their leaders celebrated in photographic portraits. In this regard they were similar to many other movements across the political spectrum, which availed themselves of the most recent technologies to reproduce and disseminate texts and images. Among the key publications that comprised a common visual core for Jewish anarchists were Kropotkin's autobiography, in Yiddish, *Kropotkin's lebens-beshraybung* (1904);[6] Alexander Berkman's *Prison Memoirs of an Anarchist*;[7] a volume documenting the persecution of anarchists in the Soviet Union from 1919 to 1939, *The Guillotine at Work: Twenty Years of Terror in Russia (Data and Documents)* by G.P. Maximoff (1940);[8] and a glossy pamphlet, the *Alexander Berkman Aid Fund, 25th Anniversary: Campaign for Political Refugees* (1946).[9] Although it is crucial to talk about abstract ideas in relation to anarchism, historians may wish, following Zaagsma, to revisit the myths and symbols of anarchism that were inextricably tied to its functions.[10] In this study I also will look beyond anarchist thought and public endeavours and discuss how essential funds for the cause were raised, which enabled the production of a stream of diverse, creative publications – even after anarchism was presumed moribund.

In this latter respect Bill Fishman was a pioneer.[11] He was interested in what made political movements tick. "It is curious," he wrote in *East End Jewish Radicals*, that selected members of the *Arbeter Frainters* Libertarians "could reconcile their anarchism with entrepreneurship." These were, after all, the good souls who facilitated the staffing of offices and the production of publications. "(Rudolf) Rocker's most devoted comrade Lief owned one of the fine Victorian houses in Bancroft Road, and later made a fortune by patenting a gyroscopic toy."[12] Although we are left to question their degree of *devotion* compared to that of Lief, Fishman also mentions Silberman, "a handbag manufacturer," and Freedman, "a successful bespoke tailor who chose to live in a more affluent area in Bow."[13] First names are not supplied for these men, and they are not listed in the book's index. Fishman insinuates, however, that Lief substantially helped Rocker, financially. Of course in order to wrest control over publishing in the East End, as the anarchists so famously did in the early twentieth century, it was crucial to have funds at their disposal. One of my objectives here is to show that photography and photographers played an outsized role in this regard. It remains difficult to prove conclusively but it seems that photographers gave disproportionately, compared to other vocational groups, towards anarchist causes. I would like to think that Bill

Fishman would not have objected to this approach, as he also was ahead of his time in thoughtfully incorporating photography, beyond simple illustrative purposes, into the study of history.

The composition of my contribution to this volume, reflecting on the fate of anarchists under the Soviet and Nazi regimes and their relationships with fellow travellers in the western democracies, has (at least) four distinct points of origin. In the spirit of those I wish to recall, who frequently defied convention, I shall break with the usual style of academic presentations and provide a hefty foreground to this study, illuminating connections to the late Bill Fishman and his work.

The first station is Madison, in the early 1980s, when I originally applied for funding to conduct research in Jerusalem for my Ph.D. at the University of Wisconsin. At that time, as a student of George L. Mosse, I was writing about the early Zionist movement in Central Europe as a manifestation of what later would be termed "diaspora nationalism." The Graduate School advisor for external scholarships was Fran Rothstein, wife of Mort Rothstein, a professor of the history of agriculture. In one of my initial meetings with Fran, she noticed that I had written my final year undergraduate essay on the relationship between Judaism and Marxism. She asked if I knew the historian Bill Fishman, and told me that she and her husband were friendly with him when he was a visiting professor in Madison some years previously. Mort had been the History Department Chair "during those tumultuous years" of the late 1960s and early 1970s.[14] She strongly encouraged me, if I ever had the opportunity, to meet Bill Fishman.

In a feat of repeated, stunning stupidity, I missed every chance to meet him, despite having moved to London permanently in 1997. I never had the good fortune, to my knowledge, to be in the same place at the same time. On two occasions, my beloved friend and colleague John Klier had arranged walking tours of the East End to be led by Bill, which either did not materialise, or else I was unable to attend.

The second launch pad for this piece is my ongoing exploration of the life and politics of Emma Goldman, the firebrand American anarchist and feminist whose own stay in London's East End was relatively brief.[15] My route from having written on Zionism and then, more broadly, representations of Jews in politics to anarchism was a bit convoluted.[16] After the demise of the USSR, when the universities in Lithuania were beginning a process of redefinition and regeneration, the University of Kaunas inaugurated an institute dedicated to the emigration of Lithuanians – which self-consciously sought to include Jews and non-Jews. The members of my department were graciously invited to its founding conference in 2001.

For Kaunas I prepared a paper about the formative stages of Emma Goldman's life and career.[17] Goldman moved, as did my own family, from Kovno (Kaunas) to Rochester, New York, in large part because it was believed that the modernised clothing factories in upstate New York might provide a better alternative to the sweating system that predominated in Eastern Europe, as well as in New York's Lower East Side and London's East End. I argued then (and later published) that

Goldman's trajectory from Kovno to Rochester was an atypical immigrant pathway – and far more important than the scholars of Goldman had surmised – in fashioning her into the kind of radical she was to become.[18]

Another project related to my hometown origins of Rochester feeds into the current project. After completing a book about the myth of "Jewish criminality" in Nazi Germany, which also has connections to perceptions of Jewish radicals, I began writing about the Jewish engagement with photography.[19] This is a field in which I have first-hand knowledge. My father had worked at Kodak Park in Rochester, from 1945 to 1983, as a metal fabricator. During the summers of my college years, in the late 1970s, I was a "melter's helper" in Kodak's main factory, in the round-the-clock operation producing the base for photographic film.

Some years after my father's death in 1995 I learned that my family's connection to photography stretched back further than a single generation. Through the initiative of a long-lost relative, Lilia Titova, I was informed that the Jasvoins, a branch of my family in Lithuania and Russia, had also been active in photography. I started, therefore, to research relationships between Jews and photography in Eastern Europe.

The book I recently completed, *Jews and Photography in Britain* (2015) was supposed to be a footnote, or a few sentences in the book I thought I had been writing about Jews and photography in Europe and America.[20] *Jews and Photography in Britain* examines how Jews revolutionised visual culture in Britain yet almost nobody noticed. One of the epiphanies that led me to look at Jews and photography in Britain as deserving its own monograph was my encounter with the historical figure Nahum Luboshez. According to none other than George Eastman, the founder of Eastman Kodak Company – who was not terribly friendly to Jews – and Kenneth Mees, who was plucked from the Wratton & Wainwright firm in London to be the first director of Kodak's research laboratory in Rochester, Nahum Luboshez was one of the most talented of the hundreds of portrait photographers in London. Luboshez, also working as a *demonstrator* for Kodak throughout Europe (based at Kodak's branch in Harrow), was a catalytic agent in the spread and improvement of amateur and professional photography, and x-ray technologies throughout Britain and continental Europe. But his name and exploits are almost nowhere to be found in the history of photography. I likewise discovered that there is barely any credit given, or research conducted, about three other seminal figures in British photography: H.A. Barnett, who had prestigious and precedent-setting London studios; Stefan Lorant, a cutting-edge photo editor, best known for *Picture Post*; and Helmut Gernsheim, a foundational collector and historian of photography, who helped create the basis for the study of photography as an academic field, as well as establishing the basis for the "art market" for photography. With few exceptions, Jews in photography were overwhelmingly progressive and occasionally, revolutionary. One of the prominent family firms that mainly served London's Jewish community, Perkoff's, was headed by Isaac Perkoff, who was a known anarchist sympathiser, as was Isidor Yog in New York, who was most famous for photographing stars of the Yiddish stage.

I came to the conclusion that the obscurity of Nahum Luboshez, who should have been illustrious, may have been partially self-imposed. His family, making their living as photographers, had run into trouble in the United States through their anarchist activity, with one relative serving time in Leavenworth prison. Although Luboshez claimed that he came to Europe in order to study art, he also may have crossed the Atlantic to escape the law. The remnants of his photographic archive in the George Eastman House Archives and the Harry Ransom Center of the University of Texas show ties to anarchism, as Luboshez produced the frequently reproduced (typically unattributed) portrait of Prince Kropotkin as well as that of the Georgian anarchist, Valdam Tscherekoff. He also has left a stunning portrait of his niece Natasha who was murdered by the Bolsheviks.[21] Although the caption supplied by Luboshez's descendants does not elaborate the circumstances of her death, she most likely was killed as an anarchist, as opposed to being a "White" opponent of the revolutionaries. In the first decade of the twentieth century Luboshez also captured political protests and the famine-ravaged landscape, including starving children, which helped precipitate the Russian Revolution.[22]

I suspect that Luboshez supported anarchism throughout his life but I have thus far found no evidence beyond his photographs and the police (and prison) record from the United States. Documents detailing his activity might have been destroyed or censored because one of his sons rose to the rank of admiral in the United States Navy. My original idea for this volume was to write about what we know, and what we still do not know about anarchism, with Luboshez as a central figure. But Nahum Luboshez, who was truly brilliant and endlessly imaginative in applications of photography, was possibly clever enough to evade authorities. If he did write in the anarchist press, or engaged in any political activity, he did so under an assumed name I have not yet detected. If he contributed to the cause, financially, he also did it under cover.

Compounding my own stupendous error in not making an effort to contact Bill Fishman was the realisation that he might have known something about Luboshez. Both of them lived in Harrow. Kropotkin also lived in Harrow when he came to London. Perhaps the reason why there is no paper trail connecting, say, Luboshez and Kropotkin, is because they encountered each other mainly in person.

My interest in, and connection to anarchism received another fillip through an effort to create, by means of an initiative of my university's computer science department, an app devoted to the history of London's Jewish East End. As part of this process, I took the team of three MS students assigned to me, Xianjun Xiang, Linda Wang, and Yining Shen, to Angel Alley – home of the Freedom Press and bookshop. As is well known to East End mavens, there is an outdoor wall display of metallic portraits of anarchists – including Emma Goldman and Alexander Berkman, about whom much of the rest of this chapter will be concerned. As I was starting to regale them with stories about Goldman and Berkman, the students loudly exclaimed, almost in unison: "Ba Jin! Ba Jin! Ba Jin!" They were thrilled that one of their favourite poets, Ba Jin – also known as Li Feigan – was prominent on the anarchist display, next to Alexander Berkman. I had never paid attention to

Ba Jin in my dozens of earlier visits. As I was to learn, the placement of Ba Jin near Berkman and Goldman was no fluke. Ba Jin and Goldman had substantial correspondence.[23] The Goldman/Ba Jin relationship encouraged me to look more closely at anarchist networks, sometimes maintained over long time spans and vast distances. There is no room for anarchism as such in communist China, but Ba Jin still has a place in its canon, as he and other anarchists were folded into the literature of communism after their own demise – and they ceased to be a threat.

The penultimate fuel for this chapter is an excellent book I reviewed recently by Kim Wünschmann on the history of Jewish prisoners in Nazi concentration camps before the Holocaust.[24] It is crucial to recall that "[m]ost Jewish prisoners of the prewar concentration camps eventually were set free; generally, release was still the rule rather than the exception" – but under the condition that they were to leave the country and never return, which became increasingly difficult in the 1930s, and nearly impossible once the war broke out.[25] In addition to her discussion of the transformation of "protective justice" into an assault on Germany's Jews, Wünschmann's study delves deeply into what actually happened to Jews in the camps' earliest incarnations, which included "abuse, isolation, and murder" to a shocking degree. "Once captured after Hitler's seizure of power, [Werner] Scholem, [Werner] Hirsch, [Erich] Mühsam, and [Hans] Litten were trophies whose maltreatment satisfied a long-held lust for vengeance on the part of the Nazi movement's paramilitary units, first and foremost the SA."[26] Reports of the gentle Mühsam's gruesome torture were horrifying to Berkman and Goldman. Berkman wrote to Michael Cohn: "He was beaten, compelled to submit to every indignity and his hair was pulled out by the handful and swastika cut on his scalp with a knife. Surely we are again in the Dark Ages. First the Bolsheviks, now the Fascists and the Nazis."[27]

Feelings for Mühsam were not just due to his reputation. Mühsam had written a personal, touching appreciation in honour of Berkman's sixtieth birthday:

> Alexander Berkman was forced to leave his native Russia because he loved Liberty; his home is in the hearts of all the peoples everywhere, although he is not persona grata with the rulers and governors of the states. Every human who loves Liberty loves him. We celebrate Alexander Berkman's sixtieth birthday because we are comrades of his ideology and the admirers of his work and his great soul. There will come a time when humanity will celebrate this brave man, Alexander Berkman, as the pioneer and great champion of its happiness; A time in which all mankind will come to admire and to love him. That time will be when Liberty has become Truth, the time of Anarchy.[28]

While Wünschmann's discussion of the often-neglected Mühsam is an important addition and correction to the historiography on modern Jewry, Nazism, and the Holocaust, it prompted my own thinking about the fate of anarchists during the inter-war years and the Holocaust. I discovered that there was little written on the subject beyond anarchist devotees. Despite earnest attempts at inclusiveness, neither Yad Vashem (Jerusalem) nor the United States Holocaust Memorial Museum (Washington, DC) has yet devoted attention to the persecution of anarchists in the midst of the Shoah.

When I was still on the hunt for Nahum Luboshez's anarchist history, I was struck by the fact that despite their intensive hounding by both the Nazis and the Soviets, and their decided unpopularity in the United States and Britain, anarchists managed to maintain institutional support structures. Besides being interested in material and visual culture, as a historian I also have been concerned with the financial support that enables political, social, and even artistic movements to arise in the first place – and then to survive. How can one understand any movement or party without learning how it is financed? This is where I found a tie between many of my concerns: photographers were apparently important in providing funding for anarchism. The largest single provider for the maintenance and work of Alexander Berkman, after his release from prison, was Modest Stein.[29] Stein made his living as an artist whose work was based largely on photography. But perhaps a more important source of income was Stein's wife, Marcia Mishkin, a successful fashion photographer. Her career was abetted by that of her brother, Herman Mishkin, the official photographer of New York's Metropolitan Opera and one of the better known "stills" photographers in the silent motion picture era.[30] I found, as well, that photographers including Senya Fleshin also offered their services to anarchists – such as did Luboshez – by providing them, most likely free of charge, with unusually good portraits.[31]

The final thread I wish to relate is a vicarious connection between Bill Fishman and myself, beyond the Madison overlap. One of the few non-academic and loyal supporters of my work, in providing necessary assistance to help defray expenses at key moments, is Mark Astaire, the husband of my wife's cousin, Liz. I have dedicated two books to Mark and Liz. An inspiration for Mark's generosity towards my scholarly work was the example of Barney Shine, a friend of his late father, Edgar, and uncle, Jarvis. Barnet Shine was the leading patron of Bill Fishman, who became the Barnet Shine Fellow at Queen Mary University of London in 1975, a post held by Anne Kershen from 1990 to 2011. *East End Jewish Radicals, 1875–1914* is dedicated "For Barney Shine without whom this would not have been possible." I do not wish to infer that I would have been left high and dry without the Shine/Fishman bond. But the support for some of my projects may have been less imaginable to Mark, without Barney Shine's enabling of Bill Fishman's historical research.

I have failed to uncover a relationship between Luboshez and Prince Peter Kropotkin beyond the fact that Luboshez took a portrait of Kropotkin and other anarchists, but I wish nevertheless to begin the expressly historical portion of this chapter with Kropotkin. His name is not often recalled in Jewish history. But he served as an important intellectual leader and symbolic rallying point for Jewish anarchists, to a greater degree and for a longer period, than has typically been assumed. Although he did not have the kind of instrumental role forged by Rudolf Rocker, Kropotkin was integrated and warmly embraced among Jews. Kropotkin's version of an overwhelmingly humanistic and universal anarchism found its greatest champion in Alexander Berkman, who – until quite recently – has been undervalued as a political actor in the United States and Europe. Berkman, similar to Kropotkin, can be comprehended as kind of messianic figure – but not in a literal sense. Both of them provided inspiration and solace to their followers through the transmission of their portraits along with their writings. One the one hand the anarchist cause was complemented by relatively good-quality photography, and on the

FIGURE 2.1 Peter Kropotkin

FIGURE 2.2 Alexander Berkman

other, the movement itself counted a few individuals, connected to photography, and to Berkman and Kropotkin personally, as their most ardent adherents.

In discussions of Jewish politics up to the mid-twentieth century, anarchism persistently resurfaces because the movement maintained a highly visible identification with Jews and Jewish interests. The infamous instances of Jewish anarchists' blatant displays of contempt for Jewish tradition, in New York and London, with cigar-smoking, *trayfe* (unkosher) banquets and marching bands on Yom Kippur, have perhaps been exaggerated due to the well-known history of Elias

Tsherikover.[32] At the time of his reflections Tsherikover had rejected anarchism and turned to increasingly insular thinking about Jewish politics coupled with religious orthodoxy.[33] There was some amount of disaffection from Judaism evident in nearly every other non-Jewish specific political stream, and the Jews were bitterly divided among themselves concerning the explicitly Jewish parties. One factor, though, that binds Jews to anarchism is messianism[34] – a concept not taken up directly by Bill Fishman. Here, however, I wish to apply messianism in the way it functioned, in a more practical way, for the Jewish masses and self-styled revolutionaries.

Since the upheavals of the 1880s, Jews who were keen to radically improve Jewish prospects were searching for someone beyond the norm, an extraordinary leader who perceived things in a different way and could propel the masses in a new direction. This modification of an expressly religious and eschatological notion of messianism might be helpful in understanding the ardent following of diverse figures such as Theodor Herzl, Alfred Stieglitz, Emma Goldman, Alexander Berkman and Walter Benjamin. It is not messianism, as in end-of-days stuff – but an articulation of discipleship for a charismatic figure who offers a bold, transcendent vision.[35] Since the seventeenth century, as Gershom Scholem showed in the case of Shabbatai Zevi, it was important both to talk about and to visualise this person who seemed cut from a different cloth.[36]

One of the reasons Berkman fits so well is because he regarded himself as part of a messianic tradition: a "Jewish Anarchist"[37] whose belief in a "Revolutionary Messiah" was tied to his Kovno childhood.[38] Berkman's prison memoirs include the following vivid reflection, which is quoted here at length because this and other religiously inflected statements are not often reproduced in the standard works of Paul Avrich or expressly anarchist movement publications:

> Involuntarily I am reminded of the old rabbinical lore: only one instant of righteousness, and the Messiah would come upon earth. The beautiful promise had strongly appealed to me in the days of childhood. The merciful God requires so little of us, I had often pondered. Why will we not abstain from sin and evil, for just 'the twinkling of an eye-lash?' For weeks I went about weighted down with the grief of impenitent Israel refusing to be saved, my eager brain pregnant with the project of hastening the deliverance. Like a divine inspiration came the solution: at the stroke of the noon hour, on a preconcerted day, all the men and women of the Jewry throughout the world should bow in prayer. For a single stroke of time, all at once behold the Messiah come! In agonizing perplexity I gazed at my Hebrew tutor shaking his head. How his kindly smile quivered dismay into my thrilling heart! The children of Israel could not be saved thus – he spoke sadly. Nay, not even in the most circumspect manner, affording our people in the farthest corners of the earth time to prepare for the solemn moment. The Messiah will come, the good tutor kindly consoled me. It had been promised. 'But the hour hath not arrived,' he quoted; 'no man hath the power to hasten the steps of the

Deliverer.' With a sense of sobering sadness, I think of the new hope, the revolutionary Messiah. Truly the old rabbi was wise beyond his ken: it hath been given to no man to hasten the march of delivery. Out of the People's need, from the womb of their suffering, must be born the hour of redemption. Necessity, Necessity alone, with its iron heel, will spur numb Misery to effort, and waken the living dead. The process is tortuously slow, but the gestation of new humanity cannot be hurried by impatience. We must bide our time, meanwhile preparing the workers for the great upheaval. The errors of the past are to be guarded against: always has apparent victory been divested of its fruits, and paralyzed into defeat, because the people were fettered by their respect for property, by the superstitious awe of authority, and by reliance upon leaders. These ghosts must be cast out, and the torch of reason lighted in the darkness of men's minds, where blind rebellion can rend the midway clouds of defeat, and sight the glory of the Social Revolution, and the beyond.[39]

Despite this unambiguous self-image of Berkman, few scholars of Jewish Studies have taken an interest in him nor in the extent to which Emma Goldman belonged to an explicitly Jewish tradition. Physically, Berkman was unremarkable. But his frequently copied image was a potent element of anarchism's arsenal, conveying an exemplary sign of moral dignity.

Kropotkin (1842–1921), was not Jewish, but clearly filled a messianic void for the mainly Yiddish-speaking faithful. In 1904 his *Lebens-beshraybung (Autobiography)* appeared in a beautifully produced yet low-priced edition, with a special foreword from Kropotkin to his Yiddish readers whom he mainly identified with the *Frayhayt* ("Freedom") group. Kropotkin expressed his profound, heart-felt gratitude for the translation and publication of his book in an accessible volume, which was somewhat ironic because the book was unusually artistic. He was enthusiastic at the prospect of his work reaching an expansive circle of readers, especially the mass of Jewish workers in Europe and the United States. While anarchism found a warm reception among the youth, he said that the appeal of the movement also extended to many other parts of the Jewish world. Such a book articulating the anarchist perspective in Yiddish was an important and even essential part of the anarchist struggle. The goal of the movement was to bring Jewry into a greater brotherhood of freedom and happiness for all. Such statements as these might be dismissed as platitudes but to Jews reading this at the time, it helped to make them feel part of a great cause.[40]

The volume features finely drawn graphics and good photographs of those who inspired anarchism, such as Alexander Herzen,[41] and the women and men who were willing to sacrifice themselves for the cause, sometimes from throwing bombs or writing what was considered to be incendiary literature. They include Jean Grave, Élisée Reclus, Peter Kropotkin's brother, Alexander,[42] and Errico Malatesta. As a continued sign of loyalty to Kropotkin, several anarchist groups would be named after him during the Second World War. Nine editions of his collected works were published between 1892 and 1932,[43] along with at least four translations of his study of trade unionism which were issued in London beginning in 1889;[44] and a memorial book was dedicated to him on his 25th *yortseyt* (anniversary of his death).[45] The Kropotkin literary societies also produced Yiddish translations that were understood as complementary to his vision, such as Sidney Webb's *History of Trade Unionism* (1920–1921), and Henry David Thoreau's *Civil Disobedience* produced in 1950 in association with the Workmen's Circle and Rocker Publications Committee.

The swift disillusion and disappointment of leading anarchists with the Soviet Union is well-known. Explicit ethical statements of Emma Goldman, Valliant,[46] Kropotkin, Tsherkesoff,[47] and others stood in stark contrast with the emerging shape of the "worker's paradise." Although there had been polemics against the Bolsheviks by their enemies from the right in the west, the intellectual challenge against communism from its left is much less known. The fact that individual anarchists and Bolsheviks joined forces, especially on the battlefields of Spain, did not prevent the inordinate persecution of anarchists under the Soviets.

While Berkman and other anarchists presented themselves as champions of humanity writ large, and their visions, including the liberation of women and the oppressed throughout the earth of different nationalities and races made them among the most egalitarian of their time, ties to the Jewish world were explicit. Jean Grave, who was not Jewish, was fond of quoting Heine. In his *Defence of Anarchism* he asserted:

> It is Heinrich Heine who cries: 'This old society has long since been judged and condemned. Let justice be done! Let this old world be broken in pieces … where innocence has perished, where egoism has prospered, where man is exploited by man! Let these whited sepulchres, full of lying and iniquity, be utterly destroyed … Ideas! these are the eternal enemy of the men in possession. The possessors want to stay where they are: Ideas must go forward.' A dagger struck down the Duke de Berry: immediately the Restoration mounts the tribune and says to a weeping country: 'The canner which struck the Duke de Berry is a Liberal idea!' A bomb explodes: immediately the third Republic ascends the same tribune and cries to a weeping country: 'The bomb which has just exploded is an Anarchist idea!'
>
> Then in the midst of the smoke of the bomb, which in our times take the place of the lightnings from Mount Sinai, M. David Raynal passes a frightful law, which is nothing else but the resurrection of the old crime of *inciting* to the hatred and contempt of the government. Only the formula is slightly modified: it is the crime of inciting to the hatred and contempt of *the bourgeoisie.*[48]

Jews are supposedly people of the book who privilege text over images. But their messianic movements have always been highly visual, such as Christianity, Sabbatarianism, and Lubavicher Hasidism. Each of them creatively and vividly pictured their messiahs and widely disseminated their images.

The volume, *The Guillotine at Work: Twenty Years of Terror in Russia (Data and Documents)* by G. P. Maximoff, produced by the Chicago Section of the Alexander Berkman Fund (1940), may now be seen as a harbinger of history that would appear decades later, excoriating both Communism and Fascism for ideologically driven slaughter. Yet along with reasonably accurate accounts and analyses, accusing the Bolsheviks of sacrificing its ideals in the interest of consolidating power and subduing its supposed enemies, it further enshrined the figures of Kropotkin and Berkman as the movement's leaders. With a portrait of Berkman by Fleshin as its lead illustration, it includes an unattributed, brilliantly composed image of the Kropotkin funeral committee, with Berkman at its centre, which exudes the solemnity, dignity, and mournfulness of expressly religious icons.[49] A number of shorter publications, often in the form of glossy pamphlets, repeated the themes of the Maximoff volume and provided updated information. In 1946 the pamphlet of the Alexander Berkman Aid Fund had on its cover a portrait of Berkman by Marcia Stein and at the end, a scene understood as the persecution of anarchists that would later be described as a classic "Holocaust" photograph. This publication testified not only to the maintenance of interest in, and loyalty to, anarchism until the end of the Second World War but also the extent to which Jewish groups, in Chicago, Los Angeles, and Detroit were mainstays of the organisation.

There was no shortage of leaders and edifying stories for their loyalists, but Berkman's proved to be one of the most compelling. The late historian Paul Avrich is part of a chain of admirers of Berkman. Along with his one-time lover and life-long friend and confidant, Emma Goldman, Berkman is the subject of a recent substantial biography by the late Avrich's daughter, Karen. In the preface, Karen Avrich writes that when her father died in 2006 after a long illness he left behind an unfinished manuscript about the passionate half-century friendship between legendary activist Emma Goldman and Alexander Berkman, a Russian-born anarchist who achieved notoriety when he attempted to assassinate the industrialist Henry Clay Frick in 1892:

> My father published a number of books on Russian history and anarchism, yet he was endlessly fascinated by the magnetic Goldman, a leading figure in early twentieth-century America, and Berkman, who served fourteen years for the attack on Frick, and was rigidly, fervently devoted to the anarchist creed. It was the story of Berkman and Goldman's intense connection and intertwined lives that my father planned to write, and he spent decades gathering material for the book.[50]

The work of the father and daughter is indeed monumental and will serve historians splendidly. The Avriches are unusual in their intellectual ardour for Berkman, because the attempted assassination has led most commentators and even historians to regard Berkman as abnormal, and not important enough to merit intensive treatment. And both Berkman and Goldman were viewed as beyond the pale of respectability on account of their aberrant sexual relations, with at one point Berkman and his cousin, Modest Stein, "sharing" Goldman.

Stein, known to his friends as Modska, is important to the lives of Berkman and Goldman, as well as to anarchism, for other reasons. Until his death in 1958 he remained one of the most critical financial backers of anarchism and occasionally expressed support for the Soviet Union, even long after he continued to live a relatively normal life. The money came from both himself and the photographic practice of his wife, Marcia, about whom little is written. It appears that she too was supportive of the cause. A closer examination of the time around the attempted assassination of Frick, in 1892, possibly shows a previously unexamined but intriguing tie to photography, which will conclude this chapter.

Immediately after the attempt on Frick's life Stein, then living in Worcester, Massachusetts, left for New York. A few months previously he had been operating a photography studio in Springfield with Goldman which did not fare well. Stein and Goldman left Springfield to open a luncheonette in Worcester, which also failed to take off. Stein later claimed that upon boarding the train his pockets were filled with dynamite sticks that Berkman had given him. Killing Frick in an explosion, at his home, was the back-up plan, should Berkman have failed in his mission. Stein, not yet knowing whether Berkman was successful, reached Frick's estate and found it well-guarded. He then took a trolley downtown into Pittsburgh, getting off at the Liberty Street station. "There," his daughter remarked, "oddly enough, he has his picture taken in Dabbs's studio, where Sasha Berkman had been photographed the previous day."[51] Berkman had been taken there the day after his arrest, by the police, in order to have a photograph not simply for identification purposes, but for a photo suitable for the press. It is indeed a fine portrait. But we do not know who the individual photographer was who took it.

The police and federal investigators, and several generations of historians, have perceived no connection between Modest Stein's mission and his visit to the studio. Dabbs's was a substantial enterprise. But perhaps there was an anarchist connection. It also fits all too conveniently with the extraordinarily friendly relations between a great number of photographers with anarchists, and Stein was well ensconced. It could be that even decades after the fact he would not have revealed full details of any transactions, or even information exchanged at Dabbs's. As a well-established business that was respected for its traffic with the hoi-polloi, it would have been a perfect cover for clandestine politics.

What is better remembered, though, is what transpired after Stein left the studio. As Stein tells it, when walking back to the trolley stop, he passed a newspaper stand. He was shocked by the headline: "WAS NOT ALONE. BERKMAN HAD ACCOMPLICES IN HIS MISSION OF MURDER. IS AARON STAMM HERE?" Avrich states that "Modska was startled." He quickly took the dynamite sticks from his pockets and deposited them in a nearby outhouse (wc). He got on the next train to Rochester, where he had family. There he met with Emma Goldman, who gave him enough money to get back to New York. One of Modska's grandsons recalled years later, his grandfather warned him that "should he ever visit

Pittsburgh" he had to watch out where he took a shit, "because somewhere out there was twenty pounds of dynamite under a toilet."[52]

The story is indeed amusing but there is a good chance it is incomplete. If Modska had stuffed the dynamite in his pockets, it is unlikely that there would have been twenty pounds of it. He was looking to blow up a substantial house, or at least a good portion of one. I would guess that when Stein had his portrait taken, he probably left a small suitcase, filled with dynamite, with an accomplice. Perhaps it was the same man, or possibly woman, who snapped the photo of Berkman the day before. We probably will never know for certain. We are left with a tale of Jews, photographers, anarchists, and loose ends. In the end, there is little doubt that photographers, well out of proportion to their numbers, helped keep the anarchist movement going. They have left historians with an unusually large cache of anarchists' portraits, which Bill Fishman might have found remarkable. Photographs of anarchists of extraordinary quality and quantity, and the men and women behind them who contributed in diverse ways to the cause, are part of the anarchist legacy that is thus far under-explored.

Notes

1 On the ground in Eastern Europe, around the time of the Russian Revolution, anarchists were accused of anti-Jewish violence – but this was a point of long-standing debate. Compared to almost any other party, however, anti-Jewish acts were considered out of character. See P. Kenez, "Pogroms and White ideology," in J. Klier and S. Lombroza (eds), *Pogroms: Anti-Jewish Violence in Modern Russian History* (Cambridge, 1992), pp. 294–6; J. Frankel, *Prophecy and Politics: Socialism, Nationalism, and the Russian Jews, 1862–1917* (Cambridge, 1981), pp. 101–2.
2 W.J. Fishman, *East End Jewish Radicals 1875–1914* (London, 1995 edition) (originally published 1975), p. 302.
3 Ibid.
4 See G.R. Esenwein, *The Spanish Civil War: A Modern Tragedy* (New York and London, 2005).
5 G. Zaagsma, *Jewish Volunteers, the International Brigades and the Spanish Civil War* (London, 2016).
6 *Kropotkin's lebens-beshraybung/geshreben fun ihm alweyn; iberzetst fun M. Kohn* (London, 1904).
7 A. Berkman, *Die Tat. Gefängniserinnerungen einer Anarchisten*, trans. Gerda Weyl (Berlin, 1927); the German edition supplies this list of major editions: American, September 1912; Yiddish, 1914; Norwegian, June 1925; English, September 1926; German, February 1927.
8 G.P. Maximoff, *The Guillotine at Work: Twenty Years of Terror in Russia (Data and Documents)* (Chicago, IL, 1940).
9 *Alexander Berkman Aid Fund: 25th anniversary, 1921–1946: Campaign for Funds for Political Refugees* (Chicago, IL, 1946).
10 See M.S. Adams, *Kropotkin, Read, and the Intellectual History of British Anarchism: Between Reason and Romanticism* (Houndsmills, Basingstoke and New York, 2015); C. Cahm, *Kropotkin and the Rise of Revolutionary Anarchism, 1872–1886* (Cambridge, 2002); R. Kinna, *Kropotkin: Revising the Classical Anarchist Tradition* (Oxford, 2015).
11 See the chapter by Wayne Parsons in this volume.
12 Fishman, *East End Jewish Radicals*, pp. 303–4.
13 Ibid., p. 304.

14 Obituary for "Rothstein, Morton" at http://host.madison.com/news/local/obituaries/roth stein-morton/article_118ae0c6-8cc9-11e2-bf65-0019bb2963f4.html, accessed 17 April 2016.

15 P. and K. Avrich, *Sasha and Emma: The Anarchist Odyssey of Alexander Berkman and Emma Goldman* (Cambridge, MA and London, 2012), pp. 325–31, 393–4.

16 M. Berkowitz, *The Jewish Self-Image: American and British Perspectives, 1881–1939* (London, 2000); *Western Jewry and the Zionist Project, 1914–1933* (Cambridge, 1997); *Zionist Culture and West European Jewry before the First World War* (Cambridge, 1993).

17 M. Berkowitz, "New York but not New York: The Jewish Immigrant Experience in Upstate New York" (unpublished paper), conference on "Beginnings and Ends of Emigration: Life without Borders in the Contemporary World," Vytautas Magnus University, Kaunas, Lithuania, 23 November 2001.

18 M. Berkowitz, "Emma Goldman's Radical Trajectory: A Resilient 'Litvak' Legacy?" in *Journal of Modern Jewish Studies*, Vol. 11 (July 2012), pp. 247–67.

19 M. Berkowitz, *The Crime of My Very Existence: Nazism and the Myth of Jewish Criminality* (Berkeley, Los Angeles, London, 2007).

20 M. Berkowitz, *Jews and Photography in Britain* (Austin, TX, 2015).

21 See description at collections.eastman.org/objects/86520/natasha-luboshez?ctx=7b8a d6d8–960f-4253–8359-bd9d8a43b4b8&idx=0.

22 Berkowitz, *Jews and Photography in Britain*.

23 "Prominent Chinese Writer Inspired by Emma Goldman," in Emma Goldman and Free Speech, The Emma Goldman Papers, available at http://www.lib.berkeley.edu/goldma n/MeetEmmaGoldman/emmagoldmanandfreespeech.html, accessed 17 April 2016.

24 K. Wünschmann, *Before Auschwitz: Jewish Prisoners in the Prewar Concentration Camps* (Cambridge, MA and London, 2015), reviewed in the *British Journal of Criminology*, Vol. 56, Issue 4 (2016), pp. 825–8.

25 Wünschmann, *Before Auschwitz*, pp. 122, 124.

26 Ibid., p. 29.

27 Quote in Avrich and Avrich, *Sasha and Emma*, p. 376.

28 Ibid., pp. 357–8.

29 Ibid., pp. 362–3.

30 D.S. Shields, *Still: American Silent Motion Picture Photography* (Chicago, IL, 2013), pp. 242, 107, 201.

31 Avrich and Avrich, *Sasha and Emma*, p. 495, n. 188.

32 YIVO (Yidishn Visinshaftlekhen Institut), *Geschichte fun der yidisher arbeter-bavegung in di fareiynikte statn*, ed. A. Tscherkover (New York, 1943).

33 See J. Karlip, *The Tragedy of a Generation: The Rise and Fall of Jewish Nationalism in Eastern Europe* (Cambridge, MA, 2013).

34 M. Löwy, *Redemption and Utopia: Jewish Libertarian Thought in Central Europe*, trans. Hope Heaney (Stanford, CA, 1992).

35 M. Powers, "*Wolkenwandelbarkeit*: Benjamin, Stieglitz, and the Medium of Photography," in *German Quarterly*, Vol. 88 (Summer 2015), pp. 271–90; W. Frank, L. Mumford D. Norman, P. Rosenfeld, and H. Rugg (eds), *America and Alfred Stieglitz: A Collective Portrait* (New York, 1934).

36 G. Scholem, *Sabbatai Sevi: The Mystical Messiah, 1626–76*, trans. R.J. Zvi Werblowsky (Princeton, NJ, 1975).

37 A. Berkman, *Prison Memoirs of an Anarchist* (London and New York, 1999, originally published 1920), pp. 83, 206–7.

38 Ibid., pp. 227–8.

39 P.A. Kropotkin, *Kropotkin's lebens-beshraybung*, unpaginated preface to the Yiddish translation.

40 P.A. Kropotkin, *Felder, fabriken un verksheper: oder industrie ferbunden mit agrikultur* (New York, 1914).

41 Ibid., p. 127.

42 Ibid., p. 65.

43 *Di entviklung fun'm treyd yunionizmus fun Peter Kropotkin* (London, 1920–21).

44 *Kropotkin-zamlbukh: gividmet dem 25ten yortsayt zint dem toyt fun P. A. Krapotkin* (Buenos Aires, 1947).
45 *Why Vaillant Threw the Bomb!* (London, 1888).
46 W. Therkesoff, *… Pages … of Socialist History: Teachings and Acts of Social Democracy* (New York, 1902).
47 *Anarchy on Trial.* Being the speeches of GEORGE ETIEVANT (sentenced to five years imprisonment on a charge of stealing dynamite cartridges), JEAN GRAVE (sentenced to 2 ½ years for publishing his famous book, Société Mourant et l'Anarchie), and CASERIO SANTO (who killed President Carnot), in 1894 (London, 1901).
48 "Jean Grave's Defence of Anarchism," in ibid., p. 5.
49 Maximoff, *The Guillotine*, p. 341.
50 Avrich and Avrich, *Sasha and Emma*, p. ix.
51 Ibid., p. 73.
52 Ibid.

Select Bibliography

Paul Avrich and Karen Avrich, *Sasha and Emma: The Anarchist Odyssey of Alexander Berkman and Emma Goldman* (Cambridge, MA and London, 2012).
Michael Berkowitz, *Jews and Photography in Britain* (Austin, TX, 2015).
Michael Berkowitz, "Emma Goldman's radical trajectory: A resilient 'Litvak' legacy?" in *Journal of Modern Jewish Studies*, Vol. 11 (July 2012), pp. 243–263.
Caroline Cahm, *Kropotkin and the Rise of Revolutionary Anarchism, 1872–1886* (Cambridge, 2002).
Ruth Kinna, *Kropotkin: Revising the Classical Anarchist Tradition* (Oxford, 2015).
Michel Löwy, *Redemption and Utopia: Jewish Libertarian Thought in Central Europe*, trans. Hope Heaney (Stanford, 1992).
Gerben Zaagsma, *Jewish Volunteers, the International Brigades and the Spanish Civil War* (London, 2016).

3

THE JEWISH HEALTH ORGANISATION OF GREAT BRITAIN IN THE EAST END OF LONDON

1923–1946

Todd Endelman

I

By the 1920s, the interest of the Anglo-Jewish elite in the behaviour of the Jewish poor of London was a long-standing concern. Predating the wave of mass migration from Eastern Europe by almost a century, it first emerged in the Georgian period, when the Jewish poor were frequently associated with disreputable behaviour. The involvement of humble, often newly arrived Jews in criminal activity and their prominence in high-profile, low-status street trades attracted the attention of Christian critics, threatening the status of well-to-do Jewish merchants and financiers, who feared being lumped indiscriminately with them.[1] Thus, for example, in 1766, when "the poor, vagabond Jews in and about London were come to such a pitch in thieving, cheating, robbing, and pilfering that the Government began to take notice of it,"[2] the *parnasim* of the Great Synagogue passed information on Jewish receivers of stolen goods to the Bow Street Magistrate Sir John Fielding.[3] They hoped that their cooperation would reduce the threat that Jewish criminality posed to the security of the community as a whole.

This established a pattern of elite intervention in the lives of the Jewish poor that continued into the twentieth century. At times when the Jewish community, especially the lowest strata, was not in the limelight and the focus of negative attention, the wealthiest stratum of the community was content to provide a minimal level of charitable assistance to the poor. They did so because religious tradition commanded the practice of *tsedakah* and because the practice was woven into the fabric of communal life.[4] It was an expression of *noblesse oblige*, a duty that accompanied wealth and respectability. However, when the behaviour of the poor attracted unfavourable Christian comment and threatened to harm their own image and status, the upper strata of the community were frequently pushed to take new initiatives to quash or reform this behaviour, hoping, thereby, to dampen the fire that was sparking Christian antipathy. The reformation of the Ashkenazi Talmud Torah in 1788, Joshua Van Oven's proposal in 1801 to create a comprehensive Jewish poor relief board with quasi-governmental powers, the establishment of the Jews' Hospital (an old-age home and trade school) in 1807 and the Jews' Free School in 1817 were all sparked by elite concern with policing and reforming the behaviour of the Jewish poor of London.[5] The elite reacted in a similar fashion a century later during the period of mass migration, when East European immigration, along with sweating and overcrowding in the East End, attracted national attention and unwanted scrutiny. Communal leaders came forward with new schemes to promote the rapid anglicisation of the newcomers while bolstering their support for existing institutions that were committed to this goal, such as the Jews' Free School.[6]

The little-known Jewish Health Organisation of Great Britain (JHOGB)[7] was also the outgrowth of 'native' Jewish anxiety about the Jewish poor. Although the concerns of its founders were not the same as those who earlier supported the Jews' Free School and the Jews' Hospital, being rooted in racial thinking and often expressed in eugenicist language, the pattern of elite intervention was similar to the interventions of the Georgian and Victorian eras. It, too, reflected deep disquiet about the ways in which poor Jews – in this case, their hygiene, sanitation, and physical and mental health – contributed to the perpetuation of negative images of all Jews, native and foreign born, rich and poor.

The story of the JHOGB begins, however, not in the East End of London but in Eastern Europe at the start of the previous century, with the establishment of the Society for the Protection of Jewish Health (*Obshchestvo Zdravookhrlaneniia Evreev*, or OZE) in October 1912 in St Petersburg. Its founders – medical men and communal workers – were motivated by both professional dedication and nationalist fervour. At a time when public debate about the fate and future of the Jews often took an explicitly biological turn, focusing on the health of the Jews, they sought to promote the bodily rehabilitation of what they considered a physically degenerate Jewish nation. Fundamental to their outlook was the belief that the Jews possessed a unique demographic, biological, and psychological profile, which was a result of their religious traditions, their persecution and marginalisation, and their confinement in cities, far from nature. Their goals were twofold. First, they promoted research on the physical development of contemporary Jewry and the history of medicine and hygiene among the Jews, thus offering a counterweight to scientific writing that stressed Jewish 'otherness.' Second, they worked to improve the physical condition of Russian Jews, primarily by remoulding attitudes and practices about hygiene, especially with regard to the health of children. They focused not on strengthening or replicating existing medical facilities but, rather, on encouraging what would today be called preventive medical measures. In the broadest sense of the term, their programme was eugenicist, seeking to combat physical degeneration by raising a new generation of healthy Jewish children. In its earliest years, for example, the OZE opened playgrounds and summer camps for children, provided school meals, operated clinics and hospitals, provided maternity and early childhood advice, and published public health pamphlets in Yiddish.[8]

The outbreak of the First World War forced OZE to set aside temporarily its initial emphases and to focus instead on emergency relief work in the Pale of Settlement, where disease, starvation, and marauding armies were taking an enormous toll. It resumed its preventive health orientation after the war but, in 1919, the Bolsheviks took control of it in their campaign against autonomous Jewish organisations. It limped along under Soviet direction until early 1921, when it was completely liquidated. By this time, however, there were OZE branches in other East European countries – most notably Poland, where the OZE branches united in 1921 to form their own Society for the Protection of Jewish Health (*Towarzystwo Ochrony Zdrowia Ludnosci Zidowskiej*, or TOZ) – and even in some West European countries. In early 1922, OZE supporters who had found refuge in Berlin formed a relief committee for victims of the pogroms in Ukraine and succeeded in obtaining the financial backing of international Jewish organisations. In December of that year, this committee convened a conference with representatives from Poland, Lithuania, London, and Berlin, from which emerged a central bureau.

In London, a group of physicians and communal workers headed by Redcliffe Nathan Salaman (1874–1955), met on 10 June 1923 at Jews' College to establish a London affiliate of OZE. In his opening remarks, Salaman explained that OZE was working to halt the biological degeneration of East European Jewry and that Anglo-Jewry was obligated to take a lead in supporting its work financially. The major address was delivered by the Odessa-born physician M. Schwartzman, head of the radiology department at the London Jewish Hospital, who stressed that the main aim of the Organisation was reviving and improving the Jewish race and thus saving it from biological degeneration. Much of his talk featured statistical evidence about Jewish mental and physical health in the newly independent successor states. Cast in the language of Jewish nationalist medical discourse, it spoke of "the great national worth" of OZE. At this initial meeting there was no discussion of health and sanitation conditions in the Jewish East End.[9]

At first, the group functioned as the London committee of OZE, disseminating information about its work and seeking donations to support its East European programmes. Early on, however, at a meeting of the council on 24 September 1923, the decision was made to focus as well on the public health of Anglo-Jewry (that is, East End Jewry). Fundraising for the central office in Berlin was not successful, however: in 1924 and 1925, the Organisation had to depend on Berlin to cover its office expenses in London.[10] In minutes and other documents from 1924, it still called itself the London affiliate of OZE, but by the spring and summer of 1925 it was referring to itself as the Jewish Health Organisation.[11] The change in self-description matched a shift in programmatic focus to the health of East End Jewry. Writing in the *Jewish Chronicle* in 1927, B.W. Lowbury (1875–1948), vice-chairman of the JHOGB, gave an abbreviated – and misleading – account of the shift. He claimed that the JHOGB was established at the 1923 meeting at Jews'

College and that when one of its chief sources of funding, the Jewish War Victims Fund, ceased its activities, the London committee found it was unable to continue its financial support of OZE and decided to turn its attention to needs nearer home.[12] Despite the shift and change of name, the JHOGB continued to affiliate with the Berlin-based OZE. Until the end of the decade, it continued to seek financial aid for OZE and, in the autumn of 1926, with the backing of Lord Rothschild, successfully solicited the support of the American Jewish Joint Distribution Committee, then headed by Felix Warburg.[13] Redcliffe Salaman, its first and only president, served as a vice-president of OZE until the Second World War.

From its inception to its dissolution, Redcliffe Salaman was the dominant personality in the JHOGB. Its activities and programmes bore the impress of his social background, his professional outlook, and his views on the nature of Jewishness. Salaman's family was part of the moneyed, native-born elite, long settled in Britain, that managed the charities, synagogues, schools, and other institutions of Anglo-Jewry. Educated at St Paul's and Cambridge, Salaman had trained as a physician at the turn of the century at the London Hospital in Whitechapel Road. During his seven years in the East End, he became familiar with the health problems of the immigrant poor and increasingly committed to working to relieve them. Immediate and sustained exposure to East End conditions also convinced him of the inadequacy of the *laissez-faire* system and led him to abandon his family's political conservatism for an increasingly interventionist social liberalism. In 1904, when he fell ill from a tuberculosis-like illness, he gave up the practice of medicine and, after time in an alpine sanatorium in Switzerland, retired to a small estate in Barley (near Royston), Hertfordshire. Left financially secure by his father, who had prospered in the ostrich feather trade and then later in property development, he lived there until his death in 1955. While he enjoyed riding, hunting and other country pursuits and devoted time to local government, serving as a magistrate for forty-three years, he also dedicated himself to communal work in London – and to research in his own garden on potato blight (how to breed potato varieties resistant to the viruses that were attacking the fields of commercial growers).[14]

Salaman's commitment to neo-Lamarckian genetics (in which there was then renewed interest at nearby Cambridge) and his own predilection to view Jewishness as a bond that was deeper and broader than the tie of religious belief and practice encouraged him to explore, as a subject of scientific investigation, the biological history of the Jews, their physical distinctiveness, and the inheritability of Jewish traits. His research, which began with the assumption that Jews bore readily identifiable physical characteristics, made him the most conspicuous Anglo-Jewish race scientist in the first half of the twentieth century.[15] While there were other Jewish scientists in Britain who shared his belief that the Jews were a biologically distinct race – some of whom also took part in the work of the JHOGB – he was the only one who wrote extensively on the topic and spoke frequently before both learned and popular audiences.

When the First World War broke out, Salaman, his health now restored, returned to medicine and served as a medical officer in the army, first in military hospitals in Britain, and then in Egypt and Palestine with one of the battalions of the Jewish Legion. His service with the Jewish Legion was transformative: it made him a fervent Jewish nationalist. While he was not an ideological assimilationist before the War – he believed in the biological distinctiveness of the Jews, after all – he was not a political Zionist either. His encounter with the Land of Israel and the pioneers working the land was eye-opening, however. It was "an experience the like of which I had never dreamed of." The young Zionists whom he met seemed to embody virility, athleticism, physical beauty, and courage and were, in his view, heralds of the transformation of the Jewish people. As he wrote to his wife, the poet and Hebraist Nina Davis Salaman (1877–1925), who shared his nationalist sympathies:

> The colonists, boys and girls, are a fine lot, and it stirs one's heart to think that these are the same blood and bone as the cringing, shuffling Halukah type which swarm in the old city [of Jerusalem]. They are straight and healthy, clean in mind and body, look you boldly in the face and smell of the earth. Somehow, good looks seems to abound among them.[16]

Like most European Zionists, Salaman believed that modernity and urbanisation were corrupting Jewish life. But he also believed, contrary to most racial doctrines, that Jews were capable of regeneration – those who were 'hucksters' in Europe could become 'aristocrats' in the Land of Israel.[17]

Salaman's concern with the biological regeneration of the Jews, which first found expression in 1918 and 1919, while serving with the army in Palestine, appeared once again a few years later in his leadership of the JHOGB. Both the OZE and the JHOGB emerged from widespread interest, indeed anxiety, in European and American medical circles, on the part of both Jews and Christians, about the physical health of the Jewish people. The biological turn in the formulation of the Jewish Question, which began in the late nineteenth century, repeatedly prompted questions about whether there were diseases or other medical conditions to which Jews were especially prone, whether these were a matter of racial inheritance and thus innate, and whether they constituted a public health threat. Allied to these questions were concerns about Jewish intelligence, temperament, and susceptibility to mental illness. In Britain, in particular, this conversation took place against the background of highly charged worries about the "racial fitness" of Britons, worries that were stoked by the British army's poor showing in the Boer War (1899–1902). Uncertain about the future of the empire and keen to halt the 'adulteration' and 'decline' of Britain's native racial stock, social reformers, medical men, and political figures embraced eugenicist ideas.[18] The East End of London as a whole (rather than its Jewish residents alone) was a particular focus of concern for them, since it had long been viewed as a site of moral and social contamination, a swamp of immorality, that posed a danger to London as a whole. For more than half a century, it was "firmly established in the public mind ... as a nursery of destitute poverty and thriftless, demoralized pauperism, as a community cast adrift from the salutary presence and leadership of men of wealth and culture, and as a potential threat to the riches and civilization of London and the Empire."[19] The movement of its economically successful Jewish residents to leafier districts in north and northwest London, moreover, left the Jewish residential areas of the East End more homogeneously poor and working class than they had been before the war – and thus, more than ever, in need of improvement and reformation in the view of the communal elite.

Such is the larger context from which the JHOGB emerged and in which it worked in the inter-war years.

II

Like OZE, the JHOGB focused on preventive health measures. Its first foray into the public health field was a series of Saturday night lectures on public health at the Whitechapel Art Gallery during the winter months of 1923–1924. The series drew appreciative crowds and was repeated in the years that followed. One series, delivered at Toynbee Hall in Whitechapel in spring 1930, with lectures by two psychiatrists, a social worker, and a social psychologist, appeared in print as *The Difficult Child: A Medical, Psychological and Sociological Problem*. In a preface to the volume, F.C. Shrubsall, senior medical officer at the London County Council, articulated the racial assumptions that undergirded much of the JHOGB's work:

> The old idea that the mind of the child is like a smooth wax tablet on which anything can be impressed is not correct – there is a certain inherited back-ground and certain traits derived from the ancestors which will come to the surface in some form; these facts must be considered by the wise parent or teacher that the best may be intensified and the less satisfactory elements reduced.[20]

The JHOGB targeted groups in the East End whose future it considered essential to the health of the Jewish people (children and adolescents) or whose work environment attracted adverse comment (garment workers and after-school Hebrew teachers). In its first year, Charles S. Myers (1873–1946), founder of the National Institute of Industrial Psychology, Reader in Experimental Psychology at Cambridge, and Cambridge friend of Salaman, along with Miss W. Spielman, investigator for the JHOGB, lectured to members of Jewish trade unions on indus-trial psychology with special reference to the tailoring trade.[21] Other speakers lec-tured on elementary hygiene and preventive medicine to Jewish friendly societies and youth clubs. In 1926, it sponsored four lectures on social hygiene at the Jews' Free Reading Room, in connection with the British Social Hygiene Council – one for men only and one for women only.[22]

From the start, the JHOGB took an interest in health and sanitary conditions in the East End's Hebrew schools (both private *hadarim* and communally supported Talmud Torahs).[23] This issue was a long-standing irritant in relations between

West End and East End Jews. For decades, the Hebrew schools of the East End were notorious for the unhealthy, shabby conditions in which they operated. Filthy, poorly lit and badly ventilated, overcrowded, lacking basic sanitary facilities, they were regarded as incubators of disease and corrupters of youthful bodies. From its first year, the JHOGB sponsored lectures for Talmud Torah teachers (the largely foreign-born *melammedim*[24] who taught in the *hadarim* were beyond their reach), their goal being the prevention of physical and mental ill-health in the next generation and the improvement of "the standard of racial physique."[25] The list of topics that the lecturers covered was extensive: the hygienic condition of books, water supply, ventilation, sanitation, artificial and natural light, personal cleanliness, student posture (especially the correlation between eye-strain and crooked backs), mental and physical fatigue, the problems of adolescence (excluding sex education), and the maintenance of discipline and order. In time, the Organisation undertook the hygienic supervision of the Talmud Torahs and those East End London County Council schools with largely Jewish enrolments and the medical inspection of their children. By May 1937, there were seventy-four schools under their supervision.

Few texts of the lectures survive. However, from the popular Yiddish- and English-language pamphlets that the JHOGB distributed in the East End, it is possible to recover how they presented their message to East End Jews. Eight pamphlets were issued in the early years of the JHOGB's work. The first, *Your Baby*, was a list of do's and don'ts. It warned mothers against drinking beer, wine and spirits while pregnant and against sleeping with their baby in the same bed lest they smother it; it urged them to breast feed their baby, to bathe it every day, and to give it as much sunshine as possible. The second, *Guides to Good Health*, stressed the importance of proper nutrition, fresh air, exercise and regular bowel movements for raising healthy children. The contents of the third, *Der weg tsum gezunt*, were similar to the second, but in Yiddish. The fourth, also in Yiddish, *Eier kind*, offered twelve rules for raising a healthy child. The fifth was dedicated to *The Care of the Eyes*. The sixth, *The Training of Children*, advised parents to avoid corporal punishment, to be firm but not overly strict, to avoid favouring one child over another, and to inculcate habits of orderliness, neatness, punctuality, and cleanliness. It also discussed good health habits for children. The seventh, *Jewish Health Sayings*, was a compendium of pithy sayings from classical Jewish texts, grouped under the rubrics Diet, Fresh Air, Sunlight, Bodily Cleanliness, Clothing, Sleep, Work, and Exercise. For example, the rubric Sleep included advice from Avodah Zarah (20b) – "a sick person sleeps better when the room is dark" – and Yoma (78b) – "do not sleep in your clothes." The eighth, *Household Pests*, advised how to deal with fleas, lice, rats, mice, cockroaches, mites, mosquitoes, beetles, ants, and flies.[26]

The advice that the JHOGB offered was, by and large, practical and uncontroversial. However, the way in which Salaman and other physicians who supported the Organisation framed their efforts was eugenicist: their aim was the improvement of "the racial physique" of the Jews. (They did not believe, like some anti-Jewish race scientists, that Jewish degeneracy was so racially embedded that it was resistant to medical and environmental intervention.) While their eugenicist perspective is not obvious in the JHOGB's popular pamphlets, it is clearly discernible in reports and lectures in which its officers reflected on their goals. In a lecture that Salaman delivered at the Whitechapel Art Gallery on 5 December 1925 – "Heredity: A Factor in Public Health" – he was explicit. While environment contributed to the formation of the individual, he explained, many troubles were hereditary in nature. Public health policy, however, failed to recognise this and worked, in effect, "to preserve the less fit," allowing imbeciles and undesirables "to produce, with dread monotony, their like." Eliminating from human stock "faulty hereditary strains" would far outstrip in effectiveness improving the external conditions of life, whether by public action or by charitable and individual effort. "Surely the time has come when the serious workers have a right to say to such people [imbeciles and undesirables], we will keep you alive but we must deny to you the privilege of reproducing your kind." Implementing such a programme would relieve society of a financial burden and eliminate "a potential mass of criminal and anti-social individuals." The Jewish community, he thought, needed to undertake "new methods." Sterilization of mental defectives was one possibility, but he conceded that public opinion was opposed to it as a violation of personal liberty. Still, he thought that much could be done without legislation and that it was the responsibility of parents to prevent damaged children from marrying. In his view, this was an especially acute problem in the Jewish community since Jews regarded marrying as a *mitsvah*[27] and forced their children into marriage regardless of their hereditary defects – with the result that "there were more mental deficients among the Jews than among the Gentiles."[28] To address this problem, Salaman proposed that the Jewish community establish a register of mental defectives, whom it would keep under surveillance, in order that any defective children to whom they gave birth could immediately be segregated and observed. That same year the JHOGB discussed the establishment of a voluntary system of "anthropometric and medical" registration and consultation for societies of Jewish adolescents – whose aim, it would appear, was to detect those young persons who should be cautioned not to marry and reproduce.[29] (There is no indication that the JHOGB ever took steps to establish such a register, for this was the last mention of it.)

It is not easy to know how many other leading members of the JHOGB shared Salaman's enthusiasm for eugenics and race science. Salaman was tireless in promoting his views about Jewish racial distinctiveness before both lay and professional audiences and they were well known. He began writing and speaking on the subject as early as 1911, and as late as December 1933 delivered a lecture on "Jewish Racial Origins" to an overflow audience at the Hebrew University in Jerusalem, where he was introduced by the German-born sociologist Arthur Ruppin, who also propagated the idea of a distinctive Jewish race.[30] Most of the JHOGB leadership probably did not share Salaman's eugenicist orientation, although most would not have been uncomfortable in speaking about the Jews as a race, as this was commonplace in scientific circles at the time. Nonetheless, their concern with the bodily health of the Jewish people was very much of the moment, for the biological turn in anti-Jewish thinking had made issues of mental and physical health central to public discussions of the fate and future of the Jews. In comparison, their Victorian predecessors, however great their concern with providing poor Jews with medical treatment, were not responding to representations of the Jewish body as uniquely or distinctively diseased.

That said, one other physician on the executive committee – Jacob Snowman (1871–1959) – was an outspoken advocate of measures to bolster the health of the Jewish people. Like Salaman, Snowman, the son of a Polish-born picture dealer, was a public figure. He was the author of two popular surveys, *Jewish Law and Sanitary Science* (1896) and *A Short History of Talmudic Medicine* (1935), both of which served as counter-narratives to the medicalised representation of Jews as diseased and a source of disease.[31] In the first, which initially appeared as two articles in *The Medical Magazine* in 1896, he argued that over the centuries Jewish law worked to preserve the health of the Jews, rendering them immune from many diseases and raising "the standard of [their] national health to a high degree." Thus, poor Jews in overcrowded slums – he cited statistics from Manchester and New York – contracted tuberculosis at a lower rate than their Christian neighbours because they were "the better fitted to resist it." Their resistance derived from their ancestors having lived for centuries in accord with the sanitary provisions of Jewish law.[32] In the second, Snowman identified a "hygienic consciousness" among the rabbis of antiquity in the "Public Health regulations" that he found scattered throughout the Talmud. For example, the rabbis praised "the tonic effect" of the air of the Land of Israel. They used the cinnamon wood that abounded around Jerusalem for fuel because they assumed that "the vapours which arose from its combustion exercised a salutary effect on the atmosphere of the surrounding districts," and they fumigated their rooms daily with "various perfumes after meals as a forerunner of ventilation."[33] Snowman also served as medical officer of the Jewish Initiation Society from 1904 to 1931 and authored and periodically updated *The Surgery of Ritual Circumcision* (1904).[34]

The fullest exposition of Snowman's eugenicist perspective on Jewish health is found in an essay that he wrote for the short-lived *Jewish Review* just before the First World War. In "Jewish Eugenics," he envisioned the task of Jewish eugenics as endowing future generations with the physical stamina, the intellectual acumen, and the moral courage to carry on the perpetual Jewish struggle for survival. Unlike full-blown ideologists of race, Snowman believed that whatever defects the Jewish people exhibited were the result of persistent persecution, not heredity. For example, he traced the frequency of insanity among Jews to their confinement to ghettos in the past and their concentration in cities in the present. Indeed, because of his adherence to environmentalism, he, like the other medical men in the JHOGB, was an enthusiast for measures to correct and improve Jewish health. Thus, the eugenic response to Jewish insanity was to encourage Jews to take up agricultural life. In this essay, as in his surveys of

the health consciousness of Jewish law, Snowman pointed to ways in which traditional Jewish practice embodied eugenicist concerns long before the modern
period. In this regard, he singled out the care Jews had always devoted to selecting
marriage partners, thus promoting unions among the best types of men and women
in the prime of their lives.[35]

One other key figure in the history of the Organisation – the psychiatrist Emanuel Miller (1892–1970) – was also sympathetic at the time to eugenics and the
attribution of cognitive and temperamental states to racial inheritance.[36] The son of
illiterate East European-born immigrants, Miller attended Cambridge on a scholarship and received his medical training at the London Hospital before serving in
the Royal Army Medical Corps in the First World War. In 1927, he became one
of two medical officers at the child guidance clinic that the JHOGB established that
year (see below) and soon became the chief medical officer, a post he held until
1940, when he resigned to serve in the Royal Army Medical Corps. Miller was a
member of the Eugenics Society, and while little is known about his eugenicist
views other than his membership, he was interested at this time in race-oriented
psychological research. An early project of his at the clinic was a study of mental
disorders of the Jews. Unfortunately, there are few archival traces of the research.
There is a note that the statistical committee awarded him £50 in July 1929 to
cover his pocket expenses.[37] The annual report of the Organisation for 1931 stated
that he was in the process of completing his investigation,[38] while the minutes of a
meeting of the statistical committee in January 1933 reported that he had completed his clinical research and now proposed to collect statistical data for England
and Wales.[39] No report or summary was ever issued. But in May 1930, while
ostensibly at work on the study, Miller offered a glimpse into his views on racial
inheritance in a lecture on 'The Jewish Mind in Health and Disease' at a JHOGB-
sponsored public meeting at Conway Hall on 'Physical and Mental Aspects of the
Jew.' While acknowledging the difficulties of assessing temperamental differences
between Jews and non-Jews and while also noting that "the same laws which
operate in the Jew are found to operate in diverse races who have been subject to
the same type of investigation," he also endorsed the then popular view that "the
Jewish child thinks verbally and a non-Jewish child pictorially." In observing
Jewish and non-Jewish children with borderline neuroses and behaviour problems,
he told the audience, he had noticed that visual imagery disappeared quickly in
Jewish children at a comparatively early age, while verbal expression (imitating the
linguistic habits of the adult) came easier to them. This explained, he added, why
musical ability was found more frequently among Jewish children, for it was nearer
to the world of mathematics and logical relationships than the visual world of
concrete things. This tendency towards realism also explained, in his view, why
Jews were such striking contributors to the sciences.[40]

The most innovative initiative of the JHOGB was the establishment in 1927 of
the first children's mental health clinic in Britain. From the start the society had
"viewed with apprehension the growth of the nervous disorders amongst the
children of this thickly populated district [the East End]," where there was not only

"an increase of psychological maladjustment in home and school producing emotional disturbance and educational disorders, but an increase in disorders of behaviour from simple refractoriness to delinquency."[41] More pointedly, the annual report for 1931 declared that "the prevalence of mental disorder alone" in the East End was "a standing menace" to the Jewish community as a whole.[42] In response to concerns such as these, in January 1926, the health committee of the JHOGB urged the establishment of a clinic for difficult and delinquent children. Planning started the following year, and the clinic opened in October 1927 in three rooms in the Jews' Free School in Bell Lane. This "temporary" arrangement lasted for ten years until the JHOGB acquired a building of its own in Rampart Street, Commercial Road, in 1937. At that time, the JHOGB, which had been headquartered in Woburn House, moved its office into the building as well. The clinic, known as the East London Child Guidance Clinic since 1932, and the Organisation's office remained there until the Organisation's demise in the Second World War. The clinic outlived its parent, however, and continued its work elsewhere in East London, where, now renamed the Emanuel Miller Centre for Families and Children, it treats disturbed children to this day.

The approach of the clinic to the treatment of children with "nervous disorders" was innovative from the start. Borrowing from methods practised in the United States, where the first child guidance clinic was established in Boston in 1921, it embraced the notion of cooperative, multidimensional treatment. It employed psychiatrists, psychologists, social workers, play therapists, speech therapists, and research psychologists who, as a team, treated the totality of their patients' needs. Treating the child in the context of his or her home setting and family background was also critical to its method. As Miller explained, often a grandparent was found to be "a potent force, perhaps a hidden one" in the working of a family and unless his or her role was addressed it was often "impossible to make headway in the elucidation and removal of the child's difficulties."[43] Children were referred to the clinic by school doctors, head teachers, probation officers, hospitals and clinics, private doctors, and parents and friends. The presenting symptoms included backwardness, lack of concentration, nervousness, excitability, restlessness, depression, bedwetting, temper tantrums, speech impediments, aggressiveness, theft, masturbation, night terrors and sleepwalking, truancy, solitary behaviour, reading disability, breathing difficulty, cyclic vomiting, photophobia, headache, temporary lapses of consciousness, and eating disorders – a list that, with one or two exceptions, would be familiar to health care professionals today.[44]

Judging by the number of children who were seen at the clinic and by the professional praise it won, it was a success. In its first two years, the clinic treated 104 children,[45] and soon there was a waiting list, leading the clinic to forgo advertising its services to local practitioners.[46] In its first six years, it treated 735 children,[47] and, in its first ten years, according to Emanuel Miller, about 1,500 children.[48] Its work attracted attention outside the Jewish community. A speaker at the fourth annual meeting in 1928 boasted that it was referred to at scientific and education congresses.[49] In January 1931, Sir George Newman, chief medical officer in the Ministry of Education, wrote approvingly in his annual report of the work of the clinic, which he described at length. He emphasised that the primary aim of the clinic was similar to that of the school medical service of the Ministry of Education: the diagnosis and treatment of early and slight departures from the normal to prevent them from becoming major abnormalities, leading to "gross aberrations of conduct, delinquency and crime."[50] That same year ten county medical officers of health visited the clinic as a group, and in May 1936, the Austrian émigré psychologist Alfred Adler visited and demonstrated his technique and method of diagnosis before a large audience.[51] Medical dignitaries graced the programmes at fundraising events. For example, in 1931, Lord Moynihan, president of the Royal College of Surgeons, told a gathering at a private home that strictly observant Jews were more resistant to the diseases of urban degeneracy than those who were lax or indifferent.[52]

The establishment of the clinic and then its expansion taxed the financial resources of the JHOGB. In March 1936, for example, a year before the launch of a major fundraising campaign, it had £61 in its bank account and £500 in unpaid bills.[53] A financial statement prepared for that campaign estimated annual income at £1,650 and annual expenditure at £2,390 – plus an existing deficit of £800.[54] The problem was both the increase in JHOGB work and the niggardliness of wealthy English Jews. From the start, Salaman complained about the difficulties of fundraising. In one notably angry outburst in 1934, he scathingly observed: "We seem to need a German crisis, a pogrom, or a Rothschild to be evicted from a restaurant before the community wakes up." Why, he asked, does the community allow its schools and religious classes to be so badly equipped and ventilated? "Are we really humbugs or do we really care for the children's health and education?" He noted that Jews took pride in how well they cared for their children, whom he described as the most overfed in the world. Yet, he lamented, it was difficult to raise money to remedy the underfeeding of poor children.[55]

Surprisingly, given the racial and national orientation of Salaman and others, the clinic selected children on a non-denominational basis. When it first opened, the majority of patients were Jewish – sixty-three Jewish children and forty-one non-Jewish children in the first two years[56] – but the ratio shifted within a few years and by the early 1930s more than half of the patients were non-Jewish.[57] If "the prevalence of mental disorder" in the Jewish East End was "a standing menace" to Anglo-Jewry and the JHOGB targeted in its other activities Jews exclusively, then why did the clinic, which received no state funds, serve all East End children in general? Unfortunately, little documentation survives that sheds light on this question. A few frustratingly brief notes in the minutes of the clinic committee prior to the opening of the clinic reveal that the question was discussed early on. Alfred Eichholz (1869–1933), Chief Medical Inspector to the Board of Education, chair of the newly created Central Committee for Jewish Education, and son-in-law of Chief Rabbi Hermann Adler, expressed the view that the clinic should not be limited to Jews. Charles Myers wondered whether non-Jews would be reluctant to send their children to be treated if the clinic was housed in the Jews' Free School and G. Chaikin responded that the London Jewish Hospital was very popular with non-Jews.[58] Other than these few remarks, there is no record of how or why the decision to treat non-Jewish children was reached.

In the absence of evidence, we can only speculate. One possibility is that most of the physicians who were active in the JHOGB did not share the eugenicist views of Salaman and others and thus were not concerned above all with the rehabilitation of the mental health of a degenerate nation or race. For them, the clinic was a humanitarian move to improve the health of children in a well-known deprived quarter of London where Jews and non-Jews lived in close proximity to each other. Another possibility is that the clinic's backers, whatever their views, saw the advantage of sponsoring a project that would cultivate goodwill outside the Jewish community and rebound to its credit. One hint that this was the case to some extent appeared in a report for the period January 1933 to June 1934. Here, after noting that more than half of the clinic's clientele was not Jewish, the report added that "this practical philanthropy" promoted "a better understanding with our neighbours in the most populous Jewish district in England."[59] Whatever the case, it was the non-denominational intake of the clinic that allowed it to survive long after the demise of its parent organisation.

III

In addition to its preventive medicine programmes and its clinical work with disturbed children, the JHOGB also sponsored research on the physical and mental health and demographic profile of London Jews. This research, like much early twentieth-century Jewish-supported research on the demography, sociology, and ethnology of the Jews, was a response to the racialised treatment of Jews in contemporary scientific literature. As Mitchell Hart explains, it was an effort by Jewish scientists to appropriate the methods and concepts of social science for their own ends, whether integrationist or nationalist. Using statistical data, much of which came from government sources, they fashioned "Jewish" narratives of Jewish race, health, crime, family life, and fertility.[60] Anglo-Jewry lagged behind the German and American Jewish communities in this kind of quantitative self-study. Although the Australian-born folklorist and historian Joseph Jacobs (1854–1916) pioneered the social scientific study of London Jews in the 1880s,[61] he had no Anglo-Jewish successors after his departure for New York in 1900. The decision of the JHOGB to initiate a research programme in the late 1920s reversed decades of neglect.

The JHOGB was explicit about its motives for sponsoring research. Its fourth annual report noted that Jews suffered collectively from the prejudices of non-Jewish investigators, whose casual observations about Jews, which were often viewed as authoritative, were merely incidental to their interest in some broader problems.[62] The rise of Nazism and domestic fascism made the need for data seem even more pressing. In 1934, when an appeal for funds for further statistical research failed, the annual report commented that this was especially tragic at the moment when Nazi Germany was spreading lies and distortions about the Jews.

Now, more than ever, it continued, there was a need for organised investigation, for establishing a clear picture of the social and economic position of the community. Unless this need was met, it feared, scientifically discredited theories would continue to poison the mind of the man in the street.[63] Two years later, when the Organisation was seeking to establish a permanent bureau of statistical information, Salaman explained to the communal leader Robert Waley Cohen (1877–1952) that the bureau would supply information to speakers and writers countering "the antisemitic campaign now raging."[64] The Ukrainian-born Leon Isserlis (1881–1966), chair of the JHOGB statistical committee and statistician to the Board of Shipping, expressed dismay at this time to Salaman at the inability of the community to grasp the urgency of the matter. In "peace time" the community suffered from a lack of numerical data when responding to everyday problems. It should now be "on a war footing," for anti-Semitism in England, even if it appeared at present "to be a cloud no bigger than a man's hand," had appeared equally unthreatening to the casual observer in Germany in 1930.[65]

A clear example of the JHOGB's attitude to research is its response to Karl Pearson's study of the intelligence of Jewish school children, based on data gathered at the Jews' Free School in 1913 but not published until 1925 to 1927.[66] Pearson, a biostatistician and Galton Professor of Eugenics at University College, London, found that Jewish girls scored less well on intelligence tests than non-Jewish girls while Jewish boys scored worse than non-Jewish boys in good schools but better than non-Jewish boys in poor schools. Since his data revealed that Jews were not markedly more intelligent than native Englishmen, he concluded that Britain would not benefit from further Jewish immigration. This conclusion, not surprisingly, alarmed the Board of Deputies of British Jews, whose assistant secretary, J.M. Rich (c. 1897–1987), turned to Salaman for advice in late 1925. Salaman then referred him to Charles Myers. Myers was familiar with Pearson's work on the intelligence of Jewish schoolchildren and was not impressed, noting that neither Pearson nor those who administered the tests at the Jews' Free School were trained in experimental psychology. Indeed, three years earlier, when Myers had asked if he could see the tests Pearson had used, the latter had made "some excuse of secrecy" and put him off from seeing them. Myers and Salaman then contracted with Cyril Burt, an educational psychologist and a pioneer of intelligence testing, who thought that the exclusion of Jews was bad eugenics policy, to supervise a new study, to whose costs the Board of Deputies contributed £30.[67] (Burt's post-Second World War studies of the inheritability of intelligence were widely discredited after his death and he was accused of deliberate fraud, at worst, or unintentional carelessness, at best.)

The new study, conducted by the psychologists Mary Davies and A.G. Hughes, tested children in three schools (the first in a good district in North London, the second in a moderately poor district in East London, and the third in a very poor district in East London). It produced very different results: Jewish children, boys and girls alike, at all age levels, outperformed non-Jewish children in all three sections of the Northumberland standardized intelligence test, regardless of the type of school.[68] Pleased with the results of the investigation, the Board of Deputies ordered fifty offprints of the report, which had appeared in the *British Journal of Psychology* in 1927. It also began cooperating with the JHOGB, which wished to expand its statistical investigations, in collecting monthly burial returns from all Jewish burial societies in the United Kingdom. This cooperation lasted from 1928 to at least 1931. The work was hampered, however, by the indifference of the burial societies, which frequently did not bother to send in the requested data.[69]

The Davies and Hughes study was not the JHOGB's only foray into the debate over Jewish intelligence. Several years later it commissioned a review of the literature on "the psyche of the Jew" and "his intelligence" by the sociologist Judah Rumyaneck (1905–1957), then a doctoral student at the London School of Economics.[70] Rumyaneck's review, published in the *British Journal of Psychology* in 1931,[71] was less suited to apologetic use than the Davies and Hughes report. While critical of the Pearson study, it was also critical of Davies and Hughes's work, largely because the investigators were unsuccessful, in his view, of holding constant the role of environment. Rumyaneck's larger point was that claims to innate psychological differences among different groups had in no way been substantiated and that no technique existed to evaluate either the alleged intellectual superiority of Jews or their allegedly unique psychological faculties. He declared untenable the once widely held conviction that heredity or nature was the dominant influence in the formation of psychological differences and intelligence. While acknowledging that Jews tended to outscore non-Jews on intelligence tests, he stressed that there was no way to prove that this was due to innate, hereditary differences and argued that environment was of overwhelming and pervasive importance. More likely, he believed, their performance was rooted "in the traditions, education and general superiority of the Jewish environment."[72] Similarly, the claim that certain kinds of nervous diseases – neurasthenia, hysteria, and melancholia – were the result of the racial character of the Jews was also unfounded. These were, he explained, urban diseases, common to all city dwellers that were daily consumed by ambition and anxiety – diseases that, in the case of the Jews, were exacerbated by their long history of exile and persecution. Yet, despite his stress on nurture over nature and his awareness that "prejudice rather than scientific acumen or dispassionate analysis"[73] shaped most assessments of temperamental and emotional racial differences, Rumyaneck did not question the meaningfulness of the very concept of race. Thus, he concluded: "An exact technique which will eliminate or make allowance for nurture, and which will secure really random samplings, will have to be devised before we range the various races in a hierarchy."[74] In 1931, Rumyaneck and his sponsors were not prepared to jettison the utility or validity of the notion of racial difference.

Rumyaneck was not alone among JHOGB researchers in affirming the primacy of environment without altogether rejecting the notion of racial inheritance. The same year that Rumyaneck published his literature survey, Maurice Sorsby (1898–1949), an ear, nose and throat surgeon, published the results of his study on the links between cancer and race. Drawing on data from London, Amsterdam,

Vienna, Budapest, Warsaw, Łódź, and Leningrad, Sorsby concluded that Jewish deaths from cancer varied from city to city and that their cancer mortality rate resembled that of the non-Jewish rate, that is, it followed a geographical rather than a racial distribution. At the same time, however, he noted that the incidence of cancer per organ was strikingly different between Jews and non-Jews. There was, for example, a low incidence of uterine cancer among Jews. This he attributed not to racial immunity, however, but to the impact of Jewish law, which promoted a high degree of "sexual cleanliness," on sexual conduct.[75] In a similar manner, the annual report for 1931 traced the higher incidence of diseases related to urban life to the fact that Jews were pre-eminently an urban people. They worked either in trades of a sedentary, indoor nature under poor sanitary conditions or in high-stress, insecure occupations that produced excessive anxiety and mental strain. Harassed Jewish parents and children alike overworked in order to overachieve, while deeply ingrained habits privileged the cultivation of the intellect over the cultivation of the physique.[76] This kind of environmental explanation was neither novel nor unique to the Jewish health movement, of course. It was a standard refrain in both integrationist and nationalist critiques of the Jewish condition from the late nineteenth century to the Second World War.

With the triumph of Nazism in Germany, the JHOGB stepped back from research that spoke to racial differences. As noted above, Emanuel Miller's investigation of the distribution of mental disorders among Jews was either never completed or never published. A study of consanguineous marriages among Jews and the pathologies associated with such marriages, conducted by L. Hermann of the Department of Social Biology at the London School of Economics and announced in the annual report for 1931, also disappeared from view.[77] The Organisation's report for the period 1 January 1933 to 30 June 1934 noted that material for the consanguinity inquiry was still incomplete, and that was the last mention of it.[78] In 1929, South African-born Meyer Fortes (1906–1983), then a psychologist at the clinic and later an eminent social anthropologist at Cambridge, proposed a study of the development of the mind in Jewish children in light of their Jewish surroundings.[79] There is no evidence that the JHOGB offered to fund it or that he even began work on the project. In any case, he resigned from the group's clinic in November 1932, when he was awarded the Rockefeller Fellowship in Anthropological Psychology, his academic focus having shifted from psychology to anthropology.[80] One indication of the Organisation's new sensitivity to the pitfalls of highlighting racial differences was an explicit statement in 1934 that there was "no such thing as a Jewish race in the biological use of the word" and that there was "no pathological condition which at one time or another was stated to be peculiar to Jews which was not found in patients who were not Jews." Of course, it acknowledged, some diseases were more common among Jews and some less common, but these differences were due to divergent habits, modes of life, and social and economic conditions. There was no need to invoke a racial factor in explaining their greater or lesser occurrence. Thus, for example, because Jews were an urban people they suffered from a higher incidence of urban-related diseases.[81]

The JHOGB's retreat from research on racial differences was not a blanket rejection of the utility of research data in the fight against anti-Semitism. The opposite was true. The challenges of both German and domestic anti-Semitism (especially Blackshirt violence) in the 1930s spurred the group to propose even more ambitious statistical initiatives. Now, however, research was to focus on the social, economic, and demographic characteristics of Anglo-Jewry. In November 1932, the JHOGB, with the support of B'nai B'rith, convened a meeting at Woburn House of representatives of Jewish groups to discuss the establishment of a permanent statistical bureau, communally funded and under the supervision of the JHOGB's statistics committee. The immediate spur to action was a concern that the Board of Deputies was considering the establishment of its own bureau, to which the JHOGB was opposed. Salaman thought that any research work that the Board, a lay, non-professional body, undertook would be amateurish. He declared that the JHOGB was ready to set up a bureau but added that it lacked the money to do so.[82] The Woburn House conference generated interest, but contributions to launch the bureau were not forthcoming. A second conference was called in 1933, at which the JHOGB offered an alternative formula for financing the bureau. Having concluded that periodic public appeals would be ineffective, given the world economic crisis and the financial demands of resettling German refugees, the JHOGB proposed that established communal institutions commit themselves to finance the bureau with regular, annual contributions.[83] This proposal met with no more success than the previous one. The gastroenterologist Hugh Gainsborough (1893–1980, né Hyman Hirsch Ginsberg), chairman of the JHOGB, told Neville Laski, President of the Board, in January 1934 that the response to the appeal for funds was "discouraging."[84] When the Board was asked for a contribution, it replied that it was impossible for it to make a financial grant to an outside body.[85]

The second proposal which suggested communal funding of the statistical bureau provoked a blistering critique of the Statistics Committee's work and a personal attack on Salaman from Simon Rowson (1877–1950, né Rosenbaum), a pioneer in the British film industry, a member of the Board of Deputies, and a one-time statistician and economic advisor to the Conservative Party. Rowson's critique identified two central problems in the statistical work of the JHOGB and, indeed, in any demographic study of Anglo-Jewry. First, the absence of a religious or racial question on the national census made it impossible to collect data that could be viewed in a comparative light, which he believed was the only measure of importance. All attempts to surmount this problem by using indirect estimates of the Jewish population and its age and sex composition were "mere second-rate makeshifts." In support of this assertion, he cited the estimate of the Jewish population in London in 1929 produced by the JHOGB's newly hired statistician Miron Kantorowitsch (born 1895, died after 1977 – exact year not recorded).[86] Second, and more fundamental, he asserted that the collection and interpretation of statistical material was both a science and an art, and that the work must be carried out in a scientific spirit without any concern that "the results might prove unpleasant and disagreeable." Having been affiliated with the JHOGB for several years, he was convinced that the group did not meet these prerequisites. The irony was that Salaman had levelled the same accusation against the Board of Deputies, viewing it as a political body unable to carry out dispassionate scientific work. Whether Rowson's specific accusations were justified or not – later Anglo-Jewish demographers acclaimed Kantorowitsch's work – he was correct in recognising that statistical research is not the value-free scientific exercise that Salaman and the JHOGB thought it was. On a personal level, he was also miffed that Salaman had removed him from the chairmanship of the JHOGB Statistical Committee when he did not agree with Salaman's views on the appropriate agency to undertake research.[87] Salaman, a representative of the old, long-settled Anglo-Jewish elite, was accustomed to having his way, while Rowson was a newcomer, the son of a Manchester butcher from Suwalki.

The failure to establish a communally funded research unit in 1934 did not lessen the felt need for data with which to respond to anti-Jewish allegations. The JHOGB (Salaman above all) and the Board of Deputies continued to discuss the possibility of cooperating. In summer 1936, Neville Laski suggested Salaman gather material on Jewish contributions to science. Salaman responded that the best strategy would be for him and the historian of medicine Charles Singer (1876–1960) to draw up a research plan and find "a younger man" to do the work.[88] Salaman used this opportunity to urge Laski once again to create a permanent statistical bureau, not a one-off committee to carry out this project. He also complained that despite the good work that the JHOGB's statistical committee had done it had received "no recognition whatever," even speculating that the Anglo-Jewish leadership exhibited "a peculiar dislike for all scientific data."[89] (His lament about the anti-intellectualism of Anglo-Jewry's leaders was a frequent one in the twentieth century.)

The Board was no more interested in 1936 in funding a permanent bureau than it had been earlier, but it did agree to award the JHOGB £500 to study the Jewish presence in the professions, hoping that the data would counter allegations that Jews were overrepresented in and even "controlled" certain fields. In its request for funding, the JHOGB reviewed its previous work, stressing the utility of statistics in anti-defamation work. Referring to the communal conference it had convened in November 1932, it emphasised that it had "endeavoured to make the delegates see that the events on the Continent created a situation which must give the greatest concern to all." It also stressed that its response in the mid-1920s to Pearson's study of Jewish intelligence (the first time that it and the Board had cooperated) demonstrated why such charges could not be left unanswered, pointing out that this could be even more widely appreciated "in the face of current racial policy" than it was at the time.[90] With funding from the Board, the Statistical Committee investigated the percentage of Jews in medicine, dentistry, law, architecture, surveying, the civil service, and teaching and research in England, Wales, and Scotland. It completed its work in February 1937. An internal Board memorandum suggested that the information would be helpful in responding to charges in the press and, as well, in counselling young Jews who were thinking of entering the professions. For example, in Manchester, where 108 of the 761 doctors were Jews, the memorandum advised that "no further entrants into that profession should be encouraged." It also recognised that other statistics should not be broadcast because "they reveal the weak points in our armour." The example it cited was the Territorial Army: there were only thirteen Jewish officers and only forty-two Jews in other ranks – in an army of 123,000.[91] (The Board assumed, like most integrationist bodies in western Jewish communities had since the late eighteenth century, that Jewish [mis]behaviour caused anti-Semitism.) The realisation that statistics could be a double-edged sword in public debate was one that had surfaced before in the deliberations of the Board. In 1934, when Laski had solicited the opinion of Leonard G. Montefiore (1889–1961), president of the Anglo-Jewish Association, about funding statistical research, Montefiore had cautioned that anti-Semites could potentially exploit such research for their own ends. He then noted that the Nazis had made excellent propaganda use of the *Die Bevölkerung- und Berufsverhältnisse der Juden in deutschen Reich* (1930) by Heinrich Silbergleit (1858–1930), chief of the Statistical Office of Berlin from 1906 to 1923.[92]

IV

The start of the Second World War ushered in the decline and collapse of the JHOGB. Its financial condition, which had never been robust, now became precarious. The demands of refugee resettlement on the communal purse became overwhelming and war-time cares all consuming. Donations to the JHOGB dried up. The evacuation of children to safer parts of the country, as well as the bombing of homes, schools, and businesses, reduced the Jewish population of the East End, dramatically accelerating a demographic trend that was already underway before 1939. With East End Jewry becoming a shadow of its former self, the concerns that led to the establishment of the JHOGB became less significant. From the start of the war, some figures within the Organisation were pressing to close it and the clinic.

Conflict within the group between its long-serving salaried secretary, David Cheyney (1893–1962), and Salaman also took a toll. The strife arose in 1941 when Cheyney charged Dr Schwartzman, Vice-Chair of the JHOGB, with misappropriating funds. Salaman agreed that some irregularities had taken place but he told Cheyney that the evidence would not stand up in a court of law and told him to let the matter drop since the accusations concerned Schwartzman's fundraising for East European Jewish relief schemes associated with ORT and OZE. Unfortunately, Cheyney was incapable of letting it drop. He became obsessed with the issue and eventually suffered a mental breakdown. In August 1943, the Organisation ordered Cheyney to close the clinic and cancel all appointments forthwith. The next month Salaman wrote to Cheyney saying that his health rendered him unfit to fulfil his duties as secretary and that the JHOGB was granting him sick leave with full pay on condition that he be examined by the king's physician, Lord Horder, who was known for his diagnostic skills. Cheyney refused to abandon his post, however, and in October Salaman showed up without warning at the office in Rampart Street, accompanied by the Organisation's solicitor, and ejected him. He took away Cheyney's keys and had the building's locks changed.[93] By then the JHOGB was largely moribund. It was formally wound up in July 1946 and its remaining funds – £356 – transferred to the Jewish Board of Guardians.[94]

The end of the JHOGB is a sad, squalid tale, which does little to enhance the reputation of any of its protagonists. This should not distract us, however, from taking stock of what its two-decade history reveals about the concerns of the medical men and communal leaders who conducted its affairs. It represented, first and foremost, the persistence of communal concern about the behaviour of the Jewish poor, which, it was believed, reflected poorly on all Jews, threatening their security and reputation. This concern was in no sense novel. However, the biological turn in anti-Semitic thinking, both in Britain and elsewhere in the West, reshaped the way in which this concern was expressed. The body of the Jew – its distinctive characteristics and vulnerability to mental and physical degeneration – rather than the disruptive social and economic behaviour of the Jew – became the focus of concern. The creation of the JHOGB is a testimony to the power of this new emphasis in thinking about Jews and to the pervasiveness of racial thinking more generally in the physical and social sciences in the decades before the Second World War. While not all of the physicians who took an active interest in the JHOGB were racial thinkers in the way that Salaman was, they were not hostile to the notion of racial difference, whether inherited or environmentally shaped. They were also receptive to the claim that the health of the Jewish people was degenerating and that preventive measures could potentially halt this trend and restore its collective health.

Little of this thinking survived the war. Nazism and the Holocaust discredited the most pernicious aspects of racial thinking.[95] Indeed, the history of the JHOGB suggests that, at least in Jewish circles, hardcore racial assumptions about the inheritance of physical and emotional traits were fading long before the start of the war. The JHOGB researchers were becoming increasingly environmentalist in their orientation in the 1930s. Even Salaman, who never completely abandoned some of his racial assumptions after the war, no longer used eugenicist language to frame the work of the JHOGB in the 1930s, as he had in the mid-1920s. Perhaps, like the proverbial canary in a coal mine, the officers and researchers of the JHOGB sensed the danger in racial thinking before others did.

Notes

1 T.M. Endelman, *The Jews of Georgian England, 1714–1830: Tradition and Change in a Liberal Society* (Philadelphia, PA, 1979), Chs 5–6.
2 William Cole, quoted in R. Leslie-Melville, *The Life and Work of Sir John Fielding* (London, 1934), pp. 260–261.
3 *Parnasim* are synagogue syndics.
4 *Tsedakah* is charity.
5 Endelman, *The Jews of Georgian England*, Ch. 7.

6 D. Feldman, *Englishmen and Jews: Social Relations and Political Culture, 1840–1914* (New Haven, CT, 1994), Ch. 12; T.M. Endelman, *The Jews of Britain, 1656–2000* (Berkeley, CA, 2002), Ch. 4; G. Alderman, *British Jewry since Emancipation* (Buckingham, 2014), Ch. 3. For the history of the Jews' Free School, see G. Black, *JFS: The History of the Jews Free School, London, since 1732* (London, 1998).

7 One possible reason that it has remained in the shadows is that the history of the Jewish East End in the inter-war years is neglected, relative to the period of mass migration. I discuss the JHOGB in another context in T.M. Endelman, "Anglo-Jewish Scientists and the Science of Race," *Jewish Social Studies*, Vol. 11 (2004), pp. 74–81.

8 N. Davidovitch and R. Zalashik, "'Air, Sun, Water': Ideology and Activities of OZE (Society for the Preservation of the Health of the Jewish Population) during the Inter-war Period," *Dynamis*, Vol. 28 (2008), pp. 128–35; M. Beizer, "OZE," *The YIVO Encyclopedia of Jews in Eastern Europe*, 31 March 2016, www.yivoencyclopedia.org/article.aspx/OZE.

9 "Di grindung-ferzamlung fon OZE in London," *Buletin fon zentral biro fon der gezelshaft dur ferhiten di gezuntheit fon der idisher befolkerung OZE*, No. 2 (June 1923), pp. 10–13. I am grateful to Zvi Gitelman for his help with this article.

10 Finance committee, minute book of meetings, 1 February 1924, 25 February 1925, 9 July 1925, ACC 3090/2, JHOGB Papers, London Metropolitan Archives (hereafter LMA).

11 Ibid.

12 B.W. Lowbury, "The Jewish Health Organisation: Its Origins and Its Work," *Jewish Chronicle* (hereafter *JC*), 25 March 1927. The Latvian-born physician Benjamin William Lowbury (1875–1948) anglicised his name, from Loewenberg, at the start of the First World War. He was the father of the poet Edward Lowbury (1913–2007).

13 Finance committee, minute book of meetings, 17 October 1928, ACC 3090/2, JHOGB Papers, LMA; Lord Rothschild et al. to Felix M. Warburg, 8 October 1926, and A.H. Levy to Felix M. Warburg, 24 November 1926, JDC Archives, New York; *JC*, 7 and 14 October 1927.

14 For biographical information on Salaman, see T.M. Endelman, "The Decline of the Anglo-Jewish Notable," *The European Legacy*, Vol. 4 (1999), pp. 62–8.

15 Endelman, "Anglo-Jewish Scientists and the Science of Race."

16 R.N. Salaman (hereafter RNS), *Palestine Reclaimed: Letters from a Jewish Officer in Palestine* (London, 1920), p. 37.

17 Ibid., p. 185.

18 R.A. Soloway, *Demography and Degeneration: Eugenics and the Declining Birthrate in Twentieth-Century Britain* (Chapel Hill, NC, 1990); D.J. Kevles, *In the Name of Eugenics: Genetics and the Uses of Human Heredity* (Cambridge, MA, 1995).

19 G. Stedman Jones, *Outcast London: A Study in the Relationship between Classes in Victorian Society* (London, 1992), pp. 15–16.

20 JHOGB, *The Difficult Child: A Medical, Psychological and Sociological Problem* (London, 1930).

21 JHOGB, *Report and Accounts, 1923–24* (London, 1925).

22 JHOGB, *Report and Accounts, 1926* (London, 1927).

23 *Hadarim* are after-school private Hebrew classes.

24 *Melammedim* are Hebrew teachers.

25 JHOGB, *Report and Accounts, 1923–1924* (London, April 1925); *Report and Accounts, 1925* (London, May 1926); *Report and Accounts, 1926* (London, September 1927); *Public Health Work in the Jewish Community: Annual Report of the JHOGB for the Year 1927–28* (London, 1928).

26 A set of eight pamphlets is found in the British Library. They are undated. Avodah Zarah and Yoma are both tractates of the Talmud.

27 *Mitsvah* is a commandment or good deed done from religious duty.

28 RNS, "Heredity: A Factor in Public Health," *The Jewish Friendly Societies Magazine*, Vol. 1 (February 1926), p. 4. This article is based on Salaman's lecture at the White-chapel Art Gallery on 5 December 1925. It did not reproduce the entire text of the

lecture. Additional remarks were included in the report of the lecture in the *Jewish Guardian*, 11 December 1925; *JC*, 11 December 1925, and *The Lancet*, 12 December 1925.

29 JHOGB, *Report and Accounts for 1925* (London, May 1926).
30 *Palestine Post*, 6 December 1933.
31 On Jewish efforts to counter medicalised and racialised anti-Semitism in Europe and America, see M.B. Hart, *The Healthy Jew: The Symbiosis of Judaism and Modern Medicine* (New York, 2007). There is a brief discussion of Snowman on pp. 99–101.
32 J. Snowman, *Jewish Law and Sanitary Science* (London, 1896), pp. 21, 24.
33 J. Snowman, *A Short History of Talmudic Medicine* (London, 1935), p. 31.
34 In December 1948, Snowman was called on to circumcise Prince Charles at Buckingham Palace.
35 J. Snowman, "Jewish Eugenics," *Jewish Review*, Vol. 4 (1913–1914), pp. 159–74.
36 On Miller, see K. Bassett's biography of his polymath son, *In Two Minds: A Biography of Jonathan Miller* (London, 2012), pp. 11–16.
37 Finance Committee, minute book of meetings, 10 July 1929, ACC 3090/2, JHOGB Papers, LMA.
38 JHOGB, *Public Health Work in the Jewish Community: Annual Report of the Jewish Health Organisation of Great Britain for the Year 1931* (London, 1932), p. 15.
39 Statistical Committee, JHOGB, minutes, 25 January 1933, ACC 3121/E03/011/01, Archives of the Board of Deputies of British Jews (hereafter BD), LMA. The survival of JHOGB documents in the archives of the BD was a result of the JHOGB soliciting financial support for its statistical programme. Given the incompleteness of the JHOGB's own papers, the BD's JHOGB files are invaluable.
40 *Jewish Guardian*, 30 May 1930.
41 Quoted in G. Renton, "The East London Child Guidance Clinic," *Journal of Child Psychology and Psychiatry*, Vol. 19 (1978), p. 309. For a historical analysis, see C.A. Reeves, "Insanity and Nervous Diseases amongst Jewish Immigrants to the East End of London, 1880–1920," unpublished Ph.D. thesis, University of London, 2001.
42 JHOGB, *Public Health Work in the Jewish Community for the Year 1931*, p. 7.
43 Quoted in Renton, "The East London Child Guidance Clinic," p. 311.
44 Clinic Committee, minute book of meetings, 24 May 1934, ACC 3090/4, JHOGB Papers, LMA.
45 *Jewish Guardian*, 1 November 1929.
46 Clinic Committee, minute book of meetings, 2 July 1928, ACC 3090/4, JHOGB Papers, LMA.
47 JHOGB, *Report for the Period January 1st, 1933 to June 30th, 1934* (London, 1934), p. 11.
48 Clinic Committee, minute book of meetings, 1 July 1937, ACC 3090/4, JHOGB Papers, LMA.
49 Jewish Telegraphic Agency, *Jewish Daily Bulletin*, 9 December 1928.
50 Jewish Telegraphic Agency, *Jewish Daily Bulletin*, 15 January 1931.
51 East London Child Guidance Clinic, "Honorary Directors' Report for 1936." The late Sarah Miller, Emanuel Miller's daughter, kindly gave me a copy of this report. Renton, "The East London Child Guidance Clinic," p. 311.
52 Jewish Telegraphic Agency, *Jewish Daily Bulletin*, 4 March 1931.
53 Executive Committee, minute book of meetings, 10 March 1938, ACC 3090/1, JHOGB Papers, LMA.
54 This document, dated 11 January 1937, was given to me by Sarah Miller.
55 Jewish Telegraphic Agency, *Jewish Daily Bulletin*, 25 October 1934.
56 *Jewish Guardian*, 1 November 1929.
57 JHOGB, *Report for the Period January 1st, 1933, to June 30th, 1934* (London, 1934), p. 11.
58 Clinic Committee, minute book of meetings, 22 June 1927, ACC 3090/4, JHOGB Papers, LMA.
59 Ibid.
60 M.B. Hart, *Social Science and the Politics of Modern Jewish Identity* (Stanford, CA, 2000).

61 J.M. Efron, *Defenders of the Race: Jewish Doctors and Race Science in Fin-de-Siècle Europe* (New Haven, CT, 1994), Ch. 4.

62 JHOGB, *Public Health Work in the Jewish Community for the Year 1927–28*, p. 9.

63 JHOGB, *Report for the Period January 1st, 1933, to June 30th, 1934*, p. 13.

64 RNS to R. Waley Cohen, 17 August 1936, uncatalogued box, file 3, JHOGB Papers, LMA.

65 L. Isserlis to RNS, 8 August 1936, uncatalogued box, file 3, JHOGB Papers, LMA.

66 For background to the Jewish intelligence debate, see G. Schaffer, "Assets or 'Aliens'? Race Science and the Analysis of Jewish Intelligence in Inter-War Britain," *Patterns of Prejudice*, Vol. 42 (2008), pp. 191–207.

67 C. Myers to J.M. Rich, 7 December 1925; RNS to J.M. Rich, 9 February 1926, ACC 3121/C08/002/001, BD, LMA.

68 M. Davies and A.G. Hughes, "An Investigation into the Comparative Intelligence and Attainments of Jewish and Non-Jewish School Children," *British Journal of Psychology*, Vol. 18 (October 1927), pp. 134–46.

69 See the correspondence in ACC 3121/E03/011/01, BD, LMA.

70 Rumyaneck, son of the Polish-born Hebraist Aaron Rumyaneck, who settled in Leeds around 1913, changed his name to Jay Rumney when he was appointed an instructor at LSE in 1934. In 1938, he emigrated to the United States, where he spent most of his career teaching sociology at what later became the Newark campus of Rutgers University. His unpublished and largely unknown dissertation, "The Economic and Social Development of the Jews in England, 1730–1860" (1933) is still worth reading.

71 J. Rumyaneck, "The Comparative Psychology of Jews and non-Jews: A Survey of the Literature," *British Journal of Psychology*, Vol. 21 (April 1931), pp. 404–26.

72 Ibid., p. 416.

73 Ibid., p. 422.

74 Ibid., p.423.

75 M. Sorsby, *Cancer and Race: A Study of the Incidence of Cancer among Jews* (London, 1931), pp. 93–4.

76 JHOGB, *Public Health Work in the Jewish Community for the Year 1931*, pp. 16–17.

77 Ibid., p. 15.

78 JHOGB, *Report for the Period January 1st, 1933, to June 30th, 1934*, p. 31

79 Clinic Committee, minute book of meetings, 21 November 1929, ACC 3090/4, JHOGB Papers, LMA.

80 Fortes later said that his experience working in the clinic turned him from psychology to sociology, as he discovered that the significant factor in the problems of the children he saw was their families. S. Drucker-Brown, "Notes toward a Biography of Meyer Fortes," *American Ethnologist*, Vol. 16 (1989), p. 383.

81 JHOGB, *Report for the Period January 1st, 1933, to June 30th, 1934*, p. 13.

82 RNS to J.M. Rich, March 1931, ACC 3121/E01/052, BD, LMA.

83 Mimeographed materials prepared for the conference are in ACC/3121/E03/011/01, BD, LMA.

84 H. Gainsborough to N. Laski, 17 January 1934, ACC 3121/E01/054, BD, LMA.

85 B.A. Zaiman to D. Tscherniakoff, 19 March 1934, ACC 3121/E03/011/01, BD, LMA.

86 This was published several years later. M. Kantorowitsch, "Estimate of the Jewish Population in 1929–1933," *Journal of the Royal Statistical Society*, Vol. 99 (1936), pp. 372–9. The Minsk-born Kantorowitsch lost his position at the Social Hygiene Seminar at the University of Berlin in 1933, found refuge in Britain in 1934, and undertook statistical work for the JHOGB, beginning that same year. This work was funded by a refugee aid group for academics and scientists with which Salaman was closely affiliated. In 1938, he settled in the United States and, on acquiring citizenship in 1945, took the name Myron K. Gordon. He was one of the pioneers of Soviet demography in the United States. M. Tolts, "For Him London was a Fruitful Transitory Stop: The Migrant's Destiny of Miron Kantorowicz," *Jewish Journal of Sociology*, Vol. 56 (2014), pp. 99–117.

Kantoroitwch carried out one other study for the JHOGB – "On the Statistics of Jewish Marriages in England and Wales," *Population*, Vol. 2 (1936), pp. 75–83.
87 S. Rowson to B. Zaiman, 12 February 1934, ACC 3121/E01/052, BD, LMA.
88 RNS to N. Laski, 1 August 1936, ACC/3121/B04/JHO, BD, LMA.
89 RNS to N. Laski, 17 August 1936, ACC/3121/B04/JHO, BD, LMA.
90 H. Gainsborough, L. Isserlis, and D. Cheyney to N. Laski, 10 September 1936, ACC 3121/B04/JHO, BD, LMA.
91 "Memorandum on Report of the Statistical Investigation Conducted by the Jewish Health Organisation," 23 April 1937, ACC 3121/B04/JHO, BD, LMA.
92 L.G. Montefiore to N. Laski, 15 January 1934, ACC 3121/E03/011/01, BD, LMA.
93 On the last days of the JHOGB, I have relied on the documents in the uncatalogued box, JHOGB Papers, LMA. The letters and memoranda in this box apparently were in the possession of Cheyney and tend to reflect his perspective on what happened.
94 RNS to the Secretary, Jewish Board of Guardians, 19 July 1946, MS 8171/51, Redcliffe Salaman Papers, Cambridge University Library.
95 However, the concept of race did not magically and suddenly disappear from the natural and social sciences. G. Schaffer, *Racial Science and British Society, 1930–62* (Basingstoke, 2008), Chs 3 and 4.

Select Bibliography

Elazar Barkan, *The Retreat of Scientific Racism: Changing Concepts of Race in Britain and the United States between the World Wars* (Cambridge, 1992).
Todd M. Endelman, "Anglo-Jewish Scientists and the Science of Race," *Jewish Social Studies*, Vol. 11 (2004), pp. 54–92.
Mitchell B. Hart, *Social Science and the Politics of Modern Jewish Identity* (Stanford, CA, 2000).
Gavin Schaffer, *Racial Science and British Society, 1930–1962* (Abingdon and New York, 2013).
Richard A. Soloway, *Demography and Degeneration: Eugenics and the Declining Birthrate in Twentieth-Century Britain* (Chapel Hill, NC, 1990).

4

THE EAST END AND THE MORAL FOUNDATIONS OF BILL FISHMAN'S LIBERTARIAN SOCIALISM

Wayne Parsons

Introduction

My first encounter with Bill Fishman came as an undergraduate when I read his great book *The Insurrectionists*.[1] I made use of it again as a postgraduate student when taking a course on socialist thought. Sadly, my annotated copy of it was liberated by a former student who took rather *too* literally my lecture on Proudhon and in particular his claim that "*La propriété, c'est le vol.*" For many years I had the good fortune to teach a course with Bill at Queen Mary and was privileged to have him as a friend for the following three decades. I want to draw upon that experience of teaching with Bill and reflect upon our conversations about his socialism by focusing on a number of points of entry into what he would refer to as "Fishmania." I argue that, although Bill did not develop an explicit philosophy *per se*, we can best understand his notion of *libertarian socialism* through three works which are critical to understanding his contribution as a historian of East London. I have chosen these particular works to serve as lenses through which to examine his thought because they were the sources to which he most often returned when we discussed, either directly or *en passant*, his socialism: *Mutual Aid* by Kropotkin, Charles Dickens's *Hard Times*, and most important of all, although not strictly a *text*, his beloved *Zeida*'s (his grandfather's) moral precepts derived from the *Torah*[2] and rabbinical literature.

I fondly remember our first meeting in the old Economics Department in Bow Road, when we divided up the lectures for the coming year. Knowing his expertise in Jacobin-Communism, I was taken aback as his face lit up and beamed with delight when I said that I would very much like to give the lecture on Kropotkin. He sat up and promptly produced a copy of *The Conquest of Bread* and gave it to me as a present when I mentioned it was the only book by Kropotkin I did not possess. I still treasure it. At that stage I had not actually read *East End Jewish*

Radicals, so he suggested I read it (*toute de suite*) if I wanted to understand his enthusiasm for the "gentle anarchist" prince.[3] In due course, I received a signed copy: and it is still one of my prized possessions. Rudolf Rocker (1873–1958), someone whom Bill greatly respected and admired, turned out to be a formidable student of Kropotkin. I then began to understand the connection – especially after he gave me yet another book, Rocker's *Nationalism and Culture* that contains numerous references to Kropotkin.[4] A little while later, he introduced me to Rocker's son, the artist Fermin (1907–2004), who also spoke about his father's admiration for Kropotkin, and it became clear to me from then onwards that Bill owed much to Rocker intellectually, and especially in respect of Kropotkin's contribution to the development of his libertarian socialism.[5] After we had given the first session of the course, Bill said that he was going to take me to meet a *real* socialist. As we made our way out of the Economics Department (then housed in what had once been the offices of the Spratts's dog food company in Bow Road) I imagined that we would end up in Freedom Books in Angel Alley, Whitechapel. Bill's *real socialist*, however, was none other than the Bishop of Stepney, Trevor Huddleston (1913–1998). We sipped tea in a small, sparsely furnished room in his house on the Commercial Road. They talked of many things: socialism, mutual aid and the *Torah*; Jesus the rabbi; and Charles Dickens. They shared their memories and stories. It was a lively and fascinating conversation between two people who clearly enjoyed one another's company. And yet this conversation, I recall, turned on just a few concepts, which I must confess I had never heard before: *tzedakah* and *rachamones*.[6] Bill and the Bishop had these concepts in common and these links made all the difference for a dialogue between a Bishop and (as Bill would say) a non-religious Jew. I thus began (slowly) to appreciate why it was that Bill had brought me along to see Bishop Huddleston. But as we left the Bishop's house that afternoon I admitted to Bill that I was slightly confused by the conversation and that I was gravely ignorant of Yiddish and Hebrew. Placing an arm around my shoulder he said: "You'll learn: keep reading your Kropotkin!"

Bill's contribution to defining a broadly based and inclusive tradition of a *libertarian* socialism, one that served to bring into focus the differences between a *libertarian* and more statist approach to politics, had room for the Christian socialism of an Anglican Bishop and the anarchism of Prince Kropotkin as well as the various libertarian strands of the British Labour movement. One of his former students in the early 1970s, the distinguished Labour politician Peter Hain (who had also, like Huddleston, campaigned against apartheid in South Africa), has spoken warmly about how he was inspired by Bill's "enthusiasm and verve" to see himself as "libertarian not a state socialist."[7] What Hain learnt from Bill as a student, I was to learn as a colleague: that there was an alternative to thinking about socialism in terms of being simplistically defined by the rather sterile and tedious arguments between different kinds of Marxism-Leninism and its social democratic variants. By contextualising the history of socialism in terms of *statism* and *libertarianism* his approach – as reflected in his recommended reading – facilitated a very different kind of understanding of the history of socialist ideas and practice. *Libertarian* socialism for Bill was, therefore, a very broad church which was inclusive of a range of thinkers and texts that were concerned with the problematics of how to have more bottom-up and decentralised structures; and the promotion of community, self-government and participatory modes of political and economic order. Above all, it was a socialism that was defined by mutual aid and the empowerment of citizens in contrast to the revolutionary Jacobin-Communism that was the subject of the *Insurrectionists*. Peter Hain's case for a distinctive libertarian tradition in socialist thought and its continuing relevance to the problems facing the Labour Party is an account which, as he acknowledges, owes much to Bill's teaching. As he recalls:

> When I was a student at Queen Mary College, … I absorbed his framework and voraciously read his recommended books. Bill's teaching revealed to me the historical framework and an explanation for the division between libertarian and state socialism … [8]

At the time when he was teaching the young Peter Hain (in 1972–1973) Bill had yet to publish his studies of East London; these came a little later. In these later books, and especially in *East End 1888*, we can discern another aspect or dimension of his libertarian socialism: as being predicated on an *ethical framework* that defined the difference between what he understood to be libertarian and statist forms of socialism. Furthermore, this ethical framework informed his opposition to all forms of *libertarianism* which conflicted with his moral principles – especially the *libertarianism* of the so-called new right and neo-conservatives. I want therefore to focus more on this largely implicit ethical framework which is manifested most clearly in his writings on East London and reflect on how we might understand his work as being grounded in a well-defined set of moral principles and a distinct philosophy of history. Furthermore, I suggest that the moral precepts of his *Zeida*, and his approach to history *qua* remembrance still have a profound and urgent relevance to the East London of the twenty-first century, as they did in the nineteenth and twentieth centuries.

Rachamones and *Tzedakah*

Let us return, therefore, to taking tea with Bishop Huddleston. What Bill admired about Trevor Huddleston was his preparedness to struggle for justice and his genuine compassion and love for the poor. He was a *mensch*: not a title Bill would lightly bestow, as he had an extensive range of far less complimentary Yiddish expressions to describe those who were the polar opposite. For Bill a *mensch* described a decent and honourable human being who had a moral sense and was not malicious or hypocritical. Bill's socialism, I discovered, was not what might be termed a *theoretical* kind of belief, nor was it easily classified or mapped on a standard ideological matrix. But Huddleston seemed to embody what being a socialist looked like. Bill would often say of himself that he was not *religious* in the sense that he believed in God, but he did believe in the existence of moral principles which he and the Bishop clearly shared. Free market capitalism was, for him, essentially *morally deficient*. Free market ideologues were to be condemned because of their misguided faith in greed and avarice and their refusal to accept their responsibility to care for the poor and the disadvantaged and to acknowledge their responsibility to promote social justice. Advocates of what he always referred to as *laissez-faire economics* were to be condemned because their beliefs were rooted in a cold-hearted utilitarianism and in a dubious form of scientism. Like Huddleston, William Booth and his Army illustrated what *real* socialism must always embody: a passion for compassion and justice. Bill was always ready to defend the role of philanthropists against those who sought to denigrate the important contribution of the "company of saints, armed with the Bible and bread basket" to promoting social justice and helping the poor.[9] At the same time, he was ready to acknowledge that philanthropists motivated by Christian ethics were "treating only the symptom, not the disease" and that they often rejected political action and the appreciation of the need for a more radical transformation of society.[10] Huddleston was much admired and respected by Bill because he understood both the importance of radical transformation and the need to address the deeper causes of injustice and poverty. As he wrote of Huddleston in the *Streets of East London*:

> From a secular point of view he is motivated by a passionate concern for the dispossessed, and a concomitant loathing for injustice perpetrated against those least capable of resisting. He regards Socialism as the practical working out of Christian philosophy in this world … He appeals for positive reforms, and where possible, implements them within the bounds of his own jurisdiction.[11]

Bill saw in such *saints* as Huddleston examples of what socialism *really* involved: compassion and a passion for justice and action to improve the welfare of all human beings in ways that respected the dignity of the individual. For Bill and the Bishop, it was the individual that mattered: and individuals should never be regarded as just part of a mass or a statistic. People like Huddleston had a bias and a preference for the poor and the dispossessed. They practised and preached what he had learnt from his *Zeida*. As he recounted:

> My grandfather was a tall, heavy-bearded, Moses-like figure. Having obtained *semicha* in the Ukraine, among our immigrant settled milieu he commanded respect and affection. His religious-based maxim and practice was never to pass a beggar without giving. He taught us our basic moral precepts of *rachamones* – compassion – and *tsedakah* – charity. Friday night was special. Back from the synagogue service *Zeida* – grandpa – would bring home with him an unexpected visitor, always a poorly clad man from the *heim* – old country. He would join us for the Shabbat meal and bed for the night on an old sofa in the kitchen. As we approached the *shul* I saw the dockers coming up the hill, and as they passed *Zeida* they would doff their hats and declaim together "Aye

Reb", not mockingly but with obvious respect. For they had seen him on many occasions being stopped by a beggar and his immediate response, a handful of small coins pressed in the beggar's hand. It was there that I learned religious tolerance.[12]

His *Zeida's* precepts would often come up when solidarity with the poor and the oppressed would emerge as an issue. Bill was far more a historian concerned with *people*, rather than ideas or theories. His interest was essentially in how ideas changed people and the ways they changed, for good or ill, the real world. He shows us the consequences that theories and ideas have for the lives of human beings, and especially for the poor and the disadvantaged. I remember once quoting those famous lines at the end of Keynes's *General Theory* about the way in which the ideas of "academic scribblers" influence "madmen in authority."[13] "Exactly," said Bill, "exactly," and then suggested that Keynes's observation also applied with equal force to mad *women* in authority as well. On the very last page of the *Streets of East London* he observes that the radical inheritance of the area accrues from "centuries of deprivation, neglect, the struggle for bread and the heartlessness of a once *laissez-faire* society."[14] As an historian he appreciated how ideas and theories changed the world for good or ill. As he also knew, however, the ideas of the libertarian socialists which he had brilliantly chronicled had manifestly failed to change the world. At the close of *East End Jewish Radicals* he recognises this fact, but draws a different conclusion:

> 'It is the unsuccessful revolutionaries who have been the chief victims of those historians who are only interested in success.' Recent investigations suggest a change of direction: that the study of failure can often be as instructive and rewarding as the study of success.[15]

For Bill, libertarians such as Kropotkin and Rudolf Rocker were *still* (like his grandfather) relevant, despite, if not *because* of, their failure to change the world. Ideas are living and active forces in the world and always have the potential to change the world. On the very last page of *East End Jewish Radicals* he quotes from Rudolf Rocker's *London Years*:

> Social ideas are not something only to dream about for the future. If they are to mean anything at all they must be translated into our daily life, here and now. They must shape our relationship to our fellow man.[16]

This is how Bill saw his libertarian socialism: as ideas that have to be taken off the page and made active in the world. And above all they must "shape our relationship to our fellow man." When I read that closing passage of *East End Jewish Radicals* shortly after our meeting with Trevor Huddleston, I then better understood why Bill saw him as a *real* socialist: he was putting his religion of charity, justice and compassion into the here and now and *shaping his relationships to his fellow men*. Socialism was not about humanity in the abstract, or academic theories, it was about human relationships. It was about what his *Zeida* taught him and the dockers' respected. Bill would often make good use of his rich vocabulary of Yiddish insults to hurl at those who embraced free market capitalism and supported the "mad woman in authority," Margaret Thatcher. He would be especially critical of those fellow Jews who expressed support for *laissez-faire economics*. Not being one to mince his words he regarded them as religious *hypocrites* for failing to appreciate what he regarded to be the utter incompatibility between the capitalism espoused by Thatcher and others and the great moral principles of his *Zeida, rachamones* and *tzedakah*.

Bill was no theorist, but he *was* a moralist. And because of this he was profoundly suspicious of economics as the dominant language of political life. His history of East London is informed by this concern for the way in which economic discourse has often served to distort our understanding of the moral and ethical dimensions of social and economic problems.

Keeping this in mind, we can appreciate that Bill's history is always written in a way to invite the compassion of the reader. In a sense we might say that for Bill his approach to history was not about standing outside from an objective position. He was no positivist. What we find in his work is more of a kind of *verstehende soziologie*: history as an ethical activity that involved looking at the world from the inside not outside. He made no apologies for his subjectivism: as an historian he "breathed, ate, laughed, wept and dreamed dreams with the immigrant poor." "For better or for worse" they were *his* people. And he was writing their history.[17] His writing seeks to enable the reader to walk in the shoes of another human being. *Rachamones* when applied in a *scholarly* sense was about writing to engage our *moral imagination*, and by doing so the reader feels compassion, and is thereby open to learning from history. *East End 1888* has no pretence or claim to be an objective book: it seeks to write a history from the inside out. It is a book which explores the vulnerability and resilience of "his people." It is an exercise of walking with them and seeing the world from their point of view. Indeed, Bill's *Into the Abyss* is in many ways a kind of an appendix to *East End 1888*, for it concerns someone (G.R. Sims) who wrote with the compassion he admired.[18] Sims, like Dickens, did not just read statistics like a Gradgrind, he wrote from the street level, not from a Blue Book. And again just like Dickens, as Bill observes, his writing "served as a catalyst for social change."[19] G.R. Sims's accounts of *London Life*, were, in short, full of *rachamones*. Sims is therefore accorded a high honour:

> Sims must lead that group of great Victorian social critics and activist reformers … whose practical efforts to alleviate the needs of the poor would lead to the early manifestations of a Welfare State. His call for State intervention to help the deprived was a manifestation of his attack on unfettered 'laissez-faire,' on moral as on enlightened self interest grounds to effect a more secure society.[20]

It is fitting that on the last five pages of *Into the Abyss* we find *Christmas Day in the Workhouse*, a poem that perfectly expresses this sense of history as about seeing the world from the perspective of a pauper rather the "guardians and their ladies." I can hear Bill's voice in the closing stanza wherein John throws back the false charity that had been served up without a care for love, mercy, justice or compassion:

> There get ye gone to your dinners,
> Don't mind me in the least,
> Think of the happy paupers
> Eating your Christmas feast;
> And when you recount their blessings
> In your smug parochial way,
> Say what you did for me, too,
> Only last Christmas Day.[21]

Unlike Marx, who also had a rabbi for a (maternal) grandfather, Bill's socialism was not about rejecting the great precepts of the *Torah*, but rather placing them at the centre of a historical method and secular ideology. All human beings had a moral responsibility, duty and obligation to: "*learn to do good, seek justice and aid the oppressed*" (*Isaiah* 1:17). For Bill the death of God did not mean that we had to abandon the morality of the Bible: he was no Nietzschean in this nor in any other regard. He was also no relativist because he believed there were indeed real and universal truths about the human condition, and that these truths were preached and practised by his *Zeida: learning to do good, seeking justice and aiding those who are oppressed*. When we accompany Professor Fishman on a walk around East London we are in no fear of becoming lost in a relativistic post-modern *cul-de-sac*, for our guide is informed by a very robust moral compass.

For Bill, therefore, socialism was essentially grounded in a sense of compassion for the poor and the disadvantaged. His gesture of always giving to a beggar – without consideration of his deserving or undeserving character – was a form of moral instruction. It was a sign that the exercise of compassion and of showing solidarity was a necessary part of living a good life and in some small way of acknowledging the primacy of the common good. All forms of social, economic and political life were deficient if they did not acknowledge that we have a moral obligation to exercise compassion and mercy. For Bill *laissez-faire* capitalism was deficient in that it manifested a gross lack of compassion. In this respect he would oftentimes refer to Dickens since *compassion* for Bill was a precept which was wholly ignored by the political economists and yet he (like Dickens) regarded it as a far more important measure of human welfare than "utility" and the "greatest happiness of the greatest number." Bill judged policy and politics by the compassion that was shown or not shown: capitalism was deficient because it was a system which was inherently compassionless. At the same time, *socialist* revolutionaries who showed no compassion towards their fellow men, or were merciless in achieving their goals were also anathema to Bill. The source of his socialism is to be found in the words of wisdom which flowed from his *Zeida*. Although Bill was what may be described a *cultural Jew*, who was to abandon his belief in the God of Abraham, he fully and warmly embraced his *Zeida's* moral principles which were about being loving, compassionate and merciful. For Bill, therefore, any ideology which has no place for his *Zeida's* precepts is truly an abomination. Bill's case against classical economics or the Manchester School was, in all essentials, that made by Kropotkin and Dickens: it had a very narrow, unrealistic and wholly inaccurate view of human nature. Bill was deeply suspicious of any ideology or theory which disregarded the capacities that human beings had for compassion, charity and mutual aid.

Bill, however, like Kropotkin, rightly judged so much of modern economics as gravely deficient in the way in which compassion was excised from the subject. As an historian of East London, *rachamones* was as important to Bill as *utility* was for followers of Bentham. *East End 1888* is, as Richard Cobb says in the foreword, a "most unrevolutionary book" because it is written with an "abiding compassion" for all those who suffered and were victims of the economic, social and political order of the day.[22] Bill's heroes had this in common: they were all human beings who had *compassion* (and not just Smithian "sympathy") and believed in social justice, and showed *verstehen*. Hence, included in the list of those who acted with compassion and showed mercy were his "Saints" who, despite the critics, went to give assistance "armed with the bible and the bread basket."[23] Bill, of course, observes that such philanthropic activity could, in reality, only "scratch the surface" of the problems which had more pernicious roots.[24] Such compassion was not enough because the power of the "established classes" was indeed "well entrenched and resilient and could contain any changes that might threaten their hegemony."[25] Compassion was necessary for socialism, but it could never be sufficient to bring about radical change. That required power, but for Bill power without compassion and mercy was the most dangerous of combinations. Bill saw the practice of *rachamones* as being central to his *libertarian* socialism. The related idea of *tzedakah* also plays a key role in the ethical framework which structures his libertarian socialism. Doubtless many well-qualified scholars would take issue with his interpretation of *tzedakah*, and *rachamones*: but he was, after all, not a scriptural scholar. Having said this, and mindful of Bill's views as to the role of the Chief Rabbi (and Bill was very fond of Geoffrey Alderman's use of the term "Chief Rabbit"), the account offered by Rabbi Jonathan Sacks seems to capture, in theological terms, a good deal of what Bill understood by the *tzedakah*.

Tzedakah is, as Sacks acknowledges, an unusual term which has no simple direct English translation because it combines *two* concepts which are normally separated out: charity and justice. Sacks argues that:

> What *tzedakah* signifies … is often called "social justice", meaning that no-one should be without the basic requirements of existence, and that those who have more than they need must share that surplus with those who have less. This is absolutely fundamental to the kind of society the Israelites were charged with creating, namely one in which everyone has a basic right to a

dignified life and to be equal citizens in the covenantal community under the sovereignty of God ... God, for the Israelites, was actively concerned in the economic and political order, especially with those who, because they lacked power, or even a "voice", became victims of injustice and inequity.[26]

Bill's understanding of the commandment of *tzedakah* was very much in keeping with Sacks's interpretation: it was not just about charitable giving to the poor, it also involved this concern with social justice. It meant that human beings have to be active in ensuring that wealth is distributed fairly and that human dignity should be respected and the powerless had to be given justice. At the same time this *mitzvah* involves a concern with human freedom and the enslavement of poverty and persecution. *Tzedakah* is not just about our responsibility to practise charity but our obligation and duty to seek the just distribution of resources and human dignity. This means, Sacks notes:

> Among other things, that my freedom is not bought at the price of yours. A society in which the few have access to good education, health and other essential amenities, is not a place of liberty. It involves the removal of barriers to the exercise of responsible citizenship. [and] ... The highest act of *tzedakah* is ... one that allows the individual to become self-sufficient ... A society must ensure equal dignity ... to each of its members. This is a constant theme of the prophets.[27]

Sacks points out that the prophets constantly reminded the powerful that politics and economics have a moral dimension because they involve justice and charity. Above all, they reminded those with power that they must show solidarity with all those they rule and are commanded to govern so as to promote the common good. The prophets spoke the great truth to the powerful: that they must love their neighbour and exercise both a personal and collective responsibility for society as a whole. And this is what makes *tzedakah* far more than charity. As Rabbi Sacks argues: "It is not merely helping those in need. It is enabling the afflicted, where possible, to recover their capacity for independent action. Responsibility lies at the heart of human dignity."[28]

East End 1888 was written in the middle of the Thatcher era and published in 1988. As a book it was speaking to the issues of the day and warning of the consequences of the belief that the free market should be allowed to function without government interference. Bill draws attention to the need to learn from history with the famous lines from Santayana: "Those who do not remember the past are doomed to relive it."[29] We can have no doubt that his strictures against those who showed little concern for justice or charity and who exhibited little by way of solidarity with the poor stand as reproaches to the politicians and others who were carrying out policies Bill considered to be revisiting the errors of the past on the people of East London in the 1980s. It has to be said he was especially angry about those members of the Jewish community who were supportive of Thatcherite economic and social policies. For Bill the principle of *tzedakah* and *rachamones* was wholly incompatible with so many of the public policies which were associated with the new-right. In this regard Bill's understanding of the problematics of realising the common good through charity and social justice was markedly different from those interpretations of *tzedakah* that would hold that free market capitalism is indeed compatible with the teachings of the *Torah*. Thus although Bill would, I am sure, have accepted Sacks's interpretation of *tzedakah*, minus "all the religious stuff," he would have disagreed with his conclusion that: "it goes hand in hand with a free market, whilst recognising that the market has inherent limits" or that "the inequities of markets are of no reason to abandon the market."[30] Bill shared Kropotkin's and Rocker's profound doubts as to the compatibility of free market capitalism with possibilities of realising a society in which mutual aid could thrive.

The Russian Prince and the East London Professor

Bill believed that those who argued the case for free market capitalism in the 1980s had a poor understanding of its *inherent limits* and the inequities and injustices which it inevitably produces. Bill rejected the underlying and dangerous logic of *homo economicus* and the perverse view that human beings were just motivated by self-interest and utility maximisation. For this reason the critical text for Bill was undoubtedly Kropotkin's *Mutual Aid*. Whereas many in the nineteenth century interpreted evolution as legitimating capitalism and the doctrine of *laissez-faire*, Prince Peter Kropotkin (1842–1921) sought to show how evolution is not simply the story of competition and struggle for survival. Kropotkin anticipated so much of the literature which was produced in Bill's lifetime to show that evolution also involves the capacity of human beings and animals to practise cooperation, altruism, reciprocity and mutual aid. This is what bothered Bill about "invisible hand" economics: it was predicated on such a narrow and shallow view of human nature. His instruction to me as a young lecturer was to "get this into the students' heads" through *Mutual Aid*.

Capitalism was morally deficient for Bill because it was predicated on a view of human nature, that *claimed* to be rational and based on science, yet which was fundamentally erroneous and misguided. For this reason (amongst others) he regarded the likes of Milton Friedman as advocating a kind of economic religion of self-interest and self-regulating markets: a religion of "leaving things alone" and not a social science. He found in Kropotkin a far more convincing account of what it means to be a human being than that propagated by the Friedmans and modern-day utilitarians. On that point, I recall telling Bill about the lecture I was about to give on cost-benefit analysis and its application to public policy and was met with the criticism that I was just "preaching the gospel of Bentham." He was right, of course.

In *East End 1888* Bill gives a kind of "looking back in anger" account of what the practice of this evolutionary ("nature red in tooth and claw") utilitarian religion actually looks like. Just as George Orwell's *1984* was about 1948, *East End 1888* was really about East London in *1988*. On another personal note I remember that, during the time he was writing the book, we regularly went to the British Museum together travelling down on the Metropolitan Line or I would pick him up from Kenton in my mini and drive to the newspaper library in Colindale. As we worked alongside one another he would frequently stop, sigh and show me a passage in a book or some statistics and draw comparisons with contemporary politics or events. On one occasion he looked across from his 1888 newspapers and read a piece on *monetarism* or "the natural rate of unemployment" that I was working on (for a book on the financial press and economic opinion) and smiled a wry smile and whispered, "*plus ça change* boy ... ." For Bill this was the great tragedy and the awful farce of the dominant economic discourse of the 1980s: we seemed to have learned nothing from history. *East End 1888* was a consciously *prophetic* book, which like Dickens's *Hard Times*, was written "for these times."

Kropotkin wanted to develop an ethical foundation for anarchism as a form of libertarian socialism. Indeed, he wanted to do for socialism what Hume, Kant and Bentham had done for liberalism: he believed that mutual aid as a factor in evolution, could provide the basis of a *scientifically* based moral philosophy. He sets this out in various places, but in its most succinct form in his essay on "Anarchist Morality." He observes that "the ant, the bird, the marmot and the savage have read neither Kant nor the fathers of the Church nor even Moses. And yet all have the same idea of good and evil." Human beings have evolved a morality and did not acquire it from some divine source: "The idea of good and evil has thus nothing to do with religion or a mystic conscience. It is a natural need of animal races. And when founders of religions, philosophers, and moralists tell us of divine or metaphysical entities, they are only recasting what each ant, each sparrow practices in its little society." The gentle anarchist believed that humanity had to liberate itself from the notion that a sense of right and wrong and good and evil have some divine origin: "The moral sense is a natural faculty in us like the sense of smell or of touch."[31]

> By flinging overboard law, religion and authority, mankind can regain possession of the moral principle which has been taken from them. Regain that they may criticize it, and purge it from the adulterations wherewith priest, judge and ruler have poisoned it and are poisoning it yet.[32]

A passage in *Mutual Aid* which sheds some light on Bill's libertarianism is where Kropotkin discusses the role of charitable associations:

> There is not the slightest doubt that the great bulk of their members are moved by the same mutual-aid feelings which are common to all mankind. Unhappily the religious teachers of men prefer to ascribe to such feelings a supernatural origin. Many of them pretend that man does not consciously

obey the mutual-aid inspiration so long as it has not been enlightened by the teaching of the special religion they represent.[33]

With this argument Bill was in full agreement with Kropotkin. His grandfather's moral precepts were indeed expressions of the mutual-aid instinct. His *Zeida's* morality was, he reasoned, the outcome of an evolutionary process, not divine commandments. But on the other hand, he was not as dismissive of the role of religion in nurturing and bringing out these "mutual-aid" feelings. Thus Bill was more ambiguous about Kropotkin's assertion (later in the same paragraph) regarding the role of the Christian Church in aiding "the State in wrecking all standing institutions of mutual aid and support which were anterior to it."[34] Bill's account of the history of the East End gives a far more positive role for philanthropy and to the work of people like Huddleston. As Cobb notes in his foreword to *East End 1888*: "On the Saints Fishman shows himself characteristically unfashionable." We do not find in Bill the rather dismissive and negative attitude towards the mutual aid deriving from a "supernatural origin" that we find in Kropotkin and Rocker. In Cobb's words, "Fishman emphasizes the extreme devotion and boundless courage of the female Salvationists in their dealings with the poor, the needy and the hopeless." As the book shows, "the Salvation Army certainly did much more to alleviate the immediate sufferings of the poor in the East End than the fashionable doctrinaire radicals." Cobb captures the essence of Bill's socialism when he says that *East End 1888* is a good book "not merely because it is compassionate, but because it is most unrevolutionary. Boots and warm clothing were a better protection than any provided by political theory or doctrinal orthodoxies."[35] But where charity and compassion were informed by *rachamones* and *tzedakah qua* justice, charity and mutual aid – Bill would commend it whole heartedly. As *Into the Abyss* shows, Sims was a supporter of charity which was about tackling injustice, and which was given with compassion, but like Bill, Sims had little time for the mean-spirited and hard-hearted charity of the condescending kind. Unlike Marx, therefore, Bill did not regard religion as a kind of political opiate. Although not a *religious* person he saw religion as practised by his saints, both ancient and modern, as having considerable potential to change the world and contribute to the building of a socialist society.

Cobb was correct, Bill was indeed an *unrevolutionary* kind of historian and an *unrevolutionary* socialist. This was because, at heart, Bill was an *evolutionary* socialist. His history of East London was informed by the belief that socialist moral precepts were to be seen in evolutionary terms. Kropotkin's *Mutual Aid* aims to show how human beings are *naturally* disposed towards the principles that may be found in sacred texts. Socialism, as Kropotkin understood it, was committed to bringing about a political, social and economic order which would be conducive to realising the potential that human beings have for love and compassion. For both Kropotkin and Bill the "death of God" as proclaimed by Nietzsche would not lead to the death of morality – in the evolutionary terms of "mutual aid" – but quite the opposite: the demise of the power of rabbis and priests would actually enable humanity to regain the possession of an innate moral sense that has been corrupted by religion. For Kropotkin evolution showed that the morality preached by religions was *natural* and not divine, thus the death of the God of Abraham and Jacob would, by definition, have a beneficial effect for the development of a socialist society free to create a new anarchist ethic. Thus for Kropotkin and Rocker, the kind of Weberian *entzauberung der Welt*, or disenchantment of the world, would not mean an end to Judeo-Christian morality *per se*, but to the demise of the claim that the compassion and charity that we find in mutual aid required any reference to a divinity.[36] If, as Kropotkin believed, human evolution has indeed been shaped by an inherent capacity of mankind to cooperate and act in reciprocal and altruistic ways, then the kind of disenchantment discerned by Weber would have the effect of *moralising* rather than *de-moralising* the world. Libertarianism was not to be confused with *egotistical individualism*. Kropotkin himself was very critical of the "narrow" and "selfish individualism" that actually "belittles" individualism of either a free market or Nietzschean kind.[37]

Bill saw the appeal of Hayekian liberalism and *laissez-faire* economics on the one hand and the emerging post-modern (Nietzschean) egoism and individualism and its accompanying relativism on the other, as *essentially* two sides of the same coin. Bill was at one with Kropotkin on this: he had little time for the individualism of the Hayekian or the Nietzschean variety. Both failed to understand the role of mutual aid in the evolutionary process. Libertarianism for Bill was not about unconstrained individualism and egotism. He was neither a positivist nor a relativist: he had a definite moral perspective and position which respected and tolerated difference and individual freedom and dignity, but within the context of there being a universal ethic of mutual aid as set out by Kropotkin. Libertarianism was not concerned with inventing your own personal morality, quite the opposite: "read Kropotkin" he would always advise those who thought they could just do what they felt was "alright." Libertarianism was not just about "rights talk," it involved "responsibility talk."

Bill found in Kropotkin a form of socialism which enabled him to reject the theism of his grandfather, whilst at the same time to accept the validity of his moral principles. Although he was, like Kropotkin and Nietzsche, of the opinion that God had indeed died, and although he could not quite understand why rational people (like me) continued to believe in God and be *religious*, he was also prepared to acknowledge that it could actually practise what it preached – just like his grandfather had done. In an edition of *Mutual Aid* published in 1939 the editor introduced the volume as "a co-operator's classic, one of the sacred texts of Marxism and socialism."[38] I am convinced that for Bill it was indeed a kind of "sacred text," for it is a book which provided him with an account of human nature that gave a scientific basis and logic for his core moral beliefs. It showed how the beliefs that his grandfather had taught him had an *empirical* foundation. *Mutual Aid* rationalised sacred commandments. An *ought* became an *is*. And, in turn, the *is* could become an *ought*.

Hard Times in 1888 and 1988

If in Kropotkin Bill found a science of evolution that could serve to support his morality and ethical philosophy, I think it was in Charles Dickens (1812–1870) that we can best understand the broader philosophy which shaped his work and his life as a libertarian socialist. It is through his Dickensianism we can enter more fully into (what he called his) "Fishmania." His views on political economy both in the nineteenth century and in the twentieth century as far as I could ascertain, were, for the most part, informed by his reading of Dickens, and especially *Hard Times*. When we would take a coffee break at the British Museum or Colindale during the period he was writing *East End 1888* we would frequently talk about Dickens and share our favourite lines. He saw ideas that were exposed by Dickens as immoral and contemptible as returning like a plague in the Britain of the 1980s. If we are to understand the essence of Bill's social philosophy and political economy, which shaped his ethical framework, I think we find it best expressed in Dickens. Bill, just like Dickens, considered the economics of the Manchester School and utilitarian "scientific" philosophy contrary to his understanding of human nature. What Bill saw in the political economy that had wrought so much misery and hardship in East London was a way of thinking about the world which was abstract, cold and calculating and devoid of compassion and consideration of justice. In a piece (entitled "On Strike") published in February 1854 in *Household Words*, Dickens sums up what he regards as the moral ugliness of the prevailing political economy. Speaking to a "Mr Snapper" whilst on a train journey to Preston he says that:

> I believe … that into the relations between employers and employed, as into all the relations of this life, there must enter something of feeling and sentiment; something of mutual explanation, forbearance, and consideration; something which is not to be found in Mr M'Culloch's dictionary, and is not exactly stateable in figures; otherwise those relations are wrong and rotten at the core and will never bear sound fruit.[39]

The consequences of this lack of feeling and sentiment in political economy were to be depicted in so many of Dickens's novels. Bill's own writings also aimed to show, as Dickens observes in "On Strike" that: "political economy is a mere skeleton unless it has a little human covering and filling out, a little human bloom upon it, and a little human warmth in it."[40] For Bill *Hard Times* captured the essence of a philosophy that was without humanity and which was predicated on "facts," "calculation" and "utility." As a socialist he believed that political economy – whether deployed by advocates of the free market or Marxists – was injurious to human beings when it was predicated on calculability and measurement and excluded consideration of compassion, sympathy, empathy and charity – in other words in which *rachamones* and *tzedakah* were absent or ignored and just "fancy." Bill saw the consequences of such a philosophy brilliantly exposed in Dickens, and experienced it for himself in the inter-war years, and lived to see it return like a thick pestilential fog in the 1980s. Jane Smiley captures the rather unconventional way in which Bill read Dickens when she observes that:

> In the 1960s and 70s, the era of the new left, Dickens was considered well-meaning but naive; his 'programme' was thought to be poorly worked out and inconsistent ... After Marxism went out of fashion, Dickens's amorphous social critique came to seem more universally true because it was not programmatic but based on feelings of generosity and brotherhood combined with specific criticisms of practices common in England during his lifetime.[41]

This is an important point in respect of understanding the logic and method of Bill's social criticism: for whom Dickens was never just well meaning and naïve. In this, as in other matters, Bill was not in step with conventional or ruling opinion amongst left-wing academics and activists. He found in Dickens a truthful and powerful critique of capitalism.

The characters of *Hard Times* in many ways personify the struggle that we find in Bill's history of East London between compassion and charity and selfishness and avarice. We encounter the utilitarian Gradgrind whose blind rationalism ultimately destroys and morally impoverishes his children and who all too late discovers that there is indeed a wisdom of the heart as well as of the head. We meet Bounderby for whom profit and self-interest are the only values that matter and who has no regard for the welfare of his workers who exist for him as simply "hands" and numbers. In Bounderby we see a human being who has no interest in remembering his past and fabricates a fiction of being an entirely self-made man. And we meet Mr Harthouse, the supreme egoist, who believes in absolutely nothing apart from himself. But we also meet people who live their lives with love and compassion and exhibit a sense of justice and fairness that is wholly absent from those, like Bitzer, who live by the laws of political economy and religion of Jeremy Bentham. And who, when asked to show some compassion by a repentant Gradgrind, informs him that, thanks to the lessons he learnt from Gradgrind and M'choakumchild, his heart is open to "Reason and nothing else." In Coketown Bill saw portrayed the moral corruption which was apparent in the history of East London, and in the realities of modern free market capitalism. But he also saw in the history of East London saints as well as the sinners: he shows us examples of real Sissy Jupes and the real Stephen Blackpools and Rachaels: people who exhibit *rachamones* and *tzedakah* in abundance and treasure their memories of good and bad times. He saw in the lives of the people of Coketown the capacity of human beings to practise the mutual aid, reciprocity and altruism that is depicted in the pages of Kropotkin.

I am reminded once again of the period in which he wrote *East End 1888* and those occasions when we discussed not the Santayana quote at the start of the book but the line in *David Copperfield* when Betsey Trotwood says: "It's in vain ... to recall the past, unless it works some influence on the present."[42] As a socialist, of course, he believed that the moral struggle we see in Dickens required more than philanthropy and the kind of reforms championed by the author of *Hard Times*. History can help us to understand the world, but the point was to *change it*. Dickens would not, like the young Bill Fishman, have actively supported the Battle of Cable Street in 1936. *Contra* Dickens, he believed that, although the saints were on the right side of the struggle for a more just and a more equitable society, it required political action to bring about a world which would be founded on the principles of compassion, love, mutual aid and the pursuit of the common good and which would challenge the power of the Gradgrinds and the Bounderbys. *East End 1888* was written to recall the past in the hope that it might work some influence on the contemporary struggle to challenge the dominance of a dangerous economic discourse.

What he shared with Dickens was a deep hostility to the onward march of the speculators, the utilitarians and the calculators in their modern incarnations as managers, target setters and number crunchers. He especially despaired at the impact that the Gradgrinds were having on the public sector – especially in education. Like Kropotkin, he believed that the *free market* economics, as described by Dickens, ignored the role of mutual aid. Significantly on this very point, Kropotkin himself was critical of Adam Smith's failure to take account of the role of sympathy that is central to the argument of the *Theory of Moral Sentiments* but that was (he believed) absent from the *Wealth of Nations*. In the *Theory of Moral Sentiments*, Smith argues that sympathy for other people is the result of the human capacity to use *imagination* as a way of understanding how people feel, and not simply exercise reason. In Dickens's reading of *laissez-faire* economics we find that Gradgrind has no time for "fancy" and "wonder." All that matters are facts, addition, subtraction and division. It is this very faculty of *imagination* that is possessed by Sissy, Blackpool and the circus folk that is absent in Gradgrind's system and catechism. What Gradgrind required were facts, not fancies: statistics and not wonder and imagination. Bill's history might also be understood in this Dickensian sense as written so as to stimulate imagination and wonder. Bill saw history as a way of learning from the past and he sought to do this by getting the reader to enter into, and imagine, the streets and the poverty and misery, but also to wonder at how, in spite of all the hardship, human beings were able to show mercy and compassion and exercise mutual aid, reciprocity, trust and cooperate and support one another. For Bill, the development of a moral sense required that human beings have *moral imagination* and this depended in turn on a *historical* imagination. If we were to successfully learn from the past we had to imagine it and enter into it, rather than stand as a supposedly objective observer. Bill was no Marxist: the past could not be objectively known, it could only be something to be imagined and wondered at and learnt from. Perhaps this is why Bill's walks were so (truly) wonderful. To walk with him around East London was to enter imaginatively into the past whilst all the time being made aware of how the history of the streets echoes and reverberates and has implications and lessons for present and future generations.

A central aspect of Bill's socialism was, therefore, the rejection of the utilitarian account of ethics and evolution. In *Hard Times* we see a world of the self-made man in which all decisions and choices can be made on the basis of rational calculation devoid of imagination and moral considerations. But, as we know, compassion and charity are, by definition, not virtues which can be cultivated simply through addition, subtraction and division. We do not arrive at compassion and charity through a cost-benefit analysis. When any form of government or economy treats human beings as just a collection of numbers and statistics then humanity is in grave danger from stupidity, tyranny and oppression. Bill saw Gradgrindism as alive and well in the twentieth and twenty-first centuries as it had been in Dickens's *Hard Times*. Any system that was grounded on the dubious calculating morality of Bentham and his ilk or which separated economics and morality was always destructive of human freedom and dignity whether it was predicated on Bounderby's faith in the survival of the fittest or the "invisible hand," or in a belief in centrally planned economy. And this defined not just his opposition to F.A. Hayek and Milton Friedman and their apostles, but also his opposition to managerialism and to communistic statism and centralisation in all its forms.

History and Remembering

Although we may discern a Dickensian quality in Bill's history of East London, his approach to history was quintessentially Jewish, as was his approach to social justice. For Bill history was about *remembering* and *memory* – or in Hebrew, *Zakhor*. After a few years of knowing and teaching with Bill I came to see his implicit philosophy of history focused on the vital importance of *remembering*. For him *remembering* was necessary for the development of the individual and collective conscience and identity. History – as memory – had a moral purpose. Above all, the lesson to be remembered was that evil had to be fought and confronted: the fight against oppression and the struggle for justice was never-ending. Without remembering and confronting the injustices and the evils done in the past there could be no justice in the present or in the future. At the same time, we also had an obligation to remember the times when human beings showed mutual aid, compassion and charity. *Remembering* was thus a defining characteristic of Bill's socialism and his historical writings.

Memory, as the work of Yosef Yerushalmi and other scholars have shown, is at the core of what it means to be a Jew.[43] The act of *remember*ing was for Bill a profoundly political act, a personal and social responsibility and not only a religious imperative. Just as we have a moral obligation and a responsibility to practise *rachamones* and *tzedakah*, we must also *remember* the past in order to make sense of our present and our future. History was not therefore about simply a chronicling of the past, it was about understanding the points in time and space at which the past, present and future all intersect and converge. I believe that is why Bill was so good at walking the streets of East London: he could tell the story of the people of that part of the world in the context of a living community which was connected with a past that was all around them and which had to be remembered, celebrated and commemorated. He was, as Beryl Bainbridge observes, "a formidable walker of the streets of his beloved East End" having "spent a lifetime retracing the footsteps of Sims and others, bringing to vivid life the history of the way things used to be."[44] The past for Bill was not therefore, as Hartley put it in *The Go-Between*, a "foreign country." The past had to be a living, ever-present and *vivid* reality which provides the foundation and source of our personal and community identity. *Zakhor* was therefore a necessary pre-requisite for *rachamones* and *tzedakah*. When we remember the past, and tell our stories about the past, we become more sensitive and aware of the present and the possibilities of the future. And we also become more aware of our personal identity and our collective, common or shared identity. For this reason, I have long considered that the lines from Ralph McTell's poignant song, *The Streets of London*, [45] at the beginning of the *Streets of East London* are really significant.

The song, which invites the reader to be led by the hand through the streets of London and be influenced by what they see, perfectly sums up Bill's approach to history. It should be read alongside the quote from George Santanya in *East End 1988*. He takes the reader by the hand and seeks to change their minds. Bill wants the reader to take a good look at the people, for "Streets without people constitute a void."[46] His history of East London is a call to remember, and a call to learn:

> Walk the streets of East London today and yesterday and you will have rubbed shoulders with Irish cockneys, Russo-Polish Jews, Chinese, Somalis, West Africans, Indians and white Anglo-Saxon Protestants … In the East End they combine to produce a marvellously colourful whole. Look at the faces of the costers and the customers that throng Cheshire Street, Club Row, Wentworth Street and Whitechapel Waste markets … Continuity is there: in the few surviving rumps of street communities, in the markets, in the pubs, in the handful of leprous, urine soaked courtyards … in the Hebrew insignia on decaying facades of the last remaining synagogues. But a crime has been committed against the past. In the race for functional conformity, and from the pressing needs for rehousing the people, the little streets and their ancient communities have fallen before the demolishers – a development now recognised too late, as an error of judgement. Juxtapose the new high-rise Bastilles against the residual one-up-one-down Victorian cottages, and one can sense the loss in human terms.[47]

The past, he says is "as inexorable as the present." And because of this *inexorability* of the past, human beings must *remember*, otherwise they will make errors of "judgement." When he spoke to me as a newly appointed professor of public policy, he reminded me of this truth about the relationship between remembering and forgetting and the inexorability of the past and present: "when policy makers don't remember the past, they fail to understand the present and make a bloody mess of the future." He saw this so vividly in the history of East London, and that is why he passionately believed history was about enabling people to remember and by remembering they could learn the importance of *tzedakah* and *rachamones*. In remembering we could more fully comprehend our obligation and our responsibility to confront evil and "learn to do good, seek justice and aid the oppressed." History as remembering was therefore absolutely essential for the cultivation of a personal and collective moral sense. So the past for Bill was not a foreign country, and therefore history – as remembering – should not become a prison or a way of building walls of hate, prejudice and intolerance. As an historian he appreciated the importance of what David Rieff has termed the "ethics of forgetting" as well as of an "ethics of memory."[48] Reading history with charity and compassion was about remembering but it was crucially also about forgiving and forgetting. Without *tzedakah* and *rachamones* human beings could easily become oppressed by their own history and memories or by the histories and memories of others. Remembering, for Bill, involved the exercise of moral and ethical judgement and above all, tolerance and the ability to walk the streets of London in a stranger's shoes.

East End 1888 and Beyond

In conclusion we can be absolutely sure that Bill's work will be read for many generations to come. It is, however, important to remember that the *principles* which informed his books will also continue to be relevant to the problems of East London. Bill's writings on East London contain truths which are, of course, universal. He saw in the lives of the people there a local example of a global history. What he has to say about the streets of Whitechapel and Bethnal Green has a relevance to other streets and other places and at other times. What he saw in the history of *his* people in the east of London was the drama of a moral conflict which was the common history of all people: the struggle for liberty and justice. In this struggle the supreme aim was to promote the formation of a society in which *compassion* and *charity* could be the guiding moral principles of political, economic and social life. And this in turn meant that history as *remembering* was indispensable to the moral progress of humanity.

Bill did not leave a theoretical or philosophical legacy, but he did give us a history of East London that is informed by deeply held moral convictions and an approach to reading and writing history which together can serve to promote a constructive dialogue between people of faith and those of none. Bill believed that the moral precepts which informed his life and his work as an historian offer hope to the East London of the twenty-first century as they did in the nineteenth century. He wrote history so that we might not forget. He lived long enough to see what happens when people fail to appreciate the role that compassion, charity and memory plays in human affairs, and what inevitably happens when we fail to understand their critical role in advancing the cause of human dignity and the common good.

Notes

1 W.J. Fishman, *The Insurrectionists* (London, 1970).
2 The Five Books of Moses.

3 W.J. Fishman, *East End Jewish Radicals* (London, 1975).
4 R. Rocker, *Nationalism and Culture* (Minnesota, 1978).
5 F. Rocker, *The East End Years: A Stepney Childhood* (London, 1998).
6 Bill, I recall, used the words *rachamonat* and *tsedoka*. In this chapter, however, we refer to the more widely used forms of *rachamones* and *tzedakah*. *Rachamones* can be understood as compassion or mercy and *tzedakah* meaning charitable giving – a moral obligation.
7 Lord Peter Hain, private correspondence with Wayne Parsons, 8 June 2015.
8 Ibid. See also P. Hain, *Back to the Future of Socialism* (Bristol, 2015) and his *Ayes to the Left*, (London, 1995).
9 W.J. Fishman, *The Streets of East London* (London, 1979), p. 50.
10 Ibid., p. 67.
11 Ibid., p. 74
12 Cited in, D. Walker, "Bill Fishman: A life dedicated to compassion and scholarship," *Jewish East End Celebration Society*, 23 December, 2014, http://www.jeecs.org.uk/news/65-bill-fishman-a-life-dedicated-to-compassion-and-scholarship (ccessed 6 March 2016).
13 J.M Keynes, *The General Theory of Employment Interest and Money* (Cambridge, 1973 ed.), pp. 383–4.
14 Fishman, *Streets*, p. 129.
15 Fishman, *Jewish Radicals*, p. 229.
16 Ibid., p. 309.
17 Ibid., p. xii.
18 W.J. Fishman, *Into The Abyss: The Life and Work of G.R. Sims* (London, 2008).
19 Ibid., p. 40.
20 Ibid., p. 90.
21 Ibid., p. 95.
22 R. Cobb in W.J. Fishman, *East End 1888* (London, 1988), p. ix.
23 Ibid., p. 230.
24 Ibid., p. 265.
25 Ibid., p. 302.
26 J. Sacks, *The Dignity of Difference: How to Avoid the Clash of Civilizations* (London and New York, 2002), p. 114.
27 Ibid., p. 120.
28 J. Sacks, *To Heal a Fractured World: The Ethics of Responsibility* (London and New York, 2005), p. 184.
29 As quoted in Fishman, *1888*, p. xiii. The quote retains the essence of Santayana's claim but the wording in the original is different.
30 Sacks, *The Dignity of Difference*, p. 122.
31 P. Kropotkin, "Anarchist Morality," (1897) retrieved on 1 March 2016 from www.sp unk.org.
32 Ibid.
33 P. Kropotkin, *Mutual Aid: A Factor in Evolution* (Harmondsworth, 1939), p. 222.
34 Ibid.
35 Cobb in Fishman, *1888*, p. ix.
36 M. Weber, *From Max Weber, Essays in Sociology* (London, 1991 edition), p. 139.
37 P. Kropotkin, in Letter to Nettlau, 1902, http://dwardmac.pitzer.edu/Anarchist_Archives/kropotkin/kropotkintonetllau3502.html, accessed 1 March 2016.
38 Kropotkin, *Mutual Aid*, p. 9.
39 C. Dickens, "On Strike," in *Household Words*, Vol. VII (11 February 1854).
40 Ibid.
41 J. Smiley, "Growing Pains," *The Guardian*, 24 June 2006.
42 C. Dickens, *David Copperfield* (London, 2004 edition), p. 356.
43 See Y.H. Yerushalmi, *Zakhor: Jewish History and Jewish Memory* (Washington, DC, 1982); E. Carlebach, J.M. Efron, D.N. Myers (eds), *Jewish History and Jewish Memory: Essays in Honor of Yosef Hayim Yerushalmi* (Boston, MA, 1998); A. Margalit, *The Ethics of Memory* (Cambridge, 2004).

44 Bainbridge in W.J. Fishman, *Into The Abyss*, p. 8.
45 Cited in Fishman, *Streets*, p. 8.
46 Ibid.
47 Ibid., pp. 8–14.
48 D. Rieff, *In Praise of Forgetting: Historical Memory and Its Ironies* (New Haven, CT, 2016).

Select Bibliography

Elishiva Carlebach, John M. Efron and David N. Myers (eds), *Jewish History and Jewish Memory: Essays in Honor of Yosef Hayim Yerushalmi* (Boston, MA, 1998).

Charles Dickens, *Hard Times: For These Times* (London, 2009).

Peter Hain, *Ayes to the Left* (London, 1995).

Peter Kropotkin, *Ethics: Origins and Development* (first published London, 1925).

Fermin Rocker, *The East End Years: A Stepney Childhood* (London, 1998).

Rudolf Rocker, *Nationalism and Culture* (Minnesota, 1978).

Jonathan Sacks, *The Dignity of Difference: How to Avoid the Clash of Civilizations* (London and New York, 2002).

Jonathan Sacks, *To Heal a Fractured World: The Ethics of Responsibility* (London and New York, 2005).

Yosef Hayim Yerushalmi, *Zakhor: Jewish History and Jewish Memory* (Washington, DC, 1982).

PART Two

Anti-Alienism, Anti-Semitism and War

5

THE REUBENS BROTHERS

Jews, Crime and the East London Connection, 1887–1911

Colin Holmes

> As long as there is the cobbled alley, one undeserted tenement left, which recalls the voices and images of the *chaverim*, I shall walk with my father.[1]

I

Bill Fishman was a rather special historian. Who can ever forget his deeply knowledgeable, highly entertaining and idiosyncratic walking tours in East London which never ceased to bring alive its varied and constantly changing history?

Whitechapel and Stepney were his stomping ground. It was here he grew up, savouring its sights, absorbing its smells, noticing its personalities.

I can still see his tall, slightly swaying figure threading its way along Brick Lane and Fashion Street. I can visualise him entering the portals of Toynbee Hall. I can hear him talking in front of the imposing edifice on Fournier Street which became a mosque in 1976 but which started its life as a Huguenot church before becoming a Methodist chapel and then in 1898 an ultra-orthodox synagogue. The changing character of this impressive building stands as an enduring physical witness to the East End providing a continuing magnet and reception centre for immigrants and refugees. I recall him once flinging open the door of the Anarchists' Bookshop in Angel Alley and proclaiming to a startled audience: "Have no fear. Fishman's here!" I remember him too, on several occasions, standing policeman-like in the middle of the swarming Whitechapel Road and holding up his hand to halt the ant-like rush of oncoming traffic. Motorists who failed to heed him would immediately have a finger jabbed in their direction and be roundly cursed with: "I'll tell the Pope about you!" Importantly, I continue also to recognise his qualities as a first-class historian displayed in books such as *East End Jewish Radicals* and *East End 1888*.[2]

Max Miller, the comedy king of the twentieth-century music hall, would often say to his admiring audiences: "There'll never be another when I'm gone, missus." He was right. The same can be said of Bill.

II

When musing on a suitable topic for a memorial volume I was taken back to 1991 when Geoffrey Alderman and I were busy seeking contributors for a *Festschrift* in Bill's honour.[3] In 1965 Bill had been appointed to a Schoolmaster Fellowship at Balliol where he became close to Richard Cobb, Christopher Hill and Jack Gallagher, and I invited Cobb – who had already written the foreword to *East End 1888* – to participate in our planned volume. Like Bill, he was known for his knowledge of life on the streets; whereas Bill focused on the East End, Cobb's chosen terrain was Paris. He seemed to be an ideal participant.

"What a very happy idea," he replied when hearing of the planned volume. He continued:

> Yesterday I suddenly had an inspiration; yes indeed I'd like to contribute to a festschrift (horrid Teutonic word) & will write a piece on Alphonse Boudard, a Paris-born former burglar and trigger-man, and now more or less a reformed character …

Against that enticing entrée he proceeded to sketch Boudard in a little more detail:

> He was born in the then very tough XIIIme arrondissement … and grew up during the Occupation. I think he fits in pretty well in my urban rogues' gallery. He is also very very funny … He was tubercular & has only one lung. He is completely apolitical and one of Nature's anarchists. Yes, I think Alphonse is my man for Bill's collection … [4]

It promised to be a fascinating contribution, the kind of discussion Bill would have welcomed and found greatly amusing. Sadly, Cobb never delivered.

But it gave me the idea that something on East London's Jewish criminals might fit the shape of the memorial volume. But on whom particularly? Bill's *Streets of East London* carried a passing reference to the Reubens brothers and they form the centrepiece of my chapter.[5] This theme takes us back to the London of a hundred years ago.

III

London, William Cobbett's "Great Wen," is today a city undergoing a massive transformation:

Just over twenty years ago nobody imagined that this grey city with 1960s tube trains, separated from the Continent only by a long traffic jam to Heathrow and then hours of dead time, would exert such attraction that a three-bedroomed house would cost £1.1m.[6]

The London which captured Bill's interest was quite different from the London of the 1960s and certainly today's capital. But there are parallels.

London has now become almost a separate state, symbolised by the power and influence of the City. But so it was a hundred years ago when it counted as "the richest … financial center in the world."[7] Today, alongside this glittering, ostentatious, staggering wealth which can be glimpsed every day in the capital, areas can still be found of acute deprivation, prolonged misery and deep poverty.[8] Those Londoners now inhabiting this "ghost" world are the equivalents of those equally faceless people who featured in the late nineteenth, early twentieth century in Charles Booth's magisterial survey, *Life and Labour of the People in London*.[9] Plus ça change.

Today London is a city of migrants. How many languages can be heard daily in the streets? In Booth's time a traveller walking its pavements would soon have noticed something strikingly similar. Liverpool might then have been the most Irish of English cities but the capital still had its attractions for those who made the challenging voyage across the water: imagine, for a moment, the psychological effect of leaving rural Mayo and entering into the world's most dizzying metropolis. These adventurous and needy Irish were not alone among London's new populations: German bankers, German sugar bakers, German clerks, Italian ice cream sellers and street musicians, added to this cosmopolitan mix. Moreover, near the docks, small groups of Africans, Chinese and Indians who worked the ships sailing daily in and out of the capital could be spotted. And, living in parallel with such incomers, from the late nineteenth century a recently arrived Jewish community had grown up which supplemented the already settled Anglo-Jewish population.[10]

The Jewish arrivals from Russian Poland consisted of both economic migrants and refugees. Russian Jews had long been confined to the western boundary of the Russian Empire in the so-called Pale of Settlement and, following the assassination in 1881 of Tsar Alexander II for which Jews were held responsible, further restrictions descended on their economic life. Rather than endure these constraints, some voted with their feet and set off hopefully, yet doubtless apprehensively, towards what they hoped and believed would be a brighter, freer life in the West. Other Jews moved westwards to escape persecution: they had simply had enough of the Cossacks and other Tsarist troops descending on their communities and bringing violence in their wake.[11]

Whereas today Germany is proving a magnet for immigrants and refugees, in the late nineteenth and early twentieth centuries, for many of these westward-moving Jews America was the *goldeneh medinah*, the golden land.[12] But migration then as now was a costly affair and some financially strapped Russian Polish Jews cut their

losses and settled in the East End of London. An estimated 120,000 Jewish newcomers came to Britain between 1870 and 1914, and the 1901 census counted
53,557 Russian Poles then living in the capital, 42,032 of them in Stepney. The
1911 census, the last before the Great War, showed their numbers in London
had grown to 68,420 and they remained heavily concentrated and visible in that
particular borough.[13]

In this area, a recognisable Jewish world came into being. The newcomers
worked in a limited range of occupations, including ready-made clothing, cabinet
making and the boot and shoe trade, where they were often employed by other
Jews. And some newcomers themselves became successful entrepreneurs, though
this aspect of the migration was less pronounced than in America. At the same time
a distinctive Jewish cultural life developed. Yiddish was heard on the streets. And
shtiebels – synagogues within houses – appeared, where observant newcomers
could practise their own forms of religion rather than what they viewed as the
Anglicised Judaism followed by the settled Jewish community. Schewzik's, the
famous Jewish ritual and vapour baths, was established at 86 and 86a Brick Lane. It
stood directly opposite the synagogue on that street and its advertising board – now
in the Jewish Museum in London – informed curious passers-by that it offered the
"Best massage in London: Invaluable Relief for Rheumatism, Gout, Sciatica,
Neuritis, Lumbago and Allied complaints." Also on Brick Lane, London's new
citizens could find and enjoy the recognisable food of their homeland at the Lodzer
Kosher Restaurant. Any of them fallen on hard times and seeking a meal could
make the short journey to the Jewish Soup Kitchen on Brune Street, Spitalfields
which, the elegant script on its decorated façade explained, had been founded in
1902 "For the Jewish Poor." By contrast, if any of London's new Jews had money
jingling in their pockets they could visit the Pavilion Theatre in Whitechapel. For
a brief time serious cultural interests could be satisfied at the Feinman Theatre.
Or, more light-heartedly, an evening could be enjoyed at the Paragon Music
Hall on Mile End Road. "The Fancy" were also catered for with the opening
in 1894 of the Wonderland as a boxing venue. Jack Berg, "Kid" Lewis and
later Lew Lazar, grew up in this Jewish East End as did the promoter Jack Solo-
mons. Here was a world within a world and that Jewish visibility was enhanced
through a noticeable attachment to socialism and anarchism. The families of
Raphael Samuel and Arnold Wesker reflected this tendency. As a result, in the
early twentieth century a discernible Jewish influence can be traced within the
British Communist Party.[14]

Bill's aged, top-hatted, battered-overcoat-wearing grandfather lived largely in
this Jewish world. So did his hard-working parents who yearned for peace and
quiet and dreamed of a better future for their children.

But alongside this society a Jewish criminal class flourished. This underworld
contained whizzers (pickpockets), shundicknicks (ponces), gonoffs (thieves),
smashers (passers of stolen money), mutchers (those who stole from drunks), spie-
lers (gamblers) as well as brides (prostitutes). And almost inevitably this small world
had its noses (informers).[15] The Reubens brothers, born in Britain to respectable

immigrant parents, plunged into the criminal sub-culture and in doing so briefly entered the history books.

IV

On 15 March 1909 the SS *Dorset* concluded its voyage from Australia and moored at London's Victoria Docks. Two crew members, William Sproull, its second engineer, who came from Jarrow, and its third mate Charles Malcolm McEachran, now on land and flush with cash, decided to go on the town in search of pleasure. They shared a meal in Aldgate and then, in the Liverpool Street area, found what they were looking for. They encountered Ellen Brooks (sometimes known as Stevens) a twenty-year-old prostitute who was accompanied by Emily Allen, two years older, who also worked the streets. The events of that evening, hazy so far, became even fuzzier. It would appear that, after drinking heavily in Houndsditch, the four went back to 3 Rupert Street where Allen lived in Room 13 with Morris Reubens. In effect, she was his girl; he ran her. Money changed hands, sexual activity occurred between the sailors and the women, and then seemingly all four went out again on the town. By now well-oiled, the party returned later to Rupert Street. At 12.40 a.m. the four were interrupted when Morris Reubens and his brother Marks suddenly showed up. The latter lived with Ellen Brooks in nearby Everard Street. He was her pimp; he controlled her. The brothers were presumably making sure their women were safe; after all, they were valuable commodities, a source of cash. Assured all was well, Morris and Marks decided – for now – to go to Everard Street and leave the prostitutes to conduct their business.

However, they claimed then to have heard a furious row between the women and their clients. Apparently the sailors were refusing to "part up" with more cash. The brothers entered the building and at some point Morris attempted to hit Sproull, described in court as "a strong muscular man" weighing fourteen stone, with a heavy leather stick made of sjambok. However his badly aimed blow struck McEachran who, believing discretion was better than valour, left his shipmate and, though drunk and wounded, staggered into the street. A police officer found him later propped against a wall on the Whitechapel Road, "dazed and a little incoherent." Meanwhile Sproull was having to contend with the brothers in Rupert Street. He might have been killed inside the house before his body was deposited in the street outside. Or he might have been dragged into the street and dealt with there. The circumstances are unclear. Wherever he was killed, an attempt was being made to suggest he had been the random victim of a passing street robbery. Allen claimed later that when the brothers returned to the room in Rupert Street she noticed Morris's stick had been broken and they also had in their possession a bloodied knife.

Clearly Sproull had been dealt with. Even so, Marks Reubens assured "Emmie" that everything would be alright. She had no need to worry. At the same time, he insisted she hide the stick and the knife behind the gas stove.

But matters soon took a new turn. The police officer who found McEachran gleaned something of what had just been happening in Rupert Street, even though the seaman was too drunk to remember the address where the dispute had occurred. The time was now 1.30 a.m. Ten minutes later a night watchman found Sproull's body lying between Rupert Street and Leman Street. He had been stabbed just above the heart and sustained a wound on his right wrist. He had also been robbed. A trail of blood led the police to 3 Rupert Street where they found Brooks, by now roaring drunk. Within minutes of their arrival the police had arrested both brothers along with Allen and Brooks. The four were taken into custody.

They strenuously denied any involvement in either murder or robbery. However on his way for questioning Morris Reubens apparently produced a gold watch and chain, saying he had removed it from "the fellow who was lying on the ground over there," to which he added "I hope he is not dead." He also attempted surreptitiously to drop a bloodstained handkerchief. This object was to feature as an exhibit at the brothers' forthcoming trial.

When the party arrived at the police station Morris, totally lacking any sense of filial loyalty, exclaimed: "I did not stab him! If he was stabbed my brother must have done it!" A mistake. At this time the police had never mentioned that Sproull had been stabbed. When Marks Reubens was questioned about the bloodied knife found in Rupert Street he admitted it belonged to him and the police believed he had recently washed his hands, presumably to remove any of Sproull's blood.

The police concluded they now had sufficient evidence to implicate the brothers in Sproull's murder, though their case was hardly watertight. Some possible key witnesses were hardly any use at all. Brooks and McEachran were too drunk to recall in detail what had happened. And Allen claimed not to have known what passed between Sproull and the brothers once they left the house.[16]

Even so, Morris and Marks were soon charged with Sproull's murder. In the East End criminal world the Reubens had apparently acquired something of a reputation not only for running girls but also, if Arthur Harding, a member of the criminal fraternity there can be believed, for garotting the women's clients. In Harding's words, the brothers' practice was to send girls "on the batter" before they "lumbered the men they brought in."[17] It had doubtless been a lucrative business. Clients paid for sex. Then they were robbed. It must have lined the brothers' pockets with a steady flow of cash they could use, via local bookies, as their betting money. It was always likely that on the night of Sproull's murder they would in any case have returned at some point to Rupert Street to fleece the sailors. But that evening matters clearly got out of hand.

The police, doubtless aware of this targeted operation about which it was naturally difficult to get people to talk, believed they could finally settle a long-standing score with the Reubens. For their part, the brothers realised the seriousness of the situation they now faced. A naïve remark Morris made to the well-known Det. Insp. F.P. Wensley – "Do what you can for us Mr Wensley, we never meant to murder the man and you don't want to see a couple of young fellows like us 'topped'" – underlines as much.[18] Their risk-taking activities had caught up with them.

V

On 22 April 1909 Morris Reubens, aged twenty-three, described as a boot sales-man, and Marks Reubens, a year younger, whom court papers listed as a coster-monger, appeared at the Old Bailey charged with murder. Emily Allen and Ellen Brooks appeared alongside them. But before the trial began, the Crown intimated it would not be proceeding against the two women. Even so, they were required to remain in court to give evidence. The brothers pleaded guilty to robbery but denied the charge of murder.

The prosecution argued that on 16 March the brothers had returned to Rupert Street with the clear intention of robbing the two sailors who had been picked up by Allen and Brooks. When Sproull had attempted to defend himself the brothers had killed him.

Arguing to the contrary, defence counsel asserted that on hearing noises in the room in Rupert Street the brothers sincerely believed the prostitutes were being attacked, went to their defence and, in the ensuing struggle, Marks Reubens had just happened to stab Sproull. It has to be wondered whether it was because Sproull and McEachran were stronger than the brothers had realised, that they had to depart from their usual practice of garotting the girls' clients into submission.

After Emily Allen had been cleared of all charges, her evidence proved crucial to the prosecution's case. She now claimed – distancing herself from events – that she had never felt threatened by the sailors. With this piece of evidence to hand and after hearing from Dr Thomas Jones, the pathologist who carried out the post-mortem examination on Sproull, that the fatal wound had been inflicted with "great vio-lence," the case against the brothers was proceeding as smoothly as R.D. Muir and Huntley Jenkins, the prosecuting counsel, could ever have hoped. On the second day of the trial the brothers declined to give evidence. But it availed them nothing. They were quickly found guilty of "wilful murder" and sentenced to death.[19]

VI

The brothers had faced a murder charge despite the absence of any evidence sug-gesting "malice aforethought."[20] Moreover, though only one of them could have inflicted the fatal blow, both were now charged with the crime. When justifying its position the prosecution drew attention to two earlier legal rulings, *Rex v Parker and Preston* (1903) and *Rex v Donovan and Wade* (1904). This complex issue, known technically as joint enterprise, was to feature later in the notorious 1953 Bentley and Craig case as well as a number of even more recent criminal proceedings.[21]

During the Reubens' trial the prosecution did whatever it could to blacken the brothers' reputations. It was suggested, for example, they had provided false infor-mation on their previous employment. Morris and Marks claimed to have worked for various employers. However, none could be traced. With the East End a buzzing hive of constant movement they might well have worked sporadically for employers who, for understandable reasons, had successfully eluded the police. But the prosecution had a strong card to play. Allen and Brooks now proved inordinately keen to avoid all responsibility for the evening's deadly outcome. It was claimed in court that Morris had lived off Allen's earnings from the past two-and-a-half years and Marks off Brooks's for the previous eighteen months. Allen even alleged it was she who paid the rent on the Rupert Street property. Morris used up most of her earnings at the racetracks.

It also became clear that the trial judge, Arthur Jelf – apparently sitting on his first murder case – was determined to send out a message:

> … in places like Whitechapel things do occur and if they are not checked and if juries are not firm in dealing with them, may grow to a very great and terrible state of things.

He had no time for the brothers and throughout the hearing leaned heavily towards the prosecution. Inspector Wensley was right to say that Jelf "took a strong line." The judge's comments on the state of affairs in Whitechapel showed, in coded form, that the trial cannot be sharply separated from the debate then taking place on alien – especially Jewish – immigration into Britain, on which tensions in London were running particularly high. It is likely, too, that this awareness influenced the collective mind of the jury.

After listening to all the evidence the jury took a mere twenty minutes to convict the brothers of murder. At which point a devastated Morris sobbed, howled and cried "Mercy! Mercy!" An equally distraught Marks screamed "If I have to die let me do so now."[22]

VII

Four days after their conviction at the Old Bailey the brothers sought leave to appeal through their solicitors Solomon Myers and Son. In particular, their situation raised the tangled issue of joint enterprise.

When finally refusing leave to appeal "the small, gaunt and somewhat short-sighted" Mr Justice Darling – regarded as "very good" in murder trials – remarked it was indeed possible to envisage some difference in the brothers' level of guilt. But any such nice distinction lay properly within the discretion of the Home Secretary.[23]

VIII

Once the case papers reached the Home Office they landed initially on the desk of Ernley Blackwell, the Assistant Under-Secretary. After reading through these details he concluded that it amounted to "murder of the worst kind committed by two men of the worst possible character." He had before him when considering this evidence a list which the police had compiled of larcenies from male clients in brothels since 1 April 1908, including examples from East London. Tellingly, one incident had occurred in 3 Rupert Street when a client had been relieved of £2 in gold and some foreign coins. Whereas the East End held out its attractions to affluent slummers who derived either vicarious or actual pleasure by frequenting its streets and back alleys, Blackwell evidently viewed it as a dangerous criminal area and threatening to the capital's social well-being. Like Mr Justice Jelf he appeared conscious of the "terrible state of things" in Whitechapel and followed the trial judge in regarding the murder as having more than a merely local significance.

Blackwell treated the brothers as part of this threatening sub-culture and went on to minute: "both men richly deserve their fate." He continued:

> It would in my opinion be most unfortunate if anything were done to loosen the deterrent effect these convictions and sentences may have upon the hundreds of others making their livelihoods in the same way as the prisoners have been doing.

Les classes dangereuses had to be kept in check or crushed.

The issue of joint enterprise also had to be considered. Mr Justice Darling had raised this matter when refusing the brothers' appeal. But Blackwell was not to be moved. In particular, he returned to the 1904 case of Rex v Donovan and Wade when, in the course of a burglary, two criminals had manhandled a houseowner who had subsequently died. Both men had been executed and Blackwell believed the Reubens case was even more serious.[24]

When the file left Blackwell's desk it passed to the "efficient, intellectually able" Charles Edward Troup who served as Permanent Under-Secretary at the Home Office between 1908 and 1922. On consideration he agreed with Blackwell's assessment. There is no surprise here. Both men were widely regarded as being tough on crime. And that stern view on capital punishment retained its supporters among senior civil servants in the Home Office for many years.[25]

Home Secretaries are invariably guided by the Department's leading mandarins and in 1909 Herbert Gladstone proved no exception. The facts of the case and the question of public policy led him to conclude that in this instance any legal arguments against joint enterprise were unsound and both men should be executed.[26] Unless the Crown intervened – which was highly unlikely – the brothers' fate had effectively been sealed.

IX

Beyond the courts and the Home Office the case attracted interest from the public.[27] As might be expected, the mother of Morris and Marks appealed for her sons. She, the matriarch of a large family – there were eight children – wrote not only to the Home Office but also contacted the King. Her wish was that at least one of her children should be spared. Joseph Reubens, a brother of the accused, also wrote in from an address in Wandsworth to plead for their lives.

The family was not alone in its interventions. Reuben Cohen, who described himself as "a life-long student of Ethics and Morality," conducted a persistent campaign on their behalf. And on two occasions, David vann Gostick from Bradford contacted the Home Office, arguing that the brothers were "impoverished, misguided aliens" who deserved to be reprieved "on account of their extreme youth" and what he called, strangely, "the complete absence of motive to kill." Hardy Summers, who wrote to the Home Secretary on 7 May, added to these pleas. His letter is of particular interest. He began by acknowledging that "it is not popular to say a good word for a Jew right now" and he himself admitted to having "no partiality for the race." Nevertheless, he urged the brothers be spared since they were victims of a "low and brutal standard of life." Stuart Samuel the Liberal MP for Whitechapel since 1900 also intervened in support of Morris and Marks.

But Blackwell in the Home Office never budged. He was generally swift in dismissing such pleas, observing on one occasion "there is nothing in these petitions that has not been disposed of the Ct of C.A."

The public's response was more complex than so far suggested, however. The passing antipathy present in Summers's intervention was reflected more fully when C.W. Rosenfeld wrote in. Ignoring the fact that the Reubens brothers were London-born, he claimed that "Years ago such a type as the Reubens was happily unknown in England but existed and does exist in Russia." He then claimed it was this "foreign lifestyle" spent in public houses, gambling dens and "living on the immoral earnings of loose women," which had sealed their fate. He was attempting here to place a safe distance between the established Jewish community and anyone touched by what he viewed as foreign vices imported from Russian Poland.

W.J. Chivers writing on 9 May was even blunter. His letter left no doubt on the strength of public feeling then circulating on the case:

> I am a Britisher and have been talking with people generally about the respite of, and possible reprieve of those two double-dyed scoundrels of Whitechapel and they all, Jews included, speak most emphatically in favour of the law taking its course.

He therefore urged the Home Secretary not to be too much influenced by "a few affluent Jews." This comment reveals a small fragment of that developing anti-Jewish sentiment which claimed the tentacles of Jews extended and fastened everywhere. Similar opinions on the alleged reach of Jew power had already been expressed by writers such as Arnold White and Joseph Banister and such sentiments provided a warm, fertile seedbed for the later reception in Britain of the extensive claim of a powerful Jewish conspiracy which appeared in *The Protocols of the Elders of Zion*.[28]

Chivers had warned about the influence of powerful Jews in protecting their own. But had he read the *Jewish Chronicle* he would have detected little sympathy there for the brothers. It incorporated them into its wider campaign against the white slave traffic. In the 1880s the widely read *Pall Mall Gazette* had mounted a noisy crusade against the trading and sexual exploitation of children.[29] But by 1909 the focus of concern, the new moral panic, had shifted away from paedophilia towards the transport of vulnerable women – Jews and others – with which Jewish traffickers had become closely identified. Or, in the words of the *Jewish Chronicle*, towards a business "too frequently found with Jews either as oppressors or victims." Against this background the paper carried a report on the "Burning Shame of a Terrible Scandal," and remarked on the prominent role played by D.L. Alexander of the Board of Deputies in a deputation to the Home Office to emphasise and discuss the problem. It went on to wish "God speed" to all those involved in fighting what it described as this sickening trade "in human flesh and blood."[30]

A few weeks later, consistent with its sense of outrage, the *Chronicle* pounced on the Reubens case which had "illumined with blood" the problem of white slavery. The paper subsequently refused to lend its support for a reprieve. The murder had revealed "moral degradation of the grossest description." The *Chronicle* further observed, significantly: "nothing we know is so likely to turn the statements of our fellow-countrymen against Jews in general as the details of the gruesome tragedy which unfolded last week." Such a reaction amounted to "a very inconsistent and illogical prejudice to be sure," the writer remarked, "but is it not to be wondered at?"[31]

X

After all this sound and fury in correspondence and newspaper comment, what happened? Shortly before the date set for his execution a desperate Marks scrawled one last painful semi-literate plea to the Home Secretary:

> I … do plead most humbly for my life which is a very young one … Should it be spared I wood make Amends for all the past, and if I ever live out of prison I wood make a God fearing citizen. As God delivered his "servant" David from the hurtful sword May he guide your heart and pardon yours most miserable servant and none that take refuge in him shall be Condemed.

His cry went unheard. He was also alleged to have apologised to Sproull's relatives. But again to no benefit. On 21 May 1909 the brothers were executed in Pentonville by Henry and Thomas Pierrepoint.[32]

XI

When the *SS Dorset* sailed into the Victoria Docks in March 1909 no one could have envisaged what followed. The ship's second engineer was soon dead, its third mate badly wounded. By May the young Jewish criminals convicted of murdering the seaman had been executed. The two prostitutes controlled by the Reubens brothers were hardly likely to experience a more traumatic time in their entire lives.

In the years of high immigration from the Tsar's Empire the Reubens brothers were not the only Jews to be convicted of murder. In 1887 Israel Lipski, an umbrella stick maker and salesman who had arrived in Britain in 1885, was found guilty of murdering his landlady Mrs Miriam Angel at 6 Battye Street, Whitechapel. She had been poisoned with acid and Lipski was discovered in her room also suffering from its effects. He denied murder and claimed both he and Mrs Angel – six months pregnant at the time – were victims of two men – his employees – whom he proceeded to name. But the authorities refused to believe him. Lipski was duly hanged on 22 August 1889.

The circumstances of his case are disquieting. This recent newcomer had little English and required a court interpreter. A particularly powerful and poignant reminder of his being a hapless alien adrift in a strange land came when the passing of the death sentence had to be translated into Yiddish to allow him to understand it. How much more had he failed to glean? He also suffered from being represented by a lawyer who was clearly intoxicated throughout the period of the trial.

His case was taken up by the *Pall Mall Gazette*; its legendary editor W.T. Stead – who later went down with the *Titanic* – was then in the middle of a long-standing feud with the Home Secretary Henry Matthews and used the Lipski case to that end. But Stead's intervention failed to move the authorities. Lipski eventually confessed to the murder of Mrs Angel – a confession welcomed by the *Jewish Chronicle* – but in 2001 a detailed examination of his case doubted that he was guilty. Lipski features in that gallery of unfortunates hanged on suspect evidence.[33] He was "not one of us;" he appears to have been regarded as easily expendable.

The following year the link between immigrant Jews and murder arose yet again but much more dramatically. Between 31 August and 8 November 1888 an unknown killer, who has passed into folklore as Jack the Ripper, murdered a number of women in Whitechapel. Each one had suffered varying degrees of mutilation. At the time someone – was it the killer? was it a hoaxer? – daubed a message, "The Juwes are the men that will not be blamed for nothing," on an East End wall. Terrified that the graffiti might result in serious riots, Sir Charles Warren, the Metropolitan Police Commissioner, ordered its immediate removal.[34] Even so, a small number of so-called "Ripper riots" did occur. And further tension resulted following a report carried in *The Times* from its Vienna correspondent of an alleged ritual murder in Cracow. Was something similar taking place in London?[35]

The haunting image of a Jewish Nosferatu-like figure stalking the streets of East London at night as a serial killer circulated even within the police force. Sir Robert Anderson, who headed the Criminal Investigation Department at Scotland Yard between 1880 and 1901, felt compelled to write later that it was "a definitely ascertainable fact" the killer was a Polish Jew. He also emphasised – perhaps to shift the police's failure to catch the murderer onto others – that it had proved difficult for the force to apprehend anyone since "people of that class (low class Polish Jews) in the East End will not give up one of their number to Gentile Justice."[36] The "them" and "us" image surfaces yet again.

Once claims or accusations are made they are often difficult to dislodge and the linking of Jews to the Ripper murders has periodically resurfaced. The image of a sadistic Jewish killer appealed later to the veteran fascist Arnold Leese who held an obsessive belief in Jewish sadism.[37] And it has appeared in the seemingly unending mass of popular literature spawned by the Ripper murders.[38]

The Lipski case and the Ripper's activities occurred at a sensitive time when the issue of alien immigration was becoming more prominent in British political debates. In 1905, however, the government passed the Aliens Act which placed certain restrictions on alien entry even though the measure did not match the hopes and expectations of many restrictionists. Alien immigration was now controlled – essentially for the first time since the French Revolutionary Wars – but it took the disruption of the First World War, the 1914 Aliens Act, the Bolshevik Revolution, and especially the tough 1919 Aliens Restriction Act, to put an effective break on Jewish immigration from the Tsar's Empire.[39]

To that time tensions remained. And various incidents thrust Russian Jews yet again into the spotlight. The year the Reuben brothers were executed, the popular press could hardly resist splashing the Tottenham Outrage across its pages. On Saturday morning, 23 January, in scenes reminiscent of the Wild West but "singularly rare if not entirely without parallel in a civilised country," this area of north London witnessed an armed robbery which rapidly turned into a double murder. Paul Helfeld and Jacob Lepidus (sometimes Lapidus), both Latvian Jews and political anarchists with East London connections, bungled what had been intended as a wages snatch. Interrupted in their endeavours, they were given chase by the police during which a constable was shot along with a young boy who happened to be present in the area. Another policeman and forty bystanders were wounded. Amazingly, the two criminals fired over four hundred rounds of ammunition during the incident. When eventually surrounded by the police Helfeld shot himself in the head and died later in hospital, Lepidus also killed himself. By any standard these were dramatic events. No wonder a documentary film of the incident soon appeared. Not surprisingly, too, these events kept the debate over alien immigration in the news. The trigger-happy Continental anarchists were far removed from British criminals. Was the country now suffering, some wondered, as a by-product of the "demoralising effects" of Tsarist policy towards the Jews and other minorities?[40]

In 1907 Joseph Conrad had published *The Secret Agent*, his novel on the perils of anarchism. With the events in Tottenham in 1909 and what soon followed, his readers could be forgiven for thinking that fantasy was rapidly becoming reality.

On 23 December 1910, just over a year after the events in Tottenham, the *Jewish Chronicle* emphasised the potential danger to the community following the murder of three London policemen.[41] Yet more deaths of men in service. They had been killed trying to prevent a meticulously planned robbery at H.S. Harris, a jeweller's shop at 19 Houndsditch. The would-be perpetrators had rented a nearby property and from there excavated a path into the shop.

Following the abortive raid the intending robbers – originally from Russia and including some Jews – fled the scene. Their apparent leader George Gardstein (he had several aliases), who had been shot probably accidentally by one of his associates when the police interrupted the robbery, was taken by his fleeing accomplices to 59 Grove (now Golding) Street, lodgings of the so-called Peter the Painter or Peter Piatkow, sometimes known as Janis Zhaklis. When Gardstein's condition worsened the women caring for him there had called a doctor, though in the event he could not be saved. The doctor had then informed the coroner of Gardstein's death and in turn the coroner had spoken to the police. Following this operation several gang members were arrested on various raids at different addresses. They subsequently appeared on 29 December at the Guildhall police court where, as in the Lipski case, interpreters had to be used. But other suspects remained at large.

On New Year's Day 1911 the police learned that others belonging to the gang had taken refuge in 100 Sidney Street. Two days later, after the evacuation of nearby residents, a posse of policemen from both the City of London force and the Metropolitan Police who had been despatched to the property, found themselves coming under heavy gun fire. So fierce was the resistance – there are shades here of the Tottenham shooting in 1909 – that, with Home Office approval, a detachment of the Scots Guards had to be rushed to the scene. A contemporary Pathé News recording captured these dramatic events and a postcard of the siege featuring the Home Secretary Winston Churchill soon appeared. He apparently relished being present at the action much to the consternation of his government colleagues. In the early afternoon the shooting intensified before the house suddenly caught fire. Eventually, two bodies, those of Fritz Svaars and William (or Joseph) Sokoloff, were pulled from the wrecked property. More arrests followed. But with one exception – which was overturned on appeal – the accused were subsequently acquitted.[42]

Even so, it is hardly surprising these serious incidents further encouraged anti-immigrant, anti-Jewish sentiment. Indeed, on this occasion, it proved a strong current to dam and along it floated a number of well-known anti-Semites. William Stanley Shaw, who in 1901 had founded the British Brothers' League in opposition to Jewish immigration from the Russian Empire, was easily and quickly tempted back into the debate.[43] Moreover, the dramatic shootings in Houndsditch and Sidney Street doubtless confirmed the opinion of the leader writer in *The Times* who in mid-December 1910, influenced by the recent events in Tottenham, had commented that Whitechapel harboured "some of the worst alien anarchists and criminals who seek our too hospitable shore. And these are men who use the pistol and the knife." The writer continued: "A savage delight in taking life is the mark of the Continental anarchist criminal."[44]

This dramatic sequence of events had just kept the spotlight on immigration from the Tsar's Empire. The recent robbers and killers were not only criminals – though a number had convictions before they landed in Britain – they were political activists. According to *The Times* they belonged to "the same clan" as the Tottenham killers. The latest events which had just involved them in London were not unusual in Russia, where opposition forces often engaged in criminal activity – bank robberies, extortion and kidnapping – to further their political aims. Stalin, "Koba," himself became involved. But in Britain it raised again the question: had alien immigration now transferred such political-criminal violence onto the streets of the capital?[45]

When the notorious siege was underway another story, once more involving the Jewish East End, began to break out and, some believe, was linked to it. On New Year's Day 1911 PC Joseph Mumford found Leon Beron (or Behren), property owner and underworld fence, lying dead on Clapham Common. He had clearly been murdered. Beron had lived in France until 1894 – the year the Dreyfus case unfolded – and then moved to London where he had a place in Jubilee Street, quite close to Sidney Street. Arthur Harding called him "the outside man" for Ruby Michaels, "the top man in Whitechapel for buying anything."[46] Beron could often be seen conducting business at the Warsaw Kosher Restaurant, often known as Snelwar's, which then stood at 32 Osborn Street at the Whitechapel end of Brick Lane. He also frequented various East End pubs well known as the haunts of fences and prostitutes. But Beron's shady dealings suddenly ended in late 1910, early 1911. Once more a criminal case had brought Jews and crime before the public – and again in dramatic fashion.

On 8 January 1911 Stinie (or Steinie) Morrison or Morris Stern, who had probably been born in Ukraine in 1879 and had then lived in Germany and France before arriving in England in 1898, was arrested by the ubiquitous Detective Inspector F.P. Wensley and charged with Beron's murder. Since arriving in London Morrison had been making his way as a petty crook and at the time of Beron's murder was living quite close to Sidney Street. On 15 March 1911 after a trial presided over by Mr Justice Darling – who had listened to the Reubens' appeal – he was found guilty of murder and sentenced to death. However, on 12 April 1911 Churchill, acting as Home Secretary, recognised the verdict was unsafe, granted a reprieve and commuted Morrison's sentence to life imprisonment. But Morrison showed absolutely no gratitude for this decision. He wrote soon afterwards to the Home Secretary requesting his freedom: failing that, he declared "You will kindly allow the death sentence to be carried out." He was clearly desperate and it becomes clear that the longer he stayed behind bars the more agitated he became. His dramatic plea-poem addressed to the authorities reveals as much:

Come, Sweetheart Death and kiss me
I'll gladly be your slave
Only hasten to release me
From this filthy living grave

His wish to be hanged and put out of his misery was always rejected. He remained in prison for the rest of his life and died in Parkhurst on 24 January 1921. He appears finally to have starved himself to death.[47]

As with the Reubens case, we are transported into the pre-1914 Jewish underworld in East London. The claims of a connection between this latest development and Sidney Street derive from the fact that when Beron's body was found the letter S appeared to have been traced on his bloodied face. Was it designed to suggest he was an informer (a spion) and possibly the one who had led the police to the house on Sidney Street? Had he been the intended fence for the Sidney Street gang but who, with the raid aborted, had earned nothing from the operation and consequently betrayed them? Was he all along a "nose," a police informer, as well as a fence? Had Morrison been recruited by unknown sources to act as the hit man? Or was he merely someone who knew of the plot to kill Beron but actually innocent of the crime? Doubts, uncertainties remain.[48]

It is clear, however, that contemporary commentators emphasised the incident centred on Jews. And, as in the case of the Reubens brothers, the *Jewish Chronicle* proved quick to distance the community from the murder which, it claimed, had illustrated "in terrible vividness the very dregs of Jewry."[49]

A specific reference to Morrison as a Jew also featured in lawyers' discussions. Edward Abinger, his counsel – who believed Morrison to be innocent – was Jewish; so was Rufus Isaacs, the Attorney General. And the former has related a conversation between the two which is suggestive of the attitudes of the Anglo-Jewish elite to the likes of Israel Lipski, the Reubens brothers, the Tottenham killers, the Sidney Street gang, Beron and Morrison. Abinger said to Isaacs, "Morrison was a Jew" and continued: "I am also a Jew, and so are you, and I am very anxious that your judgement should not be warped by any racial sympathy." The next delphic part of the conversation as relayed by Abinger is particularly interesting. "Sir Rufus smiled and, passing me his cigarette case, remarked: 'You need have no fear of that.'"[50]

Isaacs was then sailing sweetly and serenely up the ranks of the British Establishment. He suffered a setback in 1911–1912 when drawn into the murky business of the Marconi scandal.[51] But with a politician's luck he survived this unsavoury episode in British public life and eventually became Viscount Reading and Viceroy of India. He lived in a quite contrasting world, mixed with a different class of people from those Jews who inhabited the criminal sub-culture of the East End.

XII

The history of minority group crime in Britain remains in many respects an unexplored country. One suggestion has it that between 1880 and 1910 Jewish crime invariably related to fraud or white slave trafficking.[52] But even a brief survey of the East End would suggest a greater complexity. Bill Fishman wrote that in this area "petty crime was a positive necessity."[53] And as one of the disadvantaged groups living there, some Jews, recent arrivals and their children, participated in such activity. But Jews became drawn into other forms of criminality.

In the early nineteenth century, well before the notorious Krays, criminal groups who controlled and terrorised their manor and engaged in a range of activities could be found in London and also Britain's large provincial cities.[54]

In London the Sabini gang, the Italian mob, was headquartered in Clerkenwell but enjoyed a wider influence. From its early days in 1910 gang members had no hesitation in wielding the razor against their rivals and, to that end, imported recruits from Sicily to work alongside them, particularly in protection rackets. Much, but not all, of their activity, centred on the lucrative pickings to be harvested from the racetracks of southern England.[55]

Jewish criminals were also active. In the East End the so-called Bessarabian Tigers specialised in running protection rackets which pressed heavily on the takings of local restaurants – some of which had always been used for conducting criminal activity – the businesses of the area's bookies – themselves operating outside the law – and the trade of local shopkeepers. In fact, the Tigers and the Odessans, their organised contemporaries, regularly conducted "a programme of robbery, exploitation and mayhem for many years." In this area gangsters like Max Moses (known in boxing circles as "Kid" McEvoy) and Isaac ("Ikey") Bogard ("Darkie the Coon") were regularly at war over territory.[56] And Edward Emmanuel hovered as an ever-present éminence grise over this criminal world.

According to Arthur Harding, Emmanuel was the "Jewish Al Capone" indeed "the top man of the Jews," whose influence ran throughout Spitalfields and Aldgate. He had his fingers in spieling enterprises, protection rackets both in London and nearby racetracks and, as an inveterate gambler, would attempt to fix the outcome of what happened in the ring. Woe betide any boxer who refused to go down as instructed. He was also a very useful man to know. "He could be seen drinking in the 'Three Tuns' with the top detectives from the Yard" and, for an appropriate consideration of course, was known to square problems with them. Again in Harding's words, he "had the police buttoned up."[57]

At times – the 1909 Tottenham outrage underlines it – the activities of Jewish criminals associated with East London, spilled over into other parts of London. These trigger-happy North London killers were anarchists and this intermeshing of crime and politics – also present in the Houndsditch robbery and the Sidney Street siege – further heightened public fears and sharpened contemporary debates.

If many of these Jewish men and women had grown up in another place, another time, who knows how their lives might have developed? But some had witnessed or personally suffered Tsarist violence which left deep tell-tale imprints on their future lives. Others knew of such misery and repression through their family memories.[58]

As a result, alongside those tensions surrounding immigrants from Russian Poland in the housing and labour markets of the East End, as well as the anxieties fostered by cultural differences, the dangers posed by Jewish criminal activity featured in the early twentieth century debate on alien immigration.

At its most extreme it appeared in Joseph Banister's feverish self-published polemic *England under the Jews*, which first appeared in 1901:

> From Russia, Austria, Germany, Roumania and about every other country, we receive, in an increasing swarm, the precious breed of thieves, sweaters, usurers, burglars, illicit distillers, procurers, forgers, traitors, swindlers, counterfeiters, brothel-keepers, blackmailers, prostitutes, parasites, white slave traffickers, etc.[59]

Banister lived in his own frightened, frightening, paranoid world but he was not alone in discussing Jews and crime. Reflecting such public anxieties, in 1903 the Royal Commission on Alien Immigration became tasked within its wider terms of reference "to determine whether there was any truth behind the allegations that amongst [the aliens] there are criminals, anarchists, prostitutes and persons of bad character far beyond the ordinary percentage of the native population." The Committee heard conflicting voices on this matter but did express some concern at criminal activity by aliens – Jews and others.[60]

With the Reubens murder, the Tottenham outrage, the Houndsditch robbery and the death of Leon Beron on Clapham Common, the connection drawn between migration and criminality showed no signs of disappearing up to the Great War.

Eight years after the massively detailed 1903 Royal Commission, *The Times* remarked that while the majority of Jews in East London were hard-working and conscientious:

> ... East end counts among its population a large number of very dangerous, very reckless, and very noxious people, chiefly immigrant from Eastern and South-Eastern countries of Europe. The second impression will be that these people add to the difficulties of their situation by their extreme untrustworthiness, since lying, especially in the witness box, appears to be their national language.[61]

That same year Sir Robert Anderson, already noticed as heading the CID when alien immigration was at its height, wrote in the *Nineteenth Century* of the dangers created by the presence of such newcomers and the "criminal propensities and the pestilently evil influence they exercise." It appears here in a slightly coded form – hostility towards Jews often does – but there is no doubt that to Anderson aliens equalled Jews. That his essay should display little sympathy, comes as no surprise: he has been observed attributing the Ripper murders to a Jew. However it is startling to note his additional comment in the *Nineteenth Century*: "were it not for our belief in a future life we should do well to exterminate them like plague-ridden vermin."[62] Such official attitudes were often reflected in the treatment of those Jews who finished up in the dock.[63] Little wonder that in the same year M.J. Landa believed it opportune to mourn and deplore the degree of "public obloquy" Jews were currently experiencing.[64]

Within this context the Reubens brothers featured as minor players. They never created a criminal empire. Had they lived they would doubtless have continued to run a few prostitutes and featured in the 1930s among the London criminals who ventured down to the race meetings in Brighton and Lewes and inhabited the dog tracks in London and Essex. But they would never have become as influential among London criminals as the likes of the Messina brothers, Jack "Spot," Billy Hill and, later, the Krays.[65] In any case that future was not to be. They overreached themselves when still young and paid a very heavy price.

Notes

1 W.J. Fishman, *East End Jewish Radicals 1875–1914* (London, 1975), p. xii.
2 Ibid., and *East End 1888* (London, 1988). Tony Kushner's "Doing the East End Walk, Oi! Heritage, Ownership and Belonging," in the present collection, pp. 207–30 captures the importance of historical walks. See also D. Rosenberg, *Rebel Footprints* (London, 2015).
3 G. Alderman and C. Holmes (eds), *Outsiders & Outcasts: Essays in Honour of William J. Fishman* (London, 1993).
4 Richard Cobb to author, 2 May 1991. Boudard, born in 1925, died in Nice in 2000.
5 W.J. Fishman, *The Streets of East London*, with photographs by N. Breach (London, 1980), pp. 106–7. My first foray into this territory came with "East End Crime and the Jewish Community 1887–1911," in A. Newman (ed.), *The Jewish East End 1840–1939* (London, 1981), pp. 109–23.
6 S. Kuper, "Welcome to the Londonsphere," *FT Magazine* 11/12 April 2015. An extended version appears at: http://centreforlondon.org/media_coverage/welcome-to-the-londonsphere.
7 J. Schneer, *London, 1900* (London and New Haven, 1999), p. 7. J. White, *London in the Nineteenth Century* (London, 2008 ed.) and idem., *London in the 20th Century* (London, 2008 ed.), provide a general context and also touch specifically on crime and criminals in London.
8 B. Judah, *This is London: Life and Death in the World City* (London, 2016).
9 C. Booth, *Life and Labour of the People in London*, Vol. 1 (London, 1889). *Labour and Life of People in London*, Vol. 2 was published in 1891 and by 1902/3 all seventeen volumes in the series – Poverty 4 Vols, Industry 5 Vols, Religious Influences 7 Vols, plus the final volume, Notes on Social Influences and Conclusion – were available.
10 C. Holmes, *John Bull's Island: Immigration and British Society* (Basingstoke and London, 1988. Reissued 2015). Works which focus specifically on immigration into London include: N. Merriman (ed.), *The Peopling of London* (London, 1993); A.J. Kershen (ed.), *London: the Promised Land? The Migrant Experience in a Capital City* (Aldershot, 1997) and idem., *London: The Promised Land Revisited* (Farnham, 2015). The long process of migration into the capital is vividly captured in the film, *London: The Modern Babylon* (2012).
11 J.D. Klier, "Emigration Mania in Late-Imperial Russia: Legend and Reality," in A. Newman and S.W. Massil (eds), *Patterns of Migration 1850–1914* (London, 1996), pp. 21–36.
12 J. Higham, *Strangers in the Land: Patterns of American Nativism 1868–1925* (New York, 1963. First published 1955), remains a valuable source. See also T. Zaha, *The Great Departure: Mass Migration from Eastern Europe and the Making of the Free World* (New York, 2016). Issues relating specifically to Jewish migration to America are captured in Joan Micklin Silver's 1974 film *Hester Street* and in literature in Abraham Cahan's novel, *The Rise of David Levinsky* (New York, 1917).
13 *Royal Commission on Alien Immigration*, British Parliamentary Papers, IX (1903), Vol. 1, p. 14 (cited later as *RC*). *Census of England and Wales* (1911), p. 136. L. Gartner, *The Jewish Immigrant in England 1870–1914* (Detroit, 1960) remains a classic study of the newly emerging Jewish group. G. Alderman*, British Jewry since Emancipation* (Buckingham, 2014) throws a wider net over the history of Anglo-Jewry.
14 A. Godley, *Jewish Immigrant Entrepreneurship in New York and London 1850–1914* (London, 2001). Fishman, *East End 1888*, Ch. 6; Fishman, *Streets*, pp. 79, 81, 83 on

Schewzik's, the Pavilion Theatre and the Jewish Soup Kitchen, respectively. On the Jewish theatre see D. Mazower, "Whitechapel's Yiddish Opera House: The Rise and Fall of the Feinman Yiddish People's Theatre," pp. 151–83 in the present volume. On other matters see D. Dee, "The Hefty Hebrew: Boxing and British-Jewish Identity 1890–1960," *Sport in History*, Vol. 52 (2012), pp. 361–81. The Jewish influence on British Communism appears in H.F. Srebrnik, *London Jews and British Communism 1935–1945* (London, 1995). See also R. Samuel, "Family Connections," in R. Samuel, *The Lost World of British Communism* (London, 2006); S. Abramsky, *The House of Twenty Thousand Books* (London, 2014) and D. Aaronovitch, *Party Animals: My Family and other Communists* (London, 2015). The novelist Alexander Baron left a valuable memoir, "A Chapter of Accidents," which discussed his involvement in the CPGB. I am currently editing it for publication.

15 Fishman, *Streets*, pp. 101–10. R. Samuel, *East End Underworld: Chapters in the Life of Arthur Harding* (London, 1981). Samuel's archive at the Bishopsgate Institute, London contains a substantial cache of materials on criminality in East London.

16 Detail from TNA HO 144/911/178428. McEachran's dazed drunken state appears in F.P. Wensley, *Detective Days* (London, 1931), p. 85. On Wensley, known to criminals as 'The Weasel,' see D. Kirby, *Whitechapel's Sherlock Holmes: The Casebook of Fred Wensley – Victorian Crime Buster* (Barnsley, 2014). The Reubens case features on pp. 123–8.

17 Samuel, *Underworld*, pp. 126–7. C. Emsley, *Hard Men: The English and Violence since 1750* (London, 2005), Ch. 2 on garotting.

18 Wensley, *Detective Days*, pp. 88–9.

19 All from TNA HO 144/911/178428.

20 All additional court comment, unless otherwise stated, can be found in ibid. See also Wensley, *Detective Days*, p. 91; *Jewish Chronicle*, 30 August 1909 and J. Morton, *East End Gangland* (London, 2001 ed.), pp. 44–5.

21 F. Selwyn, *Gangland: The Case of Bentley and Craig* (London, 1988). The song "The Ballad of Derek Bentley" by Ewan MacColl and Peggy Seeger can be found on https://www.youtube.com/watch?v=E0u6-WgF-Fo. For further details on joint enterprise see *The Times*, 19 February 2016 and 8 March 2016.

22 *East London Advertiser*, 24 April 1909. The detail on Jelf is from Wensley, *Detective Days*, p. 91.

23 TNA HO 144/911/178428. D. Walker-Smith, *The Life of Lord Darling* (London, 1938) on Darling's career. See also *Oxford Dictionary of National Biography*, Vol. 15 (Oxford, 2004), p. 148.

24 *Who was Who* (London, 1952), p. 108 on Blackwell. TNA HO 144/911/178428, memo, 8 May 1909 contains his observations on the case. Other contemporary observers had more complex approaches to life in East London. See S. Koven, *Slumming and Sexual Politics in Victorian London* (Princeton, NJ, 2004).

25 He appears in the *Oxford Dictionary of National Biography*, Vol. 55 (Oxford, 2004), p. 446. TNA HO 144/803/134036 "List of Negroes and Foreigners sentenced to Death" (1905) reveals Troup's stern attitude towards serious crime.

26 TNA HO 144/911/178428/4 on Gladstone's response. C. Holmes, *Searching for Lord Haw-Haw: The Political Lives of William Joyce* (Abingdon, 2016), p. 347 discusses the attitude and influence of Sir Frank Newsam on later cases.

27 All the following interventions and comment are from TNA HO 144/911/178428. The individual petitions from the public are at: /36,42,43 (Mrs Reubens); /21 (Joseph Reubens); /19,32,37,38 (Cohen); /26,44 (vann Gostick); /33 (Samuel); /28 (Rosenfeld); /34 (Chivers). See I. Light, "Ethnic Vice Industry 1880–1914," *American Sociological Review*, Vol. 42 (1977), pp. 464–79 on the import theory of crime.

28 Arnold White's reflections are in *The Modern Jew* (London, 1899). Banister's musings appear in *England under the Jews* (London, 1901, 1907). On the history of *The Protocols* see N. Cohn, *Warrant for Genocide* (London, 1967). Details on its reception in Britain appear in C. Holmes, "New Light on 'The Protocols of Zion'," *Patterns of Prejudice*, Vol. 6 (1977), pp. 13–21 and, for more on earlier conspiratorial thought, idem., *Anti-Semitism in British Society 1876–1939* (London, 1979. Reissued 2015), Ch. 5.

29 F.W. Whyte, *The Life of W.T. Stead* (2 vols, London, MCMXXV). R. Schults, *Crusader in Babylon. W.T. Stead and the Pall Mall Gazette* (Lincoln, NE, 1972). *Oxford Dictionary of National Biography*, Vol. 52 (Oxford, 2004), pp. 331–3, all detail the life of the editor who launched this crusade. For a wider context see J.R. Walkowitz, *Prostitution and Victorian Society: Women, Class, and the State* (Cambridge, 1986) and P. Bartley, *Prostitution: Prevention and Reform in England 1860–1914* (London, 1999).

30 *Jewish Chronicle*, 2 April 1909. E.J. Bristow, *Prostitution and Prejudice: The Jewish Fight against White Slavery 1870–1939* (Oxford, 1982) adds a necessary perspective. C. van Onselen, *The Fox and the Flies: The World of Joseph Silver, Racketeer and Psychopath* (London, 2007), is a brilliant study of one major trafficker. See also L.P. Gartner, "Anglo-Jewry and the Jewish International Traffic in Prostitution, 1885-1914," *AJSreview*, Vol. 78 (1982–3), pp. 129-78 and L. Marks, "Jewish Women and Prostitution in the East End of London," *Jewish Quarterly*, Vol. 34 (1987), pp. 6–10.

31 *Jewish Chronicle*, 30 April 1909.

32 TNA HO 144/911/178428 and Morton, *Gangland*, p. 45.

33 His case is detailed in TNA CRIM 1/26/5; HO 144/202/A47465–1-81. *Pall Mall Gazette* 13, 15, 16, 17, 18, 19, 20, 21 August 1867 for its involvement in the case. Ibid., 22 August 1887 on Lipski's eventual execution. *Jewish Chronicle*, 26 August 1887 expressed relief at Lipski's confession. The case was raised in Parliament. See *Parliamentary Debates* (Commons), Vol. 319 (1887), cols 254, 448–9, 1102–4 for interventions on 12, 13, 14 and 19 August 1887 respectively. M. Friedland, *The Trial of Israel Lipski* (London, 2001) discusses the case and expresses reservations on the verdict. Lipski is also the subject of B. Biderman, *Eight Weeks in the Summer of Victoria's Jubilee* (Cambridge, 2012), which had appeared three years earlier under the title *The Strange Case of Israel Lipski*.

34 Fishman, *East End*, pp. 209–29 and *Streets*, pp. 101–5. A massive amount of literature exists on the Ripper, much of which speculates on his elusive identity. Early studies include R. Odell, *Jack the Ripper: In Fact and Fiction* (London, 1965) and S. Knights, *Jack the Ripper: The Final Solution* (London, 1976, 1984, 2000). The classic early study, which was not obsessed by the Ripper's identity, is R. Whittington-Egan, *A Casebook on Jack the Ripper* (London, 1975), which appeared in an expanded version as *Jack the Ripper: The Definitive Casebook* (Stroud, 2013). Other work includes D. Rumbelow, *The Complete Jack the Ripper* (new ed. Harmondsworth, 2004) and B. Robinson, *They All Love Jack: Busting the Ripper* (London, 2015). Many individuals caught up in the case appear in M. Fido, P. Begg and K. Skinner (eds), *The Complete Jack the Ripper A to Z* (London, 2010). Among the official files is TNA MEPO 3/141 on S. Montagu's offer of a reward for the Ripper's capture; it testifies to sensitivities in the Jewish community over how the situation might develop. Sir Charles Warren appears in the *Oxford Dictionary of National Biography*, Vol. 57 (Oxford, 2004), pp. 473–5. Co-existing with popular studies are more academic works such as J. Walkowitz, *City of Dreadful Night: Narratives of Sexual Danger in Late Victorian London* (Chicago, IL, 1992) and L.P. Curtis Jr, *Jack the Ripper and the London Press* (New Haven, CT, 2001).

35 Fishman, *Streets*, pp. 84–5 on the so-called Ripper riots. *The Times*, 2 October 1888 and *Jewish Chronicle*, 5 October 1888 on the Cracow incident.

36 R. Anderson, *The Lighter Side of My Official Life* (London, 1910), pp. 138–9.

37 *The Fascist*, April 1938. J.E. Morell, "The Life and Opinions of A.S. Leese: A Study in Extreme Anti-Semitism," unpublished University of Sheffield MA thesis, 1975, remains the fullest study.

38 Odell, *Jack the Ripper*, suggested a Jewish *schochet* was on the loose. C. Bermant, *Point of Arrival: A Study of London's East End* (London, 1975), Ch. 9 discusses claims that the murderer was a Jew. For later comment see *The Docklands and East London Advertiser*, 10 September 2014 for a critique of the view that Adam Kosminski, a Jewish immigrant, was the killer. This suggestion, based on an interpretation of DNA evidence, appears in R. Edwards, *Naming Jack the Ripper* (London, 2014).

39 Holmes, *John Bull's Island*, pp. 94–5, 112–4. And D. Glover, *Literature, Immigration and Diaspora in Fin-de-Siècle England: A Cultural History of the 1905 Aliens Act* (Cambridge, 2012).

40 *The Times*, 25 January 1909 and *Jewish Chronicle*, 29 January 1909. TNA MEPO 3/194 for the official file. See also J.D. Harris, *Outrage! An Edwardian Tragedy* (London, 2000). For related content see Emsley, *Hard Men*, p. 85; B. Gainer, *The Alien Invasion: The Origins of the Aliens Act of 1905* (London, 1972), pp. 205–7; and D. Cesarani, "Face has Changed but Fear Remains," *The Times Higher Education Supplement*, 27 June 2003, p. 20. See also M.H. Baylis's novel, *The Tottenham Outrage* (Brecon, 2014).

41 *Jewish Chronicle*, 23 December 1910.

42 Policemen involved in the incident proved keen to profit from their often unreliable versions of events. See Wensley, *Detective Days*, pp. 168–76; W. Nott-Bower, *Fifty-two Years a Policeman* (London, 1926); H. Brust, *I Guarded Kings: The Memoirs of a Political Police Officer* (London, 1935), pp. 90–5. V. Bailey, *Charles Booth's Policemen Crime, Police and Community in Jack-the-Ripper's London* (London, 2014), queries the influence and role of the police in the East End as opposed to that of informal social pressures in dealing with the area's problems. Later discussion of the Siege occurs in D. Rumbelow, *The Houndsditch Murders and the Siege of Sidney Street* (London, 1973, 1988 and Stroud, 2004) and C. Rogers, *The Battle of Stepney – The Sidney Street Siege: Its Causes and Consequences* (London, 1981). My article "In Search of Sidney Street," *Bulletin of the Society for the Study of Labour History*, No. 29 (Autumn 1974), pp. 70–7 discusses the official file on the incident. Churchill's view of events appears in this *Thoughts and Adventures* (London, 1948), pp. 41–8 and R. Churchill, *Winston S. Churchill: Young Statesman* (London, 1967), pp. 407–9. 'Peter the Painter,' P. Piatkoff appears in the Oxford Dictionary of National Biography, online version. Accessed 18 May 2016. E. Litvinoff's novel, *A Death out of Season* (London, 1973) derives inspiration from the siege. F. Oughton's novel, *The Siege of Sidney Street* (London, 1960) links to the film of that year with the same title. Directed by Robert Baker and Monty Berman, the script was written by Jimmy Sangster and Alexander Baron. The incident featured in Hitchcock's *The Man Who Knew Too Much* (1934). In September 2008 Tower Hamlets local authority named two apartment blocks in Sidney Street, Peter House and Painter House.

43 *East London Observer*, 24 December 1910. Holmes, *Anti-Semitism*, pp. 89–96 on the BBL.

44 *The Times*, 19 December 1910.

45 Ibid. Jacob Peters, one of the Houndsditch gang, later assumed a senior role in the Cheka before becoming another grisly statistic when in 1938 he became swept up in one of Stalin's brutal indiscriminate purges. He is the subject of two Intelligence files, KV 2/1025 and /1026. On Russian politics in Britain generally in the late nineteenth, early twentieth century see J. Slatter (ed.), *From the Other Shore: Russian Political Emigrants in Britain, 1880–1917* (London, 1984). On the anarchist political strain see Fishman, *East End Jewish Radicals*; R. Rocker, *The London Years* (London, 1956 ed.) and M. Berkowitz, "Anarchism, Jews, Relief – and Photography?: Behind the Lens and behind the Scenes, 1892–1946," pp. 29–45 of this memorial volume.

46 Samuel, *Underworld*, p. 116. Wensley, *Detective Days*, p. 110 describes him as "a quaint little Jew of Russian parentage." Arthur Harding, recollecting how Beron dressed, called him "a proper Yid." Samuel, *Underworld*, p. 134.

47 E. Linklater, *The Corpse on Clapham Common* (London, 1973) and A. Rose, *Stinie: Murder on the Common* (Harmondsworth, 1989) discuss the case. Morrison's letter demanding to be executed if not set free is in TNA HO 45/22263, correspondence 18 April 1911. His poem is readily consulted in Rose, *Stinie*, p. 163.

48 TNA HO 144/19780/210698 on Sidney Street and TNA HO 45/2261/127623 on Morrison shed no light on the question, Linklater, *The Corpse* and J.E. Holroyd, *The Gaslight Murders: The Saga of Sidney Street and the Scarlet 'S'* (London, 1960), both raise the matter. However, Rumbelow, *Houndsditch Murders*, dismisses any such link.

49 *Jewish Chronicle*, 17 March 1911.

50 E. Abinger, *Forty Years at the Bar* (London, n.d.), p. 60.

51 Isaacs's career is covered in D. Judd, *Lord Reading* (London, 1982) and *Oxford Dictionary of National Biography*, Vol. 29 (Oxford, 2004), pp. 404–11. The Marconi scandal features in K.J. Lunn, "The Marconi Scandal and Related Aspects of British Anti-Semitism 1911–14," unpublished Ph.D. thesis, University of Sheffield, 1978.

52 J.J. Tobias, "Police-Immigrant Relations in England 1880–1910," *New Community*, Vol. 3 (1974), p. 212.

53 Fishman, *Streets*, p. 105.

54 J.P. Bean, *The Sheffield Gang Wars* (Sheffield, 1981). During the inter-war years George Mooney and Sam Garvin strode across Sheffield's underworld when the city became known as "Little Chicago." Percy Sillitoe effectively broke their power when serving as Chief Constable between 1926 and 1928. He then transferred to Glasgow to tackle its razor crime, often associated with Billy Fullerton and his mob, before becoming head of MI5. On the situation in Glasgow see the novel by A. McArthur and H. Kingsley Long, *No Mean City* (London, 1935) and A. Taylor, "Street Gangs in the Interwar Gorbals: The Jewish Experience," *Contemporary British History*, Vol. 27 (2013), pp. 214–31.

55 H. Shore, *London's Criminal Underworlds 1720–1930* (Basingstoke, 2015) is a long-range study shedding light on various criminal enterprises, including the racecourse gangs. See also B. McDonald, *The Gangs of London* (Preston, 2010). On Sabini see E.T. Hart, *Britain's Godfather* (London, 1993) and *Oxford Dictionary of National Biography*, Vol. 48 (Oxford, 2004), pp. 517–9. He features slightly in Samuel, *Underworld*. Sabini was reputedly the role model for Mr Colleoni in Graham Greene's 1938 novel, *Brighton Rock*: "He was a small dark man with a neat round belly; he wore a grey double-breasted waistcoat and his eyes gleamed like raisins" (Harmondsworth, 1970 ed.), p. 63. "Crime never pays," they say, but in the 1930s he allegedly lived in a penthouse suite in the luxury Grand Hotel on Brighton sea front. *Sabini*, a film of his life, is expected soon.

56 Fishman, *Streets*, p. 106. J. White, *Rothschild Buildings; Life in an East End Tenement Block 1887–1920* (London, 1980), Chapter 3, on older residents of the East End recalling Bogard's notoriety.

57 Emmanuel's importance in the Jewish East End crime scene is emphasised in Samuel, *Underworld*, pp. 182, 204, for example. Had he lived longer Raphael Samuel would doubtless have had more to say about him. The lives of people like Emmanuel were constantly, capriciously uncertain. Rivalries, assaults and sometimes murder, were never far away. But instances of gangster cooperation did occasionally occur; in the 1920s the Sabinis and their Jewish contemporaries combined in the racecourse wars to oust the so-called Birmingham Boys – who had links with the Hoxton gang and the Elephant and Castle mob – from the southern racetracks. C. Chinn, *The Real Peaky Blinders: Billy Kimber, the Birmingham Gang and the Racecourse Wars of the 1920s* (Studley, 2014).

58 A point raised in R. Cohen, *Tough Jews: Fathers, Sons and Gangster Dreams* (London, 1996), a racy discussion of early twentieth century crime in America. Jewish criminals there also feature in R. Rockaway, *But he was good to his mother: The Lives and Crimes of Jewish Gangsters* (Jerusalem, 1993); J.J. Weismann, *Our Gang. Jewish Crime and the New York Jewish Community* (Bloomington, 1983) and N. Tosches, *King of the Jews. The Arnold Rothstein Story* (London, 2005). A representative of the "Kosher Mafia" features in Scott Fitzgerald's *The Great Gatsby* in the person of "Meyer Wolfshiem," who was seemingly based on Rothstein.

59 Banister, *England under the Jews* (1907 ed.), p. 2.

60 *RC* Vol. 1 (1903), pp. 17–19 note the concerns.

61 *The Times*, 16 March 1911.

62 R. Anderson, "The Problem of the Criminal Aliens," *Nineteenth Century*, Vol. 69 (1911), pp. 217–8.

63 Israel Lipski, who even had to contend with a drunken counsel, appears to have suffered an especially raw deal. The Reubens brothers faced a hostile judge and hardline civil servants who dismissed too easily the issue of joint enterprise. And was Morrison guilty of murdering Beron? There are suspicions here of police corruption which might have influenced Churchill in his decision to grant a reprieve. See TNA MEPO 3/1837 and

Report of the Inquiry … into the evidence given by the police at the trial of Stinie Morrison Cd 5627 (1911). But perhaps the most egregious case was Oscar Slater's. He had been born in 1870 in Oppeln and fled to Britain to avoid the military service imposed on Jews by the Tsarist government. Once here he worked variously as a bookie's clerk, bookmaker and manager of gambling clubs. He dealt in jewellery (as a fence?) and, like the Reubens brothers, had lived partly off prostitution. As a cover he posed as Mr Anderson, a dentist. He would never have entered the history books except for the accusation that he was also a killer. Like many Jewish contemporaries America fascinated him and when arriving there on a visit in 1908 he was arrested and charged with the murder of Marion Gilchrist, a wealthy spinster who lived at 15 Queen's Terrace, Glasgow. At his trial he was found guilty and sentenced to death. After being reprieved he spent the next eighteen years rotting in prison. Photographs taken before and after his release reflect much more than the expected unremitting ravages of time. Like the Reubens brothers, his reputation had preceded him and weighed heavily on the police in their enquiries. Their investigation also revealed traces of anti-Semitism. It is now claimed Gilchrist's killer was a member of her own family. See T. Toughill, *Oscar Slater: The Mystery Solved* (Edinburgh, 2003).

64 M.J. Landa, *The Alien Problem and its Remedy* (London, 1911).

65 These gangster bosses feature in D. Webb, *Crime is my Business* (London, 1953) on the Messina brothers; W. Clarkson, *Hit 'em Hard: Jack Spot, King of the Underworld* (London, 2002); idem, *Billy Hill, Godfather of London* (London, 2008); J. Pearson, *Profession of Violence: the Rise and Fall of the Krays* (London, 1995 ed.).

Select Bibliography

Colin Holmes, *Anti-Semitism in British Society 1876–1939* (London, 1979. Reprinted 2015).

James Morton, *East End Gangland* (London, 2000).

Raphael Samuel, *East End Underworld: Chapters in the Life of Arthur Harding* (London, 1981).

Jonathan Schneer, *London, 1900* (London and New Haven, 1999).

Heather Shore, *London's Criminal Underworlds 1720–1930* (Basingstoke, 2015).

Frederick P. Wensley, *Detective Days* (London, 1931).

6

JEWS AND BOMBS

The Making of a Metropolitan Myth, 1916–1945

Jerry White

I

In the opening weeks of 1943 heavy British bombing raids on Berlin received extensive coverage in the London press. The news met with mixed feelings in the East End, where satisfaction at the German capital getting its just deserts was tempered by fear of reprisals from the Luftwaffe. Many East Enders took once more to the shelters and the London Underground in readiness for a resumption of bombing that had largely ceased for over a year and a half.

An especially heavy raid on Berlin on 2 March, revealed in jaunty headlines in the evening papers, produced jitters in the East End that night, though many took the view that any reprisals were more likely on the following day. So it was that by eight o'clock on the evening of Wednesday, 3 March 1943, some five hundred to six hundred people had already entered the shelter at the unfinished underground station and tunnels at the junction of Roman Road and Cambridge Heath Road, Bethnal Green. Above ground more were making their way there when at 8.17 the air raid sirens sounded the alert, bringing hundreds of local people from their homes to the shelter; their numbers were swollen as passing buses stopped to let passengers join the crowds at the shelter entrance. Some fifteen hundred had made their way down the dimly lit staircase when at 8.27 an anti-aircraft rocket salvo was discharged from a battery a few hundred yards from the underground shelter. This was a new weapon, previously unheard locally. The noise was terrifyingly loud and unexpected and was misinterpreted by many as the sound of falling bombs. The crowd at the head of the staircase surged forward, propelled by those pushing behind. On the third step from the bottom of the flight of nineteen steps leading to the booking hall a woman, thought to have been carrying or leading a child, tripped and fell. Within seconds, ten or fifteen at the most, the staircase became "a charnel house." One hundred and seventy-three people, including eighty-four women and sixty-two children, were crushed and suffocated in "an immovable and interlaced mass of bodies" that it would take rescue workers hours to untangle. It was the greatest civilian tragedy of the British home front during the Second World War.[1]

The incident was followed by a strict news blackout as to the whereabouts of the tragedy or the numbers of casualties. In the absence of information rumours flourished. Most prominent among them, dressed as fact, travelling as fast and far as any telegraph, so that it was heard and believed "so far afield as Bristol" by 4 March, was a belief that the accident had been caused by "a Jewish panic."[2] The Ministry of Information reported shortly after that, "the trouble was occasioned by the Jews is reported from all parts of London, with the exception of Bethnal Green where there is full knowledge that any such statement is untrue."[3] For the Bethnal Green underground shelter did not serve a Jewish area, had in fact been avoided by Jewish shelterers because the Salmon and Ball public house across the road was a notorious haunt of the British Union of Fascists (BUF), and only five of the victims were thought to have been Jewish. An Inquiry into the causes of the disaster was quickly established. It took evidence in camera and when it reported to the Home Office the Inquiry chairman, a London stipendiary magistrate Laurence Rivers Dunne, roundly dismissed any suggestion that the disaster was caused by:

> … a Jewish panic. This canard had a much wider circulation [than other rumours] and was, I understand, endorsed by the broadcast utterances of a renegade traitor from Germany [William Joyce, "Lord Haw-Haw"]. Not only is it without foundation, it is demonstrably false. The Jewish attendance at this shelter was, and is, so small as to constitute a hardly calculable percentage.[4]

A relieved Home Secretary, Herbert Morrison, duly made a statement to the House of Commons on 8 April 1943, scotching the "Jewish panic" rumour, while declining to publish the Inquiry report.[5]

For some, "the decision not to publish the findings is proof that the Jews did, in fact, panic," though publication itself of course would not have prevented some keeping alive the myth. For allegations of London's Jewish population being uniquely susceptible to panic under fire went back a long way. The connection with a past conflict was explicitly made to the Dunne Inquiry by an anonymous letter writer, signing himself just "E.P.," who wrote to the Home Office on 11 March 1943:

> Being on the spot at the time of the trouble I was able to observe the cowardly display of fear by the foreign born Jews, they simply lost their heads in their desire to get under shelter causing one solid mass resulting in suffocation I remember quite well the trouble in the East End in the last War – Fear in the Jews.[6]

II

Anti-Semitism in Britain during the Second World War has been exhaustively studied by historians over the past three decades.[7] Their findings in general are not dissimilar from the conclusions George Orwell reached in an essay published in the *Contemporary Jewish Record* in April 1945 that: "There is more anti-Semitism in England than we care to admit and the war has accentuated it … " But Orwell added a rider: "it is not certain that it is on the increase if one thinks in terms of decades rather than years." Anti-Semitism, he thought, "is probably less prevalent in England than it was thirty years ago." It was not then "a fully thought-out racial and religious doctrine," but "thirty years ago it was accepted more or less as a law of nature that a Jew was a figure of fun and – though superior in intelligence – slightly deficient in 'character'."[8]

"Thirty years ago," brings us to 1915, coincidentally the year that gave Londoners their first taste of aerial bombardment in a world war, though Orwell would not have had that particular anniversary in mind. By contrast with Britain's Second World War, anti-Semitism in the First has yet to receive detailed attention.[9] In its absence there has been a tendency to infer two starkly contrasting wartime experiences of London Jewry. Compared to the vociferous anti-Semitism of the British Brothers' League and the "Chesterbelloc" years before 1914, the First World War has been cast "as a catalyst in integrating the [East European Jewish] immigrants and their children."[10]

This, though, is not the whole story. Alongside the integrating influences of Jews serving in the armed forces, and of closer involvement of Jewish organisations in the wider trade union movement and the local state, public hostility to London Jewry found new grievances and unrestrained forms of expression that seemed to many to herald collective violence. For all the elements that Orwell and the historians have uncovered at the root of popular anti-Semitism in London between 1939 and 1945 were articulated for the first time – more vociferously and outrageously – between 1916 and 1918. The discourse they originated was kept alive through the 1920s and 1930s and was revived in precisely similar terms, though far more *sotto voce*, from 1939 on. Prominent among them was the myth resurrected so powerfully in the aftermath of the Bethnal Green disaster: what E.P. called, "Fear in the Jews."

This myth around Jews and bombs did not arise overnight during the course of the earlier conflict. It took time to articulate and had origins outside the bombing campaign against London itself. But by its end, in May 1918, it had become an unshakeable legacy of London's First World War.

III

The first ever German bombing raid on London, by a single Zeppelin airship, took place on the night of 31 May 1915. The Zeppelins seemed by then long overdue. Londoners had anticipated their arrival from the early days after 4 August 1914 and naval guns to ward them off had been installed in parks and on buildings by the end of that first month. Indeed, towns along the south and east coasts had been attacked before the capital, even though London had long been recognised as the primary enemy target. That first London raid killed seven people in what would become the air war's most vulnerable metropolitan districts, those boroughs immediately north and east of the City. The victims that night included two Jewish children coming home from a cinema, who died sheltering in a doorway in Christian Street, Stepney.[11] Further raids followed in the autumn and early winter of 1915, affecting not just the East End but also the west-central districts of London, among others.

The response of Londoners to these first raids revealed no fixed pattern of behaviour, certainly no consistently robust sangfroid. Press comment was muted by censorship, just as it would be in the later conflict, but diarists and others give a mixed picture. We hear that first night of three incendiaries hitting the roof of the Empire Music Hall in Shoreditch High Street, causing damage but no fire; the manager made an address from the stage to calm nerves and the band "played lively airs while the audience left the house in an orderly manner." Not far away in Hoxton, where there was considerable damage, and in other parts of the East End, according to Sylvia Pankhurst "Panic ran rampant."[12] "People in London appear much excited," thought Viscount Sandhurst, a former military man, now Lord Chamberlain, "and there is a great rush to get into the insurance offices for houses, property, etc."[13]

Later that year, in a raid on the Covent Garden and Holborn districts on a night when the theatres were full, in some "disorder reigned;" in others the show went phlegmatically on, the performers calming nerves in the auditorium. Outside though, according to Rose Macaulay writing soon after, Chancery Lane "had been the scene of that wild terror and shrieking confusion which is characterised by a euphemistic press as 'no panic'." Viscount Sandhurst was dining that night in the Ritz and felt the same: "It is said they create no panic; I've only witnessed one raid – lots of women in tears and almost in hysterics running about not knowing what they were about." He reported, probably from others' accounts, "panic in the tube stations."[14]

Over the New Year of 1916 middle-class nervousness was widespread. "I actually met a man this week," recorded R.D. Blumenfeld, the American-born editor of the *Daily Express*, "who confessed that the Zeppelin raids made him feel so much afraid that he had decided to go and live far inland," just one of many who felt that discretion was the better part of valour.[15] In none of this do we hear mention, even the whisper, of a response in the Jewish East End, or from Anglo-Jewry elsewhere in London, different in any degree from the behaviour of cockneys on the one hand or middle-class, even upper-class, Londoners on the other.

The mood would change in 1916 but bombing, which resumed that summer and autumn, would not be the key. That was provided by the conscription of men into the armed services. Previously this had been a war of volunteers, in Britain at least. Now forced enrolment was brought in for single men from 10 February and, more controversially, for married men aged eighteen to forty-one from 25 May.

To that point the relationship of East End Jewry to the war had been complex. Some British-born Jewish East Enders had volunteered at the outset, responding among other things to a call for patriotism by the Anglo-Jewish elite of the City and West End. But many young men from the Jewish East End were foreign-born, mainly "friendly aliens" hailing from European Russia. They had fled economic dislocation and religious persecution, even pogroms, in an empire in which they were plainly unwelcome. The parents of some had migrated purposely to avoid compulsory service in the Tsar's army where Jews were universally ill-treated: when a young Jew was conscripted the prayer for the dead was said as he left home. Britain's alliance with Russia from 4 August 1914 left but a sour taste in the mouths of most East End Jews.[16]

There matters stood until 1916 and conscription, East End Jews sharing in the prosperity of wartime London, sometimes no doubt having to live with jibes in the streets against young Jewish men of military age who other East Enders thought should have been in khaki. Conscription brought this anomaly more clearly into the open. It applied only to those born in Britain. But it also redefined the position of those other young Jews who could not be forced to fight but who were well placed to take economic advantage, it was thought, of those called away. When British-born East End Jews were classified physically unfit to serve, as many were, it was interpreted as official favouritism in action. And one of the most damaging allegations, that foreign-born Jews were left at home to step into English businesses while their owners were fighting in France, began to reverberate across London, even in areas where there was not a Jew in sight.[17]

Government plans to remove this anomaly by requiring Russian men of military age to return "home" or join the British army became a matter of diplomatic discussions with Russia by July 1916. There were thought to be over 20,000 Russian Jews in Britain potentially affected by such a policy were the Tsar's government to agree to it. But the move was vociferously opposed by a Foreign Jews' Protection Committee (FJPC), claiming one hundred and twenty local affiliated organisations nationwide and with its headquarters in London. A government scheme to encourage Russian Jews to volunteer for the British army – put in place by Home Secretary Herbert Samuel, the first ever practising Jew in a British cabinet – met with only modest success. And in the House of Commons some of the die-hard xenophobes now turned their fire away from Germans and Austrians living in Britain and against those "friendly aliens," the Russian Jews.[18]

Xenophobia was at its noisiest in the East End of London. The *East London Observer*, backed up by other local newspapers, complained that while "the flower of the English race is being cut down like corn on the blood-soaked battlefields of Europe," "the Alien is to thrive and prosper in our midst," allowed "to live at ease, trade, dance and sing …" "ARE THEY COWARDS ALL?" it asked a few weeks later of "Friendly Aliens" of military age.[19] And we hear the first sounds of what in a year's time would be a cacophony: that, in living with air raids, "The mental attitude of east Londoners (except the ignorant and half-superstitious foreign element) is synonymous with that of ninety-nine per cent of the population of the

British Isles, viz., that we are going to see this thing, bad though it be, through to the very end."[20]

The position of Russian-born Jews of military age shifted considerably during 1917. News of the first Russian Revolution of February and the downfall of the Tsar was greeted with jubilation in the East End as the termination of so many years of oppression. The prospect of a return to Russia now held fewer terrors and Britain soon after concluded negotiations with the new Russian government to accept the repatriation of Russian citizens of military age not exempted from service in Britain. The Military Service (Conventions with Allied States Act) 1917 became operative towards the end of July. Applications for exemption from service were to be heard by a Special Tribunal.

Some foreign-born Jews now viewed a return to Russia with equanimity and made arrangements to do so. Many others did not. Their reasons were understandable. Most had been in the East End ten years or more, before the Aliens Act of 1905 had deterred many potential migrants from choosing Britain as a refuge. The FJPC continued to oppose compulsory enlistment despite the changed circumstances. A movement of Jews from the East End to Ireland, where conscription did not apply, became discernible. And the knowing sneers of the anti-Semites grew louder: the "Russian Jews in the East-end of London," announced *The Times*, "have prospered during the war" and "do not want to fight." "Meanwhile feeling in the East-end among the British residents is strongly in favour of the adoption of firm measures to ensure that the Russian Jews shall serve." On 30 July 1917 the FJPC offices were raided and its secretary was arrested on suspicion of conspiracy to subvert the operation of the new Act: he was interned and two months later deported to his native Rumania.[21]

The East End that summer of 1917 was in a highly excitable state. Over 8,300 Russians appealed against military service and the repatriation or service in the British army that would follow. A local magistrate who heard charges arising out of the Tribunal's proceedings recalled some years later how:

> A few solicitors specialised in this work. Subtle legal devices of many sorts were used to deflect the operation of the Military Service Acts. Conflicting and misleading accounts of what had taken place before the Special Tribunals were given in the police courts. Exemption certificates were passed from one member of a family to another. Forgery and mutilation of such documents became common …

Some who opted for the British army absconded when their call-up papers arrived; some to be repatriated failed to take the trains for Liverpool where they were to go aboard ship; some claimed to be over conscription age, their cases before the magistrates supported by "wonderful documents in foreign characters" and "aged patriarchs" who "covered their heads and swore that they had been present at the site of circumcision at places in Russia and Poland over forty years ago … ." For one cause or another, often for medical reasons, many Russian Jews were indeed exempted from service by the Tribunal.[22]

That summer also saw the resumption of air raids in a new form, by huge Gotha biplanes, faster and more manoeuvrable than the Zeppelins and carrying a larger destructive payload. Two daylight raids in June and July were the most costly of the war, with marked tragedies in the East End (eighteen children were killed in Upper North Street School, Poplar on 13 June with several others killed near Liverpool Street station).[23] Many Londoners, especially of the middle classes, felt it a good moment to take advantage of the summer weather and leave London to the bombers. But now it was the Jews of the East End – unpopular because of those conscription complications since the middle of 1916 – who were singled out for special notice.

From the middle of July 1917 "The Alien Exodus" or "Alien Wanderings"[24] – the ancient allusions all too pointed – received wide attention in the nation's newspapers and the East End press. Jewish East Enders – in reality probably Jewish Londoners from every point of the compass – were spotted joining their co-religionists in Birmingham, Leeds, Manchester, Nottingham, Cardiff and elsewhere. The coin-cidence of timing with the new conscription regulations might also have been a factor in the movement out, if only to make life difficult for the military authorities and the Aliens' Office.[25] The *Jewish Chronicle*, forced on the back foot, conceded that the dispersal might, "in unfriendly eyes, wear an unpleasant aspect," but in fact the publicity given to the Jews by hostile newspapermen served to disguise convenient "holidaying" that summer among all who could afford to indulge it.[26]

It was indeed a holiday destination that began to epitomise "the Exodus from the Ghetto," as the *Jewish Chronicle* put it in August: "Brighton is more Jewish than ever it was. Each deck-chair has its own especial minyan, and flat-owners are as envied as millionaires in Park Lane."[27] The satirical undertone was picked up by that doughty sporting journalist J.B. Booth in *Town Topics*, collected and published in the last year of the war. The object of Booth's generally good-natured "fun" (as Orwell would put it) was in fact a clueless upper-class society flapper, Miss "Billie" Tuchaud, an open-minded young woman who befriended anyone who could afford cocktails and a good dinner and who shamelessly enjoyed her war:

> Brighton yet again for the weekend … . The place was *fearfy* full, of course, and seems to be prospering madly. Indeed *on dit* that the Entertainment Committee are seriously considering the addition of two perfectly brand-new synagogues to the list of attractions. Amongst the fashionable crowd on the pier I noticed the Guggenheims (*père, mere, fils at filles*); Isidor and Leah Din-kelstein; Issy Eisenbaum; the Abraham, Isaac and Jacob families; Mossy Guts-berg (very *chic* in a light chocolate-brown, the family diamond, brocaded boot tops and dirty finger-nails) …

and with rather too much of the same.[28]

"Fun" like Booth's, though, had its limits. Things would take an uglier turn from the late September of 1917. What happened then shook the nerves of the Londoners more severely than anything that had gone before: "Probably no aspect of the raids is more vividly remembered by Londoners," it was said some twenty years later of the "Harvest Moon Raids" of 24 September to 1 October, with raids on five nights and alarms on six. On 29 September, too, the attacking aircraft comprised both Gothas and the new Giants, driven by four, five or six engines with a wingspan of 138 ft, larger than any plane bombing London in the Second World War and carrying a payload of bombs weighing almost two tonnes.[29]

In all, the five Harvest Moon raids killed forty-seven and injured two hundred and twenty-six. But it was less the damage they caused than the relentless disruption and accumulating strain, built up night after night, that people found so intolerable. Fear of the bombers' return drove more Londoners than ever before to seek shelter wherever they could find it. In July people had resorted to the underground stations in their "thousands," their depth a great comfort. Now, this September and early October, this became a mass movement, Londoners wherever they lived making for the underground to shelter, some five thousand at Elephant and Castle underground station even before the Harvest Moon raids. Even on the rainy night of 27 September when the weather made a raid unlikely, Arnold Bennett found the underground, probably at Aldwych, full of "Very poor women and children sitting on the stairs." In the lift people quarrelled with the operator, provoking an irritated response from "middle-class women saying to each other that if the poor couldn't keep to the regulations they ought to be forbidden the Tube as a shelter from raid." Queues to enter the underground now formed before dusk. By 6.30 p.m. on 1 October, some hours before a raid might reasonably be anticipated, William Beveridge "found people ensconced at Notting Hill Gate station." "Once people were admitted into the stations," recalled Caroline Playne, a social psychologist living in Hampstead, "it was almost impossible for passengers to get up or down, from or to the trains," and some platforms were made impassable and noisome (because no sanitary facilities were provided) by shelterers bedding down for the night.[30]

By the end of September, the Metropolitan Police estimated that as many as three hundred thousand a night were sheltering across the underground railway system. That was an extraordinary number. It meant that if every single Jew in London had hastened underground they would still have been outnumbered two to one by their Gentile neighbours. Huge numbers also sought shelter wherever seemed safe: a further one hundred and twenty-seven thousand, for instance, chose the London County Council schools near to them, despite the Poplar disaster of the summer. It's very plain indeed that the underground and other shelters were the resort of all sorts and conditions of Londoners in the pandemic of anxiety sweeping London. Yet very soon the only discernible underground shelterer would become the alien Jew. We can detect this rapid shift in operation through the columns of the *Daily Mail*. On 25 September it reported sympathetically on "Tube Camps. Family Parties and Comic Songs." At Oxford Circus, Tottenham Court Road and Museum stations of the Central London Underground Railway, "whole families from the Soho district" and around were camping out on platforms and passages, even bringing "rugs and mats" to provide a semblance of domestic comfort. The reporter noted some "excitement, crowding and crushing" when the alarm was raised:

> … but that phase soon passed away. The men calmed the fears of the women, and after a time stolid British silence was the prevailing note among the people. Popular songs were started, and soon the stations were echoing to rollicking choruses, while some of the more youthful in the crowd performed step dances to lighten the time.[31]

Three days later and a more sinister picture had emerged. Now the paper had discovered a "premature pilgrimage of excitable aliens to the tube stations," taking "their babies and bundles with them." "Their condition and habits are a menace to the health of passengers," the aliens uniquely filthy, it appears, in a city where millions could only with difficulty procure hot water and washing facilities.[32] Other newspapers joined in a plaint that now cast underground sheltering as unworthy of British grit: "That there was a certain amount of crowding towards these harbours of safety is a fact," admitted the *Evening Standard*; "but the bulk of the populace were not concerned in it. It was largely due to a number of foreigners."[33] No one seemed to notice that this was contradicted in subsequent issues by reports of court hearings for bad behaviour among shelterers in the underground – a drunken man at Holborn, a Lambeth Walk butcher shouting "fire!" at North Lambeth underground when "several thousands" were sheltering there, and so on.[34]

Sadly, though, those who characterised sheltering in the underground as an alien problem appeared to be corroborated by the death of Dora Kopitko in a crush on a staircase at Liverpool Street station on the night of 28 September. She was the wife of a Russian Pole, a bootmaker who could only manage to speak broken English at the inquest, and died of suffocation in a crowd that police said "consisted chiefly of aliens." In fact things might have been worse that night: "At the bottom of the stairs he [witness] could see there was a heap of women and children. They were all unconscious and the atmosphere was stifling."[35]

"Aliens" rushing to the underground coincided in the papers with an apparent rise in the numbers of "aliens" fleeing to places of safety outside London. Once more it did not matter that the Harvest Moon raids provoked an impromptu evacuation of London in every direction and in which all classes of Londoner took part. Diarists noted that Waterloo Station was "crowded with families, poor mothers and children, who are leaving London" on 2 October, people were reported sleeping out in Richmond Park, and others moved right away as far as Devon and other places if they could.[36] For the press it was only the aliens who fled. The *Daily Mail* discovered "large numbers" in Dorking, Crawley, Horsham and the "beautiful Caterham Valley," but it was Brighton that received both the largest numbers and the greatest attention, now becoming "Brightchapel" or "Jerusalem-by-the-Sea."[37] The *East London Observer* put it all together and made a historic – and sinister – point connecting 1917 with the vociferous anti-alien agitation in the East End that had led to the Aliens Act of 1905: "Brighton and the Tubes have demonstrated to perfection that what the despised and ridiculed British Brothers' League urged ten or twelve years ago is really the fact."[38]

It was around this time, with East End Jews the object of so much public loathing, that the only significant intercommunal rioting took place. That was at Blythe and Teesdale Streets, a small Jewish enclave in Bethnal Green known locally as "Jews' Island," over the weekend of 22–23 September. The main spark seems to have been over conscription of Jews into the army. There was street fighting for half an hour with two or three thousand taking to the streets to watch the action, and in truth was something and nothing.[39] But it emphasised that this was a worrying time for Jews in the East End, and many people thought there would be worse to come. Even the *Saturday Review*, the cultural journal of elite conservatism, felt able in an editorial on food waste and "gourmandising" to issue a stark warning to the Jews of London:

> The Jews, in particular, who in times of immediate profits always reap a golden harvest, are making themselves very unpopular by their loud and ostentatious expenditure. Swarms of East-End Jews travel down every evening to sleep at Brighton and come up the next morning, as they are frightened by air-raids. If these new-rich are not careful, Jew-hating leading to Jew-baiting may spring up.[40]

All this anti-Semitic polemic in the press was observed with great concern in the *Jewish Chronicle*, the unofficial voice of established Anglo-Jewry. So when a friendly and practical aid to the shelter problem emerged it was gratefully seized upon, though originating outside the Jewish community itself. One of the complications of these nervous nights in the autumn of 1917 arose from the authorities' refusal to give advance warning of raids, even though enemy aircraft were known to be approaching. Daytime warnings had been belatedly introduced after the dreadful raids of the summer and were given by maroons or "sound-bombs" fired from police and fire stations across London. But night-time warnings were thought likely to cause panic and so the first residents knew of a raid was when guns opened up or bombs fell. In these circumstances many thousands had played safe by going to the underground or shelters as darkness fell. In addition, from 1915 and subsequently, many streets and neighbourhoods across London had organised a nightly watch, where observers stayed awake by rota to rouse neighbours should firing or explosions be heard in the distance.[41]

Now, in October 1917, something similar was devised to assist the particular needs of the Jewish East End. The East End Shelter Corps was formed by Vincent Pitman and John Acton, "two worthy non-Jews" as the *Chronicle* put it, "to restore confidence, and generally, during raids and alarms, to help women, children, and infirm men by gentle persuasion and good example." It quickly became embedded into the voluntary welfare machinery of the Jewish East End, meeting at Toynbee

Hall and the Jewish Board of Guardians' offices in Middlesex Street, with Albert I. Belisha, a prominant businessman, soon to beome president and chairman.[42]

The absence of night-time warnings provoked much press criticism of the Home Secretary and Metropolitan Police Commissioner, who resolutely opposed them. Controversy continued into the New Year of 1918 though without resolution. Official policy would soon now play its part in the worst wartime tragedy of the Jewish East End, one that eerily foreshadowed the Bethnal Green disaster some twenty-five years later.

The night of Monday 28 January 1918 was unusually clear, clouds having covered London for much of the New Year so far. Clear nights favoured the bombers' chances and so a raid was anticipated. Early in the evening a crowd of potential shelterers from the Jewish and Gentile East End gathered round the locked gates of Bishopsgate Goods Station in Shoreditch. The strong arches here had been used as a shelter in the past but so much damage had been done to goods stored there, and in the absence of sanitary accommodation so much filth left behind, that the railway company would not open the gates until a formal "take cover" alert had been given by police. That would only happen when guns began firing or bombs exploded, or if the station authorities had received an indication directly from police. Three Gothas now neared London from the east. Their approach was signalled nearby with the sounding of maroons. Unprepared for this sudden noise, maroons at night-time were not part of any official policy, the crowd took this to be the first sound of exploding bombs. In a moment, hundreds of people laden with "mattresses, blankets, pillows" and other household equipment, supplemented by a queue of people across the road waiting for the Olympia Music Hall to open, rushed the station entrance. The main gates were found locked, but one side-gate was open for staff and the crowd tried to surge through it. In the melée someone fell and in the crush that immediately followed fourteen died from suffocation and many more were injured.[43]

Most of the casualties were Jewish East Enders. "Cowardly Aliens in the Great Stampede" was the *East London Advertiser*'s headline reporting the inquest on the victims. A police superintendent, keen to get in a blow about "shirkers" evading conscription, "was struck by the enormous number of young men huddled up there … . I am proud to say that we have not had the slightest trouble with the English people, but we have had a very great trouble with the foreign element" in the shelters. Other police witnesses agreed that "the panic was caused by a crowd of Russian Jews."[44] Much publicity centred on one unnamed victim: "On the body of a Jew who was killed was found £350 in gold."[45]

A month or so after the Bishopsgate tragedy the *Jewish Chronicle* noted that wartime anti-Semitism had now found a new target in "Jews and Profiteering," rationing having been introduced for many foods, and the authorities proving themselves keen to make examples of any alien found flouting the complex regulations. But in fact it would be a familiar affront that attracted most fire against London Jewry as the war drew to a close: the alien "exodus" from London and out of the reach of German bombs. It was given added zest by Bolshevik Russia's peace with Germany, signed on 3 March 1918, which rendered the East End's aliens now no longer "friendly" but merely weak-kneed neutrals.

From the middle of March, led once more by the *Daily Mail* but now joined enthusiastically by *The Times* and others, almost daily headlines complained of "Up-River Invasion. Russians in Maidenhead," of "The Capture of Maidenhead. Russians in Houseboats," and of "Maidenhead Russians. Moneyed Tailors. Capture of Trains."[46] The jocular military allusions lost their appeal when the dramatic reverses suffered by the British army in the face of the Ludendorff Offensive of 21 March soon became horrifyingly clear. But there would always be room in the papers that spring for talk of "Russians" "buying up house room" in Reading and Henley and Slough, hogging season tickets to Brighton and the upper-Thames villages and towns, snapping up seats in Pullman carriages to "eat, drink and gamble all the way up and down," eating Henley's housewives out of their sugar ration, with "the habits of the children" too horrible to specify.[47] "At present we are drifting," thought the *Mail*, "towards a violent explosion of popular resentment that may take some very unpleasant forms … ."[48]

The papers' fears of, or desires for, some form of violent explosion were not in fact realised. But in the climate of xenophobia that had driven otherwise sane Britons to a pitch of manic anxiety ever since war began, the Jews of London had been relentlessly libelled from mid-1916. Hysteria was at its most extreme in the summer and autumn of 1917 and the spring of 1918. Attacks might be directed at "foreigners," "aliens," "Russians," but all knew in fact that the target was "the Jew," whether nominally alien or British-born. Certainly that was how it was experienced, if the columns of the *Jewish Chronicle* are any guide.

The burden of this anti-Semitic discourse was that Jews were cowards, were singularly prone to "panic" and anxiety, seeking only to preserve their own skins at the expense if necessary of their neighbours. Cowardice expressed itself in the rush to the underground stations and shelters; in the flight from London–under–fire; in the evasion by fair means or foul of service in the fighting forces; in the instinct for self-preservation that led to profiteering and the hoarding of gold, in luxurious gluttony and first-class rail fare, in procuring safe house-room at whatever the cost. It was all a powerful self-sustaining myth. And it helped bolster another myth of the First World War years: that the Londoners had proved as stoic on the home front as their menfolk had on the front in France. Indeed the two myths could be opposite sides of a single coin. For it became convenient for many to scapegoat the Jews as the only cowards in London. As the popular writer Mrs Alec-Tweedie put it at the end of the war: "As to that one blot, the fevered scuttle for shelter in the Tube, the Londoner can tell you, with his hand upon his heart, that the scuttlers were mostly aliens."[49]

IV

This myth of the alien (Jewish) scuttler under fire was kept alive between the wars. It would only be another twenty-two years before German bombs began to fall on

London again and myths and memories of the Great War were vivid for anyone over the age of thirty, and handed down to all those younger. Wartime memoirs, in fact and fiction, helped keep alive the Alec-Tweedie version of the underground "filled with highly-scented aliens," as recalled by Stephen McKenna, a civil servant and writer in a memoir of 1921, and by John Galsworthy in a late Forsyte short story of 1930. The susceptibility of East End "aliens" to "panic" under fire was affirmed by H.L. Cancellor, a London magistrate, in his memoirs, also of 1930; he went on to write of "Russian Jews, who had made money out of the War," taking houses at any price to shelter in country districts, and of "Jew Boys" shirking army service to become "middlemen" and "bookmakers." William Beveridge, in his 1928 study of wartime food controls, drew special attention to prosecutions against "alien" tradesmen, some of whom were found to be "wholesalers in crime." And in his jingoistic autobiography of 1938, Captain Edward Tupper, a prominent seamen's trade union leader, spared a word for the "true British Jew" – "none worked harder" for his country during the war – while railing against the "host of foreign Jews who had no loyalties and no traditions" and who "fled in mobs from the dangers of London; mostly to Brighton." "Everybody loathed these people," he thought.[50] If we are to believe George Orwell's appraisal of British anti-Semitism written in 1945, the rise of Nazi Germany from 1933 drove hostility to Jews off the printed page. Captain Tupper showed no such inhibition.[51] There were, indeed, doubtless many ways in which false memories of Jews and bombs were kept vividly alive, and these few instances must serve as illustration only for what would surely comprise a very extensive list.

V

All the anti-Semitic myths were revived with vigour when war was once more declared. There were though differences. The intellectual climate had changed in contradictory ways. The press, local and national, was keen to downplay anti-Semitism as divisive and dangerous, and no longer acceptable given the policies of Hitler's Germany: the renamed *City and East London Observer*, for instance, was now a model of restrained community cohesiveness compared to its forebear just thirty years before. On the other hand, the BUF – which had adopted an anti-Jewish policy from 1934 – gave anti-Semitism an articulate presence on the streets of East London. Its propaganda was especially well received in Bethnal Green, Shoreditch and Hackney. The message, from 3 September 1939, that this was a "Jews' War" was chalked on walls and spread by newsletter and clearly had some purchase in London. Profiteering was another prominent attack and so was evasion of military service with Jews taking "British jobs" by staying at home while others joined up.[52]

Other Great War stereotypes were actively in play. Frank Lewey, a young cockney Labour councillor in Stepney who became that troubled borough's mayor, thought at the beginning of the war that "There was a pretty prevalent belief among numbers of Londoners that the Jews would panic if ever raiding became very bad."[53] Government too, members of the cabinet among them, shared these nervous prejudices about the Jewish East Enders – Jews still cast as "alien."[54] Once bombing began then rumours of shelter-hogging spread across London and beyond. George Orwell, weekending at Wallington, Hertfordshire, in October 1940, was told "that Jews greatly predominate among the people sheltering in the Tubes." He set out to "verify" the rumour and ten days later somehow managed to convince himself there was something in it:

> 25.10.40 The other night examined the crowds sheltering in Chancery Lane, Oxford Circus and Baker Street stations. Not all Jews, but, I think, a higher proportion of Jews than one would normally see in a crowd of this size. What is bad about Jews is that they are not only conspicuous, but go out of their way to make themselves so. A fearful Jewish woman, a regular comic-paper cartoon of a Jewess, fought her way off the train at Oxford Circus, landing blows on anyone who stood in her way.[55]

The old stereotypes proved hard to shift, for middle-class intellectual and East End cockney alike: quarrels among people queuing for shelter reportedly dragged in the Jewish origins of some of those waiting in line, in the early days of the blitz at least.[56]

Similarly too, the flight of Jews from danger, such a feature of the 1917–1918 events, was resurrected. Now it was Llandudno that was "Jerusalem-by-the-Sea." And although every Jewish family leaving London was overwhelmed by scores or even hundreds to one of their Gentile neighbours, it was "the image of the timid Jew" that stuck in the popular imagination. Even the "new-rich" Jew of the 1917 *Saturday Review* was reinvented in "the alleged ostentatious 'Golders Green' nouveau-riche Jew" of 1940–1941.[57]

At almost every turn then, even in the vicious propaganda of the BUF and other right-wing groupings, the anti-Semitic platform of 1939–1945 was built, plank by plank and nail by nail, between 1916 and 1918. Even the phrases of the discourse, word for word, might sometimes be the same. These were prejudices that, as in the case of the Bethnal Green disaster of 3 March 1943, were immune to evidence and impervious to fact: anti-Semitism, thought Orwell, "is at bottom quite irrational and will not yield to argument." Certainly the old prejudices cemented in the First World War and revived in the Second would prove hard to shake off. When the psychologist James Robb, a New Zealander, investigated anti-Semitism in the working-class streets of Bethnal Green in 1947–1949, his "extreme" Jew-haters justified their prejudice by claiming that Jews "are cowardly, did not join the army," and "ran away during the blitz."[58]

In fact, as Robb and many others of his respondents pointed out, the shared experience of the blitz in the Jewish and the wider East End revealed the courage of many Jews and cockneys while showing that not all of either was always and everywhere hero or heroine. Atavistic anti-Semites accounted for just nine of his sample of a hundred and three interviewees while forty-four, the largest group, though having some stereotyped notions of "the Jews" were not hostile to them, and eighteen were considered "tolerant."[59] "Jews are good and bad the same as anyone else," was the most frequently expressed view of this group.[60] And although some old scars stubbornly refused to heal in working-class attitudes to Jews, some of the old ghosts of the First World War were laid to rest in the Second. Despite the anti-Semitism of these years, it was in fact more the Second World War than the First that proved the catalyst in integrating London's Jewish immigrants and their children.

Acknowledgements

I'm very grateful for the assistance I have received from Darren Bryant, Ian Castle, David Feldman, Anne Kershen, Ann Stephenson, Jo Till, and the staff of the British Library Newsroom, The National Archives, and the Wiener Library.

Notes

1 L.R. Dunne, *Report on an Inquiry into the Accident at Bethnal Green Tube Station Shelter on the 3rd March, 1943* (Cmd. 6583, London, 1945), pp. 4–7. These events have recently had a fictional resurrection: see J.F. Kane, *The Report* (London, 2010).
2 TNA, HO 205/231, letter of 11 March to L.R. Dunne from Gordon Liverman, chairman of the Jewish Defence Committee of the Board of Deputies of British Jews.
3 TNA INF 1/292 part 3, Home Intelligence Weekly Report, 2–9 March 1943, pp. 194ff. See also TNA HO 205/379, Dunne Tube Shelter Inquiry, Transcript of Evidence, evidence of Police Superintendent Hill and Divisional Inspector Hunt.
4 Dunne, *Report*, p. 12.
5 *The Times*, 9 April 1943.
6 TNA HO 205/236, Anonymous Correspondence. I take it the writer was a man: he claimed he would lose his "position" if he identified himself.
7 The key text remains T. Kushner, *The Persistence of Prejudice: Anti-Semitism in British society during the Second World War* (Manchester, 1989); see also T.P. Linehan, *East London for Moseley: The British Union of Fascists in East London and South-West Essex 1933–40* (London, 1996); H.F. Srebrnik, *London Jews and British Communism, 1935–1945* (Ilford, 1995); R. Griffiths, *Patriotism Perverted: Captain Ramsay, The Right Club and British Anti-Semitism 1939–40* (London, 1998); P. Willetts, *Rendezvous at the Russian Tea Rooms* (London, 2015).
8 G. Orwell, "Anti-Semitism in Britain," in *Essays* (London, 2014), pp. 278–87, especially pp. 280, 283, 285–6.
9 There are two honourable exceptions: C. Holmes, *Anti-Semitism in British Society, 1876–1939* (London, 1979), Ch. 8; J. Bush, *Behind the Lines: East London Labour 1914–1919* (London, 1984), Ch. 6, focusing mainly on prescription; see also J. White, *Zeppelin Nights: London in the First World War* (London, 2014), pp. 84–9.
10 T. Kushner, "The Impact of British Anti-semitism, 1918–1945," in D. Cesarani (ed.), *The Making of Modern Anglo-Jewry* (Oxford, 1990), pp. 191–208, p. 200. See also Kushner, *Persistence of Prejudice*, pp. 8–9.
11 White, *Zeppelin Nights*, p. 126.
12 The best account of the raid is in F. Morison, *War on Great Cities: A Study of the Facts* (London, 1937), pp. 37ff. The music hall is in TNA, MEPO 2/1650, report from H Division, 1 June 1915. E.S. Pankhurst, *The Home Front: A Mirror to Life in England during the World War* (London, 1932), pp. 192–4.
13 W. Sandhurst, *From Day to Day: 1914–1915* (London, 1928), pp. 292–3, 11–12 September 1915.

14 Morison, *War on Great Cities*, pp. 87ff. Mrs D. Humphreys, *Recollections of a Literary Life* (London, 1936), pp. 236–7, was at Wyndham's Theatre that night. R. Macaulay, *Non-Combatants and Others* (London, 1916), p. 64. Sandhurst, *From Day to Day*, pp. 308–9, 13 October 1915. Most Londoners called the underground, the tube.

15 R.D. Blumenfeld, *All In A Lifetime* (London, 1931), p. 50 (11 February 1916).

16 Bush, *Behind the Lines*, Ch. 6.

17 Ibid., pp. 171ff.

18 For the British government's objectives see *Parliamentary Debates* (Commons), Vol. 84 (1916), cols. 178–9; Vol. 88 (1916), cols. 305–6. For the FJPC see Vol. 87 (1916), cols. 1187–8; Bush, *Behind the Lines*, pp. 174ff.

19 *East London Observer*, 2 September and 14 October 1916.

20 Ibid., 30 September 1916.

21 *The Times*, 25 July 1917. On the raid see *Parliamentary Debates* (Commons), Vol. 96 (1917), cols. 2096–7; for subsequent events see Bush, *Behind the Lines*, p. 181.

22 H.L. Cancellor, *The Life of a London Beak* (London, 1930), pp. 69–75. Much of this text is drawn from White, *Zeppelin Nights*, pp. 84–7.

23 White, *Zeppelin Nights*, pp. 212–5.

24 *East London Observer*, 21 and 28 July 1917.

25 The point is made in *East London Observer*, 28 July 1917.

26 *Jewish Chronicle*, 20 July 1917; other East Enders doing the same thing was pointed out in the issue of 27 July.

27 Ibid., 10 August 1917; a "minyan" is the ten men required for worship in an orthodox prayer meeting; the use here presumably refers to the intense competition of ten Jewish men seeking each deckchair.

28 J.B. Booth, *Miss "Billie" Tuchaud: Her Life and Letters* (London, 1918), p. 180; the 'Letters' were first published in the London weekly, *Town Topics*.

29 White, *Zeppelin Nights*, pp. 215–9.

30 N. Flower (ed.), *The Journals of Arnold Bennett*, 3 Vols. (London, 1932–3), Vol. II, p. 205. W. Beveridge, *Power and Influence* (London, 1953), p. 14. C.E. Playne, *Britain Holds On 1917, 1918* (London, 1933), pp. 147–8.

31 Aliens of any description were not mentioned in the article, even though Soho was the primary cosmopolitan district of London, with many French, Italians, Swiss and others living there.

32 *Daily Mail*, 28 September 1917; see also White, *Zeppelin Nights*, p. 88.

33 *Evening Standard*, 29 September 1917.

34 Ibid., 1 and 3 October 1917; see also 5 October 1917 for scenes at Hyde Park Corner.

35 Ibid., 1 October 1917; *East End News*, 5 October 1917; *East London Advertiser*, 6 October 1917.

36 J. Bickersteth (ed.), *The Bickersteth Diaries 1914–1918* (London, 1995), pp. 212–3; Playne, *Britain Holds On*, pp. 147–8; Anon [A. Lieck] *Narrow Waters: The Frst Volume of the Life and Thoughts of a Common Man* (London, 1935), p. 218.

37 *Daily Mail*, 27 September; see also among many others, *Evening Standard*, 21 September; *Jewish Chronicle*, 5 October 1917.

38 *East London Observer* 6 October 1917.

39 Ibid., 29 September 1917; Bush, *Behind the Lines*, pp. 181–2. For Jews' Island see Kushner, *Persistence of Prejudice*, pp. 60–1.

40 *East London Observer*, 29 September 1917.

41 White, *Zeppelin Nights*, p. 131.

42 *Jewish Chronicle*, 19 and 26 October 1917; *East London Advertiser*, 20 October 1917.

43 White, *Zeppelin Nights*, pp. 249–50.

44 *East London Advertiser*, 9 February 1918.

45 Ibid., 2 February; *Evening Standard*, 30 January 1918.

46 *Daily Mail*, 19, 20, 21 March 1918.

47 Ibid., 23 March and 3 April 1918; see also *The Times*, 22, 27, 28 March, 2 and 5 April 1918.

48 *Daily Mail*, 5 April 1918.
49 Mrs E. Alec-Tweedie, *Women and Soldiers* (London, 1918), p. 112.
50 S. McKenna, *While I Remember* (London, 1921), p. 190. "A Forsyte Encounters the People, 1917," reprinted in J. White (ed.), *London Stories* (London, 2014), pp. 275–8. Cancellor, *London Beak*, pp. 76–86. W. Beveridge, *British Food Control* (London, 1928), p. 238. E. Tupper, *Seamen's Torch: The Life Story of Captain Edward Tupper, National Union of Seamen* (London, 1938), pp. 217–8.
51 Orwell, "Anti-Semitism," p. 282.
52 Linehan, *East London for Mosley*, pp. 168–70; and for contemporary anti-Semitic opinions, V. Brittain, *England's Hour* (London, 1941), p. 94.
53 F. Lewey, *Cockney Campaign* (London, 1944), pp. 80–1.
54 Kushner, *Persistence of Prejudice*, p. 53, citing Home Secretary Anderson at a cabinet meeting, August 1940.
55 P. Davison (ed.), *The Complete Works of George Orwell. Vol. 12. A Patriot After All 1940–1941* (London, 1998), p. 278.
56 Kushner, *Persistence of Prejudice*, pp. 54–5.
57 Ibid., pp. 65–6, 71–2. Llandudno was said to be the resort of Jews fleeing the cities of the north-west.
58 J. Robb, *Working-Class Anti-Semite: A Psychological Study in a London Borough* (London, 1954), pp. 107, 109, 116–7, 209.
59 Ibid., Ch. 5.
60 Ibid., Ch. 7.

Select Bibliography

Julia Bush, *Behind the Lines: East London Labour 1914–1919* (London, 1984).
Tony Kushner, *The Persistence of Prejudice: Anti-Semitism in British Society during the Second World War* (Manchester, 1989).
Thomas P. Linehan, *East London for Mosley: The British Union of Fascists in East London and South-West Essex 1933–40* (London, 1996).
Henry F. Srebrnik, *London Jews and British Communism, 1935–1945* (Ilford, 1995).
Jerry White, *Zeppelin Nights: London in the First World War* (London, 2014).

7

WINNING THE BATTLE, BUT WHAT ABOUT THE WAR?

Cable Street in Context

Daniel Tilles

Thirty years ago, a book remarkably similar to this one was published: a collection of essays honouring the career of a British scholar of immigrant background who pioneered 'history from below,' eschewing the traditional focus on elites and instead examining events from the perspective of ordinary people. That man was George Rudé, and one of the contributors to the volume was Bill Fishman. As well as their similar backgrounds and careers, the two men shared something else in common: on 4 October 1936, both had been present at the Battle of Cable Street, the most celebrated anti-fascist event in British history, at which a crowd of over 100,000 demonstrators prevented the march of Oswald Mosley's black-shirted British Union of Fascists (BUF) through the streets of East London. Fishman attended as a local teenager, one of thousands of East End Jews terrorised by the BUF's anti-Semitic campaigning in the area; and Rudé as a newly graduated teacher, whose travels to the Soviet Union had left him, "a committed communist and anti-Fascist."[1]

It was therefore apt that Fishman devoted his chapter in that book to Cable Street. In typical fashion, he presented the event through the eyes of local residents (or "my people," as he unapologetically described them)[2] while also contextualising it and dispelling certain popular myths. Drawing on his intimate knowledge of the East End, Fishman delved into the longer-term relationship between local Jews and non-Jews before the arrival of the fascists. Dismissing facile stereotypes of ethnic conflict, he instead described a coexistence that was characterised by "reasonable amity" between residents of all ethnic backgrounds in this impoverished, diverse part of London. Yet he also admitted that Jews had created a "quasi-ghetto" for themselves, in particular due to their "persistence in adhering to 'alien' customs." This made them "vulnerable as ready-made scapegoats for local discontent," a fact that the fascists eagerly exploited when they began their East End campaign in the mid-1930s.[3] Here, however, they failed in their aim; indeed, they induced precisely the opposite effect, as was demonstrated perfectly at Cable Street. Instead of driving a wedge between different communities, they united the disparate people of East London in a shared rejection of fascism. As Fishman later told *The Guardian*: "We were all side by side. I was moved to tears to see bearded Jews and Irish Catholic dockers standing up to stop Mosley."[4]

Despite this clear sense of pride at the Jewish role in resisting the Blackshirts, Fishman strongly rejected the "interactionist analysis" that by the 1980s had become (and today remains) widespread among scholars of British fascism. This school of thought – established by Robert Skidelsky's overly sympathetic 1975 biography of Mosley – posits that Jews were themselves in part to blame for inciting fascist hostility due to their aggressive opposition to the BUF in its early days, despite Mosley's public rejection of anti-Semitism. In actual fact, as Fishman rightly noted, initial Jewish wariness of domestic fascism was completely warranted, especially given concurrent events in Germany (Mosley barely concealed his admiration for Hitler, whose portrait hung in his study). Even then, widespread and sustained Jewish involvement in anti-fascist activity began only *after* the Blackshirts commenced their anti-Semitic campaigning in the East End. "Jews, in the front line of attack," Fishman argued, "had no alternative but to resist."[5]

Fishman was also prepared to confront misconceptions common on the Jewish side of this struggle. In particular, he challenged the notion that the police were sympathetic towards the fascists and antagonistic towards their opponents, especially Jews. Though Fishman acknowledged that sometimes the police had "to be forceful in protecting the Fascists" from aggressive opposition, and that there may have been some officers who admired "the BUF's uniform, military discipline and patriotic discipline," in reality the situation was "more complex." In fact, when it came to the local police who "lived and worked among the immigrants[,] … there is a wealth of evidence" demonstrating they were "disposed to be friendly towards the law-abiding Jews."[6]

Thirty years on, I shall return to the subject of Fishman's contribution to Rudé's volume, and aim to approach it in the same spirit of challenging, contextualising and adding nuance to established historical narratives that characterised Fishman's work. In doing so, parts of his account will be updated and refined, while further layers of the mythology that have grown around Cable Street will be peeled away. Indeed, as Fishman himself observed, that mythology began to emerge on the day of the event itself. As participants celebrated their success, "wild tales, true and false, exchanged by comrades throughout that night and passed on from generation to generation, would make for the creation of another East End legend – the Battle of Cable Street."[7] If there is one fault to be found in Fishman's own telling of the history, it his over-reliance on the accounts left by these participants. While this was, at the time, a necessary counterweight to the direction of historical research into British fascism (which itself relied too heavily on the Blackshirts' version of events), Fishman swung the pendulum a little too far in the other direction. In doing so, he demonstrated both the advantages and drawbacks of people's history: by presenting events from a novel perspective he shed new light on them, but in doing so obscured parts of the wider picture.

Above all, by viewing Cable Street primarily through the eyes of those who organised and took part in the demonstration, Fishman neglected the perspectives of the other participants in the wider fascist/anti-fascist struggle: not just the Blackshirts themselves, but also opponents of the BUF who eschewed confrontational methods (who in fact made up the majority of Britain's anti-fascists), as well as the state authorities. Thus, Fishman's conclusion that Cable Street was a "humiliating defeat for Mosley" and a "turning point" after which fascism went into decline – an interpretation favoured by many participants – is at best partially true.[8] By taking a broader, longer-term view, we see that, in fact, the Battle was just one episode (albeit an important one) in a more complex ongoing relationship between fascists, anti-fascists and the state. And, although the anti-fascists clearly succeeded in their aim of stopping the Blackshirt march on the day, Cable Street actually provided a boost to Mosley in the medium term, winning him publicity, sympathy and support. Even worse, it was used by the fascists to justify launching the most intensive period of anti-Semitism in modern British history.

Prelude: The Background to the Battle

It is first of all vital to understand what the 4 October march meant for its organisers. It marked the culmination of a period of great flux for the BUF. Initially, upon forming the party in late 1932, Mosley had aimed to present an outwardly reputable brand of fascism, one he felt would be best suited to the British political environment. This strategy meant publicly disavowing anti-Semitism, claiming that his followers would use force only "defensively," and seeking a legal, electoral path to power. For eighteen months or so these tactics appeared to be working, with the party attracting a great deal of positive interest and support. It reached its peak membership of around 50,000 by mid-1934, and secured the tacit or explicit endorsement of various establishment figures, most notably the press magnate Lord Rothermere, whose newspapers, including the *Daily Mail*, provided the fascists with publicity. But these efforts collapsed following the BUF's Olympia meeting in mid-1934, when the violent treatment of anti-fascist protesters at the hands of Blackshirt stewards stripped away the party's respectable façade and pushed it beyond the boundaries of mainstream politics.

The fascists, now at their lowest ebb, were internally divided over the best way forward. One faction saw the loss of more moderate members as an opportunity. A.K. Chesterton, a leading propagandist, celebrated the departure of the "chicken-hearted democrats" and "right-wing Tories" who had swelled the BUF's ranks in its early days, but whose participation in the movement had always been "half-hearted," "unreliable," even "embarrassing."[9] He and others around him (such as Alexander Raven Thomson and William Joyce, better known today as the wartime Nazi broadcaster Lord Haw Haw) felt that no longer having to pander to such supporters could liberate the BUF to focus on propagating an authentic, radical fascist ideology.[10] They regarded anti-Semitism as central to this and, consequently, in autumn 1934 the party officially declared its opposition to Jews.

Yet, at the same time, another influential group within the BUF leadership still clung to the hope of pursuing more traditional political methods. They continued efforts to build up the party's electoral machinery and put together a plan to stand one hundred candidates at the next general election.[11] This faction sought to tone down the more extreme aspects of policy favoured by the abovementioned clique – in particular anti-Semitism – for fear of deterring mainstream support. Finally, a third group argued for downplaying ideological propagation completely, and instead wanted the party to focus its energies on the streets, through militant forms of activity such as uniformed marches.[12]

These factions each held Mosley's ear at different times and, consequently, for a period of two years after Olympia, the party struggled to settle on a stable direction. What helped to resolve this issue was the BUF's growing popularity in East London, where its active style of politics, patriotic populism aimed at the working class, and anti-Semitism struck a chord in an economically deprived area that housed the country's largest (and, as Fishman noted, still relatively unassimilated) Jewish population. It was never, of course, more than a minority who supported the Blackshirts in the East End, but it was nevertheless a significant and vocal minority. From late 1935, the BUF launched an intensive campaign there, comprising open-air meetings, marches and propaganda drives, all saturated by a crude anti-Semitism and accompanied by severe verbal and physical harassment of the local Jewish community.

Initially this activity was to some degree separate from national campaigning. But over 1936 the two increasingly aligned, as the BUF came to terms with its collapse as a national force and realised that the East End provided its most – indeed really the only – fertile territory. In June 1936, Mosley gave his first public address in the East End.[13] The next month, the party announced that it would stand six candidates in East End districts at the London County Council (LCC) elections in March 1937, in what would be the first election campaign in its history.[14] Then, in September, plans were revealed for a procession to be held on 4 October, to celebrate the fourth anniversary of the party's founding. The fact that the East End was chosen as a venue, with Blackshirts to be bussed in from around the country, was confirmation that the area had now become the party's primary focus. Moreover, the nature of its activity was a clear signal of which factions now held greater sway. Hopes of a respectable path to power had been put to one side, in favour of an approach that combined a radical, anti-Semitic fascist ideology with militant street action.

It is in this context that we can understand what the true purpose of the 4 October march was – and what it was not. Although billed as a celebration of the party's progress and a show of strength, in reality the Blackshirts would have been aware that, despite having built a base of support in the East End, they were still far outnumbered by their opponents. Moreover, those opponents had shown themselves to be increasingly willing to physically disrupt fascist events, and they would certainly be likely to do so at what was the BUF's largest ever procession, the route of which would pass through areas of high Jewish population. The fascists, therefore, knew that the march would in all likelihood provoke disruption and disorder – but this was precisely their purpose, for such an outcome was to their benefit, for three interrelated reasons.

First, by this stage the party was struggling to gain media attention. Only when serious disorder broke out at its events would the press provide coverage. One Blackshirt complained that there was a "campaign of total silence" against the BUF, with its meetings meriting attention only if "violence [was] initiated … by the extreme Left."[15] Second, aggressive opposition to the march would play perfectly into Mosley's carefully cultivated image of victimhood. He presented his party as the embodiment of the British people, whose voices were silenced and rights violated by a combination of the corrupt old political parties, the media, international financial interests and violent left-wing revolutionaries, all of whom were controlled by Jews. This sense of victimhood became a central feature of the party's political narrative, and a justification for its self-proclaimed "defensive" violence and anti-Semitism.[16] As such, when the fascists aroused violent opposition, this was portrayed as a sign of success, indicating that they were challenging vested interests. As one of Mosley's colleagues privately advised him: "The strength of a new movement is in direct proportion to the resistance offered to it."[17] Third, the fact that the BUF, which made conspicuous efforts to remain on the right side of the law was confronted by opponents who often acted aggressively and illegally, did elicit sympathy in certain quarters. For example, although the Olympia fiasco led to an exodus of respectable followers, in its immediate aftermath a stream of new members joined the BUF. In Parliament, some MPs expressed support for, or at least toleration of, its method of dealing with hecklers.[18]

Thus, the Cable Street march was not intended as a genuine show of strength; rather, it was an act of desperation by a struggling movement, which aimed to stir up aggressive opposition, especially from Jews, thereby winning headlines, sympathy and superficial substantiation for the party's political narrative. In the build-up, the BUF attempted to lay the groundwork for its depiction of the event, by stressing its peaceful, lawful intentions and drawing attention to the likelihood of anti-fascist disruption. It contacted the Commissioner of the Metropolitan Police, Philip Game, to outline a route for the march and request permission to proceed; this was later followed by a personal letter from Mosley pledging full cooperation with the police.[19] On the eve of the march, the fascist leader declared that "violence is illegal and injures our cause," and the party needed to be "clever" in its approach to Jews, avoiding "mere abuse."[20] A Blackshirt spokesman told the press that the fascists would "keep away from Jewish quarters as much as possible." The BUF's "sole object is to lay our case before the public," but unfortunately this had been threatened by anti-fascists making "the most extreme incitements to violence" and "organis[ing] … an attack on this procession."[21]

Yet behind the scenes, the fascists were openly discussing their true intentions. Police sources reported that "an influential section of headquarters" – led by Joyce and Raven Thomson – was "evolving a plan" for an anti-Semitic speech to be made on 4 October that would be "pungent" enough to provoke Jews and invite prosecution from the authorities, yet so "carefully prepared," under the advice of legal counsel, as to "leave few or no grounds for successful [legal] action." Joyce told a meeting of Blackshirt speakers that deliberately courting arrest in this manner would be used both to demonstrate "police persecution" of the fascists and to "intensify antagonism towards Jews."[22]

As this suggests, the authorities were fully aware of the fascists' true purpose – and it caused them great frustration. It is well documented that the upper ranks of the police and Home Office were hostile towards the BUF.[23] The fascists' use of anti-Semitism caused particular alarm – partly out of sympathy for the Jewish victims, but largely due to the more pragmatic concern that it was this aspect of BUF activity which was the primary cause of public disorder. Thus, in July 1936, the Home Secretary issued orders to the Metropolitan Police to "intervene promptly if they hear grossly provocative and abusive language towards the Jews," and to investigate thoroughly any allegations of assaults against Jews.[24] Yet, as much as they may have wanted to, it was hard for the authorities to go much further under the existing law. The BUF was a legitimate political organisation, whose right to free speech and assembly had to be respected, including the freedom to criticise whomever it wished, as long as it remained within the bounds of the law. Moreover, government action to restrict or prohibit the activity of a single political party would, it was feared, set a dangerous precedent. Singling out the fascists in this way would also be exploited by Mosley to his advantage, used as evidence to substantiate the image of victimhood he sought to create.

Such concerns were aired in the discussions that took place in the lead up to the fascists' 4 October march. Senior officials wondered whether "the time has come for consideration whether these entirely provocative demonstrations should not be banned," given that they were designed "merely to zig-zag through and round Jewish quarters for purposes of provocation." Game, however, warned the Home Secretary that taking action to restrict or prohibit a march simply because some local residents opposed it would make it "very difficult to draw the line between … which meetings and marches could and could not be allowed." Another senior Home Office figure, Frank Newsam, feared that banning the march on the grounds of inevitable disorder would allow Mosley to accuse the authorities of losing control of the streets. Even taking less punitive action would lead to fascist cries of "persecution." After consulting the Director of Public Prosecutions, Newsam advised that, in light of the limitations of the law, the best approach was to allow the procession to take place, but to use a police cordon to keep fascists and anti-fascists apart.[25]

What is perhaps most surprising, given that the Battle of Cable Street has become associated with confrontational opposition to fascism, is that very similar conversations were taking place within the ranks of Britain's anti-fascist organisations. They were equally aware of the BUF's true purpose in arranging the 4 October event, and keen to avoid falling into Mosley's trap by responding aggressively. Although eventually they were forced to take such a course of action, this was decided upon only at the very last minute, after all other options had been exhausted. And even then, many anti-fascists had great misgivings about physically opposing the fascist march – fears that the aftermath of the Battle proved well founded.

Although this period is remembered as one of intense conflict between the fascists and their opponents, especially Jews, in East London, in actual fact the BUF's early East End campaigning over 1935 and the first half of 1936 had met with only sporadic and *ad hoc* resistance. When Mosley gave his Victoria Park speech in June, he faced little disruption from the crowd of 15,000.[26] Even on occasions when his opponents did manage to coordinate larger-scale demonstrations, relatively few Jews participated. For example, after a mass protest outside a BUF meeting at the Albert Hall in March, there were complaints from anti-fascists at the poor Jewish turnout.[27] A Home Office official noted that the only reason the East End had not seen more serious violence was because Jews, despite deliberate and severe fascist provocation, had remained "submissive under insult."[28]

This tentative early approach stemmed in large part from a fear that responding aggressively to fascist provocation would be to play into Mosley's hands. This was precisely the warning broadcast by the Labour Party and Board of Deputies of British Jews, which advised their followers to stay away from fascist events.[29] Yet even among groups associated with a more assertive response to fascism there was a marked hesitancy to take a physical approach. The General Secretary of the Communist Party of Great Britain (CPGB), for example, warned his comrades at a central committee meeting that it would be "fatal for us … [if] opposition to Mosley is looked upon … as being in the nature of a brawl and not a real political struggle." Although the Communists should seek to "bring the masses into the fight against Mosley[,] … it is not a question of merely smashing up the[ir] meeting[s];" rather, they should make a political "case against the fascists."[30] In an internal party document laying out policies for attracting Jewish support on the back of the BUF's encroachment into East London, the author suggested that fascist violence should not be responded to in kind, but rather through press campaigns, legal action and political agitation.[31]

The same message was heard even among grassroots East End activists. Phil Piratin, a leading figure in the predominantly Jewish Stepney CPGB branch, argued vociferously for tackling the Blackshirts politically and ideologically, rather than through physical confrontation.[32] Another leading Jewish Communist in Stepney, Joe Jacobs, noted that many anti-fascists "doubt[ed] the correctness of opposing all Mosley's efforts to hold meetings," because they wanted to avoid "behaving like the Fascists themselves." Though Jacobs himself was a proponent of more aggressive action, he regarded this as a necessary evil, forced upon Jews by fascist aggression and police indifference. "This was not a question of how we attacked Mosley's forces and the police, but how we defended ourselves from them."[33]

Among anti-fascists, just as with the Blackshirts and the state authorities, the build-up to the 4 October march conformed to these longer-term patterns. Until the very last minute, it looked as though Mosley would march with little opposition. In a letter to the Home Secretary, Game confidently predicted: "I do not anticipate any serious trouble."[34] This prognosis was based on the fact that, across Britain's anti-fascist forces, there was an evident reluctance to fall into the fascists' trap by responding aggressively. The Labour Party and Jewish communal leaders pleaded with their supporters to avoid the march. The CPGB, had, before the fascists announced their plans, already arranged its own demonstration on Trafalgar Square to take place on the same day. Not only did it remain committed to this event, but it actively sought to dissuade its followers from opposing Mosley in East London. A leaflet published by its London District Committee warned: "Beware of Provocation! … Dignity, Order and Discipline must characterise the actions of the great masses of London people in their protest against Fascism."[35]

There were some, particularly among East End Jews, for whom such passivity was unacceptable. Yet even here, a confrontational approach was not initially favoured. For example, although the Jewish People's Council Against Fascism and Anti-Semitism (JPC) came to play a central role in organising the Cable Street demonstration, this course of action was a last resort, one that it took all possible steps to avoid. At first, it pursued legal avenues to have the march banned altogether. One of its leaflets called on opponents of the march to protest to their MP, mayor and the police.[36] It collected almost 100,000 signatures on a petition that drew attention to the procession's aim of "deliberate provocation" and demanded its prohibition. This was presented to the Home Office by a JPC-led deputation, which included a local Labour MP and the secretaries of the London Trades Council and National Council for Civil Liberties. Their plea was, however, rejected on the usual grounds that the authorities did not want to restrict the fascists' free speech or give Mosley an excuse to play the victim.[37]

Even then, many in the JPC's leadership continued to reject the idea of physically obstructing the procession. However, they were eventually outvoted by their more militant counterparts. Yet still a final warning was made to the authorities that disorder would be inevitable if the fascist march was allowed to go ahead.[38] The Ex-Servicemen's Movement Against Fascism, another leading Jewish anti-fascist force, was similarly split. Days before the march, debate was still raging within the organisation: many wanted to go no further than lining the procession's route and expressing opposition verbally as it passed; others favoured physical obstruction; and some even called for protestors to arm themselves with coshes and beat the fascists back.[39]

This progression towards a confrontational approach in turn influenced the CPGB's stance, as it attempted to respond to the demands of its increasingly restive East End members. Initially, while it insisted the demonstration in Trafalgar Square should still go ahead, it agreed that afterwards a march would be made to the East End to protest against fascism.[40] But eventually, just three days before the procession was due to take place, the Communist leadership relented entirely, cancelling its own event and calling on people instead to rally to the East End, with the intention of blocking the Blackshirts' path.[41] Even then, the party's organiser in East London warned its followers to "keep order" and provide "no excuse" for it to be said that "we, like the BUF, are hooligans."[42]

Aftermath: The Consequences of Cable Street

The events of the Battle itself are well known, and not worth reiterating in great detail. A vast crowd, at least 100,000 strong, gathered to block the path of Mosley's 2,000 or so black-shirted followers. However, the two opposing sides actually barely came into contact with one another. Instead, it was primarily a clash between the anti-fascists and the 6,000 police officers deployed by Game, who met strong resistance as they sought to clear a path for the pre-agreed route of the march. Having failed to do so, Game advised Mosley to call off the procession and disband his followers.

As Fishman noted, the Battle immediately began to pass into anti-fascist and Jewish lore, portrayed as a decisive victory against the fascists. Speaking at a cele-bratory meeting organised by the CPGB on the evening of the march itself, one speaker revealed that a name for the event had already been established:

> Today will go down in history as the Battle of Cable Street in the war against Fascism. The advance guard of the anti-fascists put up one of the greatest fights ever known, and succeeded in completely demoralising the Fascist ranks. ... Mosley has sustained a crushing defeat.[43]

Fishman himself, in a later interview, claimed that "Mosley's popularity began to wane after his setback in Cable Street ... Never again would the [fascist] ideology be so popular."[44] Another participant in the Battle, Ted Grant, claimed that "it induced widespread despondency and demoralisation in the [fascist] ranks;" as a result, "the East End fascist movement declined," proving that "only vigorous counter-action hinders the growth of the menace of fascism."[45] Morris Beckman, a local Jewish resident, later described it as a "watershed event" that had a "devas-tating ... effect on the fascists ... That morning proved to be the high water mark of the British Union of Fascists hubris and arrogance. Th[at] very moment ... the tide began to recede."[46] It is this image of the Battle that has become deeply rooted in popular memory.

Yet among academic historians, a rather different analysis of the Battle has developed in the three decades since Fishman published his chapter on the subject. Nigel Copsey, who has written the most authoritative work on the history of British anti-fascism, argues that the perception of Cable Street as *the* defining moment in the struggle against the BUF is unjustified. "Because [it] was such a spectacular event, its contribution to the failure of British fascism is typically exag-gerated." Moreover, a focus on the aggressive, confrontational approach epitomised by Cable Street – which, as we have seen, was not something most anti-fascists were comfortable with – has "obscure[d] ... the structure and complexity of anti-fascist opposition."[47] Within the historiography of British fascism, there is a wide-spread feeling that even the very idea of Cable Street as a defeat for the BUF "requires some qualification." In actual fact, the event gave the party a boost in terms of public interest, sympathy and membership.[48] This was, in part, because the image evoked by the Cable Street protestors – who had violently prevented a legal march from taking place – was "precisely the one that the [fascists] wished to create."[49] Worst of all, the Battle "did nothing to dampen anti-Semitic agitation in the East End" (and in fact, as we shall see, it intensified it).[50] As David Cesarani concluded: "Although Mosley's parade was blocked, violence against Jews in East London did not abate, nor did the fortunes of the BUF decline significantly. Violence continued and feelings of neglect ran high."[51]

Not all scholars adhere to such a line. Tony Kushner and Nadia Valman, for example, criticise the "fashion ... to debunk the significance of the Battle of Cable Street," arguing that historians have given undue weight to the sources left by fascists and the police, both of whom had a vested interest in downplaying the anti-fascists' victory.[52] However, Kushner also admits that the Battle has fallen victim to a complex "relationship between history, memory and myth," which are "not always happy bedfellows."[53] As such – and in light of the continued discrepancy between popular perceptions of Cable Street and academic accounts – it is vital to untangle these threads. The mythologised memory of Cable Street is important in its own right, but it must be separated from the historical reality of the event, and in particular its aftermath, which will now be examined using a range of contemporary material broader than that employed by other researchers, incorporating anti-fascist and Jewish sources, as well as those left behind by the BUF and the state.

An immediate consequence was that, just as the anti-fascists immediately began to establish their narrative of the Battle, so too the BUF set about using the event to substantiate its own, long-established image of victimhood at Jewish hands. After Game had ordered the fascists to call off their march, they regrouped outside Blackshirt headquarters in Westminster, where Mosley told them that Game's decision offered further proof "the government of Britain has surrendered to Jewish corruption." Across London in Bethnal Green, one of Mosley's East End organisers, Ernest "Mick" Clarke, delivered precisely the same message to a Blackshirt audience, proclaiming that "the marches this afternoon have been banned" because "the Government is not a British Government; it is a Jew Government."[54] The first issue of the BUF's newspaper published after the Battle declared at the top of its front page that the demonstration had been "Jewry's Biggest Blunder," and accused the authorities of "Openly Surrender[ing] to Alien Mobs."[55]

This, moreover, was no ephemeral burst of anger; rather, it marked the start of the most intensive period of anti-Jewish activity in the BUF's history, ostensibly in retaliation for the Cable Street demonstration. In the days following the Battle, a source within Blackshirt headquarters – who was secretly passing information to the Board of Deputies – revealed that the party leadership was to use the event as the basis for a "renewed anti-Semitic campaign."[56] And, true enough, over the following months Blackshirt propaganda exhibited a marked and sustained rise in the quantity of anti-Jewish rhetoric, which also became more crude and extreme in tone.[57] Even more troublingly, this language was accompanied by a growing physical threat against Jews in the East End. During his speech immediately after the failed Cable Street march, Clarke angrily declared, "by God there is going to be a pogrom ... [and] the people who have caused the pogrom to come in East London are the Yids."[58] His words proved prophetic: just a week later, inter-war Britain's most serious outbreak of anti-Jewish violence took place, in what came to be known as the "Mile End Pogrom." Newspapers reported on the "Sunday of terror in East End streets," as a couple of hundred "hooligans, shouting Fascist cries, swept down Mile End Road smashing and looting the windows of Jewish shopkeepers." As well as damage to property, Jewish-looking individuals were attacked with bottles and planks of wood, while a Jewish man and child were thrown through a window.[59] Such outbursts of violence continued sporadically over the following months. The next summer, the JPC expressed concern at the "intensification of fascist Jew-baiting and ... terrorism which appears to increase week by week."[60]

The rise in anti-Jewish activity after Cable Street was also closely tied to the BUF's campaign for the LCC elections. Among the six candidates it had put forward in East London districts were Joyce and Raven Thomson. Their prominence reflected the fact that the BUF had chosen to fight its first ever election campaign on a platform centred around anti-Semitism. Now that any ambitions of rapid national success had been abandoned, the party hoped instead to use the East End as a launch pad for progress elsewhere. In its election leaflets, the BUF declared that "no one knows better ... the stranglehold that Jewry has on our land" than residents of the East End, "who have suffered most from Jewish tyranny." They should, therefore, "send to all England the message" that by voting for fascism they can "strike the first great blow for British freedom and ... shake alien Jewish power to its foundations."[61]

Cable Street itself took a prominent place in this narrative. In a set of instructions for speakers on the LCC campaign, the BUF's propaganda department observed that local residents had been "gravely offended by the rioting of Jews and Communists last October." This "impudent use of violence on the streets ... to deny East Londoners the right to walk through their own part of London ... [had] sent a wave of anti-Jewish resentment through East London."[62] In a rallying cry on the eve of the LCC vote, Chesterton congratulated the party's followers for their "splendid success in overcoming the Jew-Red terrorism in the streets," and called on them to use the election as a chance to prove that such "riots" were the work of aliens, and should not be "mistaken for the authentic voice of British manhood." Success in East London would show that "the reconquest of Britain by the British has begun."[63]

While it would be easy to dismiss such rhetoric as mere wishful thinking on the part of the fascists, the evidence suggests that their prognosis had at least some merit. The aftermath of Cable Street saw a rise in support for the Blackshirts, in part due to their success in portraying themselves as victims of Jewish aggression. In late October, the police recorded "abundant evidence that the Fascism [sic] movement has been steadily gaining ground in many parts of East London," with around 2,000 new members joining (a huge increase, given that its estimated London membership earlier in the year had been below 3,000). Particularly prominent among the new joiners were those with "grievances against the Jews." Moreover, during this period the BUF had "conduct[ed] the most successful series of meetings since the beginning of the movement." It had been "enthusiastically received" at East End meetings that attracted audiences in the thousands, with virtually no organised opposition. The police concluded that "a definite pro-fascist feeling has manifested itself throughout the [East End] districts … and the alleged fascist defeat is in reality a fascist advance."[64]

This boost in support was enduring. At the LCC elections, which took place five months after Cable Street, the BUF received votes from over 7,000 residents in the three East End districts it contested (Bethnal Green, Limehouse and Shoreditch). This represented an 18 per cent share of the vote, and an even higher percentage among the non-Jewish population (perhaps as much as 30 per cent in Bethnal Green).[65] Moreover, given that voting was restricted to ratepayers, thereby excluding much of the BUF's disproportionately young support, the overall number of supporters in the area would have been considerably higher than 7,000. In its analysis of the election, the *Young Zionist* newspaper estimated the true figure to be at least 20,000. "Fascism is becoming a political factor," its editor warned.[66] Even a year after Cable Street, this level of support had not diminished. In the October 1937 municipal elections, which had a much broader franchise, BUF candidates received around 24,600 votes in Stepney, Shoreditch and Bethnal Green combined. In the latter district, the party won 20 per cent of the vote. The Board of Deputies warned that "the results show conclusively that … the Fascists are still a danger in the London area."[67]

It should be noted that at neither set of elections did any BUF candidate win a seat (the closest being the runners-up spot in Bethnal Green). Yet the thousands of votes it received demonstrated that the party retained a strong base of support in the area. Indeed, the period *after* Cable Street was the peak of the party's strength in the East End. And this came not *despite* the Battle, but in part because of it, with the Blackshirts successfully exploiting the event to bolster their victimhood narrative and intensify their anti-Jewish campaign, both of which won new recruits to the cause.

Some have also argued that Cable Street had one further positive consequence: by creating such disorder, it prompted the authorities to clamp down on provocative fascist activity by passing the Public Order Act (POA), which banned political uniforms, allowed the authorities to prohibit political marches in specific districts, and reinforced laws on the use of abusive language or behaviour that would be likely to lead to a breach of the peace. The POA, claimed Fishman, "proved to be most effective against the Mosleyites … [and] marked the beginning of the decline of British Fascism."[68] Yet both contemporaries and historians have been divided as to its effectiveness, which was limited at best.[69]

The BUF sought to circumvent the uniform restrictions by advising followers to wear an ordinary black shirt and tie.[70] The Home Secretary did take up his right to implement a ban on marches in East London, which he continuously renewed through to 1939. However, this action displaced the problem rather than resolving it. First, the fascists just replaced processions with outdoor meetings, which were equally provocative. In August–December 1937, the police recorded 647 fascist meetings in the East End, a 27 per cent increase on the corresponding period a year earlier.[71] Meanwhile, marches still took place around the boundary of prohibited area. In October 1937, the Blackshirts held another anniversary procession just south of the river, in Bermondsey, which attracted a huge anti-fascist counter-demonstration. The resultant violence was even more severe than at Cable Street a year earlier, with over one hundred arrested and seventy seriously injured.[72] Yet Bermondsey is today barely remembered, no doubt because it does not comfortably fit the anti-fascist narrative that the fascists were decisively defeated in October 1936. Additionally, the prohibition on East End marches was exploited by the BUF to further bolster its claims of persecution. The authorities were accused of "bowing to the dictates of Jew[s]" by preventing the lawful activity of British fascists, effectively "hand[ing] over this quarter of London to Jewry, as the[ir] own territory."[73] Police intelligence suggested that the Blackshirts were "quite relieved" when a march was banned, as it saved them the embarrassment of being vastly outnumbered by their opponents and allowed them "to raise an outcry ... that the National Government ... favoured the Jews and Communists."[74]

Finally, the POA's provisions relating to use of provocative language were difficult to implement, relying as they did on the interpretation of officers on the ground as to whether a particular speech qualified as "abusive or insulting," and whether it would be likely to incite a breach of the peace. This resulted in inconsistent enforcement,[75] and had little effect on the fascists' anti-Semitic rhetoric. Indeed, in his monthly report for June 1937, Game noted that "abuse of Jews by Fascist speakers has shown a tendency to increase." He subsequently sent an angry memorandum to his subordinates chastising them for allowing "speakers at meetings ... [to] indulge in violently abusive language without any action whatever being taken."[76] The JPC complained in 1938 that "Mosley's men are now using more provocative language at their meetings than ever before."[77]

It is also important to note that the POA was not a specifically anti-fascist measure, and was used to restrict all forms of political activity in the East End. Indeed many contemporaries suspected that the authorities were simply using fascist-related disorder as an excuse to clamp down on the left-wing activity they were really more concerned about (a charge that has received a degree of support from historians). Anti-fascist groups such as the JPC, CPGB and the National Council for Civil Liberties made precisely such complaints, while also arguing that the POA provided police with no powers to restrict fascist activity that they did not already possess and left loopholes that would allow fascists to continue wearing uniforms and holding events.[78]

Indeed, it is the attitude of such anti-fascist groups that best illustrates the true consequences of the Battle. As noted above, the JPC – which had been heavily involved in organising opposition to the BUF's Cable Street march – observed with horror that, over the following year, fascist "terrorism" of East End Jews actually "intensified." The council's leaders, many of whom had already been sceptical as to whether confrontational anti-fascism was a wise policy, now turned decisively against it. JPC publications began warning supporters that the BUF's "purpose is … to cause disorder and incite breaches of the peace"; therefore disrupting its events would be "just the denial of Free Speech that the fascists want. DO NOT FALL INTO THEIR TRAP!"[79] When some anti-fascists began organising to oppose Mosley's Bermondsey march, the JPC refused to endorse the demonstration, warning that the fascists' events were "calculated to create breaches of the peace."[80] This change was mirrored within the CPGB, which as part of its efforts to build a broad united front against fascism moved away from confrontational activity.[81] One of its leaflets called on East End Jews to show "discipline" in the face of fascist provocation; if the BUF's meetings were simply "left alone" the party would "decline."[82] The police recorded a significant drop in the disruption of fascist events over the second half of 1937, with Game concluding that anti-fascists now "realise that active opposition is more likely to assist the Fascist cause than to hurt it."[83]

Conclusion

It was this growing restraint on the part of the anti-fascists, rather than their aggressive approach at Cable Street, that did the most to weaken the Blackshirts in East London. Increasingly starved of the attention and conflict they required to sustain themselves (and also suffering financial problems and continued factional infighting), from late 1937 the fascists began to reduce their emphasis on the East End and refocus on the national stage. Even then, this was far from a defeat. Mosley's "Peace campaign" to prevent Britain going to war with Nazi Germany gave the BUF renewed relevance and impetus, with tens of thousands flocking to its rallies and membership rising to around 20,000 in 1939, its highest level since Olympia. It was only the outbreak of war, which led to the forced dissolution of the BUF, that finally brought about its demise.

This, of course, contradicts the popular perception of Cable Street as a decisive victory against the Blackshirts, evicting them from the East End and condemning them to obscurity. One reason for this contrast is the fact that the anti-fascists were successful on a second battlefront, fought not for control of the streets but of memory. For both fascists and anti-fascists, Cable Street was used to reinforce pre-existing and competing narratives. On the fascist side, it was presented as further evidence that the BUF was, like the British people, being aggressively suppressed by alien Jews. For anti-fascists, the Blackshirts were the real alien menace, invading East End streets in which they were unwelcome to preach a foreign ideology that was not wanted, but being prevented from doing so by a diverse coalition drawn from across the area's ethnic communities.

It was the second narrative that eventually won out. The BUF was soon disbanded at home and its European counterparts defeated militarily abroad, in a war that served both to discredit their hateful ideology and to render the fight against fascism not just the preserve of the left, but a patriotic duty. Moreover, a number of trends in post-war Britain saw Cable Street become, in the words of Kushner and Valman, "useable history." For British Jews, it became their Stonewall, through which they could "assert both their integration within the local community … and their demand for respect as Jews." It also allowed them to feel that they had contributed to the wider European struggle against anti-Semitic fascism. For Britons more generally, it has been used to reinforce the notion that their country is peculiarly resistant to political extremism, and especially politicised forms of prejudice, while also fitting comfortably into the growing atmosphere of multiculturalism and inter-ethnic collaboration from the 1960s onwards.[84]

However, these emphases have obscured the fact that, in the months following Cable Street, it was the fascist narrative that won out in much of East London. The violent manner in which the Blackshirts had been prevented from marching through the streets elicited sympathy in certain quarters, and was effectively manipulated by the BUF to justify a vicious anti-Jewish campaign. To be clear, this is not to endorse the fascists' version of events, which was both false and odious. Nor should it detract from the heroism of those – a young Bill Fishman among them – who bravely and justly stood up to the fascists at Cable Street, Bermondsey and elsewhere. Yet honouring their memory should not come at the expense of acknowledging historical reality.

Notes

1 W. J.Fishman, "A People's Journée: The Battle of Cable Street (October 4th, 1936)," in F. Krantz (ed.), *History from Below: Studies in Popular Protest and Popular Ideology in Honour of George Rudé* (Montreal, 1985); "Obituary: Professor George Rude," *The Independent*, 16 January 1993.
2 W. Fishman, *East End Jewish Radicals* (London, 1975), p. xii.
3 Fishman, "People's Journée," pp. 381, 383.
4 Ibid., p. 389; A. Gillan, "Day the East End said 'No pasaran' to Blackshirts," *The Guardian*, 30 September 2006, www.theguardian.com/uk/2006/sep/30/thefarright.past, accessed 6 May 2016.
5 Fishman, "People's Journée," pp. 383–4. For a critique of interactionist theories, see D. Tilles, *British Fascist Antisemitism and Jewish Responses, 1932–40* (London, 2015), pp. 24–5, 41, 75–7.
6 Fishman, "People's Journée," pp. 390–1.
7 Ibid., p. 390.
8 Ibid., pp. 390–1.
9 A.K. Chesterton, *Portrait of a Leader* (London, n.d. [1937]), pp. 119–20, 128.
10 Tilles, *British Fascist Antisemitism*, pp. 80–83.
11 *The Blackshirt*, 7 November 1936, p. 4.
12 T.P. Linehan, *British Fascism 1918–39: Parties, Ideology and Culture* (Manchester, 2000), pp. 99–103; M. Pugh, *"Hurrah for the Blackshirts!": Fascists and Fascism in Britain Between the Wars* (London, 2005), pp. 20–22.
13 N. Copsey, *Anti-Fascism in Britain* (London, 2000), p. 51.
14 *The Blackshirt*, 18 July 1936, p. 4.
15 *Mosley's Blackshirts* (London, 1986), p. 63.

16 On the BUF's anti-Semitic rhetoric and ideology, see Tilles, *British Fascist Antisemitism*, pp. 31–74.

17 Fuller to Mosley, undated, University of Birmingham Special Collections, OMD/B/7/4.

18 Pugh, *Hurrah*, pp. 161–3; Thurlow, *Fascism in Britain: From Oswald Mosley's Blackshirts to the National Front* (London, 1998), pp. 63–4; M. Pugh, "The British Union of Fascists and the Olympia Debate," *The Historical Journal*, Vol. 41 (1998); J. Lawrence, "Fascist Violence and the Politics of Public Order in Inter-war Britain: The Olympia Debate Revisited," *Historical Research*, Vol. 76 (2003).

19 TNA MEPO 3/551/2A, 5A, 11B.

20 *The Blackshirt*, 3 October 1936, p. 1.

21 *Sunday Dispatch*, 4 October 1936.

22 TNA MEPO 3/551/4B; Commissioner's Report, September 1936, TNA MEPO 2/3043/274–82.

23 R. Thurlow, "State Management of the British Union of Fascists," in M. Cronin (ed.), *The Failure of British Fascism: The Far Right and the Fight for Political Recognition* (London, 1996), pp. 29, 31–4, 42; R. Thurlow, "Blaming the Blackshirts: The Authorities and The Anti-Jewish Disturbances in the 1930s," in P. Panayi (ed.), *Racial Violence in Britain in the Nineteenth and Twentieth Centuries* (London, 1996), pp. 114–5.

24 TNA MEPO 2/3043/229–34.

25 See TNA MEPO 3/551/4C-4E and minutes sheet.

26 *The Times*, 8 June 1936.

27 Copsey, *Anti-Fascism*, p. 45.

28 TNA MEPO 2/3087.

29 Copsey, *Anti-Fascism*, p. 57; G. Alderman, *Modern British Jewry* (Oxford, 1998), p. 292.

30 Labour History and Archives Study Centre (hereafter LHASC), minutes of CPGB Central Committee meetings, reel nos 5 & 6, pp. 15–16, 6 January 1934; Copsey, *Anti-Fascism*, pp. 49–50.

31 Untitled report, 21 May 1936, LHASC, minutes of CPGB Central Committee meetings, reel no. 8, 5 June 1936.

32 P. Piratin, *Our Flag Stays Red: An Account of Cable Street and Political Life in the East End of London* (London, 1978), pp. 17–9.

33 J. Jacobs, *Out of the Ghetto* (London, 1978), p. 151.

34 TNA MEPO 3/551/4C.

35 "Beware of Provocation!" LHASC CP/CENT/SUBJ/04/04; Copsey, *Anti-Fascism*, pp. 55–6.

36 "Stop Racial Incitement in East London!" (JPC, 1936), LHASC CP/ORG/MISC/07/06.

37 J. Pearce, "The Fascist Threat," in *The Circle: Golden Jubilee, 1909–1959* (London, 1961), pp. 20–1; Parkes Library Jewish Archives (hereafter PLJA) MS116/6 AJ10; "Report of Activities: July-November 1936," PLJA MS60 17/16; Copsey, *Anti-Fascism*, pp. 54–5.

38 Pearce, "Fascist Threat," p. 20.

39 TNA MEPO 3/551/10D.

40 TNA MEPO 3/551/10D.

41 District Bulletin No 24 of London District Committee of CPGB, 1 October 1936, LHASC CP/CENT/SUBJ/04/02; TNA MEPO 3/551/10G, 10L.

42 N. Copsey, "Communists and the Inter-War Anti-Fascist Struggle in the United States and Britain," *Labour History Review*, Vol. 76 (2011), p. 199.

43 Words paraphrased in Special Branch (SB) report, 4 October 1936, TNA MEPO 3/551/11Y. The name would not, however, come into widespread use until the 1970s.

44 W.J. Fishman, "The day I fought the Blackshirts in Battle of Cable Street," *Docklands and East London Advertiser*, 29 October 2008 (accessed 6 May 2016). http://www.eastlondonadvertiser.co.uk/news/heritage/the_day_i_fought_the_blackshirts_in_battle_of_cable_street_bill_fishman_1_666798.

45 T. Grant, *The Menace of Fascism: What It Is and How to Fight It* (London, 1948), p. 42.

46 M. Beckman, *The Hackney Crucible* (London, 1996), pp. xxix, 171.

47 Copsey, *Anti-Fascism*, p. 13.
48 T.P. Linehan, *East London for Mosley: The British Union of Fascists in East London and South-West Essex* (London, 1996), p. 10. See also Thurlow, *Fascism in Britain*, p. 81.
49 W.F. Mandle, *Anti-Semitism and the British Union of Fascists* (London, 1968), pp. 54–5.
50 Pugh, *Hurrah*, p. 227.
51 D. Cesarani, "The Transformation of Communal Authority in Anglo-Jewry, 1914–1940," in D. Cesarani (ed.), *The Making of Modern Anglo-Jewry* (Oxford, 1990), p. 130.
52 T. Kushner and N. Valman (eds), *Remembering Cable Street: Fascism and Anti-Fascism in British Society* (London, 2000), p. 280.
53 T. Kushner, "'Long May Its Memory Live!': Writing and Rewriting 'the Battle of Cable Street'," in Kushner and Valman (eds), *Remembering Cable Street*, pp. 110–1.
54 SB Report, 4 October 1936, TNA MEPO 3/551/11Y.
55 *The Blackshirt*, 10 October 1936, p. 1. On fascist representations of the Battle, see T. Linehan, "Fascist Perceptions of Cable Street," in Kushner and Valman (eds), *Remembering Cable Street*.
56 Laski to Chief Constable of Manchester police, 7 October 1936, Archive of the Board of Deputies of British Jews (BDA), 1658/9/1/3/1/27, Weiner Library.
57 Tilles, *British Fascist Antisemitism*, pp. 44–6.
58 SB Report, 4 October 1936, TNA MEPO 3/551/11Y.
59 *News Chronicle*, 12 October 1936. See also *Daily Herald* and *Daily Express* of the same date.
60 "Further Disturbances in East London," July 1937, PLJA MS60 17/16.
61 *The Blackshirt*, 13 February 1937, p. 5; "London County Council Elections 1937" (London, n.d.).
62 "Speakers' Notes No 21 – LCC Elections," uncatalogued, Working Class Movement Library.
63 *The Blackshirt*, 27 February 1937, p. 1.
64 SB Report, October 1936, TNA MEPO 2/3043/262–73.
65 Tilles, *British Fascist Antisemitism*, p. 152.
66 *Young Zionist*, March 1937, p. 4.
67 S. Salomon, *Anti-Semitism and Fascism in Post-War Britain* (London, 1950), p. 2; report on municipal elections, BDA, ACC 3121/E3/245/2, London Metropolitan Archives.
68 Fishman, "People's Journée," p. 391.
69 Thurlow, "State Management," pp. 46–7; Linehan, *British Fascism*, p. 109; Copsey, *Anti-Fascism*, pp. 66–7; Pugh, *Hurrah*, pp. 173–6.
70 "Special Instructions," 30 December 1936, uncatalogued, archives of the Institute of Jewish Affairs, University College London.
71 Commissioner's Reports for relevant months, TNA MEPO 2/3043.
72 TNA HO 144/21087/41.
73 *The Blackshirt*, 26 June 1937, pp. 1, 4, 8; Commissioner's Report, June 1937, TNA MEPO 2/3043/172–7.
74 TNA HO 144/21086/146–7.
75 Thurlow, *Fascism in Britain*, p. 85.
76 Commissioner's Report, June 1937, TNA MEPO 2/3043/172–7; memorandum from Commissioner's office, 29 June 1937, TNA MEPO 2/3043/185–6.
77 *News Chronicle*, 17 June 1938.
78 "The Public Order Bill" (JPC, 1937), LHASC CP/ORG/MISC/07/06; leaflet issued by London Young Communist League, 1937, LHASC CP/CENT/SUBJ/04/03; Liberty archives, Hull University, DCL/8/5 and DCL/39/2; *New Statesman and Nation*, 31 October 1936; *Daily Worker*, 16 November 1936; Copsey, *Anti-Fascism*, p. 64; Thurlow, "Blaming the Blackshirts," p. 112.
79 "Do the Democratic British People Want Fascism?" and "Fascist Provocation" (both JPC, n.d.), LHASC CP/ORG/MISC/07/06.
80 "Debate between Mr Jacobs and Mr Renton, Whitechapel Art Gallery, 21st March 1938," LHASC CP/ORG/2/20; *The Times*, 9 September 1937.

81 Copsey, *Anti-Fascism*, pp. 49–50, 68, 72.
82 "People of East London," in Commissioners Report, June 1938, TNA MEPO 2/3043/69–74.
83 Commissioner's Reports for August and November 1937 and April 1938, TNA MEPO 2/3043.
84 Kushner and Valman, *Remembering Cable* Street, pp. 2, 4, 15, 19; Kushner, "Writing and Rewriting 'the Battle of Cable Street'," pp. 155, 165. Kushner's chapter provides detailed analysis of the evolving uses and meanings of Cable Street from 1936 to the present day.

Select Bibliography

David Cesarani (ed.), *The Making of Modern Anglo-Jewry* (Oxford, 1990).
Nigel Copsey, *Anti-Fascism in Britain* (London, 2000).
Tony Kushner and Nadia Valman (eds), *Remembering Cable Street: Fascism and Anti-Fascism in British Society* (London, 2000).
Thomas P. Linehan, *East London for Mosley: The British Union of Fascists in East London and South-West Essex* (London, 1996).
Daniel Tilles, *British Fascist Antisemitism and Jewish Responses* (London, 2015).

PART Three

Culture and Society

8

WHITECHAPEL'S YIDDISH OPERA HOUSE

The Rise and Fall of the Feinman Yiddish People's Theatre

David Mazower

Foreword

Almost thirty years have passed but I have never forgotten the shock of that day in July 1987.

I was working at the newly opened Museum of the Jewish East End and had spent almost two years researching an exhibition on the history of Yiddish theatre in London.[1] It had finally opened, and – inspired by Bill Fishman – I was leading walking tours of Whitechapel, pointing out the main theatre sites.

One balmy Sunday, around midday, we moved on from Adler Street – home of the New Yiddish Theatre in the 1940s – to Philpot Street, where Yiddish music hall flourished around 1900 in a room above the York Minster pub. Then we carried on down Philpot Street to the corner of Commercial Road to take a look at the Palaseum Cinema across the street. Semi-derelict and covered in old Bengali film posters, this sad-looking structure had a glorious past, having opened its doors in 1912 as a Yiddish opera house. Built in the then fashionable Moorish style with domes and minarets, its forgotten history was one of the revelations of our exhibition.

To my horror, as we rounded the corner and looked over to where the Palaseum should have been, a large wrecking ball was smashing into the building, and a demolition crew was securing the site. All that remained of the theatre-turned-cinema was the exposed back wall, an open stage, and a tangled pile of metal, bricks and wood.[2] We crossed Commercial Road to take a closer look and the foreman came over to talk to us. "It's a shame," he said, as I told him about the building's past, "a shame all this history's gone … . we've just broken a wall down and found the old organ." He clambered back over the rubble, re-appeared with a honey-coloured wooden organ pipe, and pressed it into my hand. "Here," he said, "a bit of history, you might as well take it."

Today that organ pipe leans against the wall by my desk, reminding me how I felt that day. The first feeling was a sharp physical pain – like a punch in the stomach. Then came anger and disbelief. How could this have been allowed to happen? Where were the preservationists and the heritage lobby? Over time those feelings were replaced by a growing sense of curiosity about the theatre's history, and a determination to tell its story. Researching it for this volume has brought the full measure of its past glory into focus. The values that made the theatre a reality – the power of working-class solidarity and belief in the dignity of an immigrant culture – were close to Bill Fishman's heart as a man and a historian. He would surely have found a grim humour in the way a *folks teater*, a people's theatre, was snatched away from its immigrant founders by the workings of the market. He might well have found a consoling word on hearing of yet another Jewish East End landmark disappearing under the wrecking ball. And then I imagine him saying: "Well, go on *boychik*, write it down, tell the story."

Prologue

A Telegram from Łódź

It all started with a telegram sent from Poland to London on Thursday, 1 July 1909. The message was terse:

> Łódź, 3.45pm. My husband Sigmund Feinman died on stage at 12 today. Dina.[3]

For Whitechapel's many Yiddish theatre devotees there could scarcely have been more devastating news. Feinman was one of the leading actor-managers of his generation, not yet fifty and in the prime of his career. He and his wife Dina had been Whitechapel's leading Yiddish stage couple for several seasons, admired and loved in equal measure. They had only just bade farewell to their East End public to travel to Poland for a season of Yiddish plays at the Grand Theatre in Łódź. The news of Feinman's demise was felt by his admirers as keenly as a death in the family. As word of the telegram spread, shockwaves rippled out into the community.

Der idisher zhurnal (*The Jewish Journal*), Britain's main Yiddish daily, led with the story on Sunday, 4 July 1909. The news dominated the front page in a black-edged report headlined "*Faynman's toyt*" ("Feinman's Death"). The paper promised details of the latest telegrams, but in truth there were few additional facts. Instead, the story reflected the swirl of speculation and the sense of grief that had gripped the district. According to the paper, angry and distraught theatre fans had smashed windows around Whitechapel, and large crowds had gathered to discuss the sensational news. *The Jewish Journal* reminded readers that Feinman's health had been poor for some months; heart problems and a haemorrhage had forced him to cancel an appearance at his own benefit night at the Pavilion Theatre,

Whitechapel. Now, it seemed, his refusal to rest and his ceaseless efforts on behalf of Yiddish theatre had cost him his life.[4]

The bad news did not stop there. *The Jewish Journal*'s editorial office had asked Dina Feinman if she would be bringing her husband's body back to London for burial. She sent another telegram with a one-word answer: "*Unmeglikh*" (Impossible).[5] The East End's Yiddish theatre faithful would be denied even the catharsis of a mass funeral; they could neither bury their stricken hero nor share in his widow's grief. Out of the despair of a community in mourning, the Feinman Yiddish Theatre project was born. It had a simple but sensational aim: to build a Yiddish drama and opera house in the heart of the Jewish East End and to give Sigmund Feinman the best memorial any actor could hope for – a theatre bearing his name.

Act One – Building an Audience

East End Beginnings: Butchers and Beer Halls

Few among the thousands of impoverished Jewish immigrants flocking into London in the 1870s and 1880s would have seen Yiddish theatre in their home towns and cities. Indeed many of them would barely have understood the concept of theatre in the language they knew as *mame-loshn* (the mother tongue). That was partly because the culture of modern theatre-going was a world away from the way of life in traditional Jewish religious communities across Imperial Russia. But it was also because the early years of mass migration of Yiddish-speaking Jews into Britain coincided almost exactly with the birth of the modern Yiddish stage in their homelands.

Yiddish theatre developed directly from the oral tradition of *shtetl* entertainers – wedding jesters and Purim players in particular. By the 1860s and 1870s, itinerant groups of young singers and actors were putting on improvised shows in wine cellars, beer gardens or firefighters' halls across Russia, delighting and scandalising audiences with songs and satirical sketches drawn from *shtetl* life. All that was needed to transform this grassroots entertainment into something akin to modern theatre was a cultural entrepreneur like Avrom Goldfaden. A rabbinical student and failed businessman who reinvented himself as an impresario and playwright, Goldfaden is almost universally credited as the creator of the modern Yiddish theatre after joining forces in 1876 with a group of travelling Yiddish players. Within a few years, posters advertising Yiddish theatre companies could be seen in shop windows, on street hoardings and on the side of horse-drawn carts from Warsaw and Lemberg to Odessa, Kishinev and Berdichev. From there, the craze for Yiddish theatre spread rapidly to the expanding immigrant quarters in cities like New York, Paris, Johannesburg and London.

The improvised atmosphere of the first Yiddish theatre productions in London's East End was recalled decades later by two veterans – the Yiddish actor Maurice Axelrod and photographer Yitskhok (Isaac) Perkoff.[6] They described an ambitious amateur production in Yoshe Shenker's beer hall in Brick Lane in February 1876. Performed on a stage made of wooden boards nailed over beer barrels, the play, *Yoysher fun ganovim* (The Honesty of Thieves), was the work of a local carpenter named Hersh Volozhiner. The play's radical message – exposing the desperate poverty of Whitechapel's immigrant workers and ridiculing the complacency of the Anglo-Jewish communal elite – so enraged community leaders that they put pressure on the Brick Lane publican to cancel further performances. In March 1880, Shenker made his tavern available again for a production of Goldfaden's play *Koldunye* (*The Witch*). By this time a few professional actors had arrived in London, and they recruited some local amateurs to join them. They played by the light of carbide lamps, and without stage decorations, but despite these limitations the show was a hit, being played twice a week for ten weeks. At the end of the run, the professional actors followed the same path as their amateur colleagues, returning to jobs in the immigrant trades, primarily tailoring.

A Prince and His Patron

For the Jewish immigrant quarter, the 1870s and 1880s were years of instability and flux, a transient time for both actors and audience. And yet, as the Yiddish journalist and playwright Shmuel Yankev Harendorf wrote:

> Every time the *kaddish* (mourners' prayer for the dead) was recited over the corpse of Yiddish theatre in London, somehow, from somewhere, new theatrical talent appeared out of nowhere to revive it.[7]

This was especially true of the moment in 1883 when Jacob Adler, the man they called *nesher hagodl* (the great eagle), alighted in London with his company. Adler was born in Odessa in 1855, the son of a grain merchant. A teenage tearaway and amateur boxer, he moved through a succession of jobs – factory accountant, lawyer's copyist, hospital orderly – while spending his evenings in Odessa's theatres and nightclubs. His promising early career as a Yiddish actor in Russia was interrupted in 1883 by news of the Tsar's impending ban on Yiddish theatre in Russia. At that point, Adler decided to join the growing tide of emigration out of the Russian Empire and try his luck in England.[8]

The arrival of Adler and his company towards the end of 1883 lifted Yiddish theatre in Whitechapel to new heights. For a brief period, it also made London the centre of the Yiddish theatre world. Adler and his company of twenty actors experienced dire poverty, but his Russian Jewish Operatic Company also found eager fans and critical success. For two years they played all over the East End in immigrant clubs and halls, and on rare occasions in larger theatres in the West End. Adler's fame attracted the attention of a local butcher and Yiddish theatre lover, David Shmit (Smith), who became his patron and business partner. Shmit converted an old Spitalfields workhouse into a theatre, the Princes Street Club, also known as the Hebrew Dramatic Club, which boasted "accommodation for upwards of six hundred persons."[9] The year 1886, when the club opened, was a momentous year for Adler. It brought personal tragedy (the death of his first wife and young daughter), local scandal (his affairs with several young actresses) and professional stardom.

These years of progress and promise came to an abrupt end during a performance of *The Spanish Gypsy Girl* on the night of 18 January 1887. Press reports over the following days talked about a broken gas bracket, a false shout of "fire," a theatre plunged into darkness when the owner switched off the gas, and then terrifying scenes as theatre-goers stampeded in darkness for the exit.[10] Seventeen people suffocated to death and the tragedy cast a bitter shadow over Yiddish theatre in London for years to come. Adler soon left for New York, taking some of his company with him, and the remaining actors returned to a hand-to-mouth existence, working at a trade by day, and putting on occasional performances in East End church halls, pubs and working men's clubs at night.

Vine Court, Whitechapel: Verdi in Yiddish

The Yarikhovski brothers from Łódź, Poland are among the most intriguing of the many theatrical personalities who passed through London towards the century's end. Yudl "Flash" Yarikhovski began working as a waiter in the *Holendishn klub* (Netherlands Club), a Jewish immigrant club in Bell Lane. His more famous brother Eliyohu Zalmen (Salomon) Yarikhovski came to London around 1889. Eliyohu Yarikhovski was a talented composer and arranger with a distinguished track record as a Yiddish theatre music director in Warsaw. In London he founded a choir to perform Yiddish songs, wrote music to the Yiddish play *Monte Cristo* and translated Verdi's *La Traviata* into Yiddish.[11]

In 1890 the brothers put on Yiddish plays in Vine Court Hall, a no-frills venue approached through a dark alley on the south side of Whitechapel Road, close to New Road. They recruited among their Polish-Jewish *landslayt* (compatriots), launching the careers of talented singers and actors like Fanny Waxman and her older brother Moyshe Dovid (Morris) Waxman. The atmosphere at an evening of Yiddish theatre in Vine Court is vividly captured in a report in *The Daily Graphic* from December 1891.[12] It describes the venue – then known as the Oriental Working Men's Club – as a large hall with a gallery and a small bar, with a capacity of about three hundred. Yiddish plays were presented every night except Friday, with the reporter noting:

> There were more Jewesses present than Jews, many carrying babies, and there were a good many very precocious little Hebrew lads who, like most of the men, were smoking. There were also some mere girls … . The play of the evening, for which there was only one hour's rehearsal, was called *The Exile of Portugal* … the hero acted with energy and feeling, as all the principals did, both men and women, and sang exceedingly well. The music consisted of selections from well-known operas.[13]

Clearly, even at this early stage, Jewish immigrant audiences had an appetite for classical opera in Yiddish translation. The reference to "selections from well-known operas" surely shows Yarikhovski's influence. It suggests that his translation of *La Traviata* was a successful experiment, perhaps even one that laid the groundwork for the project of a Yiddish opera house two decades later.

Wonderland: Home of Boxing, Variety and Yiddish Theatre

In 1896 Jonas (Jack) Woolf, a well-known East End Jewish publican and impresario, opened a new entertainment venue on the south side of Whitechapel Road, close by Aldgate. Wonderland was a cavernous hall with room for over three thousand people. It was raucous, sweaty, thoroughly working-class, and hugely popular. After a few years, Wonderland became the home of boxing in the East End, but it started as a theatre and variety hall. English music hall sketches and Yiddish music theatre frequently featured on the same programme, designed to appeal to immigrant Jew and Cockney alike.[14]

Woolf's company of London Yiddish actors was called the Oriental Hebrew Operatic Sketch Co. He freely admitted to one reporter that his actors hardly ever rehearsed and "very often hardly know what their parts are until they get on the stage," adding that Wonderland was "rather handicapped for scenery" but insisting "the audience don't care as long as the acting is good."[15] On this point Woolf was surely right; the theatre critic M.J. Landa recalled a catalogue of absurdities from the early days of Yiddish theatre in London including "Roman soldiers armed with rifles ... and a back-drop representing Windsor Castle ... shamelessly trying to pass itself off as the destroyed Temple of Jerusalem."[16] None of this deterred the immigrant audience, largely made up of workers in the tailoring, shoe-making and furniture trades. Critics could bemoan the lack of sophistication; what audiences cared about was the acting and the singing.

Yiddish Theatre in the Big Victorian Playhouses

The tide of Jewish emigration out of Central and Eastern Europe brought a fresh wave of aspiring Yiddish actors to Britain in the 1890s and 1900s. Few had any acting training, or even much formal education, but they had an abundance of raw talent and sheer theatrical *chutzpah*. The Romanian-born comedian Maurice Axelrod was known as "the Jewish Dan Leno" after the English music hall star. Song and dance man Joseph (Joe) Sherman, was another local favourite. Prima donnas Jenny Kaiser and Fanny Waxman were Whitechapel locals who had been on the Yiddish stage since they were in their early teens. Joining them were another dozen or so actor-singers who had made London their home, plus Ferdinand Staub, a highly capable and conservatory-trained pianist, conductor and musical director. Of the local Yiddish playwrights, two stand out: Nahum (Nokhem) Rakov was the author of dozens of melodramas and operettas in London in the years 1887 to 1902 before he emigrated to the United States; after

Rakov's departure, the younger character actor, singer and dramatist Joseph (Yozef) Markovitsh took his place, writing songs to order for colleagues, and a large number of dramas.[17]

The tens of thousands of Yiddish speakers in the East End were not enough to sustain a permanent theatre in this period. However, the large immigrant communities in Manchester, Leeds, Liverpool and Glasgow were also eager to see Yiddish plays, and a touring itinerary would take in all these stops and more. Paris was another regular destination for London's Yiddish actors. Jenny Kaiser toured there repeatedly in the late 1890s and early 1900s, her company of London actors taking up residence at the Théâtre Israélite in the Rue de Lancry, a narrow thoroughfare in northeastern Paris.[18]

Towards the end of the 1890s Yiddish plays began to feature at regular intervals at the two best-known East End theatres – the Standard Theatre in Shoreditch High Street (opposite Bishopsgate Goods Yard) and the Pavilion Theatre, Mile End, at the junction of Whitechapel Road and Vallance Road. Both could hold well over two thousand spectators and were among the largest theatres in London. By the turn of the century Whitechapel boasted the full range of Yiddish performance. Jacob Adler, now a huge star on New York's Second Avenue, returned to London in triumph in 1901 to star in Jacob Gordin's Shakespeare-inspired family drama *The Jewish King Lear* at the Standard Theatre. At the same time Yiddish music hall flourished above a pub behind the London Hospital; its repertoire of risqué and comic street songs drew a mixed crowd including members of two rival East End Jewish gangs, the Bessarabians and Odessans.[19]

London and New York – A Tale of Two Cities

By the 1900s the global Yiddish theatre economy was on the rise. New playwrights gave a fresh impetus to the Yiddish theatre scene in Russia and Poland. Meanwhile, fast-growing Jewish centres in Buenos Aires and Johannesburg offered new touring opportunities for Yiddish actors. But New York was fast outstripping them all. The world's biggest Jewish city had a cultural energy to rival Warsaw or Odessa and its teeming immigrant neighbourhoods supported several permanent Yiddish companies by 1900.

London's Yiddish theatre scene was more precarious. Its biggest names travelled vast distances to Europe and beyond in order to find work, but even the best of them were forced back into the tailoring workshops during quiet months. Nonetheless, it was tempting to see the rich profits to be made from Yiddish theatre in America as a harbinger of things to come in Britain. East End Jewish entrepreneurs began to look across the Atlantic, wondering if they could make the sums add up and build a new venue specifically for Yiddish plays. In 1902 a syndicate including the playwright Rakov staged Yiddish plays in the 700-seat Manor Theatre in Kenmure Road, Hackney.[20] The same year saw reports of a "Jewish theatre at Aldgate" to be built at a cost of £30,000.[21] In 1904 the local Jewish businessman Abraham Davis asked the London County Council to approve plans for the

Orient, a two-thousand-seat theatre to be built at the junction of Commercial Road and Myrdle Street. The Orient's promoters had apparently "divined the gold that lies in Jargon drama" in the course of promoting occasional Yiddish plays at the Standard Theatre, Shoreditch.[22] In the event the Orient never progressed beyond the planning stage and the Pavilion remained the main base for Yiddish theatre in Whitechapel.

Meanwhile, New York's booming Yiddish entertainment scene acted like a magnet, pulling in a stream of talented Yiddish actors, singers and dramatists from London. Dozens made the journey. Among them: Odessa-born actor and dramatist Rudolf Marks, son of a noted Talmudic scholar, who acted with Jacob Adler in London before settling in New York around 1887; child star Fanny Lubritsky and her father Isaac Lubritsky, a Yiddish theatre prompter, who left Whitechapel for Brooklyn in 1908; and the lyricist Reuben Doctor, composer of dozens of Yiddish theatre and music hall hits, and a performer in East End Yiddish variety shows for about fifteen years before he emigrated around 1910.[23] A further brain drain of Yiddish theatre talent, on a somewhat smaller scale, took place in the same period from London to Buenos Aires and Johannesburg.

By the early 1900s London's reputation in the Yiddish theatre world was as a stopover between Europe and America (or vice versa), a place where you could do good business for a few nights or weeks at most. A star actor or actress could rely on putting together a decent company from the ranks of the local Yiddish actors, but Jewish East End audiences were fickle and a guest star's novelty could wear off very quickly. And while the Pavilion and Standard theatres hosted regular nights of Yiddish drama, Whitechapel – in sharp contrast to New York's Lower East Side – still had no permanent Yiddish theatre venue.

Act Two – An Actor and His Public

Herr Sigmund Feinman

Sigmund Feinman was an imposing actor-manager of the old school, broad-shouldered and barrel-chested. With thighs that filled out a pair of tights, plump good looks, plus a fine baritone voice and a commanding stage presence, Feinman had all the attributes of the Victorian leading man. He was born Osher-Zelig Feinman in 1862 in Bessarabia, then part of the Russian Empire, today mostly in Moldova and Ukraine. Unlike most Yiddish actors, he was well-educated and came from a prosperous and stable family; his grandfather was a synagogue cantor, his father a successful trader and manufacturer. Feinman sang in synagogue choirs as a child and later joined the choir of a Yiddish theatre company passing through Kishinev. In 1886 he was recruited by comedian Sigmund Mogulesco to join a new ensemble of Romanian Yiddish stars heading for America, settling in New York and becoming an American citizen in 1896. "Herr Sigmund Feinman" was soon headlining as a romantic lead and developing a reputation as a Yiddish play-wright. Adept at reworking themes from European drama, he put his name to around twenty plays starting with *Der yidisher soldat* (The Jewish Soldier) in 1889. Several of these became hits in the Yiddish theatre in America and Europe, and four were published.[24]

Feinman was also caught up in one of the Yiddish theatre's biggest celebrity scandals – the feud that followed Jacob Adler's divorce. Adler was handsome, charismatic and – by his own admission – utterly incapable of fidelity.[25] In London, as his wife's health failed, Adler first made the fifteen-year-old actress Jenny Kaiser pregnant and then seduced (or – as he describes it – fell in love with) Dina Shtettin, another chorus girl around Jenny's age from a deeply Orthodox home.[26] After Adler's wife died, he and Dina married and travelled together to New York where their daughter Celia Adler was born in 1889. Not long afterwards, as real life mirrored Yiddish melodrama, Adler eloped with and then married the Yiddish actress Sara Heine. Dina divorced her husband but continued to act with his company out of economic necessity. In the 1890s she married Feinman and, as "Madame Dina Feinman," became one of the best-loved and most versatile Yiddish actresses.

Sigmund Feinman in London

Sigmund and Dina's marriage in the wake of her split from Adler surely served to enhance their celebrity and box office drawing power when they began crossing the Atlantic to tour Europe around 1900. By the time Feinman returned to London in 1906 after an absence of a few years, a mini-renaissance was underway in the Yiddish theatre. A company of London-based actors had taken up residence at the Pavilion Theatre in April under the name The Yiddish Operatic and Dramatic Company. Engaged alongside them were international Yiddish theatre and recording stars such as the singer Madame Zwiebel from Lemberg, Mr and Mrs Charles Nathanson from Philadelphia, and Moyshe Dovid Waxman, just back in London following a tour of South Africa. In late July, huge posters went up around Whitechapel announcing "Jacob Adler is coming!" ahead of the star's return to London after many years. His opening night at the Pavilion Theatre on Saturday, 11 August saw Adler greeted by a deafening cheer described by the *Jewish Chronicle* as a "spontaneous outburst of enthusiasm" from the packed audience.[27] By the time Feinman joined the company in September, Yiddish plays had been occupying the Pavilion more or less continuously for six months, an unprecedented run.

Feinman's first full season at the Pavilion in 1906–1907 established his reputation as the leading actor-manager of the London Yiddish stage. He spent much of the next three years in the city, taking up the challenge of educating London's Yiddish theatre public. A highly cultured man, he believed passionately that Yiddish audiences deserved to see the best of modern drama and the classic repertoire. He staged plays by Gorky and Strindberg; he starred as Othello, was fascinated by the role of Shylock and commissioned a new Yiddish translation of *The Merchant of Venice* from the London Yiddish journalist Morris Myer. He also studied the stagecraft of the famous English director Sir Herbert Beerbohm Tree and his spectacular productions went way beyond what had thus far been attempted in the Yiddish theatre in London. Another Feinman innovation was an all-female production of Goldfaden's classic *Shulamis* featuring two leading prima donnas of the Lemberg Yiddish stage as the lovers – Regina Zuckerberg as Shulamis and Frida Zwiebel as Avasholem.[28]

The London Yiddish journalist Leyb-Sholem Kreditor (Leon Creditor), a close observer of the Yiddish theatre scene, described Feinman as "*an emeser idealist*" ("a true idealist").[29] In similar vein, playwright Joseph Markovitsh described him as "a true man of the theatre, a great artist who could make stones weep with his *davening* [praying] in his play *Shabes koydesh* [The Holy Sabbath]."[30]

The lavish historical pageants and high standards of performance at the Pavilion Theatre began to attract attention well beyond the East End. The celebrated actor-manager Sir Charles Wyndham visited the Pavilion around 1907 and was reportedly "very agreeably surprised with the high class of drama and acting he saw there."[31] In 1907–1908 there were lengthy articles about Sigmund and Dina Feinman in several national magazines.[32] In March 1908 the Paris journal *La Vie Illustrée* also sent a reporter to Whitechapel to cover the phenomenon of theatre in "a Judaic-German dialect;" French readers were treated to a photo spread showcasing *The Jews in Morocco* with its "sumptuous decor, staging and costumes."[33] On another occasion in 1907 a party of British royals and aristocrats headed out east to spend an evening in the midst of the Pavilion's raucous immigrant audience.[34] At its centre was the socialite and cultural entrepreneur, Countess Gladys de Grey, known for her ostentatious fancy-dress costumes and colourful love life. Accompanying her was Prince Francis of Teck, a minor British royal with a reputation as a gambler and womaniser. They had apparently come to see Madame Feinman play the roles of both sisters in *Rachel and Leah*, a Yiddish adaptation of the popular Victorian melodrama *Hoodman Blind* in which a man blames his wife for the misdeeds of her identical-looking sister.

Dina Feinman, known as "the Yiddish Sarah Bernhardt," was perhaps the most popular Yiddish theatre prima donna ever seen in London. On one occasion in April 1909, so great was the crush to get into the gallery at the Pavilion to see her perform, that a forty-two-year-old woman suffocated to death in the middle of the crowd.[35] Madame Feinman's daughter, Celia, a rising young actress, also joined her mother and step-father in Whitechapel. She had practically grown up on stage as a child, then set her sights on a career as a teacher in America, but returned to the Yiddish theatre as a young woman, initially as Celia Feinman, before changing her name to Celia Adler.

Contemporary observers of Feinman's London years all stress the enormous effort he expended to raise artistic standards at the Pavilion Theatre. Like any true impresario he thought big, hiring top artists and spending large sums on costumes and elaborate scenic effects. But for all the respect he commanded, Feinman's efforts failed to carry the mass of London Yiddish theatre-goers with him. According to his friend Yitskhok Perkoff: "apart from a small group of sympathisers, most of the public kept their distance ... keen that the theatre should be open in case they felt like going, but unwilling to do anything to help it survive."[36] In 1908 Feinman toured alone to Czernowitz, Lemberg, Warsaw and Lithuania; in his step-daughter's words, he "needed to earn a bit of money."[37] In March 1908 the *Jewish World* reported that "it looked as if Yiddish plays at the Pavilion were to become a permanent institution among us but evidently this was not to be."[38] In a farewell speech from the Pavilion Theatre stage, Feinman insisted he hadn't lost hope of returning for another season of Yiddish plays. Shortly afterwards, he embarked from Southampton on the long sea crossing to Argentina. Meanwhile, the Pavilion Theatre reverted to English plays for a few months.[39]

Feinman returned to Whitechapel for the last time in February 1909. He told an interviewer that he was planning a "six months' season" in London, including a production of *The Merchant of Venice*; he had been studying the role of Shylock "for the past six years."[40] But after a few months, audiences once again fell away. The Yiddish journalist Leyb-Sholem Kreditor saw events unfold:

> The owner of the Pavilion Theatre began to feel a sense of dissatisfaction (with Feinman). Fewer people were buying tickets to the performances. Another Yiddish actor was playing in a second theatre, and word got around that he was quietly negotiating with the director of the Pavilion Theatre. That's when Feinman decided to leave London with his wife and family for Łódź.[41]

In fact Feinman had been succeeded as resident actor-manager at the Pavilion by the light entertainer Charles Nathanson. This was a bit like replacing Sir Laurence Olivier with Danny Kaye, and Feinman's loyal supporters were outraged at the lack of respect. Meanwhile, decades of stressful touring were taking their toll; Feinman was overweight and a chain smoker and his health was getting worse. In Louis Lipsky's thinly veiled fictionalised portrait, Dikman/Feinman returns from Argentina to a London in which "new playgoers had no taste for the old-fashioned plays [he] put on." His arrival is "untimely," he feels "a sense of failure," and his health causes alarm. "He frequented a restaurant where Hungarian food was prepared. He often ate himself sick … his bulk was enormous."[42]

Death in Łódź

In June 1909 the Feinmans travelled to Łódź to join the company run by the celebrated Polish Yiddish director Yitskhok Zandberg. According to the Yiddish theatre historian Zalman Zylbercweig:

> Feinman enchanted the critics and the public … such expressive diction, such an imposing figure had never been seen before on the Yiddish stage in Łódź … . The Company started rehearsing *Uriel Acosta* but Feinman's health was getting worse. The doctors advised him to lose weight, saying he was dangerously overweight … and so it happened that on Thursday, July 1, at midday, in the middle of the famous speech 'Yes, rabbi, I am a Jew,' in the

middle of uttering those words, he fell to the ground like a fallen tree. There was uproar. A doctor was called, but it was already too late.[43]

Yiddish theatre was popular in Łódź and thousands turned out to see Feinman laid to rest in the Jewish cemetery. There were eulogies from leading figures in the Yiddish cultural world, including actor Julius Adler and playwright Mark Arnshteyn.[44]

In London, reaction to the news of Feinman's death was coloured by the intrigues and off-stage politics that had overshadowed his final weeks in Whitechapel. As Kreditor recalled: "the Jews of the East End felt guilty. If only he hadn't gone away, or rather, if only he hadn't been allowed to leave, then perhaps this tragedy would never have happened."[45] As the news spread throughout Whitechapel on the evening of his death, crowds gathered in the streets and windows were broken – possibly during fighting by rival groups of fans. The Pavilion Theatre cancelled that evening's performance as a mark of respect. The following day, as the Sabbath came in, it held a packed memorial meeting. Morris Myer, a friend of Feinman's, launched an angry attack on Whitechapel's Yiddish theatre fans for failing to give the actor-manager their support in recent weeks.[46] He also emphasised the crude actions of rival groups of fans, reminding the audience that the Pavilion gallery youngsters had even thrown oranges at Feinman on one occasion.[47]

On the following Sunday, one of the hottest days of the summer, the vast auditorium of the Wonderland Hall on Whitechapel High Street was the scene of a mass public tribute, organised by some of Feinman's close friends. So many people wanted to pay their respects that the huge crowd overflowed into the street. The hall was draped in black crepe and dominated by an enormous photograph of the dead actor, framed in black, above a candlelit platform. A choir drawn from the Pavilion Theatre chorus sang the memorial prayer *shiviti adonai* (I have placed the Lord before me); Moyshe Dovid Waxman sang *Der forhang iz gefaln tsu fri* (The Curtain Has Fallen Too Soon), a specially composed number by lyricist Sam Levenwirth (Lowenworth); and there were more tributes from Yiddish-speaking intellectuals including Kalman Marmor and Yitskhok Perkoff.[48] It was in this highly charged atmosphere that the idea of realising Feinman's dream and building a dedicated home for Yiddish theatre in London was first raised. It came from Yosef Goldshmit (Joseph Goldsmith), a Whitechapel tobacconist and Yiddish actor who had been a regular in Feinman's Pavilion Theatre company. Goldshmit appealed to the thousands of mourners to help found a theatre bearing Feinman's name as a tribute to the great artist. He called for a statue of the dead man to be placed in the lobby and implored all those present to support Dina Feinman and the other actors. According to press reports, Goldshmit's proposal was received with enormous enthusiasm by what one reporter present described as "a wholly working-class audience."[49]

Meanwhile *Der idisher zhurnal* (*The Jewish Journal*) served up a steady stream of supposed scoops about Feinman: his life was said to be insured for £7,000; his body was going to be brought back to London for burial; and the Britannia

Theatre in Hoxton had been booked for Madame Feinman's imminent return appearance in London.[50]

The Feinman Yiddish Theatre Society

Within weeks a group of East End theatre-lovers had set up an organisation to channel these emotional appeals into practical steps. The Feinman Yiddish Theatre Society was chaired by Alexander Kennard, a local businessman and music-lover. Originally from Odessa, Kennard was the owner of Elman Bros, a Whitechapel piano showroom. The Society held regular meetings in the York Minster pub behind the London Hospital and began to collect money towards its goal of building a theatre in Feinman's honour. Larger public meetings were held at the Pavilion Theatre and in July 1910, "The Feinman Yiddish People's Theatre Company Ltd" was formally registered. Kennard was the Chairman, heading a board of directors made up of local businessmen, including a leather merchant and a funeral director. Few among the board members had any professional involvement in the theatre. One of those who did was Isaac Perkoff, a Russian-born former anarchist whose St Petersburg Studios was one of Whitechapel's best-known photography businesses. Under the name "*Der vaytshepeler filosof*" (The Whitechapel Philosopher) Perkoff was also a columnist in the Yiddish press. He was close to many Yiddish writers and theatre figures including the dramatist Avrom Goldfaden, who on several occasions stayed at Perkoff's family home in Lea Bridge Road, Lower Clapton.[51]

The Feinman Company signed a lease option on the site of the old Teetotum billiard saloon at 226, Commercial Road, between Anthony Street and Fenton Street. It announced a share issue of twelve thousand £1 shares, giving it a paper valuation of £12,000, and issued an upbeat prospectus explaining the business potential of a new Yiddish theatre:

> The Yiddish theatre at the present time is flourishing at all important centres on the Continent and in that part of the United States where Jews reside … the Jewish population of London, numbering over 180,000 is not only ripe for such an Institution, but in the view of the directors there exists a demand in that direction for the elevation of the masses.[52]

It went on to claim that the Pavilion Theatre had been attracting 35,000–40,000 people a month in recent seasons, and had only been prevented from turning a profit by the high cost of renting the theatre. Turning to their new venture, the directors anticipated an annual income of £12,500, annual expenditure of about £9,500 and an annual dividend to shareholders of about twenty-five per cent.[53]

In the months that followed, the dream of building a theatre to honour Feinman, together with the promise of a sound investment, attracted hundreds of shareholders. Their details, meticulously listed in the Company's records, show them to be a cross-section of what at the time was often called the respectable working

class. Among a random sample of two hundred and thirty shareholders we find one
housekeeper, one milkman, one stick maker, three barbers, five grocers, five
tobacconists, six cigarette makers, six boot-makers, seven furriers, eight merchants, fifteen dealers, and no fewer than one hundred and nine tailors. About
seventy-five per cent of shareholders lived in the East End, and most signed up
for just one or two shares. The Company's directors invested ten pounds each
and two people bought shares to the value of fifty pounds – the Anglo-Jewish
aristocrat Sir Francis Montefiore, president of the English Zionist Federation, and
Oscar Baumgart, another prominent Whitechapel photographer. Other shareholders included the Yiddish playwright Sholem Asch (one share), the Yiddish
stage star Boris Tomashefsky (ten shares), and the local Yiddish actors Samuel
Goldenburg (one share) and Moyshe Dovid Waxman (thirteen shares). Con-
spicuously lacking were West End Jewish business owners, and wealthier or more
anglicised Jews.

Building the Temple

With its fundraising target some way off, the Feinman Company nonetheless hired
an architect and a firm of builders. By 1911 they had approved a design for "The
Temple of Art," a wide-fronted theatre in the Oriental or Moorish style with a
domed roof and two minarets. Building work commenced on the site in May
1911.[54] In the same year, the Company also began promoting Yiddish plays to
publicise its cause. Feinman's step-daughter, "Miss Celia Feinman" appeared under
the Company's auspices as the orphan in Jacob Gordin's play of that name at the
Pavilion Theatre on 18 July 1911. Given the circumstances – the man who had
brought Celia Feinman up as his own daughter was dead even if her real father was
alive – the choice of play made sound box office sense. On top of that, Celia had
inherited Jacob Adler's looks and talent, and the poster featured a large photograph
of her in a white dress, looking wide-eyed, helpless and far younger than her
twenty-two years.[55]

Towards the end of September 1911, a large festive crowd gathered to see Sir
Francis Montefiore lay the foundation stone for the Feinman Theatre. Flags and
banners were hung across Commercial Road and festooned the theatre's construction site. Montefiore used his speech to emphasise the important role he hoped
the Feinman Theatre would play in strengthening the religious and racial feelings of
the local Jewish population. Other speakers addressed the ideological opposition in
some sections of the Anglo-Jewish community to the very idea of a Yiddish-
language theatre. Another Theatre Board member, Henry Harris JP, argued from a
position of practical necessity, saying "it would be at least two centuries before they
would be able to say that no Yiddish was wanted here."[56] Joseph Cowen, a leading
English Zionist and close associate of Theodor Herzl, said he "might have wished
that Hebrew should be the medium used, but they had to deal with the facts
and the Yiddish-speaking public comprised thousands of their people." It was a
relatively faint echo of the bitter language and culture wars raging elsewhere in the

Jewish world between rival supporters of Yiddish and Hebrew. Nonetheless, it was hardly the ringing endorsement of Yiddish that the occasion warranted.

As Montefiore's speech suggests, the dominant ideology behind the Feinman Theatre project might be characterised as Jewish cultural nationalism. Most of those involved with the Company were sympathetic to Zionism and strong believers in Jewish national rights. That was equally true for the music director Samuel Alman as it was for Yiddishists like Morris Myer and Isaac Perkoff, both one-time anarchists, now moving towards Labour Zionism. The chief promoters of the Feinman scheme also shared a common artistic vision. Their Temple would be a place of pure art, unashamedly highbrow. The management placed articles in the local Yiddish press, promising the public that there would be no place for *shund* (trashy theatre) or *purimshpileray* (cheap clowning) – the sort of dismissive terms intellectuals used for the popular Yiddish theatre of light operetta and cut-and-paste plots.[57]

This elitist vision attracted the derision of one of Whitechapel's most barbed satirists – the journalist and medical doctor Avrom Margolin, who went by the pseudonym *Avreml* or Little Abie. Margolin poked fun at pretension and pomposity on the immigrant cultural scene in his biweekly magazine *Der blofer* (*The Bluffer*) and he had the Feinman Company squarely in his sights. The front cover caricature of the very first issue, dated October 1911, featured a bloated version of the theatre in Commercial Road.[58] Two box office counters are open for business. The window selling tickets for *Hamlet* has one lonely customer. At the other window, the queue for *Shmendrik* (one of Goldfaden's most popular comedies) stretches down the street. The caption rams the point home: *Hamlet* will be played to an empty house with a lone *griner* (newly arrived immigrant) thirsting for high culture; by contrast, *Shmendrik* is "*ful gepakt mit moyshes*" ("packed full of Moyshes"), using the actors' half-affectionate, half-contemptuous slang for the devoted gallery regular. And Margolin's conclusion: "*der vilen fun folk hot geziegt*" ("the people's will has triumphed"). Rubbing salt into the wound, the cartoon's punning title cleverly mocks the theatre's grandiose name: *Dos tempel fun kunst* (The Temple of Art) has become *Dos tepel fun kunts* (The Pot of Magic).

Over the next six months, as construction proceeded and the handsome structure took shape, it was clear that the Feinman Company's success would depend on its ability to establish a sound financial base for the venture. The projected share capital was £12,000. That would have been enough to cover the anticipated expenses and avoid taking out a mortgage on the building. But in reality the Company fell far short of this figure. The final number of shareholders was two thousand, share income never exceeded £4,500 and many of those who pledged to buy shares ended up paying by instalments and never paid the full amount owing.[59] Attempts to recruit prominent Jews as shareholders were repeatedly rebuffed. Israel Zangwill wrote back saying "Let the Whitechapel ghetto itself create the institutions it requires." Ahad Ha'am frostily replied: "Nobody can deny that a theatre is a good thing but it all depends what sort of theatre it is. If it's a bad one, then better not to have it at all."[60] By the time the theatre opened, the Company still owed thousands of pounds to its builders, architect and two of its directors.

FIGURE 8.1 Sigmund and Dina Feinman looking every inch the successful actor–manager and glamorous leading lady. A studio portrait by the New York photographer A. Hurdus, *c.* 1900.
(From the Archives of the YIVO Institute for Jewish Research)

FIGURE 8.2 Front cover of the Whitechapel Yiddish satirical journal *Der blofer* (The Bluffer), October 1911. The cartoon lampoons the grandiose ambitions and elitism of the Feinman Theatre directors. The *Tempel* (Temple of Art) has become a bloated *tepl* (little pot) and, in a cautionary tale of two box offices, *Hamlet* attracts a lone punter whereas the popular Yiddish operetta *Shmendrik* fills the house.

(Courtesy of the National Library of Israel, Jerusalem)

Photo by Record Press.

FIGURE 8.3 The Feinman Theatre in Commercial Road, East London, photographed in March 1912. The brightly painted sign above the entrance says "The Temple of Art" in English and Yiddish. Such unabashed self-promotion was unusual in a city where Jewish institutions typically kept a fairly low profile. (Courtesy of the Jewish Museum, London)

As a result of the funding shortfall, building plans were scaled down dramatically. The Company's first submission to the London County Council in October 1910 showed a venue with a capacity of 1,850. By July 1911 the revised plans had reduced that figure by a third to 1,250. The theatre that was finally built held only 900 people and consisted of stalls, pit and circle.[61] In the effort to slash costs, the gallery had been sacrificed. Not only did this drastically reduce the number of cheaper seats, it also amounted to a betrayal of the theatre's many working-class supporters. The gallery audience could be boisterous and over-familiar, but its partisan involvement was an essential ingredient in the special atmosphere that struck all first-time visitors to a Yiddish theatre. The Feinman Company said it planned to add a gallery later when funds permitted, but the news immediately soured popular goodwill towards the project. As Morris Myer put it:

> So in the end they built a People's Theatre that wasn't really for the people (*a folks teater, ober nisht far'n folk!*) ... and the popular mood quickly cooled towards the People's Theatre.[62]

FIGURE 8.4 A scene from *King Ahaz*, the opening production at the Feinman Theatre in
March 1912. Samuel Alman's Yiddish opera on a Biblical theme featured an
international cast of singers, lavish sets and this towering statue of the pagan idol
Moloch.
(Courtesy of the Jewish Museum, London)

Yiddish Opera or Yiddish Theatre?

Behind the scenes, the tightening financial situation also served to sharpen the
conflict between board members with competing visions of the Company's artistic
policy. From the start the chairman, Alexander Kennard, had imagined the Feinman theatre primarily as a Yiddish opera house for East End Jews unable to afford
the prices of Covent Garden or the London Opera House. It was his idea to raise
the curtain on opening night with the world's first original Yiddish grand opera.
King Ahaz was a Biblical extravaganza by a rising star of synagogue music – the
London-based choirmaster Samuel Alman. Kennard hoped to follow Alman's
opera with some of the great classic operas in new Yiddish translations. Morris
Myer, one of two literary advisors to the Company, fundamentally disagreed with
Kennard's plans. "Even the richest nations have to subsidise opera" he cautioned:
"Who will subsidise opera in Whitechapel?"[63] Myer, active on the London Yid-
dish theatre scene as a critic and translator, felt strongly that the Feinman Company
should focus its efforts on theatre. This dispute, fundamental to the direction and

FIGURE 8.5 Russian baritone Yosef Vinogradov (Joseph Winogradoff), photographed in
Isaac Perkoff's St Petersburg Studios, Commercial Road, in 1912.
(From the Archives of the YIVO Institute for Jewish Research)

FIGURE 8.6 The Yiddish actor Leyzer Zhelazo, photographed in Russia a few years
before he was recruited by the Feinman Theatre.
(From the Archives of the YIVO Institute for Jewish Research)

financial health of the Company, was never resolved. The Feinman Theatre would recruit two full companies which would alternate in repertory.

Both camps pushed ahead with equally ambitious plans. For his star opera singer and stage manager, Kennard approached one of the leading lights of the Imperial Opera in St Petersburg, the Russian-Jewish baritone Yosef Vinogradov (Joseph Winogradoff). Growing up in a Yiddish-speaking home in Vilna, Vinogradov had trained as a synagogue chorister before completing his music education in Odessa and Moscow. In his mid-forties, he was in the prime of his career as a Russian and international opera soloist and had spent several years starring at The Royal Opera House, Covent Garden.[64] But Vinogradov had no qualms about swapping the West End for Whitechapel, finding the idea of a Yiddish opera house irresistible:

> The idea appealed to my Jewish national feeling and my artistic ambition … a Yiddish opera house! Musical parity with all other nations! How often had I dreamed of just this in the two decades of my artistic career! How often had I spoken of this with my Christian and 'half-Jewish' colleagues who insisted that it would never happen … that Yiddish was not a suitable language for the world's best-known musical pearls![65]

Vinogradov was a proud advocate for Yiddish. The Feinman Company had originally written to him in German, to which he had replied: "Write to me in plain Yiddish. Jewish people should write in Yiddish. What use is German?"[66] Now, facing the prospect of a one thousand rouble fine for breach of his Russian contract, Vinogradov played sick; he pretended he was recuperating in Switzerland and made his way to London, arriving a few weeks before opening night.[67]

Not to be outdone, the directors in charge of handling recruitment of the theatre company also aimed high. A few years earlier the young dramatist Perets Hirshbeyn (Peretz Hirshbein) had founded a Yiddish Art Theatre in Odessa. It attracted some of the best young Yiddish directing and acting talent in Russia but the company disbanded in 1910 after two years on the road. Their breakup was the Feinman Company's opportunity. Several of the top stars of the Hirshbeyn Troupe now signed contracts to come to London. They included Leah Noemi, one of its most promising younger actresses, and the character comedian, singer and actor Leyzer Zhelazo. However, the headline signing from Hirshbeyn's ensemble was undoubtedly Jacob (Yankev) Ben-Ami. Like Vinogradov, Ben-Ami was a brilliant artist whose career in Russia had been hampered by anti-Jewish prejudice and laws. A yeshiva student turned actor, Ben-Ami had turned down an offer to audition for Stanislavsky's Moscow Art Theatre academy because he refused to contemplate converting to Christianity (an almost obligatory step to gain a resident's permit in Moscow). Like Vinogradov, Ben-Ami was attracted by the vision and ambition of the Feinman Company and he also agreed to come to London.[68]

The three stars of the Hirshbeyn troupe were supplemented by some of the best of the London Yiddish actors. Their ranks included Moyshe Dovid Waxman and his sister Fanny Waxman, whose fine voice made her capable of joining both the opera and the drama company. Joining them was another local actor, Samuel Goldenburg. A former music student at the Warsaw Conservatory, Goldenburg had come to London in the 1900s to escape Russian military conscription. When professional jealousies kept him out of the Yiddish theatre in Whitechapel, he started an amateur theatre group that performed at a radical club in Jubilee Street. Goldenburg would go on to have a distinguished acting career in Yiddish and English in America. But it was Sigmund Feinman who had recognised the young man's ability and brought him into his company at the Pavilion Theatre.[69]

With both opera and drama companies finally taking shape, the Feinman Company looked ahead to the opening weeks of their programme. No expense was spared: an orchestra of twenty-four was hired, and scenery and costume designs for *King Ahaz* were based on the art collection at the Victoria and Albert Museum.[70] Meanwhile, the building team worked round the clock to finish the theatre's interior. "On entering" wrote Morris Myer, "you are greeted by the glow of the Star of David, painted in gold above the stage."[71] There was a growing sense of pride at the prospect of finally accomplishing their goal. Alexander Kennard spoke of:

> A theatre that is intended to appeal musically to Jews only, and which is run by Jews, controlled by Jews, has an entire working staff of Jews, and whose artists, both in the orchestra and on the stage, are of the same religion.[72]

Behind the scenes, however, the reality was rather different. Vinogradov was shocked by the chaos he found backstage, the poor state of the theatre's administration, and the magnitude of the task in front of him. Still, he threw himself into rehearsals for Alman's opera and for the production to follow it – Verdi's *Rigoletto* with a new Yiddish libretto also by Alman. Among Vinogradov's many tasks was that of coaching the singers; he recalled later that "many of the English-born ones had very poor pronunciation in Yiddish, and their voices needed a lot of work."[73] Ben-Ami meanwhile rehearsed the opening theatre production. *Der vilner balebesl* (*The Little Householder from Vilna*) was the work of a young Polish-Yiddish author, Mark Arnshteyn, the story of a nineteenth-century cantor from Vilna who cannot cope with the psychological effects of success as an opera singer in Warsaw. It was almost certainly the first production in Britain of this classic of the modern Yiddish stage.

As opening night approached, the Company's finances remained a source of great concern with thousands of shares still to be sold. Visiting journalists were told of plans for a subscription scheme and the Company's Secretary sounded confident about the future: "So far our wealthier co-religionists have shown the cold shoulder" Jacques Horchower told the *Jewish Chronicle*, "but we shall get them later on."[74] It was to prove an optimistic prophecy. The journalist A.B. Levy, who attended the first performance, and took a keen interest in the theatre's fortunes, provided a more sobering assessment: "The wealthy and anglicised in the community were unsympathetic, simply because they despised Yiddish."[75]

Act Three

Opening Night

As The Temple of Art finally shed its scaffolding in the days before the gala opening, one thing was clear: the Feinman Company had created an exotic jewel of a building. At first glance it resembled a mosque or an Ottoman steam bath rather than a Jewish theatre. On its roof two slender minarets soared into the Commercial Road skyline, topped by ribbed domes pulled into points like upturned Chinese lantern flowers. The minarets flanked a central dome above the theatre's wide entrance, with smaller domes at each corner. A banner sign ran almost the full width of the building with large gold letters proudly announcing The Temple of Art in English and Yiddish at its centre, and *Faynman idish folks teater* (Feinman Yiddish People's Theatre) stretching across the sign from right to left.[76] Backstage, a bust of Feinman reminded the actors of his presence.[77]

Anxious to ensure that suitable decorum prevailed in The Temple of Art, the management appealed to their customers through the pages of the Yiddish newspaper *The Jewish Journal*, placing this announcement two days before opening night:

> Worthy audience … the success of the Yiddish theatre depends very much on your behaviour during the performance. We appeal to you: take your seats before the curtain rises … . be calm and quiet … do not applaud before the curtain falls … you are also warned not to shout and not to whistle … . Don't bring any nuts or oranges … please do not forget that the Yiddish People's Theatre is a temple and make sure that an atmosphere of holiness prevails.[78]

The theatre finally opened its doors on the evening of Saturday, 16 March 1912. Police had to keep order as crowds surged into Commercial Road and the surrounding side-streets. "There was a festival mood in the Jewish neighbourhood" wrote Vinogradov, adding "Whitechapel had surely never seen so many motor cars, horse-drawn carriages with servants, hansom cabs and fancy buggies."[79] The audience included Rothschilds and Montefiores. Congratulatory telegrams arrived from Dina Feinman, dramatist Sholem Asch and novelist Israel Zangwill. Sir Francis Montefiore addressed the packed theatre, and then the curtain rose on *King Ahaz, a Grand Yiddish Opera in 4 Acts*.

Samuel Alman, the opera's Ukrainian-born composer, was the choirmaster and organist at London's Duke's Place Synagogue.[80] A graduate of the Odessa Conservatory, *King Ahaz* was his first opera, based on a story by the nineteenth-century Hebrew writer Abraham Mapu. Set in ancient Jerusalem, its heroes were Oziel and his wife Miriam, who resist the cult of idol worship that has spread under the rule of Ahaz, the heathen king. The unlikely story of a Yiddish opera house in one of the poorest parts of East London attracted critics from the leading English newspapers. They were fulsome in their praise for Alman's music, the excellent singing, lavish production and the theatre itself. Perhaps more than anything they were intrigued by the audience. The *Daily Sketch* marvelled:

> It is probably the first time in the history of the world that the occupants of the stalls at grand opera wore cloth caps and drank beer, but this is looked upon as quite commonplace in the Commercial Road. Beer and sandwiches, indeed, were the order of the evening.[81]

For the next few weeks all appeared to go smoothly. Despite high admission prices, the theatre was packed for most performances. The opera company had another triumph with its world premiere of a Yiddish-language version of Verdi's *Rigoletto* (in Alman's translation) in April. "Nowhere except in Covent Garden could one hear in England a company of such brilliant talents as in this Yiddish theatre" wrote the *Daily Chronicle*, calling the production "one of the most notable operatic triumphs in this country."[82] The *Jewish Chronicle* agreed, complimenting Alman on a libretto "with surprisingly successful results … his version appeared to fit the musical accent admirably and to run easily."[83]

The drama company received equal acclaim for its opening production of *Der vilner balebesl* (also billed as *Der zinger/The Singer*) on 25 March 1912. Ben-Ami played the chazan/opera singer torn between duty in Vilna and fame in Warsaw. Playwright Mark Arnshteyn was in the audience, having been invited to London to work with the actors on his play. The drama company went on to produce around twenty plays in total, including several new to East End Yiddish theatre, including Herman Heyermans' *Ghetto*, Hirshbeyn's *Der tkies-kaf* (*The Handshake*), and Jacob Gordin's *Der Unbekanter* (*The Stranger*).

Trouble Backstage

Behind the scenes, however, months of over-spending and poor financial management were starting to catch up with the theatre's management. Just two weeks after the gala opening, one prominent shareholder, photographer Oscar Baumgart, asked to cash in his fifty pound investment. He received no payment, but was assured by Chairman Alexander Kennard that his money was safe. Baumgart was right to be suspicious. As accountants later found out, the company had kept no systematic financial records since September 1911 and was now hopelessly in debt.

By early May the financial crisis burst into the open. In letters to the press, Mr Kennard admitted the theatre was in a "dire position" and facing severe financial strain.[84] He appeared to lay some of the blame at the feet of orthodox Jews, saying the theatre was losing £150 per week by remaining closed on Friday night and Saturday afternoon in accordance with the Jewish sabbath. On Sunday 5 May 1912, the directors held a public meeting in the theatre to try to quell what they termed "the false rumours spreading around the East End."[85] Kennard admitted the Company faced a £6,000 shortfall but insisted that this problem could be overcome. He said that the theatre's chief creditor, Messrs Kirk the builders, were content to wait until the Company could secure a mortgage on advantageous terms. To those who were unhappy with the high ticket prices, he announced reduced prices for midweek shows. The key thing, he said, was for people to continue to support the theatre. Finally, Mr Kennard unveiled a new star attraction – the actor Maurice Moskovitch appeared on stage to loud applause. The popular star would, he said, be taking over the drama company and would open the following night with Strindberg's play *The Father*. Moskovitch had been hired at great expense to improve the theatre's fortunes. In Myer's view, his huge wages only worsened the situation.[86]

For the time being, the Feinman Company's shareholders seemed placated. But within days a very different sort of drama engulfed the East End. On 8 May 1912 over six thousand Jewish tailoring workers gathered in the Great Assembly Hall, Mile End and voted for industrial action in support of their striking co-workers in the West End. The tailoring trade was the backbone of the East End economy and this was the start of the biggest strike in the industry's history.[87] It was to last for weeks, bringing economic stagnation to East London and real hardship to thousands of families. Mindful that fully half their shareholders worked in the trade, the theatre's directors acted swiftly to make their sympathies clear. They announced that proceeds from the following two performances would be given over to help the striking workers.[88] It was good public relations, but yet another drain on the finances.

As the tailoring strike took hold, there was yet another piece of bad news. The Temple of Art was about to face some serious competition. Adverts in the Yiddish press announced that the American Yiddish theatre star Joseph (Yozef) Kessler would be opening on 3 June at the Empire Theatre, Mile End, a large playhouse just ten minutes walk away.[89] Meanwhile the woman who the Feinman Company's directors had counted on to be their biggest box office draw, the bereaved actress Dina Feinman, was still mid-ocean, having spent longer than expected recuperating in Atlantic City. She finally arrived in England on Monday, 20 May and was welcomed with a reception at the Three Nuns Hotel in Aldgate.[90]

In May 1912 the Feinman Opera Company introduced the one-act opera *Cavaleria Rusticana* by Mascagni and *The Macabees* by Anton Rubinstein, both in new Yiddish versions. The drama company, now under Moskovitch's direction, presented mainly the Gordin repertoire. Dina Feinman finally made her long-awaited debut at the end of May in Gordin's play *Di yesoyme* (The Orphan), reprising the title role in which she had made her name in London. Morris Myer, writing under his pen-name of *Kritikus* in *The Jewish Journal* praised her acting but with reservations. Madame Feinman, he opined, was better suited to comedy than tragedy and had picked up the American habit of playing to the audience rather than immersing herself in the role.[91]

In early June 1912, there was one last burst of artistic creativity with the premiere Yiddish production (and possibly the first UK production) of Israel Zangwill's play *The Melting Pot*. Moyshe Dovid Waxman and Dina Feinman starred in the leading roles: Waxman played David Kechana, a Jewish composer and survivor of the Kishinev pogrom, now settled in America; Feinman played his lover, the daughter of a Russian baron who was one of the pogrom organisers. Moskovitch had apparently left the company by this point, and Ben-Ami was relegated to a supporting role. The Zangwill premiere coincided with the opening week of Kessler's rival Yiddish theatre company at the Empire. Kessler had hired local actors who mostly played the popular repertoire: the comedian Joseph Sherman, actress and singer Jenny Kaiser and the brothers Joseph and Harris Fineberg. The programme changed nightly, featuring the staple musical comedy and melodrama repertoire alongside occasional performances of Kessler's trademark adaptations of *Hamlet* and *Othello*. The battle lines were clear: on one side an Art Theatre with a limited repertory of Yiddish opera and modern drama; on the other side a company of comedians and light entertainers playing popular hits. By the end of the month the *Jewish Chronicle* was reporting that "so great has been the success of Mr J. Kessler's season of Yiddish plays at the Mile End Empire that it is the intention of the management to prolong the season indefinitely." And, rubbing salt into the wound, it added that "arrangements have been made for a company of Yiddish operatic singers to sail from New York immediately."[92]

Crisis and Closure

Kessler's popularity probably sealed the Feinman Theatre's fate. The management reduced ticket prices still further, but by mid-June the Company was back in the headlines once more. On 16 June its shareholders held a crisis meeting. In an emotional speech, Dina Feinman expressed her disappointment with the Whitechapel audience, saying she had expected to be received with love and excitement like in the past, not with cold hearts. Shareholders appointed an Inspection Committee from within their ranks to investigate the true state of the Company's finances. Its members included Alderman Billings, a member of London County Council, and the Yiddish journalist Solomon (Shloyme) Dingol, later well-known as the editor of the New York Yiddish daily *Der tog* (*The Day*). Morris Myer suggested that the Company immediately address one of its chief failings – the lack of a clear separation between the management of the theatre and the artistic leadership of the opera and drama companies.[93]

By the end of June 1912 all future performances at the theatre were cancelled. The Inspection Committee commissioned an auditor's report which was presented to another shareholder meeting on 2 July 1912. This report revealed a catalogue of mismanagement and incompetence. Company cheques worth over £200 had bounced, some staff had not been paid for weeks, and the company's books were in a poor state. The managing director and company secretary resigned. But there were still hopes that the theatre could be saved with effective management and the meeting ended by discussing how the company could be put on a sound footing.[94] However, other shareholders had had enough. The very same East End Jews whose enthusiasm and belief had helped build The Temple of Art now decided to take legal action to close it down and recover their money. On 11 July

1912 Oscar and Bertha Baumgart petitioned the High Court to wind up the Feinman Company. It was bad enough, in their view, that the Company was insolvent and unable to pay its debts. However, they had also learned that the Company had done a deal with its builders to defer payment by making them, not the shareholders, its primary creditors to the tune of £3,500. To add insult to injury, the Company was still trying to sell more shares. This, said the Baumgarts, was nothing short of fraud, and it was time to declare the Company bankrupt. The High Court ruled in their favour. On 23 July 1912 it ordered the Feinman Company to be wound up and placed in the hands of the Receiver.[95]

This was not quite the end of the story. Some months later, the Receiver put The Temple of Art up for auction. The Company's directors were determined to buy back their theatre and make a fresh start. They were confident they could secure it for close to the starting price of £6,000 and even found a willing bene-factor – the American soap millionaire and philanthropist Joseph Fels.[96] A good friend of photographer Yitskhok Perkoff, Fels sent a representative to bid at the auction. To everyone's surprise, a rival East End Jewish consortium bid against them, upping the price first to £7,500, then £8,500. At that point, Fels' agent stormed out of the auction, furious at the rivalrous London Jews.[97] Months later the Temple reopened as the Palaseum Cinema. Locals boycotted it for many weeks in protest at what they saw as the new owners' treachery.[98]

The dream of presenting Yiddish opera in the East End stayed alive for at least eighteen months. In 1913 the Pavilion Theatre management announced: "Great Attraction! Easter Monday, March 24 for six nights ... The First Yiddish National Grand Opera Company." With Vinogradov (stage director), Alman (music direc-tor) and Kennard all involved, this was the Feinman Theatre's opera company in all but name. They put on eight shows in six days – two performances each of Gou-nod's *Faust*, Rossini's *Barber of Seville*, Verdi's *Rigoletto* and Alman's *King Ahaz*, in the Yiddish versions previously staged in Commercial Road.[99] And in October 1913, at a meeting in Aldgate, Mr Kennard said he was in touch with "some business people who wished to revive the idea of a 'people's theatre'."[100]

It took the Receiver three years to untangle the financial mess left by the Fein-man Theatre's management. It remains unclear as to whether the shareholders and creditors ever got their money back. What comes through loud and clear in the Jewish press, however, is the deep sense of anger, shock and disappointment that followed the theatre's dramatic closure only four months after its doors opened.[101] Some of the shortcomings and setbacks were clear – the insufficient take-up of shares, lack of support from the wealthier sections of British Jewry, financial mis-management, gross over-spending and over-ambition, the tailors' strike, and the competition from a rival company. Other factors were less obvious. Morris Myer identified not only a financial crisis but what he termed a moral crisis, a steady alienation of working-class support that followed a succession of snubs and mis-calculations by the theatre's management.[102] The rhetoric of a people's theatre for an audience of immigrant workers was not matched by the reality. The highbrow artistic tastes of the Temple's directors were always going to end in commercial suicide. London's Yiddish theatre audiences simply moved elsewhere: within months of the Temple's downfall, two rival companies – Moskovitch at the Pavilion Theatre, and Kessler in partnership with Dina Feinman at the Mile End Empire – were both doing good business.

In retrospect, the Feinman Theatre was the product of two overlapping cultural trends, which came together in the East End in the years before the First World War. Ideas of cooperation and working-class self-help gave rise to institutions like the Jewish hospital, the *Arbeter Ring* (Workers' Circle) and the *Arbeter Fraynd* (Workers' Friend) anarchist club and publishing house. At the same time the Yiddish art theatre movement flowered briefly, influenced by trends in Russian theatre and the new social plays of Gorky, Ibsen, Shaw and others. Feinman's sudden death in 1909 was the spark that made The Temple of Art possible. But its failure was a colossal blow to those who sought to educate the taste of London's Yiddish theatre-goers. There would be other visionaries, other actors and impresarios with high ideals, but never again would Yiddish theatre in London see such an ambitious venture or attract such a galaxy of international theatre and operatic talent. The Temple of Art would remain the only purpose-built Yiddish theatre ever constructed in western Europe, and one of only a handful of such buildings anywhere in the world.

The Palaseum Cinema added a "cinematograph chamber" for film projection in 1913, an enlarged balcony in 1919, and an organ in 1927.[103] It closed in 1960, re-opened as the Essoldo Cinema in 1961, and then reverted to the Palaseum in the 1970s, screening Bollywood movies. As the years passed, the domes and minarets crumbled and weeds began to sprout from its facade. By the 1980s, like a rich man turned pauper, the grimy Palaseum was unrecognisable as the handsome Moorish-style edifice of its early years. It finally closed in October 1985, was demolished in 1987, and a five-storey residential block with two ground-floor shop units went up on the site in 2008.[104]

With more awareness of its unique history, and with the support of a more historically minded local council, The Temple of Art could easily have been saved and restored. After all, its inspirational message – that working-class communities need arts venues and culture just as much as wealthier areas, and can achieve extraordinary things by coming together with a common purpose – is as valid today as it was in 1912.

Epilogue

A Grave in Łódź

Nowhere gives such an abundant sense of the teeming Jewish presence in prewar Poland as the old Jewish cemeteries in Warsaw and Łódź. In summer, their tall trees shade the walkways below, creating green oases of contemplation amid the cacophony of city life. On either side of paths the length of airport runways, gravestones lie half-buried in carpets of weeds. Some of the names are sharp and clear, others worn beyond recall. Together they amount to a lexicon of a vanished world, a lost civilisation of writers, shopkeepers, rabbis, doctors, wagon-drivers, political activists, innkeepers, cabaret singers, tailors, lawyers, architects ... and Yiddish actors.

On a visit to Łódź a few years ago I went in search of Sigmund Feinman's resting place. As my guide, I had a copy of the photograph taken in 1911 at the stone-setting and reproduced in a reference work by the Yiddish theatre historian Zalmen Zylbercweig.[105] It shows an imposing monument on a raised platform with a round column about four metres tall, truncated at the top. A smaller cut-off column leans against the main one. Decorative features include a stone lyre and a plaque in the shape of an open book, with the Yiddish words *zayne verk* (his works) and the titles of several of Feinman's plays. Also shown in the photograph are Feinman's widow Dina, and her daughters Celia and Lily, together with the Łódź Yiddish theatre director Yitskhok (Isaac) Zandberg.

Unable to locate the grave, I sought the help of the cemetery's Polish caretaker. We found the site eventually but it looked nothing like the photograph. The smaller column was still leaning at an angle, but the ornate memorial had collapsed almost completely, leaving a pile of moss-encrusted stones. The freshly chiselled Hebrew letters visible in the photograph had worn away to almost nothing. However, as I prised some moss away from the stone plaque two words emerged. They spelled out *Shabes koydesh* (Holy Sabbath), the title of one of Sigmund Feinman's most popular plays.

Notes

1 "Yiddish Theatre in London, 1880–1987," at the National London, London, 30 June to 8 August 1987. Review articles included: C. Osborne, "The Theatre that Is No More," *The Daily Telegraph*, 7 July 1987, Arts; N. Khan, "The Day the Theatre Died," *New Statesman*, 10 July 1987; C. Armitstead, "Where the Player Was the King," *Ham and High*, 26 June 1987.
2 For a photo of the theatre mid-demolition, see *Jewish Chronicle*, 24 July 1987, London Extra section.
3 *Der idisher zhurnal (The Jewish Journal)*, 4 July 1909.
4 Ibid.
5 Ibid.
6 Sh.Y. Harendorf, "*Yidish teater in London*," (Yiddish Theatre in London) in *Yidn in England (Jews in England)*, (New York, 1966), pp. 226–9.
7 Ibid., p. 239.
8 J. Adler, *A Life on the Stage* (New York, 1999).
9 D. Mazower, *Yiddish Theatre in London*, (London, 1996), p. 32.
10 *Reynolds Weekly Newspaper*, 23 January 1887; Z. Zylbercweig (ed.) *Leksikon fun Yidishn Teater (Encyclopedia of the Yiddish Theatre)*, 6 Vols (Vol. 1, New York, 1931; Vol. 2, Warsaw, 1934; Vol. 3, New York, 1959; Vol. 4, New York, 1963; Vol. 5, New York, 1967; Vol. 6 Mexico City, 1969), Vol. 2, pp. 1503–4.
11 S. Perlmuter (Perlmutter), *Yidishe dramaturgn un teater-kompozitors* (Yiddish Playwrights and Theatre Composers) (New York, 1952), p. 319. L. Prager, *Yiddish Culture in Britain, A Guide* (Frankfurt, 1990), p. 700.
12 "A Foreign Jews' Theatre in Whitechapel," *The Daily Graphic*, 1 December, 1891.

13 Ibid.
14 Poster for Wonderland attractions "Whit Monday May 25th and during the week," (n.d. but 1896) author's collection.
15 "A Visit to Wonderland," *The Golden Penny*, 17 December 1898, pp. 591–2.
16 M.J. Landa, *The Jew in Drama* (London, 1926), pp. 285–6.
17 On Rakov see Prager, *Yiddish*, p. 541 and Perlmuter, *Yidishe*, pp. 184–8; on the others, see Mazower, pp. 80–7.
18 Information from copies of Paris Yiddish theatre posters 1899–1905 in author's collection (originals in the collection of the Bibliothèque Nationale, Paris).
19 B. Leeson, *Lost London, the Memoirs of an East End Detective* (London, 1934), pp. 113–8.
20 *Jewish Chronicle*, 2 May 1902.
21 Ibid., 10 June 1904.
22 Ibid. Davis is probably the builder and developer Abraham Davis of 19–20 Aldgate, who in 1905 built the Moorish-style Arcade on the south side of Fashion Street, off Brick Lane. See http://www.british-history.ac.uk/survey-london/vol27/plate-49#h3-0004, accessed 11 August 2016.
23 On Doctor, see http://www.milkenarchive.org/people/works/all/857/Reuben+Doctor#/people/view/all/857/Reuben+Doctor/full, accessed 24 May 2016; for the others see Prager, *Yiddish*, pp. 426–7, 440.
24 Zylbercweig, *Leksikon*, Vol. 2, pp. 2544–60; Vol. 6, pp. 5165–72.
25 See Adler's autobiography, note 8 above.
26 On this episode, see Adler, *A Life*, pp. 291–304. Adler writes that Kaiser was "very young when I met her, sixteen or seventeen at most" but my research in UK archives suggests she became pregnant at fifteen and was sixteen when their son was born in 1884.
27 *Jewish Chronicle*, 27 July 1906 and 17 August 1906.
28 Zylbercweig, *Leksikon*, Vol. 4, p. 2551.
29 L.Sh. Kreditor, "*Yidish teater in London,*" (Yiddish Theatre in London) in *Hundert yor yidish teater* (Centenary of Yiddish Theatre) (London, 1962), p. 16. For more on Kreditor, see Prager, *Yiddish*, p. 383.
30 D. Mazower, "Stories in Song, the *melo-deklamatsyes* of Joseph Markovitsh," in J. Berkowitz (ed.), *Yiddish Theatre, New Approaches* (Oxford, 2003), pp. 123–4.
31 *Jewish Chronicle*, 9 July 1909.
32 "Behind the Scenes at London Theatres: II," *The Lady's Realm* Vol. 23 (1908), pp. 421–428; A. Ellis, "The East-End Jew at his Playhouse," *Pall Mall Magazine*, Vol. 16 (1908), pp. 173–9.
33 *La Vie Illustrée*, no. 492, 20 March 1908.
34 *The Bystander*, 18 September 1907.
35 *Jewish Chronicle*, 16 April 1909.
36 Zylbercweig, *Leksikon*, Vol. 4, p. 2552.
37 Ibid.
38 *The Jewish World*, 13 March 1908.
39 Zylbercweig, *Leksikon*, Vol. 4, pp. 2551–2.
40 *Jewish Chronicle*, 19 February 1909.
41 Kreditor, "*Yidish,*" p. 16.
42 L. Lipsky, "The Circle of a Life," in *Tales of the Yiddish Rialto* (New York, 1962), pp. 36–7.
43 Zylbercweig, *Leksikon*, Vol. 4, pp. 2554–5.
44 Ibid.
45 Kreditor, "*Yidish,*" p. 16.
46 Morris Myer was a labour activist, editor of a number of Yiddish daily newspapers, including from 1913, *Die Tsayt (The Jewish Times)*. He became vice president of the Federation of British Zionists and a member of the Board of Deputies of British Jews.
47 *Der idisher zhurnal*, 5 July 1909.
48 Zylbercweig, *Leksikon*, Vol. 4, p. 2555.

49 *Jewish Chronicle*, 9 July 1909; on Goldshmit, see Prager, *Yiddish*, p. 287 and Zylbercweig, *Leksikon*, Vol. 2, p. 1376; Vol. 6, p. 4872.

50 *Der idisher zhurnal*, 5 July 1909.

51 On Perkoff, see Prager, *Yiddish*, pp. 512–3 and Z. Reyzen, *Leksikon fun der yidisher literatur, prese un filologye* [Encyclopedia of Yiddish literature, press and philology], (Vilna, 1930), Vol. 2, pp. 946–9.

52 A copy of the Prospectus is in the Gaster Papers at University College London Library.

53 Ibid.

54 *Jewish Chronicle*, 19 May 1911.

55 Poster of Tsili Faynman in *Di Yesoyme* (The Orphan) at the *Pavilion Theatre*, 18 July [1911], YIVO poster collection.

56 *Jewish Chronicle*, 22 September 1911.

57 *Der idisher zhurnal*, 7 March 1912.

58 *Der blofer* is in the collection of the Jewish National Library, Jerusalem. See Prager, *Yiddish*, for entries on *Der blofer* (p. 164) and Margolin (p. 437). I am grateful to Vivi Lachs for bringing this cartoon to my attention.

59 *The Standard*, 12 March 1912; *Morning Leader*, 15 March 1912.

60 Zylbercweig, *Leksikon*, Vol. 6, p. 5171.

61 LCC (London County Council) Minutes of Proceedings from October 1910 to February 1912, and Palaseum Plans in London Metropolitan Archives.

62 M. Myer, *Idish teater in London (Yiddish theatre in London)* (London, 1942), pp. 245–6.

63 Ibid.

64 Yosef Vinogradov papers, YIVO Archives, New York.

65 Vinogradov, *Di ershte proben tsu shafen a yudishe opere* (The First Attempt to Create a Yiddish Opera), Der Moment, Warsaw, 7 January 1925 (press cutting in Vinogradov archive in YIVO, no page number).

66 Mayer, *Idish*, p. 276.

67 Vinogradov, *Di ershte proben*.

68 On Ben-Ami, see Zylbercweig, *Leksikon*, Vol. 1, pp. 184–7. His papers are in the YIVO Archive.

69 Zylbercweig, *Leksikon*, Vol. 1, pp. 271–2; Vol. 6, p. 687 and Prager, *Yiddish*, p. 283.

70 Vinogradov, *Di ershte proben*.

71 *Der idisher zhurnal*, 22 February 1912.

72 *Jewish Chronicle*, 22 March 1912.

73 Vinogradov, *Di ershte proben*.

74 *Jewish Chronicle*, 8 March 1912.

75 A.B. Levy, "King Ahaz and the Apaches," *Jewish Chronicle*, 4 June 1965.

76 Mazower, *Yiddish*, p. 72.

77 *Jewish Chronicle*, 29 March 1912.

78 Ibid.

79 Vinogradov, *Di ershte proben*.

80 For Alman's biography, see *Cantors' Review*, no. 13, April 1974, pp. 17–22.

81 *Daily Sketch*, 18 March 1912.

82 *Jewish Chronicle*, 19 April 1912.

83 Ibid.

84 Ibid., 3 May 1912.

85 *Der idisher zhurnal*, 6 May 1912.

86 Myer, *Idish*, p. 250.

87 For details of the 1912 tailors' strike see, A.J. Kershen, *Uniting the Tailors: Trade Unionism Amongst the Tailoring Workers of London and Leeds* (Ilford, 1995), pp. 153–6.

88 *Der idisher zhurnal*, 8 May 1912.

89 Ibid., 26 May 1912.

90 Ibid.

91 Ibid., 30 May 1912.

92 *Jewish Chronicle*, 28 June 1912.

93   *Der idisher zhurnal*, 17 June 1912.
94   Ibid., 3 July 1912.
95   Zylbercweig, *Leksikon*, Vol. 6, pp. 5165–72.
96   Joseph and Mary Fels papers at the Historical Society of Pennsylvania http://hsp.org/
     sites/default/files/legacy_files/migrated/findingaid1953fels.pdf, accessed 23 July 2016.
97   Myer, *Idish*, p. 251.
98   Zylbercweig, *Leksikon*, Vol. 6, p. 5171.
99   4-page Pavilion Theatre brochure in English, March 1913, author's collection. There
     were at least two publishing ventures devoted to opera in Yiddish: in 1908 the New
     York-based Jewish Libretto Publishing Company published a handful of Yiddish
     booklets devoted to famous operas, including *La Traviata* and *Aida* by Verdi. Each
     booklet includes the lyrics of selected arias in Yiddish translations by Hilel Vikhnin.
     Another series of small song sheets, published in Vilna c. 1924 under the umbrella title
     of *Muzik far alemen* (Music for All) contained Yiddish translations of individual arias.
100   *Di Tsayt* (*The Jewish Times*), 22 October 1913.
101   See for example *Jewish Chronicle*, 16 August 1912.
102   Myer, *Idish*, pp. 243–52.
103   For the building's history as a cinema, and a photograph of the exterior *c.* 1970, see
     http://cinematreasures.org/theaters/31416, accessed 24 February 2016.
104   http://www.mizen.co.uk/commercial-rd-london-e1.html, accessed 24 February 2016.
105   Zylbercweig, *Leksikon*, Vol. 4, p. 2557.

Select Bibliography

Der idisher zhurnal [The Jewish Journal] (London, 1905–1914).

David Mazower, *Yiddish Theatre in London* (London, 1996 ed.).

Morris Myer, *Idish teater in England* [Yiddish Theatre in England] (London, 1942).

Sholem Perlmuter (Perlmutter), *Yidishe dramaturgn un teater-kompozitors* [Yiddish Playwrights
     and Theatre Composers] (New York, 1952).

Leonard Prager, *Yiddish Culture in Britain, A Guide* (Frankfurt, 1990).

Zalmen Zylbercweig (ed.), *Leksikon fun yidishn teater* [Encyclopedia of the Yiddish Thea-
     tre], 6 Vols (Vol. 1, New York, 1931; Vol. 2, Warsaw, 1934; Vol. 3, New York, 1959;
     Vol. 4, New York, 1963; Vol. 5, New York, 1967; Vol. 6 Mexico City, 1969), Vol. 2,
     pp. 1931–1970.

9

THE METROPOLITAN RHYTHM OF STREET LIFE

A Socio-spatial Analysis of Synagogues and Churches in Nineteenth-century Whitechapel

Laura Vaughan and Kerstin Sailer

I The Time and the Place, 1899

The German sociologist Georg Simmel wrote in 1903 how the city functions as an alienating environment that is strikingly different from the village or the town: in the city the individual has to adjust to the "metropolitan rhythm of events."[1] Simmel's proposition that the nature of the urban setting means that every street crossing creates an intensified tempo "of economic, occupational and social life"[2] is examined here to see the way in which East London functioned – as it has done so now over several centuries – to provide a specifically urban setting for incoming religious minorities to settle and form a community. This chapter focuses on Whitechapel in the year 1899, around a decade later than Charles Booth's first poverty survey and in the year in which the update to his great map of poverty was drawn up.[3]

The period leading up to 1899 was one of great upheaval for the inhabitants of the East End of London. As Fishman shows in his seminal *East End 1888*,[4] a massive influx of Jewish Eastern European economic migrants and refugees led to the area east of the City of London becoming known as "Little Jerusalem."[5] They had fled severe restrictions under Russian law, with confinement to areas reserved for Jewish residence within the Russian Empire, from the early nineteenth century onwards as well as violent anti-Jewish persecutions, which came to a peak following the assassination of Tsar Alexander II. Although there are no precise numbers for the Jewish presence in the area, the 1891 census shows a threefold rise of Eastern Europeans resident in England and Wales, with a total of 45,808 across the country, many of these in the Whitechapel area.[6] Russell and Lewis state that "There is no available material for anything like a trustworthy statistical estimate of the number of immigrants who come here to stay. Such evidence, however, as is obtainable, points to the fact that the influx of Russian and Polish Jews had increased to a considerable extent in the last few years."[7] Pre-existing slum conditions that had caused great suffering to the previous generation's Irish incomers were worsened by ever-increasing overcrowding for the area's latest inhabitants.[8] By the time of Charles Booth's first poverty survey in the 1880s, work and dwelling conditions were found to be shockingly poor. Indeed, despite fears of poverty (and the poor) having been stoked by a sensationalist press, its true extents were little understood until Booth's maps made poverty "seem a problem that could be addressed, rather than an insurmountable crisis." [9]

The morphology – the physical form and layout of the city – was itself viewed by the general public as a source of the immorality of its inhabitants, and considered to be a significant obstacle to policing.[10] Booth's maps, which showed the gradations of poverty and prosperity from the warmer shades of red and pink for streets above poverty, through purple to the colder shades of blue and black for streets below poverty (see Figure 9.1, which shows a greyscale reproduction of the printed coloured map) were able to lift the curtain of image and stereotypes and create an informed basis for new legislation to alleviate the situation of the East End, leading to a series of legislative acts that sought to tidy up the rookeries and streets of the area.[11] The year 1899 marks the end of a period during which many slum clearances had taken place, with the erection of new model dwellings in locations such as Flower and Dean Street alleviating the physical condition of housing in the area, although doing little for the most impoverished in the area, who were unable to pay the required regular rents demanded by the dwellings' landlords. The clearance of the notorious Old Nichol slum and its replacement in 1900 by London County Council's first housing estate – the Boundary Estate – is an important example of this initiative.[12]

In George Duckworth's account of his walk with Superintendent Mulvaney, head of Whitechapel Division of Police on 7 January 1898, he reports that the district was "very peculiar" in its being a "hybrid" district with a large number who couldn't speak English. Polish Jews and Russians who had "come over" were "mostly strong socialists," whose "first inclination in coming over and finding their liberty is to break out … ."[13] The street setting in which they found themselves was one of tightly packed houses, workshops, factories and shops, set on narrow streets leading off the broad thoroughfares of Whitechapel Road and Commercial Road East. The vicinity of Fieldgate Street, with its shops and four-storeyed buildings used by mantle and corset makers, included also the Great Eastern Dwellings, which was protected by a "court entered by iron gates ('necessary to prevent prostitutes from using the place in the evening')."[14] Booth's poverty maps illustrate that the policeman's perception of his beat's population as being "hybrid" was similar to the streets, which ranged from reasonably comfortable shops on the main roads to miserable tenements on the back streets, never more than a few turnings away. Elsewhere, Duckworth reports:

[a] Great mess in Jewish streets – fishes heads, paper of all colours, bread … orange peel in abundance. The constant whirr of the sewing machine or tap of the Hammer as you pass through the streets: women with dark abundant hair, olive complexions, no hats but shawls – Children well-fed & dressed. Dark beards, fur caps & long boots of men – The feeling of being in a foreign Town.[15]

The apparent foreignness of the town is evident from this eyewitness account, but it leaves open the question of the extent to which the most hidden aspects of Jewish life – in clubs and schools, let alone in synagogues – was apparent to their fellow Whitechapel inhabitants.

II The Study

The year 1899 is also significant due to it almost coinciding with the publication of *The Jew in London*, a joint effort by a Jewish and non-Jewish pair of authors to uncover some of the reality of life in the area.[16] The current study builds on previous research that used the book and its map of "Jewish East London," which showed the patterns of Jewish immigrant settlement in the area. This research found that the Jewish settlement in a tight spatial cluster on the edge of the City of London constituted a strongly supportive milieu of co-religionists whose communal institutions – from clubs, hospitals and schools to dozens of synagogues – were situated so as to make the most of the local street network's pattern of connectivity.[17] The layout of the East End was such that its main streets were well connected to London's economic heartland, allowing for trade and other economic activity to take place, whilst the back streets facilitated a quieter setting for immigrant communities' less public activities. The research concluded that this area of the East End operated as a mechanism for acculturating immigrants into society by allowing them to form a network of self-support whilst building connections to the wider neighbourhood through participation in the local spatial economy. Subsequent research has found that the synagogues of the East End were by far more secluded than earlier Huguenot chapels and other churches.[18] The object of the current study is to assess the exact position of synagogues within their urban setting in order to establish if their location had any systematic relationship with the social and economic context of those streets. In order to further validate this analysis, in addition to studying all synagogues in the district, the analysis was carried out comparatively for all churches within the study area.

The study focuses on an area of Whitechapel within the parishes of Mile End New Town and St Mary Whitechapel (see Figure 9.1) which had a high Jewish presence, serving as an ideal case for examining the spatial and social setting of synagogues at the time.

The study drew on a variety of maps and data sources, starting with the large-scale Goad Fire Insurance plans, which were used to map building outlines and streets.[19] The study area was also selected due to it being the only one in the vicinity which Goad updated in 1899. Missing data on the urban built fabric and information on the streets surrounding the plans were completed with historical maps of East London.[20] The Goad plans also provide a categorisation and description of historical land uses (see Figure 9.2). All synagogues and churches that appeared within the study area were identified on the Goad Plan and, along with the land use functions of adjacent buildings, were recorded within a geographical information system (GIS). The Goad plans were cross-referenced with lists of

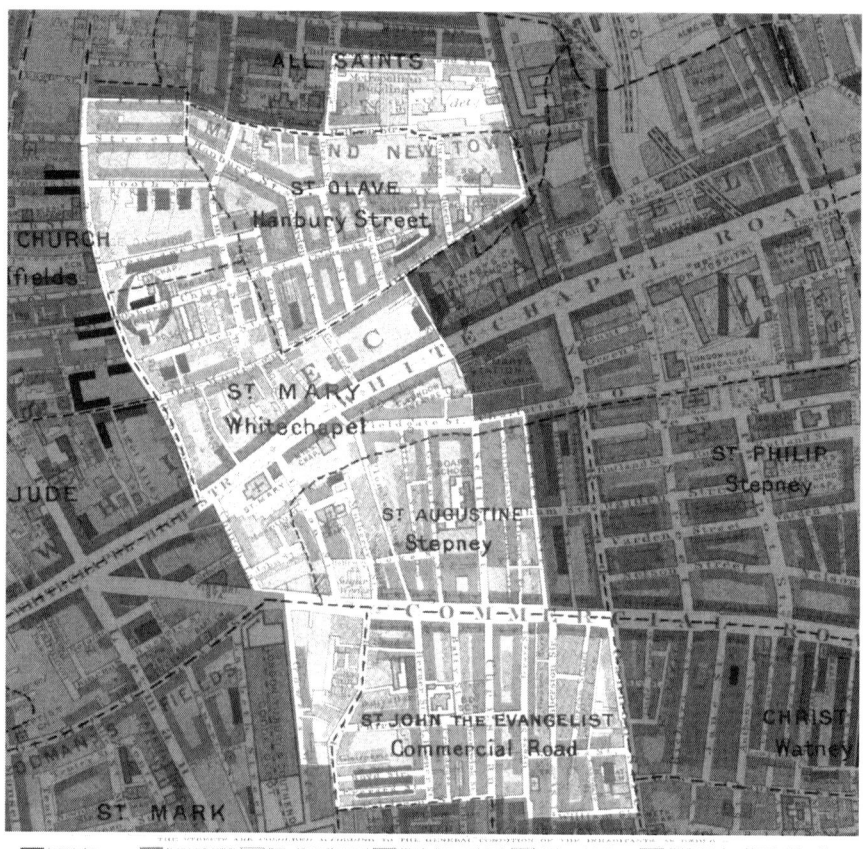

FIGURE 9.1 The study area – captured by a section from the Booth map of poverty
        1898–9. Maps from Charles Booth's *Inquiry into the Life and Labour of the*
        People in London (1886–1903)
Courtesy: London School of Economics. For colour version see the LSE website
http://booth.lse.ac.uk.

locations of synagogues from other sources in order to obtain information on date
of foundation and affiliation.[21] In total, there were fourteen synagogues and seven
churches recorded by Goad in the study area (see Table 9.1), though any existing
smaller one-room synagogues or other more temporary arrangements are not captured here, due to there being no historical record of their precise spatial location.

An important aspect of the study was a consideration of how the religious buildings
in the late nineteenth century communicated their presence to their surroundings, raising
the question of how visible the synagogues were to their neighbouring streets. In order
to address this question, the study was designed to analyse the embeddedness of the
Jewish community within wider society by taking account of how the street setting
provided opportunities for contact between Jews and Gentiles.[22]

The visibility and presence to the street for both synagogues and churches was established by drawing isovists and analysing their shape and extents. An isovist captures the visual field of an individual or object.[23] It marks the directly visible area from and around a vantage point. To construct isovists as realistic representations of a building's presence on the street, four distinct types of buildings were identified: 1) *Prominent* and *purpose-built* structures, which could be recognised at a distance due to their size, distinctive style and décor; 2) *Converted* buildings, many of which would have been religious buildings of another denomination, also visible from afar; 3) *Passage* types: buildings situated in courtyards with no direct access or façade to the street. Access instead was through a passage, often with signs on a street façade indicating the presence of a synagogue. 4) *Hidden*: these are synagogues located in courtyards with neither direct access to the street, nor any visible sign to the street. They were often accessed through shops or workshops. Figure 9.2 shows examples of all four types while Table 9.1 lists the classification of all religious buildings within the study area.

A recent book on urban Jewish culture in this period indicates the importance of Yiddish shop signs, billboards or newspaper stands as "visible markers" of a Jewish territory,[24] raising the question of how visible the synagogues were, given that they would only have needed to have advertised their presence to the Jewish community itself (or indeed only to their own congregations). Therefore, in addition to their visibility the analysis also enquired to whom they were likely to have been visible (whether to Jewish people or the wider community) and whether the degree of visibility changed according to the type of synagogue, the situation of the street or the degree of poverty within the area. The *hidden* synagogues may not intentionally have been located in a completely invisible setting. Indeed considering the ramshackle nature of the premises of all six examples, it seems likely that they were not hidden by intention but simply were located wherever financial circumstances allowed them to be.

The classification of all religious buildings within the study area (Table 9.1) demonstrates that the most common type amongst synagogues was Hidden (6), followed by Passage (5), Prominent (2) and Converted (1). In contrast, nearly all the churches were Prominent, with only a single Mission Hall hidden behind the street building line.

The isovists were drawn according to a careful consideration of what was the likely visibility of, on the one hand, a prominent building such as a church with a spire and, at the other extreme, a synagogue with no sign on the street to indicate its presence.

1) *Prominent* and *Purpose-built* Structures and 2) *Converted* Buildings

In the case of the first two types isovists were drawn from all the faces of each building's façade and extended until they met another building. To ensure the visibility of a façade was appropriately modelled according to human perception, we used an angle of 170 degrees (since façades would not be recognisable from a completely obtuse angle). All but one of the seven churches plus two synagogues in the study area fell into these two categories.

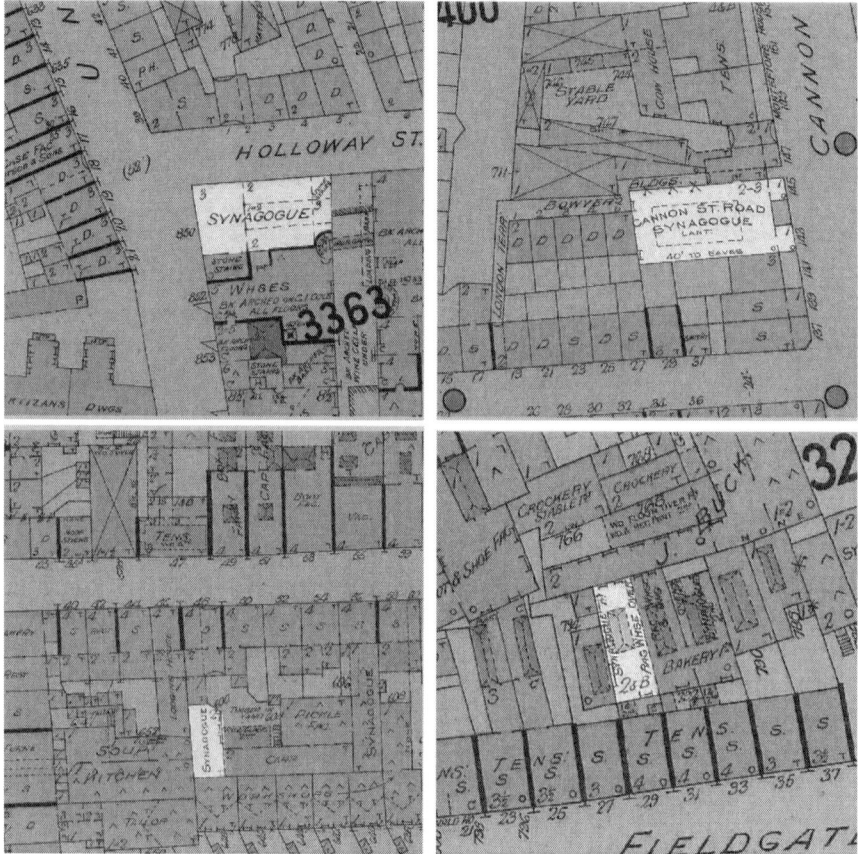

FIGURE 9.2 Four types of synagogues, showing from top-left to bottom-right, examples
of prominent, converted, passage and hidden types featuring on the Goad
Plan of 1899, sheets 336, 339, 320 and 323, respectively
© Crown copyright and Landmark Information Group.

3) *Passage* Buildings

In the case of the passage type of synagogue, a photograph dating from c. 1959 of
one of the synagogues, *Chevrah Shass*, provided evidence for the way in which such
synagogues announced their presence to the street, with a sign bridging the passageway at the point at which it met the street – this being the first point of connection
between the synagogues and the urban environs. As can be seen in Figure 9.3b,
an isovist was constructed from the passageway opening towards the street. Since a sign
would be neither legible at a great distance, nor readable at an obtuse angle, two
further limitations were introduced: first, that isovists were constructed at a degree
of 135 (rather than 170 degrees as above);[25] second, isovists were ended after 70
metres, given that any distance beyond this the sign would cease to be readable.[26]

TABLE 9.1 List of synagogues and churches within the Whitechapel study area

	Building	Name	Address	Position on street
1	Synagogue	*Chevra Torah*	Booth Street 20	Prominent
2	Synagogue	Cannon Street Road Synagogue	Cannon Street Road 143	Converted
3	Synagogue	Plotsker	Commercial Road East 45	Hidden
4	Synagogue	Mile End New Town Synagogue	Dunk Street 39	Passage
5	Synagogue	Crawcour Synagogue	Fieldgate Street 29	Hidden
6	Synagogue	House of David United Brethren Chevra	Fieldgate Street 33	Hidden
7	Synagogue	Fieldgate Street Synagogue	Fieldgate Street 41	Passage
8	Synagogue	Great Garden Street Synagogue	Great Garden Street 9–11	Passage
9	Synagogue	Greenfield Street Synagogue	Greenfield Street 81	Hidden
10	Synagogue	Brothers of Konin	Hanbury Street 48	Passage
11	Synagogue	The Brethren of Suwalki Synagogue	Hanbury Street 56	Hidden
12	Synagogue	*Chevrah Shass*[27]	Old Montague Street 42	Passage
13	Synagogue	Limciecz Synagogue	St Mary Street 3	Hidden
14	Synagogue	New Hambro	Union Street 850	Prominent
1	Church (Congregational)	St John the Evangelist	Grove Street 861	Prominent
2	Church (Anglican)	St Olave	Hanbury Street	Prominent
3	Church (various)[28]	Trinity Chapel	Hanbury Street 211	Prominent
4	Church (unknown)	Unknown (Gospel Hall)	Osborn Place 879	Hidden
5	Church (Anglican)	St Augustine's	Settles Street 882	Prominent
6	Church (Catholic)	German R.C. Chapel	Union Street 760	Prominent
7	Church (Anglican)	St Mary's	Whitechapel Road	Prominent

The last category of hidden synagogues was excluded from the isovist analysis, since they would not have any visible presence on the street.

In order to assess whether there were measurable differences between the street setting of synagogues and churches, additional data were captured from key historical sources for all buildings situated within the religious building isovists. Three different street block classifications of the buildings in the visual field of a synagogue or church were analysed:

1. Land use: namely the numbers of dwellings and non-domestic buildings according to the Goad Plan information (although much more detailed land uses were recorded for exploration at a future date).
2. Poverty as determined by the Charles Booth survey in six classes ranging from red (middle class) through pink, purple and then to the poverty classes of light blue, dark blue and black.[29]
3. Percentages of Jewish population showing proportion of Jews to Gentiles in six bands from 0–5 per cent to 95–100 per cent, from dark red to dark blue.[30]

FIGURE 9.3A An isovist drawn from passage entrance to Montague Street synagogue (*Chevrah Shass*) drawn on the Goad Plan of 1899, sheet 322
© Crown copyright and Landmark Information Group.

FIGURE 9.3B A photograph *c.* 1950 showing the *Chevrah Shass* Synagogue, Whitechapel, London, with a sign in Hebrew and English above the passage entrance; marked up with the measurements that were used to calculate assumed readable distances for all passage-type synagogues; *c.* 1946–1959. Artist: John Gay.
© Heritage Image Partnership Ltd/Alamy.

III The House of Assembly

In the first century and a half since the readmission of Jews to England in 1656, only a handful of purpose-built synagogues were erected in London. Aside from the Sephardi Bevis Marks, which was situated in a relatively hidden location on the edge of the City of London, these comprised the Great in Dukes Place; the Hambro, ultimately located in Fenchurch Street; and the New in Hambro Street.[31] Sharman Kadish describes how following the establishment of the United Synagogue movement in 1870 – set up to centralise resources for the funding of new synagogues – a "Golden Age" of synagogue architecture emerged, leading to a "boom [in the] erection of large-scale synagogues." These so-called cathedral synagogues, whose style of worship and architecture was in tune with the state church model, were set up to cater to an increasingly acculturated, English-born Jewry.[32]

In contrast, the synagogue in East London Jewish life was not purely a place of worship.[33] Anne Kershen describes how "it was almost a second home, a club and some-time friendly society which might provide benefits during sickness, unemployment and old age."[34] The East End practice of praying in smaller, self-organised synagogues represented an alternative institutional structure, with some synagogues formed as benefit societies, which organised the collection of dues for payment in the case of sickness, temporary incapacity and old age – hence the naming of many of these as *chevra*.[35] In some of these cases, as was the Eastern European practice, the congregants of one synagogue might be made up of members of the same trade; the *chevra* also assisted in negotiating a way into a new urban environment by providing a familiar social and cultural network for the newer immigrants.[36] As the meaning of the Hebrew *beit knesset*, or house of assembly, would suggest, it served as a community gathering place and was one of several aspects in which East End Jewish immigrants lived in a specifically Jewish milieu of "workplace, synagogue, theatres[37] and clubs, shops, politics or in the home."[38] Notably though, the synagogue was very much a male domain, with minimal (or no) accommodation for women congregants, other than in segregated galleries, or even entirely separate domains situated above the main men's hall.

A handful of the East End's medium-sized congregations worshipped in converted buildings previously used by other denominational groups, such as chapels or Mission Halls,[39] but most East End synagogues were *shtiebels*, or small synagogues.[40] In their most restricted incarnations they were simply temporary prayer rooms, set up at the back of workshops or living spaces. An anonymous account in the *Jewish Chronicle* of a visitor to a sick woman in Hanbury Street highlights how impoverished some of these settings could be. He described his climb up a steep staircase into what he thought initially was a bedroom, only to discover that it doubled as prayer hall, with an Ark (containing the holy scrolls of the Torah) and Reader's Desk: "the room was not only a kitchen and a bedroom, it was also a Shul … ."[41] Many poorer congregations made do with temporary conversions of an area within houses. These congregations might total only ten men (a *minyan*), the minimum quorum necessary for prayer.[42]

The eleven hidden and passage type synagogues in the study area (out of fourteen in total) emphasise the predominance of *shtiebels* over more prominently placed and visible synagogues in the East End overall. Historical evidence shows that most synagogues were accommodated in the sort of piecemeal extensions, lean-tos and other haphazard structures that according to Booth fell into three types: "the building of small houses back to back, fronting on to a narrow footway, with small courts utilising space at the rear of rows of housing; the building of workshops at the back and solid … extensions backing onto a house into another street."[43] In one example, the synagogue at 35 Fieldgate Street was said to be approached "through a somewhat dingy passage … built in the same way as many workshops in the locality on what was originally an open space at the back of the house."[44] In many ways these constructions were the only way the burgeoning population could be accommodated in the tight confines of the area, since very few open spaces had been left by the previous generation's infilling of small cottage properties with housing.[45] The Goad plans for 1899 Whitechapel in fact show remnants of that previous generation's less intensified industrial nature being intermingled amongst the area's workshops and tenements (see "cow house" and "stable yard" featuring in the Goad Plan for Cannon Street Road synagogue in Figure 9.2).

The Federation of Minor Synagogues was established in 1887 to draw together the East End's small synagogues under an umbrella organisation, with the professed aims of attracting formally trained preachers, to have representation at the established central Jewish organisation – the Board of Guardians – to organise ritual slaughter and to fund burials.[46] Reading the *Jewish Chronicle* of the preceding years indicates that it was also a response to a growing belief that the unaffiliated synagogues would delay assimilation of the new immigrants and attract anti-alienism for the community overall. In this context, the erection of model synagogues could be viewed as a form of "architectural colonialisation"[47] that would bring west London modes of behaviour to the streets of East London. The impact it was likely to have had on making the Jewish presence in the vicinity more visible is illustrated in the analysis of prominent synagogues in the next section.

The model synagogues were also constructed to improve problems with the unsanitary nature of some of the buildings as well as the risks related to overcrowding (such as upper storey doorways opening outwards onto staircases).[48] The Fieldgate Street synagogues in the bottom-right example in Figure 9.2 show such a layout, with a skylight apparently being the only source of lighting. Beatrice Potter described such a setting in 1887, where she found that:

> It is a curious and touching sight, to enter one of the poorer and more wretched of these places on a Sabbath morning. Probably the one you will choose will be situated in a small alley or narrow court, or it may be built out in a back yard. To reach the entrance you stumble over broken pavement and household debris; possibly you pick your way over the rickety bridge connecting it with the cottage property fronting the street. From the outside it appears a long wooden building surmounted by a skylight, very similar in construction to the ordinary sweater's workshop. You enter; the heat and odour convince you that the skylight is not used for ventilation. From behind the trellis of the 'ladies gallery' you see at the far end of the room the richly curtained Ark of the Covenant you may imagine yourself in a far-off Eastern land … At last you step out, stifled by the heat and dazed by the strange contrast of the old-world memories of a majestic religion and the squalid vulgarity of an East End slum.[49]

Despite the Federation's records showing several of the synagogues in the study area having been incorporated by the year 1899, Booth's notebooks show that whilst some of the buildings had met the standard demanded by the organisation, many of them were located in rundown premises on or near to highly impoverished streets, confirming the findings of our own sample area. Booth's researcher reports that Booth Street, for example, was comprised of three-storeyed buildings containing Jews, in tailoring and shoemaking occupations, with a decent purple classification (namely, just above the three poorest classes). Yet, the street opened up to Booth Street Buildings with:

> Rough and … poor Jewish inhabitants, … broken windows stuffed with rags, dirty, no curtains or blinds to windows only a bit of stuff drawn across lower half, ragged dirty children … Corners of the yard used as urinals, 'stench in hot weather' … .[50]

Great Garden Street's situation was worse still:

> Across Great Garden Street, the [east] corner of which both on the [north] and south sides are brothels, thieves, prostitutes and bullies, Black. In map Purple.[51]

Our analysis of the street setting of the study area's fourteen synagogues, compared with the seven churches in the area demonstrates that this juxtaposition of poverty and religion was not incidental. The poverty classes of the streets of all synagogues and churches observed in the study area indicate subtle differences between synagogues and churches: while mixed populations (shown in purple in Booth's maps) can be found across the sample, the lowest poverty class (marked in black and classified as "vicious, semi-criminal") can only be found amongst the synagogues sample (*Chevra Torah* and *Chevrah Shass*), while the better-off classes (marked in red and classified as "middle-class, well-to-do") are exclusively in the vicinity of churches within the sample (St Augustine's, German Roman Catholic Chapel and most notably St Mary's) – see Figure 9.4.

Interestingly, differences among the synagogues were found, too. The three synagogues visible from afar (*Chevra Torah*, Cannon Street Road Synagogue and New Hambro) were the only synagogues in the study area in close proximity to the class marked in pink by Booth (labelled as "fairly comfortable, good ordinary earnings"). Specifically in the case of Cannon Street Road, as a synagogue converted from a church, it makes sense to find its proximity to a higher class. Thus, the evidence tells us that some of the synagogues created a visible interface to different segments of the population. What is clear is that simply equating the presence of synagogues with poverty in the surrounding population would be misleading.

A similar picture emerges when the location of synagogues and churches is compared to the composition of Jewish population. A clear pattern can be found:

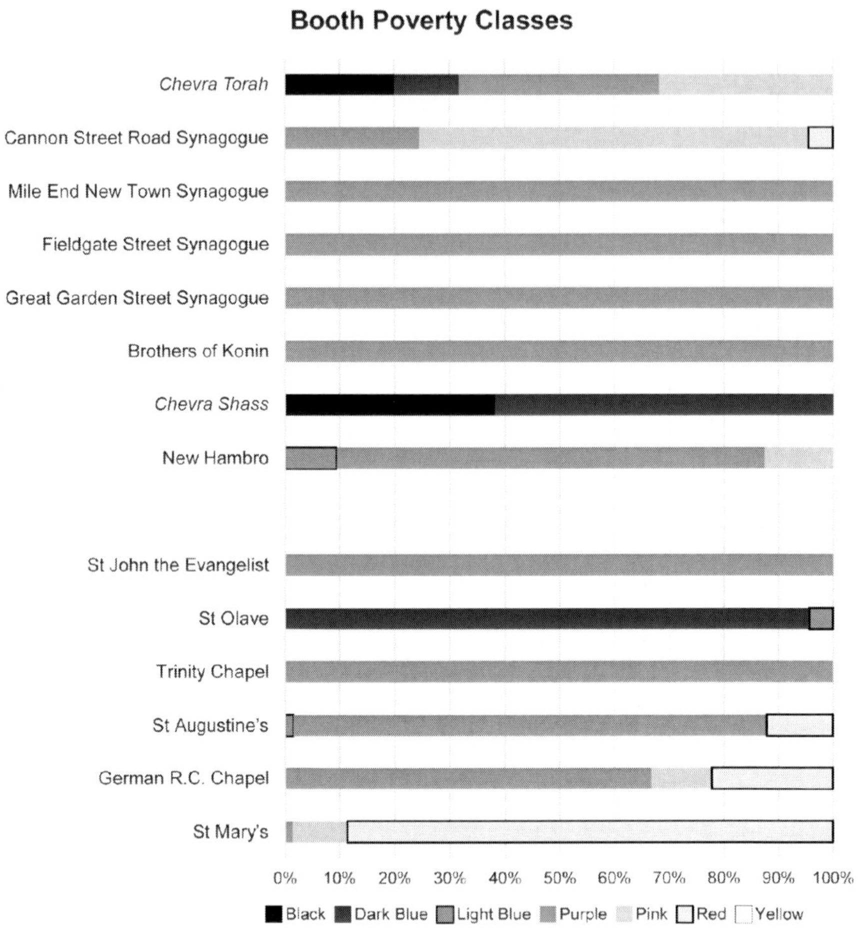

Booth Poverty Classes

Chevra Torah

Cannon Street Road Synagogue

Mile End New Town Synagogue

Fieldgate Street Synagogue

Great Garden Street Synagogue

Brothers of Konin

Chevra Shass

New Hambro

St John the Evangelist

St Olave

Trinity Chapel

St Augustine's

German R.C. Chapel

St Mary's

0%   10%   20%   30%   40%   50%   60%   70%   80%   90%   100%

■ Black ■ Dark Blue ▨ Light Blue ▨ Purple ░ Pink ☐ Red ☐ Yellow

FIGURE 9.4 Bar chart showing the proportion of Booth Poverty Classes in the visual fields of synagogues (top) and churches (bottom); the yellow category of 'Upper-middle and Upper classes' was not found in the sample.

all churches were within the vicinity of lower percentages of Jewish population (lower than 75 per cent Jewish); in contrast, all synagogues (but one) show at least 75 per cent Jewish population in the directly visible neighbourhood. This evidence suggests that the synagogues communicated their presence to a predominantly Jewish population and were not visible to the Gentile population to the same degree. It seems that religious practice, living and working were very closely intertwined, evident in patterns of spatial clustering.

IV Society: Together But Apart

It was emphasised at the beginning of this chapter that the densely woven streets and closely packed buildings of the East End created a setting in which the Jewish community had a large variety of its activities within reach from each other. The large concentrations of Jewish presence on a relatively small number of streets around the area suggests a high cohesiveness to their settlement. Nevertheless, the map of Jewish East London plays a visual trick, emphasising the relatively few dark, 95–100 per cent Jewish streets clustered in the westerly edge of the East End, rather than the many streets in which Jewish inhabitants featured alongside the non-Jewish population.[52] Booth's notebooks confirm how both poverty and prosperity, on both mixed or exclusively Jewish or Irish streets, intermingled turn by turn around the district. It is because of this spatial complexity that there is a need for a thorough understanding of the way in which Jewish spatial solidarity, enacted through its communal institutions, was visible to the community at large.[53] To what extent did the synagogues play a role in making the community visible?

Analysis of the visibility of religious practice in London's East End shows a significant difference between churches and synagogues. First of all, six of the seven churches in the study area were prominently positioned, while only a minority of the synagogues (three out of fourteen) enjoyed a similarly exposed and visible position in the urban fabric. Further analysis shows important variations in the size and shape of the relevant isovists (namely, visual fields; see Table 9.2). Isovist areas for the synagogues range from 74 sqm for the smallest (Great Garden Street Synagogue) to 2570 sqm for the largest (*Chevra Torah*), while those of the churches range from 930 sqm (Trinity Chapel) to 24,501 sqm (St Mary's). While there is an overlap of isovist size in the mid-range,[54] synagogues tended to have smaller isovists than churches and thus clearly show less visibility of the religious practice at street level, especially if one takes account of the fact that a large number were completely invisible and not included in this analysis. Even more telling are the differences regarding the longest length of the isovist. This measure indicates prominence and visibility, since longer isovists mean that the building is visible from further afield. With the exception of *Chevra Torah*, all synagogues were characterised by a significantly shorter isovist length (28–133 metres) than the churches in the study area (139–1093 metres).[55]

As the most prominent religious building in the study area, St Mary's takes on a special role in this analysis. It was described as a "noble spire" visible from a distance "far above the houses of the populous and struggling district around, a striking and commanding feature visible far and wide" (Figure 9.5). The description also demonstrates the strikingly different street setting from many of the synagogues: "Through the crowded streets of loungers, well-to-do church-goers of the middle classes are wending their way to morning service."[56] This particular position of St Mary's is clearly reflected through the data analysis of this study: it has the largest isovist area and length (see Figure 9.6 and Table 9.2); it has the

TABLE 9.2 Properties of visual fields of the synagogues and churches in the sample

	Building	Name	Isovist Area [sqm]	Longest length of isovist [m]
1	Synagogue	*Chevra Torah*	2,570	287
2	Synagogue	Cannon Street Road Synagogue	2,268	267
3	Synagogue	Plotsker	—— [Hidden]——	
4	Synagogue	Mile End New Town Synagogue	206	45
5	Synagogue	Crawcour Synagogue	—— [Hidden]——	
6	Synagogue	House of David United Brethren Chevra	—— [Hidden]——	
7	Synagogue	Fieldgate Street Synagogue	1,353	85
8	Synagogue	Great Garden Street Synagogue	74	28
9	Synagogue	Greenfield Street Synagogue	—— [Hidden]——	
10	Synagogue	Brothers of Konin	142	38
11	Synagogue	The Brethren of Suwalki Synagogue	—— [Hidden]——	
12	Synagogue	*Chevrah Shass*	483	60
13	Synagogue	Limciecz Synagogue	—— [Hidden]——	
14	Synagogue	New Hambro	1,795	133
1	Church (Congregational)	St John the Evangelist	962	160
2	Church (Anglican)	St Olave	3,644	284
3	Church (various)	Trinity Chapel	930	139
4	Church (unknown)	Unknown (Gospel Hall)	—— [Hidden]——	
5	Church (Anglican)	St Augustine's	2,798	280
6	Church (Catholic)	German R.C. Chapel	2,921	192
7	Church (Anglican)	St Mary's	24,501	1,093

FIGURE 9.5 St Mary's Church, Whitechapel, c. 1900[57]
© Ian Galt/Museum of London. The banner on the side is advertising sermons in
Yiddish.

highest proportion of middle-class populations in its visible neighbourhood; and
shows the lowest percentages of Jewish populations nearby. It stands in stark contrast to the majority of the synagogues, which were characterised as mostly small,
hidden and make-shift, communicating their presence to the street in a much more
subtle way, if at all.

Another significant result of the analysis is that despite the presence of twenty-
one religious buildings in the study area and some very prominent and large isovists,
not many of the visual fields overlap. Where synagogues are clustered spatially, for
instance in Hanbury Street or Fieldgate Street, many of them are hidden or barely
visible to the street. It is mainly the churches that are visible to each other, for
instance inside the visual field of St Mary's, the German Roman Catholic Chapel
can be seen as well. Likewise, there was inter-visibility between St Olave and
Trinity Chapel in Hanbury Street. The only visibility overlap between a church
and a synagogue was present in Union Street (see street running north-south in the
centre of Figure 9.6), where the New Hambro (in the southern end of Union
Street) and the German Roman Catholic Chapel (in the street's northern end)
communicated their presence to the same shared neighbourhood, which was part

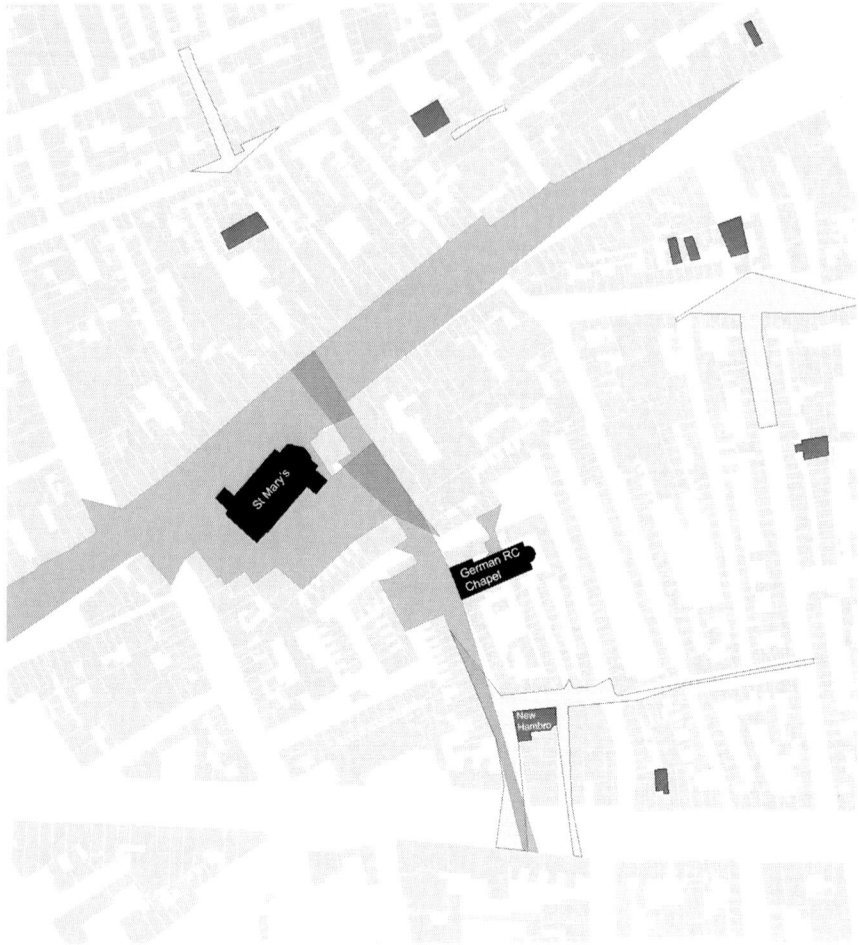

FIGURE 9.6 Overlapping isovists in the vicinity of Union Street with St Mary's church and German R.C. chapel as well as New Hambro synagogue marked.

Jewish, part Gentile and generally relatively prosperous according to Booth's poverty classifications (purple and pink). The New Hambro was one of only two of the fourteen synagogues prominent in the area and given that it was a transplantation of a synagogue originally situated in the City of London, it is unsurprising to find it being the outlier from this point of view also.[58]

V Conclusion: The 'Intensified Tempo' of Urban Life in Whitechapel

Simmel argued that urban life was a distinctly different manner of living, constituting an intensified tempo, whereby the narrow streets of the city paradoxically free one spiritually from the small-mindedness of small town life. At the same time, we have shown here how the street setting (as well as the mode of organisation) of small synagogues meant that they created an interior world, which allowed the Jewish community – in all its multiplicity – to negotiate its way into the urban environment "by providing a familiar social and cultural network."[59] It has been proposed that the variety of religious institutions since the inception of settlement in London's East End were due to "the particular structure of urban space in this area … [enabling] a state of co-presence which is shaped by the specific pattern of space of the area, which is integrated at a large scale, but locally segregated,"[60] suggesting that the relative seclusion of the areas of concentrated Jewish settlement allowed them to shift from the public, urban realm into the more Jewish milieu of the area's back streets. Our analysis here confirms this feature. It shows that the interfaces between Jews and Gentiles, between poor and well-off, and between synagogues and churches, followed subtle spatial patterns, characterised by both segregation and integration in a densely populated community, with the majority of synagogues having little visual prominence to streets with a low Jewish presence, nor to the more prosperous streets in the area.

Whitechapel comprised an open network of streets, some connected with the wider sphere of the city, with others quieter and more remote from city life. The lack of strong boundaries to the area meant that alongside the close-knit social circles of the Jewish community, were myriad opportunities – at least in principle – to encounter people from other backgrounds. While the home remained a "fortress" against an alien world and the synagogue formed a place of exclusively Jewish space, often hidden from the outside world, the main point of connection to wider society was the street – "a meeting place for peoples of different cultures."[61] Arguably, contact between Jew and Gentile worked in concentric circles of increased levels of encounter, from the domestic realm and religious sphere, where the worlds were apart, through to the streets themselves, which ranged from back streets with little likelihood of interaction – and hence a perception of foreignness and a "world apart" – to the truly urban thoroughfares, where one's foreignness could dissipate within the "metropolitan crowd." This characteristic is arguably what explains the vital importance of the "distinctively urban" aspect of London: the city serves as an integrating device – like many other nineteenth-century cities – to bring disparate people together.[62]

Simmel wrote how "the deepest problems of modern life derive from the claim of the individual to preserve the autonomy and individuality of his existence in the face of overwhelming social forces, of historical heritage, of external culture, and of the technique of life."[63] He is pointing out a general truth that applied just as well to the East End in 1899: the nature of urban space was that it could provide a setting in which the Jewish immigrants could preserve their autonomy and individuality, sometimes connecting with the city at large and sometimes seeking out the sanctuary of Jewish life in the largely exclusive preserve of the synagogue. Yet importantly, this study has shown a divergence within the sample of fourteen synagogues found within the study area. Although our research shows that the majority of synagogues within the study area were exclusive in the way in which they set themselves apart visually and physically from the mixed streets of the area, the purpose-built "New Hambro" on the corner of Union Street and the converted premises of Cannon Street Road synagogue (founded 1899 and 1895, respectively), represent the start of a process initiated by earlier generations of Jewish immigrants in London, to move from back street, hidden locations, into prominent buildings with a clear architectural identity.

This process sits well within the spatial logic of the wider range of public-facing institutions that the Jewish community had at this time. As Gidley has written, "in that historical moment, the East End hosted a complex web of contentious, subaltern, multi-lingual micro-public spaces" which included posters advertising English products in Hebrew script [i.e. in Yiddish], street corners and parks, "which functioned as open air debating societies" and other places for quasi or actual political activity, such as "working men's clubs, reading rooms, mutual aid associations and friendly societies." Whilst the majority of synagogues were exclusively Jewish spaces, Gidley suggests that the transformation of the profane attics and backrooms into temporary synagogues: sacred spaces of prayer, learning and "Talmudic dialogue" were part and parcel of the way in which the Jewish population created spheres of engagement with both local London issues as well as with transnational politics, given that they served as meeting places for political discussion as well.[64] Thus, even within the supposedly singularly, exclusively Jewish domain of the synagogue, the world outside was never completely cut off.

Acknowledgements

The authors are grateful for the sterling efforts of our research assistant, Ms Blerta Dino, Ph.D. student within the Space Syntax Laboratory, Bartlett School of Architecture, University College London, in preparing the GIS data and carrying out the preliminary analysis for this project. Some of the initial findings were presented at the Urban History Group conference in Cambridge, March 2016. We are grateful also for the helpful comments from the audience members there.

Notes

1 G. Simmel, "The Metropolis and Mental Life (Original German, 1903)," in Kurt H. Wolff (ed.), *The Sociology of Georg Simmel: Translated, Edited and with an Introduction by Kurt H. Wolff* (New York and London, 1950), pp. 409–19.
2 Ibid.
3 C. Booth, *Life and Labour of the People in London*, 17 Vols (3rd series ed., London, 1902).
4 W.J. Fishman, *East End 1888: A Year in a London Borough among the Labouring Poor* (London, 1988).
5 R. Lichtenstein, *On Brick Lane, a Chronicle of Changes in the East End* (London, 2007).
6 A.J. Kershen, *Strangers, Aliens and Asians: Huguenots, Jews and Bangladeshis in Spitalfields 1660–2000* (London, 2005), p. 140.
7 Fishman, *East End*, p. 131 states that a dozen years earlier, Charles Booth estimated the Jewish population of Whitechapel to be 28,790, although the Russell and Lewis 1901 publication stated that the difficulty of any precision in numbers, other than that there

had been a considerable increase in the past few years, remained. C. Russell and H.S. Lewis, *The Jew in London (with a Map Specially Made for This Volume by Geo. E. Arkell)* (London, 1901), p. 7.

8 B. Walter, "England People Very Nice: Multi-Generational Irish Identities in the Multi-Cultural East End," *Socialist History Journal*, Vol. 45 (2014), pp. 78–102.

9 M.A. Kimball, "London through Rose-Coloured Graphics: Visual Rhetoric and Information Graphic Design in Charles Booth's Maps of London Poverty," *Journal of Technical Writing and Communication*, Vol. 36 (2006), pp. 353–81.

10 R. Evans, "Rookeries and Model Dwellings: English Housing Reform and the Moralities of Private Space," *Architectural Association Quarterly*, Vol. 10 (1978), pp. 25–35.

11 L. Vaughan, "Mapping the East End Labyrinth," in A. Werner (ed.), *Jack the Ripper and the East End* (London, 2008), pp. 218–37.

12 M. Hebbert, *London: More by Fortune than Design* (Chichester, 1998), p. 53.

13 C. Booth, "Poverty Series Survey Notebooks (Online Archive)," booth.lse.ac.uk, B350, pp. 43, 45, accessed 23 June 2007.

14 Ibid., B351, p. 37.

15 Ibid., B351, p. 47 also cited in V. Bailey, *Charles Booth's Policemen: Crime, Police and Community in Jack-the-Ripper's London* (London, 2014), p. 95.

16 C. Russell and H.S. Lewis, *The Jew in London*.

17 L. Vaughan, "The Relationship between Physical Segregation and Social Marginalisation in the Urban Environment," *World Architecture*, Vol. 185 (2005), pp. 88–96.

18 A.J. Kershen and L. Vaughan, "There was a Priest, a Rabbi and an Imam … : An Analysis of Urban Space and Religious Practice in London's East End, 1685–2010," *Material Religion*, Vol. 9, Issue 1 (2013), pp. 10–35.

19 Charles E. Goad produced detailed (scale 1:1056, namely 1 inch to 88 feet) and coloured plans of urban areas in Britain between 1885 and 1970 to assess the risk of fire for fire insurance companies. This study used Goad Fire Insurance plans, Vol. 11, sheets 320–4 and 336–9; copyright and database right Crown Copyright and Landmark Information Group Ltd.

20 The maps, dated 1864–1911, were provided by the Ordnance Survey/EDINA Digimap service.

21 The lists featured in J. Glasman, "London Synagogues and the Jewish Community, c. 1870–1900," unpublished M.Sc. Dissertation (Bartlett School of Architecture, University College London, 1982), whilst Sam Melnick, a synagogue historian, provided access to his list of "Sites of Synagogues 1800 to 1940" through personal contact with the first author in 1990.

22 Gentile is the term used in the Jewish East London study to describe non-Jewish people. In fact, this would have covered many different groups.

23 Originally defined by M.L. Benedikt, "To Take Hold of Space: Isovists & Isovist Fields," *Environment and Planning B*, Vol. 6 (1979), pp. 47–65.

24 T. Metzler, *Tales of Three Cities: Urban Jewish Cultures in London, Berlin, and Paris (1880–1940)* (Wiesbaden, 2014), p. 139. Indeed, shop signs continue to be a subject of discussion regarding signs of the presence of a "foreign" culture in public space, as discussed by Hall and Datta in their study of contemporary London; S. Hall and A. Datta, "The Translocal Street: Shop Signs and Local Multi-culture along the Walworth Road, South London," *City, Culture and Society*, Vol. 1 (2010), pp. 69–77, or in the study of contemporary Sydney, Australia by A. Wise: "Foreign Signs and Multicultural Belongings on a Diverse Shopping Street," *Built Environment*, Vol. 37 (2011), pp. 139–54.

25 This was established experimentally by a researcher noting signage sizes, distances and angles at which urban signage could still be read.

26 Based on research on the readability of signage and relevant distance thresholds, the formula presented in Kuhn et al., 1997 was applied, which suggests a readable distance of 3.6 metres per cm of size of font used on the sign. B. Kuhn, P. Garvey, and M. Pietrucha, "Model Guidelines for Visibility of on-Premise Advertisement Signs," *Transportation Research Record: Journal of the Transportation Research Board*, Vol. 1605 (1997), pp. 80–7.

An image of the *Chevrah Shass* served as an example of contemporary signs indicating passages to synagogues, where a distance threshold of 70 metres was established.

27 The normal transliteration to English spells chevra, but this is the spelling used by the synagogue (see Figure 9.4).

28 This church had different denominations over time including Calvinist, Independent and Congregational; from 1862 it was known as Trinity Congregational Church. Source: Survey of London, Vol. 27, pp. 265–88.

29 These were the Charles Booth's Maps Descriptive of London Poverty, 1898–9, digitised and made available by the London School of Economics library's Charles Booth Online Archive project http://booth.lse.ac.uk, accessed September 2015.

30 The map, published in Russell and Lewis (1901), was drawn by George Arkell, a cartographer who also worked on the Booth maps. According to the book (p. xxxiv), the main source of information on Jewish presence in each street was the London School Board, along with the Superintendents of Visitors of the Tower Hamlets and Hackney Divisions. The School Board provided data on all families with children under fourteen, distinguishing between Jewish and non-Jewish children by forename and surname and observance of Jewish holidays, extrapolating from households with Jewish children to all households within the street (or for long streets, within the street section). The area was divided into six classes, of which the three in shades of red denoted a Jewish minority presence in a given street (whereby the darker the colour, the lower the proportion of Jews) and the three shades of blue did the same in reverse (the darker the blue, the higher the concentration of Jews).

31 Kershen, *Strangers*, p. 85.

32 S. Kadish, "Constructing Identity: Anglo-Jewry and Synagogue Architecture," *Architectural History*, Vol. 45 (2002), pp. 386–408.

33 The decision to form independent, self-governing prayer houses, rather than join those affiliated to the United Synagogue was due to a variety of reasons: cost (the membership charges would have been prohibitive for the new immigrants), logistics (there were very few such synagogues within walking distance of the East End, which would have limited access for the orthodox practice of not travelling on the Sabbath and indeed there was limited leisure time to attend services at any distance from the workplace), but most importantly it was a matter of difference in style of service; the formal Anglo-Jewish practice would have been very much at odds with the less decorous style of worship familiar from Eastern Europe.

34 Kershen, *Strangers*, p. 86. See also this chapter, Table 9.1, where Limciecz Synagogue is one of many examples of the time of the "fusing of *der heim* with the here" whereby smaller synagogues would name their congregation after the town of origin of its founders.

35 A *chevra* (plural: *chevrot*) is the Hebrew and Yiddish word for a social or voluntary association for religious purposes often forming the congregation of a small synagogue. Many East London *chevrot* were just as much friendly societies as synagogues, set up to assure funds for funerals and burials. Although the term *shtiebel* is frequently used interchangeably with *chevra*, it simply denotes a small synagogue (from the German *Stüberl* which means small room).

36 Metzler, *Tales of Three Cities*, p. 129. See also R.P. Kalman, "The Jewish Friendly Societies of London, 1793–1993," *Transactions of the Jewish Historical Society of England*, Vol. 33, 1992–1994 (1995), pp. 141–61.

37 See D. Mazower's chapter on Yiddish theatre in this volume, pp. 151–83.

38 T. Kushner, "Jew and Non-Jew in the East End of London," in G. Alderman and C. Holmes (eds), *Outsiders & Outcasts: Essays in Honour of William J. Fishman* (London, 1993), pp. 37–8.

39 An example of building adaptation of this nature is revealed by the newspaper report of a dispute over a bill from an architect commissioned to "convert business premises in Hanbury Street into a synagogue … to look at the buildings and see if they could be altered as desired" (*Jewish Chronicle*, 23 October 1896).

40 See note 37 for meaning of *shtiebel*. The transliteration from Yiddish follows various English spellings. We have standardised these, except when quoting directly.
41 "A Humble Chevra Room," *Jewish Chronicle*, 23 August 1895. *Shul* is the Yiddish word for a synagogue.
42 Beatrice Potter reporting for Charles Booth, C. Booth (ed.), *Life and Labour of the People in London* (I–IV; London, 1889–93). Vol. I, pp. 572–3, as quoted in Fishman, *East End*, p. 167. Beatrice Webb (née Potter), an important social scientist in her own right, assisted Charles Booth in his investigations.
43 C. Booth (ed.), *Life and Labour of the People in London*, Vol. 1, p. 31, as quoted by J. Glasman, "Architecture and Anglicization: London Synagogue Building, 1870–1900," *Jewish Quarterly*, Vol. 34 (1987), p. 18.
44 Federation Minutes 19 January 1897, quoted by Glasman, "Architecture and Anglicization," p. 18.
45 J. Glasman, "Assimilation by Design: London Synagogues in the Nineteenth Century," *Immigrants and Minorities*, Vol. 10 (1991), p. 183.
46 *Jewish Chronicle*, 21 October 1887.
47 Glasman, "London Synagogues," p. 57.
48 *Jewish Chronicle*, 7 March 1890, reports that the Federation's Honorary Architect had found a number of synagogues to be "dangerous," requiring the urgent material assistance of the Federation. His report on the decrepit built fabric of two of the synagogues in Fieldgate Street stated that it was "only a matter of time" before an accident were to happen, due to women rushing down the staircase from the gallery, where the door opened the wrong way.
49 C. Booth (ed.), *Life and Labour of the People in London*, Vol. I (London, 1889), p. 170.
50 C. Booth, "Poverty Series Survey Notebooks (Online Archive)," B351, p. 151.
51 Ibid., p. 133. "Bullies" at this time this would mean either a ruffian hired for purposes of violence or intimidation or a protector of prostitutes. The reference to black and purple in the notebooks is due to the 1898–9 survey being a revisiting of the earlier, 1889 survey. Here the notes are indicating that the 1889 survey classified the street as purple, but it was being reclassified downwards to the lowest classification, black.
52 See for example the notebook entry for Brushfield Street: "West along Brushfield St. North up Gun St. very rough. Mixture of dwelling houses and factories … a Jewish common lodging at the N.W end. Where the Jew thieves congregate … South of Brushfield St. Gun Lane is rougher than the north end. Street narrow. Loft across from wall to wall. Old boots & mess in [street]. Dilapidated looking: ticket of leave men living here: at least dark blue on map purple. But it is not a street particularly noted for prostitutes! At the North end is Fort St. Fairly well to do. Pink rather than purple of map: Jew middlemen live here … Duke [Street] has houses on East side. The west side is all factories & warehouses. Character [dark blue to light blue,] in map purple. The coster flower & fruit sellers in Liverpool St. come from here! Inhabitants are a mixture of Jews & Irish." C. Booth, "Religious Influences Survey Notebooks," (Online Archive), B351, pp. 100–1.
53 Vaughan, "Physical Segregation and Social Marginalisation," *World Architecture*, pp. 88–96.
54 This overlap means that a t-test indicating differences of sizes of isovists between synagogues and churches is not statistically significant, indicating that size of the isovist alone is not a definite predictor of religious building type.
55 In this case, the t-test delivers statistically significant results, i.e. isovist length is indicative of building type. In addition, the three churches of Anglican denomination (St Mary's, St Olave and St Augustine's) have the longest isovist lengths among the churches, pointing to subtle differences among the sub-sample of churches.
56 H. Walker, *East London: Sketches of Christian Work and Workers* (London, 1896). There are no obvious page numbers in this source.
57 This image of St Mary's shows the church tower with a huge banner advertising Yiddish sermons. According to the Museum of London caption, "On Saturdays at 5.00pm, addresses to the Jewish community would be made from St Mary's open-air pulpit.

Special services for Jewish festivals would also be conducted, read in Hebrew and German, and sermons preached in English and Yiddish. Up to 500 people would make up the congregation" (http://www.museumoflondonprints.com/image/141270/john-ga lt-st-marys-church-whitechapel-c-1900, accessed 8 April 2016. St Mary's seems to have formed part of the effort that the Anglican Church devoted at that time (almost totally unsuccessfully) to the conversion of the immigrant Jews. Indeed, Bill Fishman quotes the American Missionary Societies' analysis of the cost of doing religious work around the world, which listed the outlay required for "converting a Jew" to be $2,800 in contrast with an African, $14 and so on up the scale to "A Chinese, $100." Fishman, *East End*, p. 173.

58 Another point of difference was that the New Hambro was a constituent member of the United Synagogue movement, rather than the Federation of Synagogues.

59 Metzler, *Tales*, p. 122.

60 Kershen and Vaughan, "There was a Priest, a Rabbi and an Imam ... ," p. 31.

61 Kushner, "Jew and non-Jew," p. 39.

62 B. Hillier, "The Architecture of the Urban Object," *Ekistics*, Vols 334 and 335 combined (1989), p. 18.

63 Simmel, "The Metropolis," p. 409.

64 B. Gidley, "Cultures of Translation: East London, Diaspora Space and an Imagined Cosmopolitan Tradition," in N. Sigona et al. (eds), *Diasporas Reimagined: Spaces, Practices and Belonging* (Oxford, 2015), pp. 38–9.

Select Bibliography

Robin Evans, "Rookeries and Model Dwellings: English Housing Reform and the Moralities of Private Space," *Architectural Association Quarterly*, Vol. 10 (1978), pp. 25–35.

Judy Glasman, "Assimilation by Design: London Synagogues in the Nineteenth Century," *Immigrants and Minorities*, Vol.10 (1991), pp. 171–211.

Bill Hillier, "The Architecture of the Urban Object," in *Ekistics*, Vols 334 & 335 (January/ February 1989 & March/April 1989), pp. 5–21.

Anne J. Kershen, *Strangers, Aliens and Asians: Huguenots, Jews and Bangladeshis in Spitalfields 1660–2000* (London, 2005).

Tobias Metzler, *Tales of Three Cities: Urban Jewish Cultures in London, Berlin, and Paris: 1880–1940*, (Wiesbaden, 2014).

George Simmel, "The Metropolis and Mental Life (original German, 1903)," in Kurt H. Wolff (ed.), *The Sociology of Georg Simmel: Translated, Edited and with an Introduction by Kurt H. Wolff* (New York and London, 1950), pp. 409–19.

10

DOING THE EAST END WALK, OI!

Heritage, Ownership and Belonging[1]

Tony Kushner

I

"Lambeth you've never seen … Why don't you make your way there?" To Tom Harrisson and Charles Madge, co-founders of Mass Observation, the lyrics of Douglas Ferber's hit song, "Doing the Lambeth Walk," from *Me and My Girl* (1937) revealed much about Britain in the late 1930s. If, they posited,

> … the song had been a rumba and the words had been 'Cuba you've never seen,' there would be reasons of distance to explain why only a few people have seen Cuba or know what it is like. But Lambeth is not so far away, and there is the equivalent of Lambeth round every corner.[2]

To them it reflected the ignorance of one section of British society (the elite) about the other (the working class) and how it lived and thought.

Nevertheless, these radical and unorthodox anthropologists of Mass Observation also recognised the particularity of Lambeth as a "Cockney area, south of the river" and traced the origins of the song to the music hall traditions connected to that specific part of London.[3] An Observer from the organisation went into a local pub there and, when asking how long they had been doing the Lambeth Walk, was told: "Oh years ago when we were little shirt buttons. Fifty years ago. We used to call it the jig."[4] Tracing its origins to the Irish jig, the black American "Cake Walk" (which in turn owed much to the "ceremonial dances of the Seminole Indians"), and the coster traditions of the music halls, Mass Observation was torn between acknowledging its diverse origins and evolving nature and viewing it as an expression of essentialised Cockney culture.[5]

Mass Observation carried out its ethnographic fieldwork most famously in Bolton, or what it called "Worktown" (alongside its northern sister,

"Holidaytown" or Blackpool).[6] Less known is its base in the East End of London.[7] One reason for its presence there was to study anti-Semitism amongst the "tribes" of this infamous area. To Mass Observation, these consisted mainly of Cockneys and Jews whom they would study "quite objectively" to reveal the "differences and similarities."[8] That these were not mutually exclusive categories did not occur to the leaders of Mass Observation. As the writer Julian Franklyn noted in response:

> Some Jews (in fact many) are Cockneys, not only because they were born within the sound of Bow Bells, as the saying has it, but because for several generations the Cockney environment has been assimilated.[9]

Franklyn described himself as "a Jew and a Cockney. A disbelieving Jew and a suspicious Cockney … ."[10] To Harrisson and Madge, Lambeth represented the true Cockney whereas the East End of London was mixed with different tribes who led separate if similar lives.[11] Overall, in their mind, the area produced a confusing ethnographic picture. In this, they were at least in partial agreement with one of Mass Observation's harshest critics who described their East End research as superficial, tendentious, inaccurate and untruthful "tripe:" "No Londoner living East of Bloomsbury has in my experience ever described himself or his neighbour as a 'cockney'."[12]

In reality, the cultural life of *Me and My Girl* represented the cosmopolitan and regionally varied nature of interwar Britain and beyond. The show's impresario was the managing director of the Locarno Dance Halls, C.L. Heimann, who had come to Britain in the 1920s from Denmark allegedly without a word of English. Lupino Lane, who took the part of Bill Snibson, the Cockney hero of the musical and also partly responsible for its catchy tune, was of British-Italian heritage. Noel Gay, who co-wrote the tune, was originally Reginald Armitage and born in Wakefield.[13] The song and dance itself became a global phenomenon extending to New York, Paris, Budapest and Prague – so much so that it was banned in Nazi Germany because of its alleged Jewish and "Negro" sexualised influences which led it to become even more popular there as a form of everyday resistance.[14]

One reason for the Nazis' anxieties was the climax of the "Doing the Lambeth Walk" chorus, with its emphasised "Oi." Originally, Mass Observation reported that "Wo-up" and not "Oi!" was the original exclamation point of the dance.[15] In popular culture, the new wording linked it for some to a Jewish discourse. Indeed, it was often essentialised as part of what Sander Gilman has labelled the "Jew's body" and performed by "Hebrew comedians."[16] In its anti-Semitism research, Mass Observation found that "Oi" was associated with a "lewd comedian … Typical lower class Jewish wit."[17]

Lupino Lane was adamant that there was "no special reason" why the character Bill Snibson came from Lambeth: "it was pure chance … [he] might have been Hoxton or Stepney."[18] But for all the ambiguity of origins that the "Oi" added, setting it south of the river and not in the East End was important for the success of the song and the musical. As Bill Fishman emphasised, the East End had *too many* associations and mythologies associated with it, most notoriously Jack the Ripper, to make it "unknown territory."[19] Spitalfields especially, is, as Anne Kershen notes, "a landscape composed of myth and reality," notorious as "'deprived, dangerous and exotic … ' 'a jungle', 'a bazaar', 'an abyss', words which instantly conjure up images of poverty, violence and otherness."[20]

It was also the case that the diversity of its population made constructing a stereotypical English Cockney in Spitalfields much harder than the superficially less cosmopolitan Lambeth. In the East End, not only did many Jews define themselves as Cockneys, but they might well be mistaken for other groups of migrant origin – Franklyn suggested Italians or Greeks.[21] "Doing the East End Walk, Oi," would have to wait a further generation or so from the 1930s, and then it would be through tours round the neighbourhood and faux heritage, and not in the form of an internationally successful and much-revived musical.[22] Nevertheless, post-Second World War walking tours of the East End had deeper roots in heritage construction which can also be traced to Mass Observation.

Julian Franklyn had queried of the paid investigators of Mass Observation in the East End: "who *are* these 'innocents abroad'?"[23] Following a trip to the New Hebrides earlier in the 1930s, Tom Harrisson had boasted about his ability to pass as a "local" whilst living with the "last remaining cannibals in the South Seas." It was, he took pride in telling his followers, "hardly the usual thing for an English-man to go native – especially to go cannibal."[24] Closer to home, as Franklyn cruelly but perhaps accurately noted, the organisation never quite got to grips with observing the cannibal tribes of Britain.[25] But in the East End project, alongside Harrow-educated Tom Harrisson was Nina Massel, a young local Jewish commu-nist who later wrote powerful descriptions of the impact of the blitz in Stepney.[26] Nevertheless, Harrisson was the dominant force. For all his efforts at "objectivity," Harrisson followed in the footsteps of other English middle-class writers including Dickens, Mayhew, Potter and Booth, as well as Jack London from abroad, who had come to visit or live in the East End, and see for themselves its poverty and violence first hand as journalists, flâneurs or social activists. Indeed, from the second half of the nineteenth century, the East End was at the heart of what Seth Koven has called the process of "slumming" with all its sexualised associations.[27]

It was through Tom Harrisson and his Mass Observation work that the first formally recorded "tour" of the East End took place using modern technology. In one of the earliest BBC television documentaries, Harrisson led viewers around the places and personalities of the area.[28] Sadly the film itself does not survive but the script is preserved if not in full verbatim form. Entitled *East End*, it was broadcast on 12 July 1939. It was framed by a discussion between the "outsider" Harrisson as the ethnographer and the locally rooted Mrs Green, a "typical" East Ender to whom he will reveal the world which only a street away from her house remains a foreign territory.

For Mrs Green, her neighbourhood is unremarkable. But to Harrisson "this East End of London is just as interesting to me as the Arctic or Pacific Islands were when I was an explorer."[29] Mrs Green replies that she has not seen "any wild animals roaming round here" to which Harrisson is keen to emphasise that it is still "full of the unknown" beyond the lives of her next door neighbours.[30] What follows is Harrisson's desire to show both the normality and strangeness of the East End – a template for the wider work of Mass Observation. The organisation itself was formed out of a frustration and a fear that politicians and the media were alienating the British people from one another, leading also to an ignorance of the growing international crisis.

In his notes on the script, Harrisson emphasised how the East End was the entrance to a great port city, with the docks dropping off people from "every maritime nation on earth." As a result, "a huge mixed population has silted up, to make the most varied, colourful confusing hubub in the world."[31] To him this was a vision of peaceful co-existence as global conflict threatened:

> In the East End today the League of Nations works in fact. People of every colour and tongue live and work and drink and play darts side by side. The East End, a million people without a park or a hotel, is the one place where anyone can look like almost anything on earth, yet go unnoticed and unwatched.

Sentimentally, and no doubt fictionally, to illustrate its diversity Harrisson took delight in informing the viewers that on his first night in the East End, and asking for directions, the "first I asked turned out to be a negro. The second a Chinaman. The third a Jew. The fourth a Cockney."[32]

In many respects, Harrisson's film was years ahead of its time, moving beyond the portrayal of the East End as dangerous, diseased and subversive and emphasising instead the positive immigrant contributions to the area from the Huguenots onwards, as well as its everyday normality. Even so, there is a hierarchy of belonging established, with Mrs Green as the Christian Cockney at the apex and those most marginal at the bottom who were presented literally as "the colour of the East End." With regard to the latter, "First and nearest to the sea [is] the Lascar. He works his way in as a sailor, heavy sea work, and he comes to anchor almost imperceptibly in the East End … happy to sleep on the shelves of empty shops and without any centre. The film must then move swiftly so as 'not to lose [the] racial link'."[33] It did so by pitting Lascar transcience against the Chinese Limehouse.

As late as 1926, travel writer H.V. Morton had claimed in *The Nights of London* that Limehouse was like the "native quarter of an Oriental city" and that coming from the West End, he "could not have travelled farther from the London that most of us know."[34] Faced with the reality that this "special Chinatown" was in fact in decline and rather mundane, Harrisson's film initially emphasised the "otherness" of this small area through "Chinese music, exotic, rapid, elaborate" and then proceeded to debunk popular (and its own) mythology. Harrisson was to ask "Is Limehouse really as romantic as it is painted?" but to do so with "deliberate naivety," similarly raising without conviction questions about the presence of drugs and secret societies in its streets of Chinese concentration. In fact, the difference in settlement patterns between the Chinese and Lascars was decided in advance.

Before the interviews had been carried out in their appropriate locations, representatives of the two "races" would be chosen with the following criteria: "Contrasting with the lascar we want a pretty clever Chinaman."[35]

Mrs Green and Harry Haynes, a Cockney docker, were at the top of the ladder in terms of being fully grounded in the East End, with the descendant of a Huguenot, Mr Lucking (a silk weaver) just a fraction below them. The "coloured races" were firmly at the bottom of the race ladder, leaving somewhere in the middle the Jews who were "The greatest race of the East End, after the Cockney."[36] Their intermediate and ambivalent status was amplified by the three Jews chosen to give their testimony. First was Basil Henriques, from one of the oldest Anglo-Jewish families, who was at the heart of elite social work in the area. The public school educated Henriques (like Harrisson, at Harrow) possessed the same status of authority in the documentary as the leader of Mass Observation and he presented the official view of the Jewish establishment about the working-class Jews of the area. Tellingly, it is only Henriques's testimony and that of the Cockney docker, alongside the commentary from Harrisson, that is fully preserved in the transcript. According to Henriques "Most Jews in East London today want to assimilate in every way, except in religion. The average Cockney has respect for another man's religion."[37]

The interviews that followed of Wolfe Michaels, a Jewish upholsterer and Mike Sterne, a market stall holder in Petticoat Lane, did not fundamentally query Henriques's simplistic analysis. Even so, they illustrated the poverty of the area and the struggle to survive within it. Although the BBC instructions for the film suggested shots of foreign-sounding shop names for the Jewish section, the two Jewish workers were presented as being rooted and an integral part of the everyday life and economy of the East End.[38] Echoing the defensive approach of Basil Henriques, Sterne is presented as offering a "fair deal" to his customers and Michaels is determined to stay there, in spite of the struggles to make a living.[39]

Harrisson's documentary confirms a normative "Cockney" narrative of the East End, but also lightly queried its own assumptions. For example, the Lascar, Mr Singh, was settled in the East End and had brought his wife and children to live with him. Thus he was not the transitory figure suggested in the treatment of the film.[40] And there are points at which essentialist readings of "Cockneydom" *were* explicitly challenged – the barrel organ playing the tune of the "Lambeth Walk" is used to show East Enders of *all* backgrounds uniting in strike action and it then merges into the "noises of Petticoat Lane," becoming one voice, that of the "medicine man [who] claims to cure the blues of every nation" (possibly the racing tipster, Prince Monolulu).[41] If somewhat unevenly, Harrisson's film predates the path-breaking exhibition, *The Peopling of London: 15,000 Years of Settlement from Overseas* (1993–1994), the first to show the full diversity of the capital's past.[42] Each section of this Museum of London exhibition was accompanied by various ethnic renditions of *Maybe It's Because I'm a Londoner*, Hubert Gregg's song which was first performed in 1947 by Jewish East Ender, Bud Flanagan.[43] Many visitors found the repeated "strains in various guise" of this number highly irritating.[44] Its purpose, however, as with the use of the *Lambeth Walk* in Harrisson's film half a century earlier, was, in the words of curator Nick Merriman, to "*challenge* the idea of what it means to be a Londoner. We want to show that, ultimately, all Londoners have come from overseas."[45]

Harrisson ended his programme on an optimistic note: there *was* local racial prejudice but it did not prevent people living side by side in relative harmony. Moreover, the poverty, pain and overcrowding did not cancel out the hallmark of the East End which was its vitality, "its tremendous interest in being alive." Yet it was perhaps Harrisson's desire to emphasise the positive attributes of the place that made him fail to realise its dynamism. In the documentary, for example, Petticoat Lane is presented as unchanging through the centuries: "it seems to me that the market now must be much the same as it ever was."[46]

II

Mass Observation's own work in the blitz was to chronicle the devastation caused to the area which would irretrievably mark it. But there were earlier tendencies from the interwar period, especially in relation to the declining Jewish presence there, that the intense bombing simply accelerated. If at its peak the Jewish East End had over 100,000 residents *before* the blitz, this number had declined already to around 60,000.[47] By 1945, the Jewish East End had become a shadow of its former self; a change that had to be confronted on a practical level within British Jewry immediately after the war. More generally, it is still being worked out in the twenty-first century through many different forms of cultural representation and practice.

In the later 1940s, the Jewish population of the area was still 25,000, one-quarter or one-fifth of the number at its peak before the First World War. As A.B. Levy noted in his *East End Story*, published in 1950, based on articles in the *Jewish Chronicle* two years earlier, "Stepney [still] holds as many Jews as Leeds."[48] Immanuel Jakobovits, later to become Chief Rabbi of the United Congregations of the Commonwealth, also commenting in 1948, stated:

> The most distinguishing feature of the East End of today is certainly its astounding multiplicity and variety of synagogal, social and educational institutions. Although more Jews are now living in North and North-West London than in the East we still have here the greatest number of Synagogues [and] the *Beth Din*.

Jakobovits then went on to list the presence of major burial societies, educational establishments as well as many of the social institutions such as the Jewish Board of Guardians and youth organisations. "Hardly any of these have joined the general human exodus to the Promised Land of North-West London."[49]

To this list, Levy added the importance of the East End for Jews coming back "to buy or sell, study or teach, go to work or to play, arrange a burial or a marriage, visit a parent … plan a *simcha*, or order a tombstone."[50] And yet there is in his *East End Story* a fatalism that the Jewish East End was in essence over: "If you have not been in East London for some years and now pay an evening visit to Whitechapel Road or Commercial Road you will find the pavements that once bustled with promenaders strangely empty." The same was true of the synagogues which once "thronged" and now mustered just a *minyan* or two.[51] And whereas Mass Observation and Tom Harrisson had viewed the Lascars and other non-white groups as just (exotic) tribes of the East End, Levy explicitly connected the decline of the Jews with what he labelled the rise of the "dark-skinned neighbours."[52]

The visitor to the East End might be reassured to find the presence of *Mezuzahs* on doorposts as an "accurate sign of Jewishness."[53] In fact, according to Levy, they would be mistaken: "The Muslim name over a shop; or the actual emergence of turbaned Sikh … controvert the implication of the tiny metal symbol on the door."[54] Christian Street in Spitalfields was now "not so completely the misnomer it used to be," and there Levy observed, using the phrase that Enoch Powell would make infamous two decades later, "some picaninnies and Jewish tots [are] busily playing together."[55]

Famously, Russell and Lewis in their study, *The Jew in London* (1900), included a map of the streets of East London, colour coded to show the concentration of Jewish residents.[56] This sociological device was not designed for the tourist. In contrast, Levy's *East End Story* included four simple maps designed as an aid to the visitor in finding or relocating Jewish places of interest. In the first, devoted to Bishopsgate and Aldgate, the sites were illustrated not for their ongoing religious or secular functions, but as acts of memory with the depletion of the Jewish population in mind:

> When you come eastward through the City in search of the Jewish East End, two of the most important landmarks exemplify the two reasons for dispersal: the synagogue at Bevis Marks has lost nearly all its congregants – they have moved to distant neighbourhoods; the congregants at Duke's Place have lost their synagogue – it was bombed and burned.[57]

In Whitechapel, the map is accompanied by the comment that "those two bearded figures a few yards away are not Jews but Sikhs."[58] The map for Mile End notes that the Great Assembly Hall is "now a gaping shell."[59] Thus rather than an encouragement to visit a declining world, Levy's *East End Story* was more a warning in preparation for loss and decay if those who had known it at its peak should stumble back into the neighbourhood.

More optimistically, there were still those keen to pursue the image of the East End as a melting pot where all races and religions lived, played and worked together in harmony. Harrisson's documentary intended to feature Father Groser, an East End clergyman who helped to combat Mosleyite anti-Semitism in the area during the 1930s by bringing together the area's Jews and non-Jews, especially in housing protests.[60] Groser's approach was continued after the war by the Council of Citizens of East London which through research, publications and educational initiatives worked to bring all the population together and to fight against different forms of racism and the rebirth of British fascism.

The Council aimed to show the long tradition of migration to the East End and how much each group had contributed to its distinctiveness. In *The Story of Our Streets* (1950), Chinese, Danish, English, Huguenot, Irish, Jewish, Saxon and Swedish linkages were emphasised from Adler Street through Fashion Street to Zangwill House.[61] The approach of the Council was summarised by its patron, Earl Attlee: "Though there have been some lapses, due mainly to external influences, East Londoners have been conspicuous for their exhibition of toleration. People of various races and religions have learnt to live together and to appreciate the qualities of others."[62]

The Council's publication and Harrisson's film are indicative of early concerns to promote the area as having a history of racial harmony. But there was also in *The Story of Our Streets* an apprehension that the rapidly "changing face of East London," much of which was desirable to remove the "traces of the past … which was sad and ugly," would also erase its immigrant histories. Its author noted, for example, that "One hopes that when the names are changed to suit the changed nature of the street surroundings, those of Canton and Pekin will not be displaced as they are among the few records left of the Chinatown of bygone days."[63] He wondered, with blitz and slum clearance in mind, how many of the houses of Huguenot master weavers of Spitalfields survived, emphasising the huge losses that had taken place of the area's oldest buildings.[64]

Harder to imagine in 1950 was the ending of the Jewish connections to Petticoat Lane market. *The Story of Our Streets* noted that it was not until the eighteenth century that Jewish immigrants first became prominent there but now "the initials P.L. written in Hebrew characters are used to indicate an East End origin."[65] Even the sombre tone of A.B. Levy's *East End Story* could not refrain from celebrating the spark of "The Lane" on a Sunday morning and the insults of the Jewish traders: "Come on, come on, you miserable lot of *schleppers*, what's the matter with you today? You make me tired! Forty-five years I've been standing here in the Lane – no wonder I'm tired." Even Prince Monolulu makes an appearance, "assuring in a high-pitched harangue, which includes a Yiddish phrase or two, that he's 'gotta horse'."[66]

As late as 1989 it was suggested that three-quarters of the market stall holders were Jewish even if "the once distinctive Jewish flavour of the Lane is … harder to find."[67] In his 2012 satirical explorer's guide to the "backpassages" of the East End, Alan Gilbey highlights the stark decline of that intimate linkage:

> In 1880 there were forty-six thousand Jews living in the East End. By 1900 there were one hundred and thirty-five thousand. Today there's a man called Morrie who sells string down Petticoat Lane and that's about it.[68]

Whilst Gilbey's statistics could be queried for overstating and then understating the spectacular rise and fall of the Jewish East End, his overall picture is correct – a population estimated at 7,500 in 1985 thereafter continued its noticeable decline.[69]

In its portrayal of loss and destruction during the Second World War, the focus of A.B. Levy's *East End Story* was *British* Jewish history, and especially that of the world made by East European Jews. The Holocaust features only once and is confined to the section on the Jews Temporary Shelter with mention of a couple who were "in the concentration camp of Auschwitz." There are sad stories of these survivors, but they are presented by Levy as being "other" to the East End. They thus pass through emphasising "transmigration and temporary shelter" as they await "the Queen Elizabeth for New York."[70] They are part of a longer story of movement *through* the locale but not integral to Levy's narrative.

The erasure of the Jewish East End and that of East European Jewry are thus not explicitly or even implicitly connected by Levy. But for the writer Joseph Leftwich, with his strong cultural links to the continent, the two were linked and inseparable. Wandering round Spitalfields in 1949 and the damage inflicted on it, Leftwich reflected that "It was Hitler, who destroyed so much of Jewish life, who also destroyed the [Jews'] Free School, in the Blitz of 1940 … The school has never been reopened."[71] For some in the Jewish world, postwar melancholia relating to the East End also led them to ponder on the passing of an even greater world and from which the former had emerged.

III

For those second generation Jewish East Enders writing after Levy and Leftwich in the 1950s and 1960s, varying from Arnold Wesker to Bernard Kops to Wolf Mankowitz, the interwar years were remembered through a mixture of anger at its poverty and anti-Semitism alongside nostalgia (political and cultural) for a world that had largely disappeared. The dominant note is that of Kops who in 1956 in *The Hamlet of Stepney Green*, "laments a world that has passed away." His character Sam, a "pickled-herring seller of Wentworth Street," is lost in time: "Whatever became of Whitechapel? Teeming with people, so gay, so alive … where are they?"[72] In his 1963 autobiography, Kops writes of his family who moved not to the gilded suburbs of *Golders* Green but to *Bethnal* Green, a mile or so from their original East End home. In spite of its proximity, "I could hardly bear to visit Stepney Green [his pre-war neighbourhood] any more. The air was thick with ghosts."[73] Similarly, Mankowitz's *The Bespoke Overcoat* (1956) is set in the postwar era and consists of a conversation between a Jewish tailor and Fender, a Jewish shipping clerk who has passed on, both reminiscing about the past and a world in which poverty did not undermine their dignity.[74]

In the 1960s, as James Jordan has illustrated, on radio and television the BBC brought back famous East Enders – Jewish and non-Jewish – including Jack Warner and Bud Flanagan, to visit the area and comment on change. In 1962, Flanagan presented an optimistic picture: the "Jewish people in my day, down there, they just strove to get out of the neighbourhood and they did." Flanagan was sure the same would be true of its more recent immigrants: "it is just the same to me – but with different people."[75] The singer and actress Georgia Brown was more hesitant in a 1968 television documentary. This programme focused on immigrant succession, and the challenges facing the newcomers from Pakistan and India who were fast replacing the Jews. She wondered whether separation or the melting pot was the answer to the rise of Powellite racism, emphasising the alleged problematic difference of the area's non-white newcomers.[76] That the Jews, in essence, had had their "turn" was not queried in these programmes which tended, unlike Norman Cohen's *The London Nobody Knows* (1967), to ignore the elderly Jews who were left behind in the race to the suburbs.[77]

These literary works of the 1950s and broadcasts of the 1960s were cultural products of, or reflections on, a talented second generation of East European Jews. None of them suggested rescuing what was in danger of being lost in terms of physical reminders of the past as the postwar redevelopment of the East End gathered momentum. In 1966 and 1968 *Jewish Chronicle* special supplements similarly marked the "passing of the 'golden age' of East End Jewry" but saw no need to preserve its buildings.[78] Commenting on the decline of the *chevras*, writer Chaim Bermant declared that "There are many Jews in the East End, but no Jewish life."[79] By the 1970s however, when the Jewish population was less than a tenth of its height half a century earlier, and the religious and commercial pull of the area for those from outside had also diminished, the first efforts were made to preserve the past and to revisit it in the form of self-reflexive commemoration and heritage conservation. It appeared in individual initiatives, organisational structures and key publications, not all of which, however, saw the preservation of that past as either possible or desirable.

From a literary perspective the most important of these was Emanuel Litvinoff's *Journey Through a Small Planet* (1972). Litvinoff was born in Whitechapel in 1915 to Russian immigrant parents. His autobiography is evocative but lacks any hint of sentimentality about the hardship and pain of his East End upbringing in Bethnal Green. The book was prompted by a visit, probably in the 1960s, from a Swedish author, Alvar Alsterdal, who "asked me to take him round the Jewish East End." Like the BBC documentaries of the same decade, on his return Litvinoff focused on the ethnic succession that had taken place. There were one or two Jewish shops and bakeries surviving "but instead of the old Yiddish newspapers on the counters there were others printed in Urdu. In Old Montagu Street, the very heart of the original Jewish quarter, nothing was left of the synagogue but a broken wooden door carved with the Lion of Judah."[80]

Litvinoff returned to his former tenement and rediscovered the initials which he had carved on the window ledge after failing a scholarship exam. Opening the door he "expected to see that same unhappy, resentful boy emerge to wander disconsolately into the street." Instead, an elderly man greeted him, expecting a visit from the council sanitary department. Echoing Kops a decade earlier, Litvinoff recorded, "I felt indescribably bereaved, a ghost haunting the irrecoverable past."

His response was to return to the comfort of his home in Hertfordshire and to begin a memoir, "'My East End Tenement' [*Journey Through a Small Planet*], grew out of that beginning."[81]

It is significant that both Kops and Litvinoff linked, directly or indirectly, the "irrecoverable past" of the East End with the "irrecoverable loss" of the Holocaust. European Jewish life, whether in the former pale of settlement or transported west, was over and it led to a profound melancholia in their work. Less deeply and with greater sentimentality, Harry Blacker's *Just Like It Was: Memoirs of the Mittel East* (1974) also implicitly connected the two. Echoing Leftwich, he categorically stated that "The Mittel East of my memoirs is no more. It was murdered by Hitler's Luftwaffe and quietly buried by the march of time and redevelopment."[82] An artist and cartoonist, his memoir is heavily illustrated with drawings that are fixed firmly in what he described as "then."[83] *Just Like It Was* had no intention of encouraging the reader to revisit the sites of Blacker's youth.

More ambiguous was another illustrated reflection on the East End of the past, *Say Goodbye: You May Never See Them Again*, also published in 1974. In this collaboration between Arnold Wesker and artist, John Allin, the "old" East End is evoked, but the vivid colours of the latter's paintings suggest that the past is not yet passed. The dialogue between Wesker and Allin provides the heart of the text as they pondered how to represent recent history and link it to the present. From the start, Wesker emphasises the dilemma:

> It's a trap, the East End, to be sentimental and full of cosy longing for the "good old days" … I mean, *I* may have loved it … written about it with love, but my family remember it with misery. *I* may be riddled with nostalgia, hoarding the past as though it were food for a time of famine, but not them … [84]

Wesker is adamant, however, that looking back with love is not sentimentality, "That's looking back with dishonesty" to which the non-Jewish Allin responds by asking: "Can't you sentimentalize the East End by always making it slummy, though? … I like painting the past with dignity."[85] Importantly, their endeavour was also a warning about the future and the dangers of the ongoing destruction of many of the buildings featured in the text. It laments "the continuing destruction, begun in the Blitz, of one of the most fascinating parts of London."[86]

By the later 1970s, what had been an admonition with Wesker and Allin, was being put into active conservation work with the past and present melded into one. It was expressed in another collaborative project between writer and artist in *The Streets of East London* (1979). Here Bill Fishman, historian of, and educator in, the East End, especially its radical Jewish past, worked with photographer Nicholas Breach juxtaposing black and white images of "then" and "now" in a politically committed text. Continuity, emphasised Fishman, born in the East End during the early 1920s and a witness to the Battle of Cable Street, was there "in the few surviving rumps of street communities, in the markets, in the pubs … in the Hebrew insignia on decaying facades of the last remaining synagogues." But, he added, "a crime has been committed against the past. In the race for conformity, and from the pressing needs for rehousing the people, the little streets and their ancient communities have fallen before the demolishers." Much still remained and Fishman and Breach wanted both to conserve what was left and, to the "curious and the imaginative," offer a "pleasurable feast" – a "voyage of discovery into a unique past and present."[87]

For the first time, *The Streets of East London* provided maps and itineraries for formal walking tours of the East End, taking in "Victorian and Edwardian Spital-fields" and "Whitechapel and Mile End." The stories they incorporated were inclusive, including those of migration (Jewish and other), poverty, crime (from the Ripper murders to the Krays), radicalism, social protest and reform. Deeper elements of the area's history such as the second parliament of Edward I in Stepney Green were placed alongside the neighbourhood's Jewish writers, Bernard Kops and Arnold Wesker, to indicate how they were in no way alien to its deep history.[88]

This was innovative heritage work, avoiding any elitism or nostalgia and inte-grating migrant history into general narratives unapologetically and without any form of special pleading. It went alongside Bill Williams's similar work in Man-chester leading to the formation of the Manchester Jewish Museum (1984) and, at a national and historiographical level, that of Colin Holmes who became the first professional scholar of immigration in the British past.[89] At a grassroots level, Fishman's work inspired the formation of the Jewish East End Project (JEEP) in 1978. The initial aim was to train tour guides "for youth groups and visitors wishing to explore the Jewish East End." The hope was to inspire an interest in roots from those whose family origins were in the area, but also to address the needs of the remaining and largely elderly Jewish residents of the area, largely neglected in reflections on the East End. JEEP's slogan was "our future was our past" and through carrying out oral histories and documenting the area, heritage preservation was to the fore. Indirectly it led to the formation of the Museum of the Jewish East End (1983), which, reflecting the changing nature of London Jewry, was situated not in the place of its focus but many miles away (both spiri-tually and physically) in Finchley. The walking tour had become an active agent in the attempt to strengthen Jewish identity in an increasingly secular age and to present that particular history to a wider audience.[90]

Whilst Monty Richardson (youth worker founder of JEEP) and Bill Fishman's parents were of immigrant origin, the major impetus for it and the projects that followed were from those of the third generation who had been born in suburbia and away from the original immigrant settlement areas, and also non-Jews of a similar age. Such work climaxed with the Jewish East End Celebration (1987) which featured innovative exhibitions on everyday life and events, including walking tours, that were rooted in the area. But that the talent and energy of the Celebration was not nurtured and maintained reflected the marginality of its sub-ject matter both in the world of heritage generally and the priorities of British Jewry specifically.[91] Indeed, that only a minority would identify as strongly as the founders of JEEP was reflected in the struggle in both Manchester and London to create museums of the Jewish immigrant past. Nevertheless, progress was made in preserving some buildings in the 1980s and 1990s (if many others, in the secular and religious realm were lost, including the Feinmann Yiddish People's Theatre, built in 1912 and demolished in 1987).[92]

Such work went alongside encouraging and recording the written and oral testimony of those who had occupied (or continued to occupy) the streets in which they were located. Thus, from the late 1970s, Bill Williams in the north and Bill Fishman in the East End established the walking tour as an art form where the relevance of the past to the present was performed culturally and politically. As artist and writer Rachel Lichtenstein (who was deeply influenced by Bill Fishman) noted, these were "more than just historical tours. [Bill was] engaged with the contemporary world around him."[93]

IV

The maverick medievalist Colin Richmond has urged the historian to understand where it happened and the "necessity of 'being there'."[94] That was the advice too of Colin Holmes when I was embarking on my doctorate in the early 1980s on twentieth-century British anti-Semitism. For any research on this topic the East End of London would be central, and it was experiencing Bill Fishman through a walking tour of Spitalfields in 1983 that my appreciation of the importance of "place" was enhanced. With Fishman, this was heritage as lived experience where impromptu digressions from its residents, including the homeless, were encouraged. It went alongside a requirement to look carefully at the built landscape and to recognise the layers of history represented in each building and every street.[95]

In 1986 I began a fellowship at the University of Southampton and developed a course, inspired by the work of Bill Fishman, Bill Williams and Colin Holmes, on the history of migration in Britain from the mid-nineteenth century to the present. A walking tour of the East End was, from the start, an integral part of the student experience. It was first led by Bill Fishman's successor at Queen Mary College, David Cesarani,[96] and then by Bill's young protégé, Alan Dein, who had played a key role in the early years of the Museum of the Jewish East End, founded by Rickie Burman, formerly of the Manchester Jewish Museum.

Alan, following his mentor, had become centrally involved in the difficult task of getting buildings listed, such as the exterior of the Jewish Soup Kitchen in Brune Street.[97] One of the most talented oral historians to emerge in the late twentieth century, his walking tours incorporated testimony, photographs and documents to make the fast-changing streets of the East End come to life for a generation of students to whom this was foreign territory chronologically, geographically and experientially.

As with Bill Fishman and Bill Williams, the success of Dein's tours required a knowledge of the present as well as the past, and a familiarity with those who lived in the neighbourhoods – both then and now. For students trained rigorously in historical methodology who accompanied Dein on his walks the following dialogue in the late 1990s outside what was formerly the United Workmen's and Wlodowa Synagogue in Cheshire Street was perhaps as bewildering as it was entertaining. The building, a synagogue since 1910, was in terrible disrepair and on the verge of demolition, which eventually occurred in 2002 to become yet more "luxury flats" in Spitalfields. In spite of this dilapidation and risk, the students clambered in through a hole in its roof to explore the remnants of the synagogue interior. The "owner," in effect the squatter of the site, told the Southampton party that after the war the building had housed Holocaust survivors passing through Britain. Asked how he knew and could be sure – academic questioning he clearly regarded with contempt – his response said much about ownership of the past – in this case literally as well as metaphorically:

1. Born and bred here.
2. I'm a Jew.
3. I make my business to know such things.[98]

This was the same building whose interior had been lovingly created by the father of Harry Blacker and his contemporaries: "After a hard day's work, he would come home, eat his dinner and then go off to the site, where he and many other craftsmen worked until midnight making seats, cupboards, doors, and an ark and *bima* for the proposed synagogue."[99]

In the second decade of the twenty-first century, the last fragments of the United Workmen's and Wlodowa Synagogue have long since gone and Cheshire Street as a whole has become gentrified with bijou fashion shops and no evidence of its former history at the heart of the Jewish East End – whether religious or secular (in the form of a bath house). Even its once infamous informal market is on the edge of extinction. The last section of this chapter will deal with how "the walking tour" has dealt with the remarkable changes that have overtaken Spitalfields and other parts of the East End in recent years. Put boldly, are the aims of JEEP, the Jewish East End Celebration and more broadly the vision of Bill Fishman, now redundant in the light of this transformation?

V

The history of the East End involves constant flux, conflict and solidarity, ethnic succession and persistence. It is a complex mix of roots and routes – the latter a result of both choice and pressure to leave. In the 1960s and 1970s, recognition that the Jewish East End was a shadow of its former self seemed to contemporaries easier to accept with the presence of another vibrant group – Bengalis from the region of Sylhet.[100] From the early 1980s, however, concerns grew that the growth of the City of London eastwards and later Docklands from the west, was beginning to push out the Bengalis and their children. For the first time, it was not new migrants but offices and the wealthy middle classes who were beginning to shape the identity of Spitalfields.

In 1989, the coordinator of the Spitalfields Small Business Association was anxious that, unlike previous refugees and migrants in the area, "this time around the Bangladeshis won't have the same opportunity, because they're being squeezed out by the City."[101] Her fears have subsequently been realised. Slow at first, the pressure to create new office space has intensified in the twenty-first century and the area has changed dramatically. Increased rents and house prices have pushed out and alienated many Bengalis and also a generation of grassroots artists who were drawn to the area from the 1980s through its short-lived affordability and cosmopolitanism.[102]

In 1969, a guide to the East End concluded that "much of it is ugly and sordid. Slums still exist and will continue to exist into the foreseeable future. Places like Brick Lane are not, in any way, attractive."[103] Less than half a century later, it is ironic that this street is the heart of an area that has become a major tourist attraction. In the late twentieth century, attempts were made to create "Bangla-town," an East End version of "Chinatown," as a tourist trap.[104] This proposal generally irritated the local Bengali community who were frequently bypassed in the rebranding of Brick Lane. Banglatown was in fact inaugurated in 1997 but never really took off as a heritage branding in the eyes of the general public. Muhammad Haque of the Committee for Bangladeshis' Rights argued in 1990 with regard to the "unrepresentative and ghettoising tag 'Banglatown'," that "ordinary people have not been consulted to this harmfully divisive label."[105] Whilst the "curry mile" of Brick Lane continues to attract tourists, it is now its Georgian architecture, art, music and club scene and upmarket shops that have made the East End a "happening place" – edgy but largely without the danger it represented to "respectable" society from the Victorian era onwards. This rapid gentrification has divided opinion and this tension is also apparent in the world of heritage and the walking tour.

To Rachel Lichtenstein, who moved to the area where her grandparents had lived and worked in the interwar years, by the 1990s the transformation was too much and she closes her rich account of Spitalfields, past and present, by acknowledging the end of an era: "My time on Brick Lane seemed to have reached its natural end."[106] Alan Dein, who had introduced her to Spitalfields and to his mentor, Bill Fishman, is of similar mind. "Bill's passion for connecting his-tory to the very streets we were standing on was already legend [in the 1980s], and he was delighted that someone still in their 20s was also passionate to learn, and to tell the story too." Then the Jewish Soup Kitchen was still functioning with its weekly parcels and:

> There were still a number of extant Jewish clothing and retail businesses around Brick Lane … [In Gunthorpe Street] the old East End of Israel Zangwill, Jack London or Arnold Wesker felt so palpable. Scroll on a quarter of a century and the same street now feels more like … a fashion shoot or an art installation. It's like the mystery and the grit has been replaced by a film set.[107]

It is significant, therefore, that Alan Dein and Rachel Lichtenstein, the direct heirs of Bill Fishman, have stopped taking walking tours of the area. Even in Alan's last years of leading my Southampton students in the early twenty-first century, it was clear that "place" was being replaced by "text" as his readings grew longer and the walking element diminished proportionally. It is perhaps no coincidence that Nadia Valman, who took part in one of the later tours, has developed an "app" of Zangwill's Spitalfields which incorporates a rich range of primary materials.[108] Creatively using Israel Zangwill's satire *Children of the Ghetto* (1892) as a "walking guide to the Jewish immigrant subculture of Victorian Spitalfields," the app puts the novel "in dialogue with … oral history sources," alongside digital sources such as photographs and museum objects.[109] As with the earlier writing of Rachel Lichtenstein, or the ongoing blog of The Gentle Author, who is attempting to describe "the exuberant richness and multiplicity of culture in [Spitalfields],"[110] texts – whether visual or written – become a way of dealing with the dissonance of the streets in relation to then and now. Both utilise new forms of electronic communication and social media. Indeed, Nadia Valman is insistent that "Digital technology offers a new way to capture and preserve these many competing pasts [in the East End] while remaining in immediate contact with present lives."[111] Whilst both Valman and The Gentle Author encourage their audience to experience the streets themselves (the former through a GPS device and the latter in a published collection of his blogs which provide two such detailed walks for his readers),[112] perhaps too much imagination is now required to leap across time and context compared with when Spitalfields was still a poor migrant area. Despite the valiant efforts of Valman and The Gentle Author to connect Spitalfields' past and present, theirs ultimately is a task as thankless as that of Sisyphus – if coming from a genuinely creative and humanistic impulse rather than paying the price for former misdeeds.

Yet the market place for heritage walking tours of the area (minus Dein and Lichtenstein) thrives as never before. Jewish East End tours continue and have now become routine and "standardised."[113] Nostalgia plays its part in explaining why these are relatively popular, but so is the more critical search for roots and identity that had motivated JEEP to promote such walks from the late 1970s onwards.[114] David Rosenberg's *East End Walks* provide an alternative to them. They are explicitly aimed at "Bringing London's radical history to life" and are part of a "History from Below" international network of "historian-activists, artists and agitators."[115] Here there is a direct link to the approach of Bill Fishman with anarchist heroes such as Rudolf Rocker and the Battle of Cable Street featuring prominently. The narrow focus, however, differentiates them from the wider interest of Fishman in the street and the people beyond those explicitly involved in revolt and resistance. As Roger Mills notes, there are "other stories of Cable Street in London's East End apart from the famous Battle."[116]

These are quibbles, however, in the light of what is the dominant subject matter and approach to East End tours since the last quarter of the twentieth century. All other walks are vastly outnumbered by those devoted to Jack the Ripper which total over eighty a week and are often found backing up on one another like planes in a stack over Heathrow.[117] Whereas the Museum of Immigration, which has been in the making for a third of a century at 19 Princelet Street in Spitalfields continues to flounder, that commemorating Jack the Ripper opened in the summer of 2015 and flourishes, ironically in Cable Street, which whilst associated with the sex industry after the Second World War, had no connection to the murders in Whitechapel.[118] In the "Ripper" walking tours, much to the dismay of local residents, visitors expect and are given gruesome descriptions of the murders carried out in 1888, regardless of taste, awareness of the lives of the murdered prostitutes or historical accuracy.[119]

Whilst Bill Fishman's original walking tour guide of 1979 did not avoid mention of the Ripper's victims, his aim was inclusivity – to emphasise the poverty and danger of the area and how tension and fear could be directed against vulnerable minority groups. But the market place for heritage rarely allows such sensitivity. Returning to Alan Dein's walking tours in the late 1980s and 1990s, a former student remembers with some remorse, when confronted with "an old crumbling synagogue" and the Jewish soup kitchen, trying to "push the subject matter onto Jack the Ripper where we could and Alan would allow."[120] Another also confesses some quarter of a century after the tour, that then he was "more interested in Jack the Ripper than the immigrant history."[121] That they still have memories of that immigrant past through the streets and buildings and their inhabitants is, however, a reflection of the potential of the walking tour to evoke and connect. Indeed, a former student of Indian origin recalls, "being struck by the East End. The trip made me realise and appreciate the rich history of migration which the East End has seen over the years which I guess is also a reflection of the UK as a whole."[122]

In contrast to such exploitation of the East End's unsavoury past, an alternative emphasis on heritage has developed, most notably in the form of *The Back Passages of Spitalfields*. This tour and its associated literary work, which involved a collaboration between Alan Gilbey and the actor Steve Wells, parodied the "Ripper tours" while providing a critical approach to East End history that consciously avoided either nostalgia or muckraking. Immigrant succession is present but not at the cost of ignoring racism, poverty and rebellion in the area. The most important influence Gilbey acknowledges, not surprisingly, is Bill Fishman, reflecting not only his commitment to the lives of ordinary people but also his renowned impishness. Gilbey notes that Fishman was "a man who told off Gilbert and George [who live in a renovated Georgian property in Spitalfields] when they tried to stop him doing a talk outside their house."[123] It was not for them to end freedom of speech. Yet again, it is significant that the *Backpassages* tours have also ended – there is a limit ultimately to how far satire can maintain itself against the dominant forces that they ridicule.

Gilbey's reference to the battle of Fournier Street between an elderly Jewish anarchist professor and Gilbert and George poses the underlying questions, who owns the past and the contemporary spaces in which it took place? After all, walking tours are not neutral events without consequences. In fact, both guides and customers have been attacked on "Ripper tours,"[124] and reflecting more complex tensions, a group of Americans led by Bill Fishman was verbally assaulted in the early 1990s by some young Bangladeshi men at a time of heightened tension over the Gulf War. The meeting place for the tour was Whitechapel underground station which is also "a busy shopping area used by local Bangladeshis." As John Eade notes, "it provided an illustration of competing appropriations of the same space."[125] Spitalfields is fast losing its Bengali presence, but issues involving alcohol and sexualised images and behaviour still cause tensions between "locals" and visitors. The politics of the past also have not gone away.

VI

How to represent and preserve the Jewish Soup Kitchen in Brune Street is a good example on which to end this discussion. It is now luxury flats and through the humanistic approach of The Gentle Author, an attempt was made to connect Linda Carney, who used to work in Brune Street above the soup kitchen in the 1960s, with a resident of one of the flats that now occupies that space, banker Kweku Adolobi. When they met Linda bridged the gap by talking about the area as a melting pot where all races – black and white, Jewish and non-Jewish – mixed, worked together, partied and married. "I could see Kweku's eyes widening at Linda's open-hearted enthusiasm." Kweku shows Linda round his flat and she is not alienated: "It feels strange but homely, because it is so familiar."[126] "Unfortunately Kweku is now in prison, having been jailed for seven years after losing UBS £1.4 billion as a rogue trader."[127] The Gentle Author has no space for a discourse on the moral implications of Adolobi's crime nor did the press coverage of the scandal connect the social housing origins of his luxury home to its less affluent past. Bizarrely the London *Metro* and the *Daily Telegraph* both place it in Shoreditch and not Spitalfields.[128] A few years earlier, in an article on the role of charities in *The Guardian*, the building was used to illustrate the need for "caring capitalism" in the twenty-first century. It was framed, however, to reveal only the last two words of its frontage, removing the word "*Jewish.*"[129]

The Jewish Soup Kitchen closed its doors in 1991. Early walking tours with Alan Dein would sometimes coincide with elderly Jews collecting their food parcel from the building. This was not quite the ethical awkwardness, for example, of taking part in a walking tour of a Cape Town township, but it revealed the potential danger of voyeurism as ordinary people, often elderly and neglected, gained not only material support but also a sense of community in this weekly ritual, but were watched in this process.[130] Since its closure the dilemma for the walking tour is now to connect to the poverty once, but no longer, represented by this "must visit" building in East End heritage.

As just another gentrified property, the Jewish Soup Kitchen is in danger of having its history deracinated, but even when confronted with its troubled past, there is still the problem of connecting it to its current City occupants. Nadia Valman's "app" attempts this through use of a museum image of the soup kitchen's tally board to show its strict adherence to administering aid "scientifically" and through "procedural correctness."[131] Yet away from this app, the building is now more likely to feature in "lifestyle" sections of colour magazines for those rede-signing their own period properties. According to one property commentator, it now has "the feel of some very exotic, chi-chi Balinese hotel" – a comment that was positive rather than ironic. A similar lack of awareness and connectivity was apparent in the remarks of developer Dominic Brown who was proud of the apartments' "modern monastic" kitchens.[132]

VII

In the second decade of the twenty-first century, recognising the growing tourist presence in Brick Lane, Tower Hamlets Council produced a "cultural trail" for the casual visitor who was not part of a formal tour. This history is not challenging as its presents a comfortable multiculturalism which has made for the "richness and complexity of the area's character": "Flemish, French, Russian, Bengali, Protestant, Jew and Muslim – Brick Lane has welcomed all these people over time." There is no recent rupture, however: "Now it is also home to a diverse mix of fashion, art, entertainment, retail and start-up businesses." Here, the City of London, rather than causing a break with the past, is part of it: the trail is funded by the Bishop's Square development.[133]

In fact, each newcomer group to the East End has faced hostility from those who regard themselves as representing its "true" character. It is a repetition wonder-fully parodied by Richard Bean's play *England People Very Nice* (2009) which includes the wonderful lines: "Fucking frogs! My grandfather didn't die in the English Civil War so's half of France could come over here and live off the soup." Jeremy Gavron's powerful and disturbing novel of Brick Lane, *An Acre of Barren Land* (2005), offers a similar message.[134] But is that process of rejecting the latest newcomers what is happening now in relation to the middle classes who are so prominent in the Spitalfields of the twenty-first century? This possibility cannot be discounted.[135]

This is the first time that non-migrants coming to live in the area have become the major catalyst for change. The cultural and financial gap between the City and Spitalfields is fast disappearing. In 1968, two Jewish Petticoat Lane market stall owners, Jo and Jack Joseph, created "Cockneyland" – an attempted rival to Disney-land in a "neglected area on the tourist map." A "Cockney Tavern" was created selling jellied eels accompanied by music hall songs. If nothing else, the repre-sentation of the Josephs as "true cockney[s]" put to rest the assumptions of Tom Harrisson and Mass Observation fifty years earlier about labelling and Jewish belonging in the area.[136] But if "Cockneyland" failed, the East End as theme park has succeeded today, including the restoration of a Georgian house in Folgate Street representing a fictional Huguenot family which has been described by Iain Sinclair as "some self-knowing pantomime."[137] In this respect, I would conclude pessimistically that now possessing some of the highest property prices in the world's most expensive city, "doing the East End walk," as imagined by Bill Fishman, is under threat – and this at a time when the area itself is awash with tourists and tours. As he would have said to me when learning of the sums involved in buying flats or renting property in the former slums and homes for the dispossessed in Spitalfields such as the Providence Row Night Refuge: *Oi Veys Mir, Boychik!*

Notes

1 This chapter is dedicated to the memory of the great historians Bill Fishman and David Cesarani. It is also in gratitude to Alan Dein who led evocative and inspiring tours of the East End for my students over two decades.

2 T. Harrisson and C. Madge, *Britain by Mass Observation* (London, 1986 [1939]), p. 142.

3 Ibid., p. 140. For a wider analysis of their work on the Lambeth Walk, see N. Hubble, *Mass Observation and Everyday Life: Culture, History, Theory* (Basingstoke, 2006), pp. 157–64.

4 Harrisson and Madge, *Britain*, p. 144.

5 Ibid., p. 148.

6 G. Cross (ed.), *Worktowners at Blackpool: Mass Observation and Popular Leisure in the 1930s* (London, 1990); D. Hall, *Worktown: The Astonishing Story of the Project that Launched Mass Observation* (London, 2015).

7 J. Hinton, *The Mass Observers* (Oxford, 2013) at least mentions their less-known East End work. See T. Kushner, *We Europeans? Mass Observation, 'Race' and British National Identity in the Twentieth Century* (Aldershot, 2004), pp. 82–99, for a more thorough treatment.

8 Mass Observation Archive (M-O A) FR A12. The Mass Observation Archive is now located in The Keep Record Office, Brighton, Sussex.

9 Franklyn commentary, 12 April 1939 in Board of Deputies of British Jews Defence Committee records, C6/10/26, Wiener Library.

10 Ibid. He later wrote *The Cockney: A Survey of London Life and Language* (London, 1953).

11 For more on the origins and use of the appellation 'cockney', see this volume, A.J. Kershen, "From East End 1888 to East End 2016," pp. 1–21 and G. Stedman Jones, "The 'Cockney' and the Nation, 1780–1988," in D. Feldman and G. Stedman Jones (eds), *Metropolis London: Histories and Representations since 1800* (London, 1989), pp. 272–324.

12 Anonymous critique in Board of Deputies Defence Committee archives, C6/10/26.

13 D. Furber, who wrote the lyrics, was born in London. His family origins are unclear.

14 Harrisson and Madge, *Britain*, p. 163.

15 Ibid., p. 150.

16 S. Gilman, *The Jew's Body* (New York, 1991), Ch. 1.

17 M-O A: Topic Collection "Antisemitism," Box 1, File G.

18 Harrisson and Madge, *Mass Observation*, p. 159.

19 W.J. Fishman, *East End 1888* (London, 1988).

20 A. Kershen, "The Migrant at Home in Spitalfields: Memory, Myth and Reality," in K. Burrell and P. Panayi (eds), *Histories and Memories: Migrants and their History in Britain* (London, 2006), p. 97.

21 Franklyn, 12 April 1939 in C6/10/26.

22 R. Samuel, *Theatres of Memory* (London, 1996), pp. 390–400.

23 Ibid.

24 T. Harrisson, *Living Among Cannibals* (London, 1943), p. 7.

25 Kushner, *We Europeans?*, Ch. 3.

26 M-O A: Topic Collection Air Raids, Box 9 File T.

27 S. Koven, *Slumming: Sexual and Social Politics in Victorian London* (Princeton, NJ, 2004), esp. Chs 2 and 5.

28 *Radio Times*, 7 July 1939.

29 *East End*, BBC, tx 12 July 1939. Partial script in M-O A: TC Anti-Semitism Box 1 File E. Reproduced with permission of Curtis Brown Group Ltd, London on behalf of The Trustees of the Mass Observation Archive. On Harrisson more generally, see J. Heimann, *The Most Offending Soul Alive: Tom Harrisson and His Remarkable Life* (London, 2002).
30 *East End* script.
31 Harrisson's notes, in M-O A: TC Anti-Semitism Box 1 File E.
32 Ibid.
33 Ibid.
34 Reproduced in H.V. Morton, *H.V. Morton's London* (London, 1940), p. 317.
35 *East End* script.
36 Ibid.
37 Ibid.
38 BBC Written Archives, *East End* film.
39 *East End* script.
40 Ibid.
41 Notes on *East End* film. See *I Gotta Horse: The Autobiography of Ras Prince Monolulu, as told to Sidney H. White* (London, 1950).
42 *The Peopling of London*, Museum of London, November 1993 to May 1994.
43 Bud Flanagan, *My Crazy Life* (London, 1961), p. 193.
44 Visitor comments book, *Peopling of London*, Museum of London.
45 Merriman quoted in K. Cracknell, "Because I'm a Londoner," *Spotlight*, 11 November 1993.
46 *East End* script.
47 D. Munby, *Industry and Planning in Stepney* (London, 1951), pp. 13 and 36 and T. Kushner, *The Persistence of Prejudice: Antisemitism in Britain during the Second World War* (Manchester, 1989), p. 50.
48 A.B. Levy, *East End Story* (London, 1950), p. 98.
49 I. Jakobovits, *The East End and the Anglo-Jewish Community* (London, 1948), pp. 9–10 based on a lecture given at the Great Synagogue, 7 March 1948.
50 Levy, *East End Story*, p. 99.
51 Ibid., p. 1. A *minyan* is the ten adult males required for the celebration of public worship in an Orthodox service.
52 Ibid., pp. 95–7.
53 A *Mezuzah* is a piece of parchment inscribed with biblical passages fixed to the outside and inside doorposts of a Jewish home.
54 Levy, *East End Story*, p. 63.
55 Ibid., p. 95.
56 C. Russell and H.S. Lewis, *The Jew in London* (London, 1900).
57 Levy, *East End Story*, p. 2.
58 Ibid., p. 12.
59 Ibid., p. 68.
60 Notes on *East End* film. It is not clear from the script whether the interview with Groser was included.
61 *Our East London: The Story of Our Streets* (London,1950). This was the third bulletin of its schools' committee.
62 In foreword to *Our East London: A Study of Diversity* (London, 1963), p. vii.
63 *The Story of Our Streets*, p. 22.
64 Ibid., p. 21.
65 Ibid., p. 9.
66 Levy, *East End Story*, p. 13.
67 *Jewish Chronicle*, 10 February 1989.
68 A. Gilbey, *East End Backpassages: An Explorer's Guide* (London, 2012), p. 45.
69 B. Lantin, "A Bird's Eye View of the East End," *Jewish Chronicle*, 6 December 1985.
70 Levy, *East End Story*, p. 42.

71 J. Leftwich, "The Passing of Jews' Free School," *Zionist Review*, 29 July 1949. In fact the school subsequently reopened in Camden Town as *JFS Comprehensive* in 1958 and moved to Kenton in North West London in 2002. For a history of the school, see, G. Black, *JFS: The History of the Jews' Free School, London, since 1732* (London, 1998).

72 B. Kops, "Preface," and *The Hamlet of Stepney Green* in idem, *Four Plays* (London, 1964), pp. 9, 42.

73 B. Kops, *The World is a Wedding* (London, 1963), p. 135.

74 W. Mankowitz, *The Penguin Wolf Mankowitz* (Harmondsworth, 1967), pp. 257–8.

75 "Our East End, BBC Home Service," 16 January 1962, quoted in J. Jordan, *More Than One Pair of Eyes: Transitional Transnational Identities in Georgia Brown's East End*, forthcoming.

76 *One Pair of Eyes*, BBC 2 television, 17 August 1968 analysed in Jordan, *More Than One Pair of Eyes*.

77 *The London Nobody Knows* (1967). See J. Bennett, *E1: A Journey Through Whitechapel and Spitalfields* (Nottingham, 2009), p. 62 on the East End sections of this documentary.

78 B. Lewis, "Of industries and immigrants," *Jewish Chronicle Supplement*, 14 January 1966.

79 C. Bermant, "The Conventicles," *Jewish Chronicle East End Supplement*, 21 June 1968. *Chevras* were "small societies" set up by Jewish immigrants often in private houses for worship and communal centres.

80 Author's note in E. Litvinoff, *Journey Through a Small Planet* (London, 2008 [1972]), p. 2.

81 Ibid., p. 3.

82 H. Blacker, *Just Like it Was: Memoirs of the Mittel East* (London, 1974), p. 14.

83 Ibid., p. 12.

84 A. Wesker and J. Allin, *Say Goodbye: You May Never See Them Again* (London, 1983 [1974]), no page.

85 Ibid.

86 From the cover of the 1983 edition.

87 W.J. Fishman and N. Breach, *The Streets of East London* (London, 1981 [1979]), pp. 10, 14–15.

88 Ibid., pp. 134–7.

89 B. Williams, "Heritage and Community: The Rescue of Manchester's Jewish Past," in T. Kushner (ed.), *The Jewish Heritage in British History: Englishness and Jewishness* (London, 1992), pp. 128–46; C. Holmes (ed.), *Immigrants and Minorities in British Society* (London, 1978) see also his later, and still unsurpassed, *John Bull's Island* (Basingstoke and London, 1988, and reprinted 2015).

90 H. Karsh, "The Jewish East End Project of the Association for Jewish Youth," in A. Newman (ed.), *The Jewish East End 1840–1939* (London, 1981), pp. 323–6; R. Burman, "The Jewish Museum, London," in J. Martin and L. Steadman (eds), *Treasures of Jewish Heritage* (London, 2006), pp. 10–19.

91 See T. Kushner, "The End of the 'Anglo-Jewish Progress Show': Representations of the Jewish East End, 1887–1987," in idem (ed.), *The Jewish Heritage*, pp. 94–100.

92 D. Mazower, "Curtain Drops on Old Theatre," *Jewish Chronicle*, 24 July 1987. See also Mazower's chapter in this volume, pp. 151–83.

93 R. Lichtenstein, *On Brick Lane* (London, 2007), p. 20.

94 C. Richmond, *Doing History* (Woodbridge, 2012), p. 214.

95 This would have been in summer 1983. For Bill Fishman's insistence on helping out those living on the street, which was very much part of these early tours, see Lichtenstein, *On Brick Lane*, p. 25.

96 This tour featured David's deep knowledge and remarkable energy. I remember David in what would have been the spring of 1987, climbing up a lamp post in Spitalfields and bantering with builders who were helping to further the encroachment of the City on the East End. See *Jewish Chronicle*, 14 October 1988 for a photograph of him in action in similar guise, a year later.

97 Alan Dein features prominently in Lichtenstein, *On Brick Lane*, especially Chapter 7.

98 Conversation with the "owner" of the synagogue on a walking tour with an Alan Dein and my students, c. 1999. I have photographs of the last days of the synagogue from these tours. See also Lichtenstein, *On Brick Lane*, p. 195 in relation to Daniele Lamarche who had photographed the decaying building.

99 Blacker, *Just Like It Was*, p. 22.

100 C. Adams, *Across Seven Seas and Thirteen Rivers* (London, 1987).

101 Quoted in D. Sharrock, "City and Boundary," *The Guardian*, 12 April 1989.

102 Lichtenstein, *On Brick Lane*, Ch. 20.

103 R. Curtis, *East End Passport* (London, 1969), p. 96.

104 D. Jones, *Exploring Banglatown and the Bengali East End* (London, 2005?).

105 *The Guardian*, 8 June 1990. See also "Battle Cries in Banglatown," *The Guardian*, 5 June 1990.

106 Lichtenstein, *On Brick Lane*, p. 327.

107 Alan Dein, email to the author, 13 June 2016.

108 Launched formally in July 2016. See http://www.qappsonline.com/apps/zangwills-sp italfields, accessed 26 June 2016.

109 N. Valman, "Walking Victorian Spitalfields with Israel Zangwill," *Interdisciplinary Studies in the Long Nineteenth Century*, no. 21 (2015), pp. 1–15.

110 See "In the midst of life I woke to find myself living in an old house beside Brick Lane in the East End of London: My Promise," by the Gentle Author, 26 August 2009, http://spitalfieldslife.com./my-promise, accessed 26 June 2016. The Gentle Author is best known as the keeper of a blog "Spitalfields Life" which records life in the East End of London. See http://dontdoitmag.co.uk/spitalfields-lives-an-inter view-with-the-gentle-author, accessed 14 September 2016.

111 Valman, "Walking Victorian Spitalfields," p. 12.

112 The Gentle Author, *Spitalfields Life* (London, 2012), pp. 410–20.

113 This is the phrase of Isabelle Seddon, a registered independent guide who regularly takes tours consisting largely of Jewish people whose ancestors were from the East End, or who are foreign tourists of Jewish origin, around the area, starting at the Whitechapel Art Gallery and taking in the Jewish Soup Kitchen, the site of the Jews' Free School and Brick Lane and its tributary streets. Conversation with the author, London, 21 June 2016.

114 See *Jewish Chronicle*, 15 July 2011 for a Zionist Federation promoted tour.

115 See http://www.eastendwalks.com, accessed 26 June 2016.

116 Back cover of R. Mills, *Everything Happens in Cable Street* (Nottingham, 2011).

117 Bennett, *E1*, p. 73.

118 *The Guardian*, 30 July 2015; *Evening Standard*, 7 and 16 October 2015.

119 Bennett, *E1*, p. 73.

120 Paul Israel, email to the author, 23 June 2016.

121 Rob Alder, email to the author, 23 June 2016.

122 Anita Parmar, email to the author, 6 July 2016.

123 Gilbey, *The Back Passages*, p. 166.

124 Ibid.

125 J. Eade, "Adventure Tourists and Locals in a Global City: Resisting Tourist Perfor- mance in London's 'East End,'" in S. Coleman and M. Crang (eds), *Tourism Between Place and Performance* (New York, 2002), p. 137.

126 The Gentle Author, 'Linda Carney, Machinist,' 19 March 2010, http://spitalfieldslife. com/2010/03/19/linda-carney-machinist/, accessed 26 June 2016.

127 Ibid., response 17 February 2014. Adolobi was released from jail in 2015 and in 2016 lost his appeal against deportation.

128 *Metro*, 16 October 2011 and *Daily Telegraph*, 21 November 2012.

129 *The Guardian*, 3 June 2009.

130 J. Kossoff, "Tears and Fears after East End 'Soup Kitchen' Closes," *Jewish Chronicle*, 4 October 1991.

131 Valman, "Walking Victorian Spitalfields," p. 9.

132 T. Blanchard, "Interiors: Kitchen Confidential," *The Observer Colour Magazine*, 2 February 2002.

133 Author site visit to Brick Lane, 21 June 2016.

134 R. Bean, *England People Very Nice* (London, 2009), p. 17; J. Gavron, *An Acre of Barren Land* (London, 2005).

135 The Gentle Author, *Spitalfields Life*, p. xvi.

136 Curtis, *East End Passport*, pp. 23–7.

137 Bennett, *E1*, p. 70 and Lichtenstein and Sinclair, *Rodinsky's Room*, p. 8.

Select Bibliography

William J. Fishman and N. Breach, *The Streets of East London* (London, 1979).

Alan Gilbey, *East End Backpassages: An Explorer's Guide* (London, 2012).

A.B. Levy, *East End Story* (London, 1950).

Rachel Lichtenstein, *On Brick Lane* (London, 2007).

The Gentle Author, *Spitalfields Life* (London, 2012).

Arnold Wesker and John Allin, *Say Goodbye: You May Never See Them Again* (London, 1974).

AFTERWORD

Colin Holmes and Anne J. Kershen

Bill Fishman left a valued legacy, especially on the history of the Jewish East End, which provides the central if not the only focus of these memorial essays. But it needs to be remembered that his work transcended religious boundaries. He remained curious about all aspects of life in that quarter of the capital, from the *schwer und bitter* to the joyous and celebratory. And as a giver, not a taker, he was always encouraging of others. As a result, numerous professional scholars and amateur investigators have been continually inspired by his books, journal articles, walks and lectures to undertake their own forays into the East End. In that sense his legacy lives on.

INDEX: PEOPLE

INDEX: PLACES

INDEX: SUBJECTS